Daniel Burnham and Louis Sullivan

Daniel Burnham and Louis Sullivan

Personal Histories of Two Icons of American Architecture

TRYGVE THORESON

3 FIELDS BOOKS
An imprint of the University of Illinois Press

3 Fields Books is an imprint of the University of Illinois Press.

Manufactured in the United States of America
1 2 3 4 5 C P 5 4 3 2 1
∞ This book is printed on acid-free paper.

Library of Congress Cataloging-in-Publication Data

Names: Thoreson, Trygve author
Title: Daniel Burnham and Louis Sullivan : personal histories of two icons of American architecture / Trygve Thoreson.
Description: Urbana : University of Illinois Press, [2026] | Includes bibliographical references and index.
Identifiers: LCCN 2025032298 (print) | LCCN 2025032299 (ebook) | ISBN 9780252049538 cloth | ISBN 9780252089183 paperback | ISBN 9780252048685 ebook
Subjects: LCSH: Burnham, Daniel Hudson, 1846–1912 | Sullivan, Louis H., 1856–1924 | Architects—United States—Biography | Architecture and society—United States—History—19th century | Architecture and society—United States—History—20th century | LCGFT: Biographies
Classification: LCC NA737.B85 T49 2026 (print) | LCC NA737.B85 (ebook)
LC record available at https://lccn.loc.gov/2025032298
LC ebook record available at https://lccn.loc.gov/2025032299

The manufacturer's authorized representative in the EU for product safety is Mare Nostrum Group B.V., Mauritskade 21D, 1091 GC Amsterdam, The Netherlands.
Email: gpsr@mare-nostrum.co.uk

"Curiosity seemed to be Louis's ruling passion; always he was seeking, finding something new, always looking for surprise sensations, always welcoming that which was fresh and gave joy to the sight."

—Louis Sullivan, 1922

"One cannot plan cities if one does not believe in life."

—Sigfried Giedion, 1941

"I am impressed with Chicago . . . such buildings, such noise, such people."

—Paul Bourget, 1893

Contents

Acknowledgments

MANY DEBTS ARE OWED to individuals and groups who contributed, whether they knew it or not, to the gestation and development of this project. Here let me just name a few of the most obvious contributors.

First and foremost would be JT de la Torre at the Ryerson and Burnham Libraries of the Art Institute of Chicago. JT's patience, diligence, and kindness have made him a joy to work with throughout this long process. Jessica Smith and others at the library have also been uniformly helpful in locating and making available to me the collections' abundant resources on both Burnham and Sullivan. The Art Institute's Dave Hofer was a model of patience and efficiency in gathering and transmitting the images that have greatly enhanced the finished product.

Illinois historian James Edstrom, my former colleague at Harper College, has encouraged my pursuit of the project from its inception. His enthusiasm for the project and willingness to offer a close and critical reading of the entire manuscript as well as to construct the index has left me debts I can never repay. Likewise, Harper's instructor on Chicago's architectural history, Tom Roth, kindly agreed to read the manuscript, and his involvement and encouragement and willingness to act as a sounding board has been greatly appreciated. I should also take a moment to acknowledge the humanities program at Harper College under the then-leadership of Judy Kaplow. It was the opportunity Judy gave me to teach a second-semester humanities survey course that first awakened my interest in Burnham's and Sullivan's contributions to Chicago's architectural history and that ultimately, over several years, led to this book. Finally I thank Terry McIntyre, Harper's former instructor in world religions, for taking that original walk with me down

Michigan Avenue to locate and examine Burnham- and Sullivan-specific sites. Thanks to Terry for his interest in the project and his friendship.

My thanks go to several members of the helpful staff at Columbia University's Avery Library: Dylan Rosenlieb, Teresa Harris, Shelley Hayreh, Margaret Smithglass, and former curator Janet Parks, who, I believe, just happened to stop by on the last day of my visit there and took some time to help resolve a small but sticky question. Alison Hinderliter of the Newberry Library in Chicago also went beyond the call of duty in helping me track down an elusive biographical source, and so also deserves my thanks, as do the Newberry's Kristin Morrison and Catherine Gass.

In Henderson, New York, Robert E. Aliasso Jr. took time out of his day to show me Daniel Burnham's boyhood home and to patiently answer my questions. At the Henderson Historical Society, Elaine Scott and Jon Marie Pearson were most gracious and eager to guide me to sources about their town and its most famous native son. I was unable to meet with town historian and president of the Society Eric Anderson other than via indirect email exchanges, but Mr. Anderson should know that his associates were generous in giving me time and attention during my brief visit.

At the Evanston History Center, housed in the historic home of Daniel Burnham contemporary (and briefly the Burnhams' neighbor) Charles G. Dawes, Kris Hartzell and Grace Lehner graciously provided materials related to Burnham's domestic life in Evanston.

In Owatonna, Minnesota, Glenda Smith of the Chamber of Commerce was most helpful in arranging for a visit to the town's extraordinary National Farmers' Bank and for putting me in touch with local tour guide Matt Jessop, who consented to conduct a full tour for just two people, my wife and myself. A summer 2023 trip through Iowa awakened equal helpings of generosity from several persons working in extant or converted Louis Sullivan banks, all of whom were eager to share their stories, experiences, and expertise. There were too many of these folks for us to track their names during brief encounters, but I am grateful to all the people I met in Iowa—in particular, personnel currently staffing Louis Sullivan bank buildings in Cedar Rapids, Grinnell, and Algona—for sharing their information and enthusiasms. I had similar instructive encounters with those who staff and care for the Sullivan structures in Ohio and Indiana.

At the Chicago Architecture Center, I have had the pleasure of much informal and valuable information-sharing with my volunteer colleagues, all of whom function under the supportive leadership of Director of Volunteer Services Caroline Duda and Volunteer Services Coordinator Cole Christian. Learning Services Coordinator Paul Neumann has also been a pleasure to work with. I have also benefitted in multiple ways from the many walking tours I've taken with highly knowledgeable docents at the CAC. Many thanks to all the fine people—including the many inquisitive and knowledgeable guests from near and far—who make my time spent at the Center so enriching.

At the University of Illinois Press, I have had thc pleasure of working with several dedicated professionals. Acquisitions editor Martha Bayne first took an interest in bringing this project into the public space. Tad Ringo, senior editor at the Press, helped guide the manuscript to completion. Copyeditor John Gehner brought a deft hand to the task of clarifying, simplifying, and adding a touch of grace to a sometimes heavy-handed prose style.

Daniel Burnham and Louis Sullivan

Introduction

A FEW YEARS AGO, I happened to be on a tour of downtown Chicago that included a stop at the Sullivan Center, originally the Schlesinger and Mayer department store, designed by Louis Sullivan. In tracing the intricate floral patterns of Sullivan's grand two-story ironwork, I was surprised and delighted—and a little puzzled—to learn that some architectural historians and critics claimed that Sullivan created buildings such as this under the influence of the nature-obsessed American transcendentalists of the nineteenth century.

How could that be? I wondered. Elaborately intertwined botanical motifs rendered on hard architectural surfaces were obviously not original with Louis Sullivan. They had a long history stretching back over the centuries, from the Corinthian capitals of ancient Greece and Rome through the carved portals of medieval cathedrals and beyond.

So—really? Commercial buildings that owed some kind of visible debt to the unique expression of Ralph Waldo Emerson's spiritual musings or perhaps the "Orphic sayings" of the slightly dotty transcendentalist gadfly Amos Bronson Alcott? Department stores and banks modeled in some sense after the quasi-religious teachings, poems, essays, and aphorisms of East Coast sages of some fifty years in the past? In Chicago of all places? Hard to imagine Emerson or Alcott or Margaret Fuller or Henry Thoreau having much to say about such things as hollow-tile fireproofing or the array of problems involved in erecting enormous structures on compressible soil, which were among the central preoccupations of Chicago architects of the time. Even Sullivan's cross-city rival, the notable architect and pragmatic city planner Daniel Burnham, as I soon came to learn, was deeply devoted to the teachings of Emerson's favorite mystic philosopher, Emanuel Swedenborg, and would occasionally claim that he could locate Swedenborg's transcendentalisms in his stone-and-steel building designs and his forays into urban planning.

What began as a passing twinge of curiosity before long developed into a desire to find out more about where these ideas and enthusiasms came from and how the personal experiences and beliefs reaching back into their earliest years left a mark on the personalities and legacies of both immensely consequential architects.

Along the way, I discovered that the up-and-down life of Louis H. Sullivan resulted in no shortage of individuals eager to mine that biographical mother lode. The narrative arc of Sullivan's life, after all, resembles something close to the form of a Greek tragedy: extraordinary early success, multiple conflicts and grievances often aired in public forums with passionate intensity, a melodramatic decline and fall, with a strong dose of hubris contributing to the painful trajectory of his final years. The startling image of the once imperious and revered master reduced to begging his former apprentice Frank Lloyd Wright for enough money to keep him going for one more month has the irresistible appeal of a daytime television drama.

And then there's the work—original, daring, strange, sometimes extravagantly over the top—that some have dubbed "Sullivanesque." Few people doubt the inventiveness of the work or the lasting impact of his example on several well-known twentieth-century architects.

Thus Hugh Morrison's *Louis Sullivan: Prophet of Modern Architecture* (1935) was merely the beginning of a parade of full-length biographical treatments and critical studies with strong biographical components. Other accomplished writers and scholars include John Szarkowski (1956), Willard Connely (1960), Sherman Paul (1962), Narciso G. Menocal (1981), David S. Andrew (1985), Robert Twombly (1985), Lauren S. Weingarden (1987 and 2009), Hans Frei (1992), Mario Manieri Elia (1996), Nancy Frazier (1999), David Van Zanten (2000), Patrick F. Cannon (2011), and Tim Samuelson and Chris Ware (2021). Of these, Twombly's *Louis Sullivan: His Life and Work* remains the definitive biography. And to this list could be added Frank Lloyd Wright's heartfelt tribute *Genius and the Mobocracy* (1949) and the numerous influential books and articles on architecture in which Sullivan and elements of Sullivan's life are highlighted, including academic pieces by Paul E. Sprague and Robert R. Warn, essay collections like *Louis Sullivan: The Function of Ornament* (1986), and Lewis Mumford's *The Brown Decades: A Study of the Arts in America, 1865–1895* (1931).

Though equally famous in Chicago architectural circles, Daniel H. Burnham has excited far less interest in the details of his personal history. To date book-length biographical studies of Burnham number exactly three.

In 1921 Charles Moore, Burnham's close associate on the Washington, DC, city plan and the editor of the 1909 *Plan of Chicago,* published his two-volume *Daniel H. Burnham: Architect, Planner of Cities.* Not until 1974 was Moore's work superseded by Thomas S. Hines's *Burnham of Chicago: Architect and Planner.* With a second edition published in 2009, it remains even today—like Twombly's *Louis Sullivan*—the standard, comprehensive treatment of its subject's life and work and a model of in-depth scholarly research. In 2003 Kristen Schaffer's lavishly illustrated *Daniel H. Burnham: Visionary Architect and Planner* introduced striking full-color images to complement and expand on the story of the legendary architect.

All of these book-length studies—whether focused on Sullivan or Burnham—mix biographical information with critical and explanatory commentary on the two architects' professional achievements, with major emphasis on the structures and plans and architectural concepts they left behind. All of them cover the men's youth and formative years in just a few pages or a chapter or two, then they move quickly to devote maximum space to the years of greatest influence and accomplishment, beginning in the late 1870s into the 1880s and '90s and beyond.

As chapter one explains in more detail, this book has a somewhat different scope and purpose. As a humanities professor with a background in literary studies, I was initially drawn to the stories of these two individuals less by the details of the built environment they helped construct than by an interest in the array of influences—cultural, personal, literary, intellectual—that seemed to have formed them, along with the remarkable confluence of historical forces that pulled them together and pushed them apart.

The result? This book.

1

Uncle Dan, Beloved Master

IN THE MID-1890S a promising young architect named Frank Lloyd Wright received a dinner invitation to the home of Chicago real-estate lawyer Edward C. Waller, "the handsomest person and most aristocratic individual [Wright] had ever seen." To get there, he traveled west of the city to River Forest, one of many comfortable suburban communities then growing rapidly to accommodate the host of well-to-do Chicagoans who sought to shelter their families in spacious, elegant houses at a safe remove from the dust and turmoil of the teeming industrial city. Wright himself had just overseen the completion of one such River Forest home, known then and now as the "Winslow House," after his client, ironwork manufacturer William Winslow. Winslow House was the young architect's first independent commission and, as he later acknowledged, the first in the "Prairie Style" for which he was to become famous.

Wright was ushered into Waller's cozy library, where Waller locked the door behind them, and "sitting there, handsome, jovial, splendidly convincing, was 'Uncle Dan,'" Daniel Burnham, renowned local architect and director of works for the monumental World's Columbian Exposition that had recently wrapped up on Chicago's South Side.[1] Burnham had the manner and look of a successful self-made man entirely at ease with his privileged position of power and influence: middle-aged, mustachioed, a genial presence whose thick frame bespoke the kind of hearty diet that marked a contented exemplar of Gilded Age prosperity.

For one brief summer in 1893, the Chicago World's Fair had been the center of the city's and the world's attention. It presented a largely unified complex of exhibition buildings and forums in a rigidly controlled, mostly whitewashed classical style approved by prominent New York architects and executed under the direction of Burnham. He and an army of workers and associates had accomplished the miracle of bringing the fair to completion, even without the assistance of Burnham's esteemed partner and innovative designer and architect, John Wellborn Root. In 1891 at the age of forty-one, Root had died suddenly of pneumonia just as planning for the fair was getting underway.

In the comfort of Waller's home, Burnham made an offer Wright would never forget. Four years in Paris's famed École des Beaux-Arts, then two years in Rome, a guaranteed position with Burnham's firm on his return, and support for Wright's wife and children for the duration of his time abroad. All expenses paid.

"It was more than merely generous. It was splendid," wrote Wright.

It was also an offer Wright felt he could not accept. He had just struck out on his own after leaving the service of a rival firm, Adler and Sullivan, where his mentor and "Lieber Meister," his beloved master Louis Sullivan, was still basking in the afterglow of his widely lauded designs for Chicago's Auditorium Building and the extravagant, color-splashed Transportation Building that was, for many visitors, the most exciting architectural feature of the fair.

According to Wright's 1932 memoir, his reasons for declining closely mirrored his master's famous later denunciations of the fair's tightly controlled classical motifs, which had been executed in accord with the ideals and architectural practices of the conservative École. "I've been too close to Mr. Sullivan," Wright explained. "He has helped spoil the Beaux Arts [design style] for me."

"You are loyal to Sullivan, I see, Frank," countered the congenial and apparently unperturbed Burnham, "and that is right. I admire Sullivan when it comes to decoration. Essentially he is a great decorator. His ornament charms me. But his architecture? I can't see that. . . . I can see all of America constructed along the lines of the Fair, the noble 'dignified' classic style. The great men of the day all feel that way about it—all of them."

"No," countered Wright. "There is Louis Sullivan, he doesn't. And if John Root were alive I don't believe he would feel that way about it."

Waller and Burnham continued to try to persuade the young architect—by Wright's account with charm and quiet persistence—but without success. Wright felt the weight of the occasion, he said. He saw the road sketched out by Burnham as one that would lead inexorably to personal influence, prosperity, and security for himself and his family. But it was "too easy and unexciting" and "all untrue." It placed architectural creativity behind a locked door.

There in one brief—and perhaps embellished and self-serving—anecdote, Wright accurately uncovered several key elements in the attitudes, personalities, and beliefs of two iconic figures in the history of American architecture: Daniel Hudson Burnham, the jovial, clubbable, socially adept manager of men, architectural collaborator and urban planner; and Louis Henry Sullivan, the prickly, idiosyncratic iconoclast and advocate for artistic independence and a "new" democratic American architecture rooted in nature's organic patterns.

To some present-day observers, as Wright was suggesting, these two contemporaries would seem to stand in stark opposition. In many ways their contrasting traits fit neatly into either of two persistent stereotypes of the master architect: the inspiring corporate team leader and the tortured, uncompromising, solitary artist dedicated to a uniquely personal vision.

Burnham was, to be sure, of the first type: the consummate team manager and collaborator. He was among the first architects to build a practice around a large group of talented professionals responsible for managing a heavy workload of significant projects. By the 1890s, Burnham was presiding over Burnham and Root, one of the largest architectural firms in the world.[2] He nurtured a stable of loyal assistants who remained with him over decades, some of whom continued the work and values of the firm long after his death.

Sullivan, by contrast, fit the role of lonely visionary. The Adler and Sullivan firm employed numerous draftsmen and assistants at the height of the firm's success. But even in those flush times, Sullivan remained a distant and sometimes irascible boss who expected and demanded first-rate work according to his own high and distinctive standards. Some employees in later years expressed positive, respectful memories of their time under Sullivan, but Wright felt Sullivan "had no respect whatever for a draughtsman . . . [n]or, so far as I could see, for anyone else except the 'big chief'—Dankmar Adler—whom he trusted and loved."[3] One such draftsman, William L. Steele, who worked for the firm in the post-Adler days, professed admiration for Sullivan's "vigorous personality," but noted that when Sullivan entered the office, "at the first brisk swing of the outer door we instantly subsided in graven images of unremitting toil. . . . Louis' methods with his draftsmen were severe. We did not love him, but we had a great respect for him."[4] Once Adler left the firm in the mid-1890s during an economic downturn, the partnership lost its most client-friendly face. Sullivan's commissions dried up, placing a continuing strain on the company's finances, which led to inevitable attrition. It didn't help that, when Adler sought to return, Sullivan refused to reunite with his "big chief"—trust and love be damned.

Burnham's entire professional career benefited from numerous sustained friendships and partnerships with leaders of business and industry, neighbors, politicians, artists, musicians, and others. He gave advice freely, played golf relentlessly, hosted social events at his Evanston estate, traveled widely, engaged in countless civic improvement projects in Chicago and elsewhere (often uncompensated), attended concerts conducted by his friend Theodore Thomas, and happily took on leadership roles in professional committees and organizations. He got along with just about everybody. Not long after Frank Lloyd Wright turned down Burnham's handsome offer in no uncertain terms, Burnham could be found recording in his diary an enjoyable holiday sleigh ride with "Mr. and Mrs. Frank Wright."[5] "Uncle Dan" was not just Wright's nickname for him; it was, Wright insisted, what just about everyone in Burnham's professional orbit called Dan Burnham.

With Louis Sullivan, it is hard to shake the image of a lonely, haunted individual, a man prone to hours-long monologues after the workday, articulating his philosophies on craft to the young Frank Wright. He seemed more at ease at his worktable or trimming roses in his isolated Southern getaway than lighting up cigars or proposing toasts with the titans of Chicago industry and politics. Solitude, he declared, was a prerequisite for the formation of a great mind.[6]

As several biographers have shown, Burnham was a hands-on boss, an active participant in formulating design elements and details of individual projects, but he was equally willing to defer to and accept the directives of clients or the judgments of respected associates such as a John Root or Ernest Graham. "The only way to handle a big business is to delegate, delegate, delegate!" he's reported to have said.[7] "Individuals are nothing," he declared on another occasion, for a spirit of collaboration, once established, creates a force "strong enough to carry men entirely outside of themselves and often into an atmosphere to which they are entirely unaccustomed." In such circumstances, "when opportunities come, they are always met."[8]

Louis Sullivan was deeply committed to his singular artistic vision and openly contemptuous of what many of his contemporaries were doing. The typical architect of his time, he said, "neither works, thinks, lives, nor conceives." He is a mere "trafficker in styles."[9] "None of his contemporaries ever won from Louis Sullivan much but contempt," said Wright, with the exception of the famous master of American Romanesque H. H. Richardson, though, added Wright, "he was not so hard on John Wellborn Root."[10]

The death of cherished partner John Root had been a crushing blow to Burnham, but Burnham went on to make a triumphant reputation with the success of the Chicago World's Fair. His reputation grew continuously thereafter until his death, even if the inventiveness and creativity that Root had brought to the team gradually seemed less and less to characterize the work of Burnham and Company, as Burnham's conservative temperament and inclinations gradually asserted themselves. By contrast, Sullivan's separation from Adler in 1895 ultimately proved to be the first step in an irregular but inexorable decline in his professional fortunes, brought about in part by a stubborn resistance to compromise in matters of design and artistic control.

Burnham enjoyed a rich and expansive family life, including an enduring marriage to the daughter of his first prominent client. Sullivan married relatively late in life, a marriage that lasted ten years, did not include a household with children, and ended in a poisonous mix of drinking, depression, divorce, and, ultimately, extreme poverty.

Late in their professional lives, Daniel Burnham's influence and fame had a global reach. He engaged in city planning for locations as far apart as San Francisco, Washington, DC, and the Philippines. Louis Sullivan's commissions during this period were largely concentrated in the American Midwest. In the final years of his life, most of his notable projects were for small rural banks and savings institutions in Minnesota, Wisconsin, Iowa, and Ohio.

So, yes, they were very different personalities whose careers took them to very different places. But to think of them in such one-dimensional terms is to do a disservice to them both. In the latter decades of the nineteenth century and first decade of the twentieth, Daniel Burnham and Louis Sullivan occupied professional pathways that sometimes crossed and sometimes diverged, encountered each other in many of the same social and professional circles, and enthusiastically participated in an architectural renaissance in a city that pioneered a host of advances in building construction and design. For years, their offices were within blocks of one another. Burnham and Root and Adler and Sullivan learned from each other, as did other Chicago architectural firms living through this intensely creative and innovative period.

When the owners of Sullivan's Schlesinger and Mayer's State Street department store—known to generations of Chicagoans as the Carson, Pirie, Scott and Company Building and now called the Sullivan Center—planned an addition, Burnham's firm extended the building as an almost seamless expansion of Sullivan's vision, with only minor departures. When the architects of the 1893 Chicago World's Fair first convened in January of 1891 in the offices of Burnham and Root, it was Sullivan who sat, apparently without complaint or cavil, as secretary and earnest contributor. Though Burnham was Sullivan's senior by ten years, professionally the two were very much equals contributing to the extraordinary creative explosion that first brought Chicago architecture to the attention of the world. As Wright reported, Burnham expressed admiration for Sullivan's skill in ornamentation, and in an era when decorative finishes were considered important features of the highest forms of architecture, his admiration may have been stated sincerely and without an intended note of condescension.

In fact, both men began their Chicago apprenticeships within five years of each other and in the same shop, the offices of William Le Baron Jenney, the Civil War engineer who gained lasting fame in the design and development of the skyscraper. Their early work as architects owed much to a shared admiration for one of the premier figures of the day, Boston's H. H. Richardson, and the massive, rough-finished masonry style of the Richardsonian Romanesque. Their brief stays with Jenney signaled another shared trait from their early years: a spotty educational record filled with false starts and sudden departures. At the same time, each stop along the way included valuable lessons that the two men later acknowledged and reflected on in their years of triumph.

After the fire of 1871, Chicago was a blank slate upon which both architects could draw, and they found the prospect inspiring and energizing. "Make no little plans; they have no magic to stir men's blood" is the phrase associated with Burnham, but similar calls to boldness and daring permeate Sullivan's writing. "Here in Chicago," he wrote during this period, "the freedom of thought and action should be not only maintained, but held sacred. . . . These men . . . have in themselves qualities as noble, daring, inspired as ever quickened knights of old to deeds of chivalry."[11] Even late in life, in the same book in which he famously and bitterly denounced the disastrous influence, as he saw it, of Burnham's fair on American architecture and city planning, Sullivan recognized in Burnham "a man of fixed determination and strong will . . . a man who readily opened his heart if one were sympathetic," a person with whom one could exchange "enthusiasms, prophecies, ambitions, and even confidences."[12]

Sullivan is often hailed as the prophet of an "organic" architecture that attempts to fuse the world of nature into structures made of masonry, glass, and steel. Repeatedly in his writings he insisted that architects must return to and seek inspiration from nature. Burnham's interest in nature was just as strong and heartfelt but was less connected to a conception of organic architecture than to a more conventional commitment to incorporating the actual presence of nature into a well-planned cityscape or the surroundings of a domestic residence. It was Burnham's *Plan of Chicago* that envisioned a chain of parks, lagoons, and boulevards for Chicago that would bring "the sweet breath of plant life so abundant in nature and so agreeable to man" for "those who seek the refreshment of the parks," with vast masses of flowers "stretching broadly along the shores of the lagoons" to create a "possible paradise."[13]

Their attachment to nature can be attributed in part to their exposure to the ideas and attitudes of the Romantic movement of the early nineteenth century, in particular to the transcendental idealism of such figures as Ralph Waldo Emerson and Walt Whitman. Nature, for these and other romantics, was infused with spiritual force. Among their common influences Burnham and Sullivan would count the eighteenth-century Swedish philosopher Emanuel Swedenborg, a scientist and religious mystic whose claims to having found a pathway that connected the familiar world of our material existence to a heavenly realm occupied by angels and an array of benevolent spiritual forces exerted considerable influence over nineteenth-century thought. Burnham professed Swedenborgian views his entire life. During a hospital visit late in Burnham's life, biographer Charles Moore said he recalled "Uncle Dan" discoursing on the subject of Swedenborg so convincingly that Moore felt he "came away strengthened in purpose." A few days later, Moore listened again as his friend held forth on "the infinite possibilities of the material expression of the spiritual."[14]

As for Louis Sullivan, we know he was familiar with Swedenborg, even if he had no direct ties to any Swedenborgian congregation. He mentioned the Swedish mystic's theory of correspondences as early as 1887 in a talk he gave to the Illinois Association of Architects, and much later he approvingly linked Burnham's Swedenborgianism to the sympathetic open-heartedness he found in "Uncle Dan," despite their real differences in matters architectural.[15] Sullivan's biographer Robert Twombly and critic Narciso Menocal describe the effect of Swedenborg's teachings on Sullivan. In particular, Twombly and Menocal argue that Sullivan was deeply affected by the Swedenborgian view that "universal rationality . . . comes into harmony with the masculine principle of the cosmos, and emotion, or love, with the feminine." They contend that Sullivan gradually came to the view that, in designing buildings, the "female" principle of subliminal emotion should dominate and should conceal the "masculine" geometry that provides an underlying principle of order.[16] "The heart in you is the woman in man," Sullivan insisted to the mostly male readership of *American Contractor*. For architects and designers, the feminine principle can serve as "the hidden wellspring of Intuition and Imagination."[17]

That a true artist could and should invest material forms with spiritual, transcendent power was a core belief for both Burnham and Sullivan. Equally important for both men was their conviction that American architecture should express the ideals and practices of democracy. Democracy, Sullivan declared in a variant on his most famous dictum, is a function seeking a form, and a truly independent and original American architecture must express the essence of Democratic Man, an idea he repeated often in a lifetime of writing about architecture.[18]

For Burnham, though speaking from his privileged perch among the city's commercial and professional elite, the classical public structures he envisioned for his city were designed not as palaces to segregate rulers from the ruled but as magnets to draw the citizenry together to inspire, to heal class divisions, and to join in the adventure of self-government. His passionate classicism was more closely allied to the ideals of the Roman Republic than to the autocratic power of imperial Rome. He imagined that his reshaped downtown, with its grandiose civic center (never built), "would be what the Acropolis was to Athens, or the Forum to Rome, and what St. Mark's is to Venice—the very embodiment of civic life."[19] As Joan Draper has noted, Burnham and his civic-minded friends envisioned these monumental structures as "active agents of democracy and antidotes to problems resulting from mass immigration and strife between labor and capital," designed to "inspire civic pride in the hearts of the masses."[20] His vision was not without a touch of naïve idealism. In Thomas Hines's succinct characterization, Burnham could champion pragmatic efficiency and "'the people's interests' in elitest terms of the most luxurious, aristocratic taste."[21]

Architects are necessarily pragmatists. They must answer to, and balance, the push and pull of multiple demands of owners and clients; the challenges of physical environments; the myriad complications inherent in the availability, cost, and properties of building materials; the difficulties imposed by the varied interests and capabilities of workers and contractors; and the unpredictability of acts of God. But they are also conscious of their aesthetic role. Building design is rarely exclusively utilitarian; it is, for its most significant practitioners, an art form. Burnham and Sullivan both considered themselves creative artists. Burnham's interest in the fine arts was a permanent feature of his character. He was a skilled watercolorist and a steadfast devotee of the symphony, the opera, theater, ballet, sculpture, and painting. When Burnham resigned his position as head of the 1893 fair, the board of directors lauded his administrative work but emphasized his close attention to the artistic distinction of the project.

When the project began, they recalled, "no man had any proper conception of what was to be. It was to be grand and beautiful, but how vast its grandeur and beauty was to be . . . no one had ever dreamed. You were . . . charged with the duty of choosing the designers and artists of the great undertaking and of harmonizing and carrying out their great conceptions."[22] For his part, Burnham tended to speak less of the fair's miraculous logistical feats of construction than of its extraordinary artistry. Yes, the great work had "brain, muscle, material, and the means of rapid transport . . . instantly at command," he wrote. "But that which is wonderful, and which I can scarcely believe . . . is the noble artistic result."[23] Visitors to the fair tended to agree. Many came away marveling not so much at the technical achievements showcased in the exhibit halls but at the transcendent beauty of the glowing White City, which magically materialized for one brief, unforgettable summer beside a dirty, congested, and strife-ridden industrial city.

The architect as artist received even more insistent expression in the writings of Louis Sullivan. In his autobiography, to take just one of hundreds of similar examples, Sullivan, referring to himself in the third person, recounted that "as buildings varying in character came to his hand . . . his conviction increased that architectural manipulation, as a homely art or fine art must be rendered completely plastic to the mind and the hand of the designer; that materials and forms must yield to the mastery of his imagination and his will."[24] Architecture was a technical endeavor but equally an artistic pursuit. From the very beginning of his career to its end, Sullivan devoted himself uncompromisingly to architecture as an art form.

The manifold works and influences that these two men were responsible for have been well and thoroughly documented and analyzed. The list of materials at the end of this book would be a good starting place for those who wish to explore in depth their specific artistic and technical contributions to the fields of architecture and urban planning. This book has a different emphasis. It focuses primarily on the personal histories of these two men: the sources of their dreams and ambitions, their family lives and friendships, their interests and passions, their disappointments and tragedies, the points at which their lives intersected and diverged, their place in the social and communal life of Chicago and the other locations in which they worked and lived.

Why examine these unique individuals side by side? As key figures in the first great flowering of Chicago architecture, Burnham and Sullivan are often seen by historians and others as representing two sides in an ongoing argument over the proper direction for American architecture and design: Burnham the great architectural leader and collaborator, the ultimate organization man; Sullivan the independent and uncompromising thinker and artist devoted to a unique personal vision. Such is the case with the imaginative depictions of the two men in Erik Larson's bestseller *Devil in the White City.* And Thomas Hines ends his magisterial biography *Burnham of Chicago* by pointing to Sullivan as Burnham's "erstwhile antagonist in life and in death," and concludes, "The Sullivans and Burnhams of our history have been different and distinct voices, separate and unmergeable. As students of history, we accept that and continue trying to understand them both."[25]

Aspiring architects and artists could plausibly read these two figures as object lessons in the perils and possibilities of navigating uncertain career paths, which have been the lot of those seeking recognition in these fields throughout history. Burnham-style collaboration may sometimes mean acceptance of compromise and movement toward preserving time-honored conventions and customs. Following that route can often bring financial success and great acclaim among one's contemporaries, but it may also result in reputational loss once the fashions change and the public looks to new avenues of expression and innovation. Insistence on realizing a unique personal vision can result in lost commissions and even the kind of extreme poverty Louis Sullivan experienced in his last years, but it can also bring post-mortem fame and expanding influence.

If you were to ask today which of these two architects—Burnham or Sullivan—is now considered the greater, more original artist in architecture, Sullivan would likely be given pride of place. Still, Burnham's legacy remains a force to be reckoned with, whether in terms of the lasting impact of the Chicago World's Fair, the pioneering approaches to city planning, or the buildings that in recent years have steadily begun to re-earn our admiration. As young men, both harbored essentially the same ambition: to achieve unquestioned preeminence in the field of architecture. What is the best way to achieve such a lofty goal? To seek "starchitect" status as a singular figure in the history of architecture? Or to embrace a leading role in the teamwork inevitably required in this most collaborative of all arts? A close look at the choices these two individuals made along the way might offer a useful starting point for conversations surrounding questions such as these.

Finally, these two contemporaries are interesting in themselves, apart from their professional achievements. Anyone who cares about the material reshaping of Chicago during this seminal period in the history of the city is likely to wish to know more about the personal stories behind the two most recognized names from this place and time in American architecture, each in his own right. At its heart, this book will attempt to answer two foundational questions that guide all biographies. What were these individuals like, and what ideas and cultural forces engaged them? How their works and creations figured into their personal stories is an important part of the picture, to be sure, but brief discussions of selected key works will be presented in the larger context of the lives they lived. Burnham and Sullivan have become iconic figures in the history of American architecture, often remembered only in connection with their famous aphorisms. There is room for further inquiry beyond the public personae and material legacies.

2

"There Was a Child Went Forth"

1846–1850s

IN 1846, THE YEAR IN which the architect and city planner Daniel Burnham was born, the United States was still an awkward adolescent of a country that remained largely rural and agricultural with a loosely connected network of small towns, farms, dirt and wood-plank roads, and intermittently navigable rivers.

Only about fifteen percent of the population lived in cities. The largest city in the country, New York, had a population of roughly 400,000, about three times the size of the next largest city, Baltimore. By comparison, greater London at the time was home to well over two million souls. The revered founding fathers of the Republic—the Jeffersons and Madisons and Adamses—had only been in their graves for a decade or two. Their presence on the national stage was a living memory in the Burnham family, two of whose members—Daniel's great grandfather and great-great grandfather—had served in the Continental Army during the Revolutionary War.[1]

In the month of Burnham's birth, General Zachary Taylor, under the direction of President Polk, succeeded in taking Monterrey from the Mexicans. It was the first major victory in the Mexican War, a conflict that would ultimately lead to the United States' annexation of vast portions of modern-day California, Utah, New Mexico, Arizona, and Nevada. The city of San Francisco—where Burnham would, from a panoramic perch on Twin Peaks, later engage in an ambitious plan to redesign the central city—held fewer than one thousand inhabitants and was still known to residents as Yerba Buena. It would technically remain under Mexican control until the signing of the Treaty of Guadalupe Hidalgo in 1848.

In the drowsy river town of Hannibal, Missouri, the father of a young Sam Clemens, John Marshall Clemens, was joining with other members of the community to plan a new railroad from Hannibal to St. Joseph, Missouri, one of a growing number of efforts from similar groups across the nation to harness the still newfangled Iron Horse to the cause of regional prosperity. The establishment of a railroad, thought the local boosters, had the potential to ignite the growth of new Midwestern metropolises, as was already starting to happen throughout the region. Judge Clemens's son, later to be known to the world as Mark Twain, was at precisely this time pursuing youthful adventures with his Hannibal gang and developing a crush on the lovely Laura Hawkins. She would later be immortalized as Becky Thatcher in *Tom Sawyer,* Twain's iconic novel of frontier boyhood.

Of course as Sam Clemens himself would later recognize, the joyous liberties he and his young companions enjoyed in antebellum America were reserved for whites only. In 1846 the stain of slavery was deeply imprinted on the American social fabric, lamented by many but assumed by many others to be part of the natural order of things stretching back to the ancient world and frequently justified by political leaders, preachers, and others who were wont to cite classical philosophers and passages in scripture. In the year Daniel Burnham was born, the escaped slave and antislavery activist Frederick Douglass was abroad, marveling over the difference between the kind of treatment he received in Britain and Ireland and what he was accustomed to in the United States: "I employ a cab—I am seated beside white people—I reach the hotel—I enter the same door—I am shown into the same parlour—I dine at the same table—and no one is offended. . . . I find myself regarded and treated at every turn with the kindness and deference paid to white people. When I go to church, I am met by no upturned nose and scornful lip, to tell me—'we don't allow niggers in here.'"[2] It was in Britain where sympathetic antislavery activists raised enough money for Douglass to finally succeed in officially purchasing his freedom. But legalized freedom remained the exception, not the rule, for African Americans in the United States.

For enterprising white men, on the other hand, there were plenty of places that promised almost unlimited opportunity. Some three hundred miles north of idyllic Hannibal, a true metropolis-in-the-making was rising on the banks of a great lake and an unprepossessing streamlet much less impressive than the mighty Mississippi. Chicago in 1846 was already, in Nelson Algren's memorable phrase, a "city on the make." Founded as a town of three hundred in 1833, by 1837 it had gained enough population (four thousand) to be declared a city, and by the time of Burnham's birth, the count had reached into the tens of thousands. In 1846 Cyrus McCormick was making plans to move his ever-expanding reaper works to occupy the land just north of the mouth of the Chicago River, alongside lumber yards, grain elevators, docks, warehouses, and other building blocks of a burgeoning industrial, agricultural, and commercial center.

One prominent visitor during this period characterized the river as a "sluggish, slimy stream, too lazy to clean itself" and noted that "the three thousand houses, in which the people lived were almost entirely small timber buildings, painted white, and this white much defaced by mud." The city's streets were unpaved, covered with deal boards from house to house, the boards resting upon cross sills of heavy timber to create so-called plank roads. Beneath these roads, on a low-lying lakeside plain, lay standing water, and "as the sewers from the houses were emptied into them, a frightful odor was emitted in the summer causing fevers and other diseases. . . . Of architectural display," said this commentator, "there was none."[3]

The primitive state of Chicago's built environment near mid-century was hardly surprising. Builders and carpenters had become accustomed to performing their work in this ramshackle frontier town when and how they pleased, generally paying more attention to speeding up the process and turning quick sales than to creating structures of permanence or artistic distinction. John Van Osdel, a transplanted New Yorker, recalled that it had been only two years previous to the time of Burnham's birth, in the winter of 1844, that Chicago builders thought to ask him to open an architect's office. Van Osdel agreed to do so but only after receiving their assurance that they would not "make any drawings or construct any important building, without a plan." Careful architectural planning, it seems, had never been a priority.

After all, said Van Osdel, "No one had ever used an architect, and it was difficult to convince proprietors of the necessity of such a branch of the builders' business."[4] One architect who came on the scene in the latter part of the century claimed that before the Great Chicago Fire of 1871, as much as ninety percent of all buildings in the city had been built by non-architects. The same architect conveyed the story of one such improviser, a local merchant who designed and built his own two-story house. He neglected to include an interior staircase, leaving only one way to access the second floor: by ladder through an outside window.[5] It was in such a wild-west environment that Van Osdel—who would go on to a long and distinguished architectural career and would be known to history as Chicago's first, and for a time only, true architect—lived and worked.

In September of 1846, a thirty-seven-year-old Abraham Lincoln won his first seat in the US House of Representatives. Some ten years earlier as a member of the Illinois House, he had voted in favor of the construction of the Michigan and Illinois Canal, the creation of which was to have significant impact on the growth of Daniel Burnham's and Louis Sullivan's

Chicago. During the same state legislative session, Lincoln was one of only six representatives to refuse to support a resolution condemning "abolition societies" since, as most of Lincoln's fellow legislators believed, owning slaves was considered a sacred property right in the slave-holding states.

On the day Daniel Burnham was born in 1846, the New England transcendentalist and writer/philosopher Henry Thoreau had taken a temporary break from his experiment in solitary living on Walden Pond and was plumbing the spiritual depths of the natural world in the Maine woods. In Maine he sought out encounters with the native peoples, marveling at the devastating effects of white encroachment on indigenous cultures. He commented on the built environments around him everywhere he traveled. The Indians, he said, had been ill-served by the intrusion of European style architecture on their communal life: "I observed some new houses among the weather-stained ones, as if the tribe had still a design upon life; but generally they have a very shabby, forlorn, and cheerless look, being all back side and woodshed, not homesteads, even Indian homesteads. . . . The church is the only trim-looking building, but that is not Abenaki, that was Rome's doings. Good Canadian it may be, but it is poor Indian." A Roman church plunked down among the native peoples of the Maine wilderness! More respectable than this, asserted Thoreau, would be a "row of wigwams, with a dance of powwows," even if it were to include "a prisoner tortured at the stake."[6]

The shelters we build for ourselves and others was a recurrent subject in Thoreau's musings, which is not surprising for one who constructed a small, assertively simple cabin in the Walden woods and thought deeply about his interactions with the built and unbuilt environments all around him. Thoreau was thoroughly possessed by what might be called the "organic imagination." The boundary lines between man-made structures and nature and human and animal life were, to him, quite thin—in fact, nearly nonexistent. Long before Louis Sullivan formulated his theories on organic architecture or gave the world his famous "form ever follows function" dictum, Thoreau wrote, "What of architectural beauty I now see, I know has gradually grown from within outward, out of the necessities and character of the indweller, who is the only builder—out of some unconscious truthfulness, and nobleness." Simplicity and truthfulness of design, insisted Thoreau, will only follow from an "unconscious beauty of life." "The most interesting dwellings in this country," he went on, "are the most unpretending." The decorative details that architects typically heaped onto their buildings were "literally hollow" and could easily be stripped from the surface in a September gale.[7] Better to allow ornamentation to grow naturally out of the personality and preoccupations of the dweller.

Thoreau was not alone in calling for a native, non-imitative architecture. The sculptor Horatio Greenough, Thoreau's contemporary and fellow New Englander, voiced similar sentiments in a series of critical essays rediscovered, collected, and published in book form in 1947. The "principle of structure" we see throughout God's creation and that we should make our own, wrote Greenough, is the "unflinching adaptation of forms to functions." He asked builders to experiment with forms not based on classical models and instead counseled, "let us consult nature . . . in the assurance that she will disclose a mine richer than was ever dreamed of by the Greeks." He declared that we instinctively perceive beauty in whatever is natural and organic; when non-functional, "inorganic" embellishments are introduced, architecture takes its first step downward.[8]

As Greenough and Thoreau looked around the built environment of Concord and Boston, they saw housing and business structures that were mostly modest efforts to reproduce the styles of their European forebears. Many private residences in New England followed the eighteenth-century custom that reached back to medieval Europe: a skeletal rectangular framework of heavy timber and laboriously crafted mortise-and-tenon joints topped by steeply pitched roofs. The walls and floors of the house would hang from this heavy, solid core. An exception to this practice was just then beginning to come into widespread use in Chicago, where light, wood-frame "balloon" structures—with wall frames constructed of easily assembled, nailed-together, lightweight studs—were now going up at a rapid pace. Well-to-do Easterners would often choose to express their wealth through elaborate classical stone or brick mansions, with Greek columns rising over elaborate porches or supporting elegant porte cocheres that provided shelter for carriage stops at the side entrance. Commercial buildings would be wood frame or masonry, the latter in the cities perhaps rising as high as five or six stories. Decorative elements, for those who could afford the individual craftmanship required, would typically be inspired by historical European models. Roadways would be mostly dusty and manure-filled, often nearly unpassable when heavy rains turned them to mud. Towns tended to grow outward from a water's edge, often—as in Chicago's early years—with little attention given to long-term, formal city planning.

It was into this kind of easygoing, largely unregulated, and unplanned world—in a country on the brink of transformative turmoil and change—that Daniel Burnham was born on September 4, 1846. Like Thoreau's Concord, Burnham's birthplace—the town of Henderson in upstate New York—was essentially a rural village with a population of just over two thousand. The railroad would soon reach the area by way of a terminus, a mere ten miles away, in the town of Sackets Harbor on Lake Ontario, where military shipyards had been established. Ships would embark for trade and passenger traffic to upstart Chicago and, ultimately, venerable New Orleans.

The Burnhams had long been New Englanders. Their American roots reached back as far as 1635, when Thomas Burnham first arrived in the colonies and established a family home in Ipswich, Massachusetts, only thirty-plus miles from Thoreau's Concord. Several generations later, Nathan Burnham, Daniel's grandfather, removed the family from Vermont to Henderson, probably in search of new business opportunities. The family's male members had long devoted themselves to a mix of occupations typical of the time: the law, farming, mill ownership, storekeeping—whatever the Burnham men thought they needed to do to survive and prosper.

Daniel Burnham's maternal grandfather, Reverend Holland Weeks, was a popular and respected minister in the Congregational Church of Abington, Massachusetts, until he began to openly question such concepts as the trinity and eternal damnation. His apparent drift toward the newly imported doctrines of the Swedish philosopher/mystic Emanuel Swedenborg eventually led to his expulsion from the Abington pulpit. His heterodoxy was a daring move at the time and not for clergy who were faint of heart. Weeks's daughter Elizabeth (Daniel's mother) said that during the period of this controversy, certain bold and like-minded young ministers would come to him to "have their horns put on"—in some eyes the equivalent of forging an alliance with the devil.

After moving to Henderson, Rev. Weeks organized the town's first Swedenborgian congregation, a thirteen-member group that called itself the Society of the New Jerusalem. His grandson Daniel Burnham Jr. characterized Weeks as "very set in his opinions," [a man who] "admitted no half-way course; the thing with him was either right or wrong." He must have been a formidable, perhaps somewhat frightening, personage to those around him. "He knew little of children," observed his grandson, and "attending rigidly to their morals seems to have been his only care for them."[9] Weeks's serious commitment to his faith finds expression in the lines from the Old Testament inscribed on his grave marker just outside of Henderson: "Oh, how love I thy law, it is my meditation all the day."

Daniel was the sixth of seven children born to Edwin and Elizabeth Burnham: Edwin Jr., Romeo, Ellen, Mary, Lewis, Daniel, and Clara. The house in which Daniel was born still stands in Henderson. It was originally constructed in 1818 by woolen-mill owner Chester Norton and is known today as the Norton-Burnham house, an imposing two-story vernacular structure composed of local Trenton limestone, much of which was likely quarried onsite. The house bears a rigidly symmetrical front façade suggestive of the severe Federal colonial style of the time. Other classical elements include a semi-elliptical fanlight window over the wide front entrance and side gables enhanced by vertical oval windows, a "fan sash" decorative element characteristic of the Federal style. The home remains in private hands, with the current owner overseeing preservation of several original elements, including hand-hewn oak mortise-and tenon beams and rafters in the attic with "all joints tight, no sagging, and very strong wood remaining."[10]

Little is known of Daniel's experiences during the eight years spent in Henderson. The countryside was forested then, as now, and in many places largely undisturbed by human settlement. It's not too much of a stretch to infer that young Daniel in Henderson experienced the same kind of Tom-and-Huck boyhood that so many white youngsters across the land enjoyed and would remember with fondness, filled with outdoor adventures in field and forest, brief but formative friendships, and irksome chores.

The Burnhams were a typical upstate New York family preoccupied with the practical business of getting ahead. Daniel's father Edwin had navigated a series of financial ups and downs through a series of business enterprises,

Daniel Burnham's childhood home, Henderson, New York. (Photo by Loslazos is licensed under CC BY-SA 4.0.)

including a brief stint as a steamship company employee in Michigan and a couple attempts at storekeeping in New York. His daily affairs, however, did not preclude him or his family from involvement in the philosophical and religious currents of his time and place. Religion provided the near-universal intellectual and cultural structure within which American families functioned. In the Burnham household, Edwin and wife Elizabeth, the dutiful daughter of Rev. Weeks, devotedly followed the Swedenborgian faith. To understand Daniel Burnham, man and architect, it is necessary to understand the pervasive impact of Swedenborg's ideas on the whole Burnham family. It is not too much to say that Swedenborg's spiritual idealism had an impact in shaping the vision of the architectural cityscapes that Daniel Burnham helped design in America and abroad.

Emanuel Swedenborg (1688–1772) was a Swedish scientist, political figure, and religious mystic whose theology eventually found a ready home in both the rationalist temper of the Enlightenment *philosophes* and the emotional and intuitive visions of Romantic poets and artists of the late eighteenth and early nineteenth centuries. Swedenborg's early reputation was founded on empirical works of natural science and engineering. In 1716 his expertise in the areas of metallurgy and mining was recognized in his appointment by the king of Sweden to serve as the chief assessor of Sweden's Board of Mines. He served several terms in a chamber of Sweden's legislature, the House of Nobles. Soon thereafter he also published studies in anatomy and physiology, advancing theories that sometimes broke new scientific ground in those fields.

Swedenborg's wide-ranging scientific interests and deep curiosity about the inner workings of the human body led to a desire to explore a dilemma that had bedeviled philosophers and theologians over many centuries: the relationship between body and soul. For many Europeans of this period, both among the people at large and among the intellectual elites, the existence of an immortal, foundational spiritual self—a soul—within each human being was taken as an obvious truth, confirmed by our own intuitive perceptions and by centuries of religious indoctrination. Our consciousness, our emotions and affections, and our unique personal characteristics had to add up to more than a mere random churn of chemicals within the brain and bloodstream. Every human being possessed an indefinable, transcendent spiritual inner self—of this few had any doubts. Swedenborg saw his inquiries into the nature of the soul as an extension of his studies of anatomy. Understanding how the parts of the body worked together led to a desire to know how those body parts related to that mysterious spiritual force within. Unlike most religious thinkers, however, Swedenborg did not see the soul as literally supernatural, something that existed beyond and apart from the material worlds of nature.

His belief was direct and certain. To Swedenborg, the soul was virtually inseparable from the body. The two were closely united, with soul as the indispensable governing force. As Swedenborg's biographer Signe Toksvig put it, to a dualist such as Descartes the soul was a kind of Cinderella outside the palace; Swedenborg, in this sense something close to a monist (a believer in only one universal reality), invited Cinderella in and made her queen.[11] This close interweaving of the spiritual with the material provides the key to much of the complex theology that Swedenborg would spend the latter years of his life developing in a voluminous series of written works. Among some of his foundational—and in some quarters controversial—conclusions:

- God is One, the traditional doctrine of the Trinity is wrong; Father, Son, and Holy Spirit are simply different dimensions of a single deity.
- Vicarious atonement is a myth; Christ's death had nothing to do with the erasure of anyone's sins.
- The will is free to choose good or evil.
- Souls naturally seek community with like souls, here and in heaven; some souls may choose their own "hell" through selfishness, others may ascend to the higher realm of "heaven" by embracing a loving orientation toward others, and for most this division will persist in the afterlife.
- "Correspondences" between the spiritual and material worlds are all around us if we have eyes to see them (e.g., every material action and object expresses a corresponding spiritual truth: a tree may represent spiritual growth, water may represent the cleansing power of truth, biblical passages contain spiritual messages beyond their literal meaning).
- Good souls express themselves through good works.
- Angels and spirits of departed loved ones are all around us and are engaged in continuous interactions with each other.
- Souls of men and women will enjoy eternal marriage in heaven, and they will live much as they chose to on earth and in a familiar earth-like environment.

Swedenborg's proofs for all of this? His own scientific and philosophical studies as confirmed through direct, personal interactions and discussions with angels and spirits, both in his waking life and in dreams.

The powerful appeal of such doctrines should be clear. Swedenborgians believe that individuals have agency to live the lives their souls choose. Traditional burdens of sin and guilt are largely lifted and do not depend on any external authorities for "absolution" or forgiveness of sins. There is a hell, but it is not a place of fire and eternal physical punishment. It's a kind of deeply unhappy and unproductive mental state only for those whose souls are foolish enough to pursue selfish goals and ignore the many "correspondences" that God uses to provide guidance for lives well lived. The force that animates God's universe is love, and after death we can choose to join the universal currents of love and enjoy an eternity of bliss in communities of liked-minded souls, including those of our departed loved ones. Husbands and wives who achieved this unity of souls on earth will continue their loving partnership in heaven, while mismatched earthly souls will unite with their true soulmates in the afterlife, a happy coming together for which Swedenborg coined the term *conjugial love.* Heaven will present us with a new but familiar reality enhanced to a degree previously unavailable to us. As an example, Swedenborg asserted that our sensory perceptions will be heightened in the afterlife, including seeing colors more vivid than, and totally unlike, any we had ever seen on earth.

Swedenborg's description of the physical environment awaiting us in the world of spirit had particular influence on the man who became one of the nation's premier architects and city planners. In our lives there, he declared, we will live in purified and idealized versions of the constructed environments we enjoyed on earth. We will live in houses much like those we previously inhabited, recognizable structures complete with walls, chimneys, kitchens, walkways, gardens, trees. In other words, our souls will not take the form of disembodied ghosts wandering an ethereal realm of pure intellect. Quite the contrary, our heaven will be tactile and architecturally familiar. We will live in communities large and small, actively pursuing our interests and personal associations in recognizable towns and landscapes.

Among many other things, heaven will be an architect's dream world: spirit infused in a beautifully constructed material environment. And every object, every detail, in our heavenly houses will both reflect the predilections and desires of our individual minds and correspond to our uniquely experienced spiritual "goods." As Swedenborg wrote, the angels he conversed with told him that in heaven all things inside and outside of their beings "correspond to the interior things which they have from the Lord, the house itself in general corresponding to their good, the particular things inside of a house to the various things of which their good consists. . . . These are what the angels perceive when they behold what is around them, and thus their minds are more delighted and moved by them than their eyes."[12] In other words, buildings in heaven possess more than mere sensory or artistic appeal; they almost literally glow with spiritual and moral content.

Swedenborg was widely respected during his lifetime as an impressive intellectual and political figure, but his forays into theological speculation and his detailed accounts of routine encounters with spirits—including reported personal conversations with the spirits of Moses, Jesus, Martin Luther, Saint Paul, and John Calvin, among others—led some contemporaries to question his sanity. Nonetheless, not long after his death, Swedenborg societies and churches sprang up in England, Holland, and America. The church remains active in the present day, with churches numbering in the thousands under a variety of names: The New Church, The Swedenborgian Church, and General Church of the New Jerusalem.

It is abundantly clear that Swedenborgian thinking and ethics permeated the Burnham household as Daniel was growing up. The family even had indirect ties to New England transcendentalists, including some who moved in Thoreau's Concord circle. In 1844 the Swedenborgian minister George Field stayed for a time with "our brother in the church, Edwin Burnham" shortly after visiting Brook Farm, the famous utopian experiment in communal living inspired by the transcendentalists.[13] Brook Farm participants, visitors, proponents, and interested well-wishers included George Ripley, Margaret Fuller, Nathaniel Hawthorne, Orestes Brownson, and other notable figures, many of whom earnestly hoped to remake the American social fabric in novel ways that would unite the worlds of spirit and nature.

The best-known proponent of the union of spirit and the natural world at this time in America was the Sage of Concord, Thoreau's friend and mentor, Ralph Waldo Emerson. Emerson's sometimes enigmatic but impassioned epigrams could have come directly from the mouth of the most orthodox Swedenborgian, especially on the subject of correspondences: "Particular natural facts are symbols of particular spiritual facts," Emerson famously declared, and "behind nature, throughout nature, spirit is present."[14] Emerson specifically pointed to Swedenborg as one of his "representative men," a figure possessing the visionary power of "the mystic," a "colossal soul" who saw that "a certain vastness of learning, or quasi omnipresence of the human soul in nature, is possible."[15]

The entire Brook Farm and transcendentalist enterprise was of particular interest to clergymen and heterodox religious thinkers, so it is not surprising that Swedenborgians such as the Burnhams would find kindred souls within those circles and would have contacts that reached out across the state and region. Daniel Burnham's parents had established themselves as prominent local leaders within the sect. As Thomas Hines notes, "though less renowned than Nathaniel Hawthorne and other 'celebrities' of Brook Farm, Edwin and Elizabeth Burnham became, over the years, quietly modest 'celebrities' of the New Jerusalem Church, in Detroit, New York, and later in Chicago."[16]

Emerson and Swedenborg were influential figures within the vast intellectual and religious currents in which the Burnhams immersed themselves, part of the larger impulse in the first half of the nineteenth century that we have come to know as the Romantic movement. At its roots, Romanticism was a reaction against an overly mechanistic view of human nature. Romantic poets and philosophers celebrated those elements of our experience that seemed beyond the reach of rational analysis and explanation. Intuition, emotion, ecstatic visions, and the realm of dreams were all seen as areas worthy of exploration, perhaps leading to a transcendent state that could open a new and transformative spiritual dimension to the world in which we lived. The idea of an "organic" approach to artistic creation, based in part on deeply felt, unmediated experiences in a natural environment, was entirely congenial to thinkers in the Romantic and transcendentalist mode.

It is difficult to overstate the ways in which religion and various transcendental philosophies, mainstream and other, permeated almost all aspects of nineteenth-century American life. Western New York state, in particular, was fertile soil for the growth of nonconformist religious thought. Among the movements fostered in the regions and towns not far from Henderson: Joseph Smith's Mormonism, the Second Great Awakening of religious revivalism, the Oneida Society (an experiment in communal living not unlike Brook Farm), and the millennialist sect called the Millerites.

The religious impulse was strongly represented in the world of architecture as well. In 1859 when Burnham was twelve years old and Louis Sullivan was just two, the thirty-seven members of the recently formed American Institute of Architects (AIA) gathered in New York City. J. Coleman Hart read a paper that put religious feeling squarely at the center of his profession: "Religion is the mother of architecture," he intoned, and "[e]ach style of architecture owes its existence to the religion which is coeval to it." From Greek and Roman temples to medieval churches and cathedrals, in Hart's view, true architects have formulated styles that express spiritual aspirations, and these are the only creations worthy of the name of architecture. Hart roundly rejected an earlier—and less memorably alliterative—version of Sullivan's "form follows function" formula. "It has become quite common to say," he noted, "that 'Architecture is the art of constructing a building so as to express the uses and purposes for which it was designed.'"[17]

Nonsense, Hart argued. By this measure, the rudest hovel that served its essential purpose of providing shelter would compare to the most magnificent structures in the history of civilization. "A sugar-house may show by its various stories and ill-proportioned windows the uses for which it was constructed; yet no gentleman here will say that *that* is architecture."[18] Presumably speaking for most or many of the members present, Hart instead preferred the view of the widely revered English architectural critic John Ruskin. As Hart pointed out, Ruskin argued that architecture was an art form devoted to creating "edifices raised by man for whatsoever uses, that the sight of them contribute to his mental health, power and pleasure." We create structures, according to Ruskin, to house our spiritual selves, not merely to serve our bodily needs. Notice that here, "whatsoever uses" we may choose to include in our houses, those utilitarian functions are subordinate to the mental pleasures to be derived from living in them. Hart specifically cited Emerson as approving a similar philosophy of architecture: "verbose, transcendental, and perhaps obscure, but it approaches nearer to what architecture means in our day than [other] definitions."[19]

Daniel Burnham's mother Elizabeth was perhaps the most appealing and influential carrier of one version of the Swedenborgian spiritual message to the young boy. She learned early to take a leading and energetic role in household affairs, having been called upon to look after her father Holland and brother after the death of her mother Harriet and the marriages of her older sisters. Before leaving her home to marry Edwin, Elizabeth served her father as "both cook and housekeeper and something of a farmer as well."[20] Like many women of her time, after starting a family of her own, she was expected to oversee much of the religious and cultural upbringing of the children. Although she readily adopted her father's Swedenborgianism, her religious influences were not confined to the Weeks side of the family. Elizabeth's mother, Harriet Hopkins, was the daughter of Samuel Hopkins, a well-known Calvinist theologian who Daniel believed had served as the model for the extremely pious and self-sacrificing Reverend Hopkins in Harriet Beecher Stowe's novel *The Minister's Wooing.*[21] Like her father Holland, Elizabeth's maternal grandfather was once dismissed from his post in a church he had long served for rigidly espousing doctrines that did not sit well with many in the congregation.

It is easy to find examples of the family's singular devotion to Swedenborg's teachings. When Daniel was two, Elizabeth wrote her daughter Ellen that "if you are in the habit of simply observing every thing that is taught you from a love of *obedience*, you will soon see the *reason why* I should like to have you read some of Swedenborg's writings also *every day*, say two or three nos. [numbered passages], in any book [by Swedenborg]." To develop such habits, Elizabeth assured her, would offer a "golden opportunity" to be instructed "in all the most important things that renders [*sic*] a woman truly amiable and useful."[22]

Later on in a letter to her eldest son Edwin Jr., as he began to venture forth in life, she admonished him to "guard every thought, word, and action and not let any unworthy thing have a dwelling place with you." She told him that with his new career in Boston would come "an opportunity to see what the New Church really is" and "judge for yourself in regard to many things that are matters of controversy." In words that echo Holland Weeks's gravestone message, Elizabeth was quite explicit on what young Edwin's priorities should be. While some souls wish to govern themselves by laws of their own devising, she hoped her son would be "one that will love Heavens [*sic*] just law & love to be governed by the *law*." Elizabeth's concern received instant reinforcement in a note added by her husband Edwin Sr. "We rejoice most sincerely at your good prospects and present advantages—But we rejoice more at your appreciation of them, and your acknowledgement of their heavenly origin," he told his son.[23]

Like her Puritan forebears and her husband, Elizabeth Weeks Burnham saw success in life as linked to, and in many ways dependent on, faithful adherence to the values and tenets of one's religious upbringing, a perspective that clearly influenced young Daniel. At the same time, and unlike her stern and scholarly father Holland, Elizabeth was remembered by her children and grandchildren as a loving and delightful presence in the home. She was not a beautiful woman and "not fond of [high] society," said one, but "she had a reserve fund of merry wit and fun-loving, to which she often resorted under trying circumstances 'to carry her through'" combined with an "ever ready sympathy with others."[24] In her later years, some of her son Daniel's high-powered associates, such as the renowned artist Francis Millet, were said to seek her out in the Burnham home in suburban Chicago to spend time talking and joking with her.[25]

Elizabeth was similar to her clergyman father in an apparent unwillingness to accept traditional dogmas at face value. "To her dying day," said her grandson, "she showed a remarkable openness of mind, with readiness to welcome progressive thought in any direction." When called upon to list the characteristics Daniel Burnham inherited from his mother, family members offered a set of virtues that would have been the familiar stock-in-trade to any nineteenth-century eulogist—courage, clear judgment, ready sympathy, sincerity and truthfulness, moral responsibility—but notably added "progressiveness."[26] The willingness to entertain new and perhaps controversial ideas, and even publicly embrace them, was a familiar attitude among the immediate descendants of the independent-minded Reverend Holland Weeks.

Elizabeth became the driving force behind the family's eventual relocation to Chicago. In 1854 Edwin proposed a move to nearby Rome, New

York, but Elizabeth pushed for a more radical break and an abrupt uprooting of the family to the rapidly growing city of Chicago. "When it was a question of the children," said Dan Jr., "[Elizabeth] always made the decisions." Edwin's brother Dyer, now established in a law practice in Chicago, suggested that Chicago offered better opportunities in education and "a better society for [the children] to grow up in." Edwin dutifully set forth to explore the area on his own and briefly acquired part ownership in a stone quarry in Joliet, Illinois. He soon accused his partner, a man named Skelly, of dishonesty and immediately sought to return to New York with the intention of buying a small farm with his remaining money. The determined Elizabeth, however, lost no time in breaking up the house and sending all their furniture to Chicago. Accepting the inevitable, Edwin returned to the midwestern city and quickly managed to establish himself in the wholesale drug business there.[27]

The city the Burnhams would enter was transitioning from its rough and scattered pioneer beginnings into a growing metropolis, but architecturally it remained largely the undistinguished conglomeration of structures Van Osdel had encountered some ten years earlier. The year before the Burnhams arrived, one early commercial publication had called for a sophisticated architecture worthy of Chicago's recent emergence onto the national scene. In so doing, the writer spiced up the call for better buildings by employing the not-at-all-subtle imagery of sexual allure. The city was changing so rapidly, he said, that he was "forcibly reminded of the figure of a young and beautiful damsel whose rounding form and budding proportions are fast bursting from the limited and straining vestments which sufficed her girlhood and demanding a costume of more flowing dimension and costly texture."[28]

The person who would later do so much to redesign that costume, Daniel Burnham, started his Chicago schooling at age eight in Snow's Swedenborgian Academy on Adams Street between Dearborn and State. Thereafter he would attend two public high schools in Chicago.

By 1855, the year in which the Burnhams completed the move, much had changed in America and in Chicago since the time of Daniel's birth. The first telegraph line reached the city in 1848, the same year that the Illinois and Michigan Canal opened and the Chicago Board of Trade was established.[29] Under the determined entrepreneurship of William Ogden, Chicago's first mayor and the future founding president of the Union Pacific Railroad, railroads were rapidly extending out from the city. By 1857 Chicago would lie at the heart of more miles of track than any other locality in the world, with nearly a hundred trains entering and leaving daily.[30] The city that had become a crossroads of trade because of linked water routes

Daniel Burnham at age twelve. (Charles Moore, *Daniel H. Burnham: Architect, Planner of Cities* [Boston: Houghton Mifflin, 1921]. Ryerson and Burnham Libraries Book Collection, Art Institute of Chicago.)

was rapidly establishing itself as the rail center of the American heartland and consequently a nexus of trade and manufacturing.

Within and outside the city, the cultural and political landscape was changing as well. Following federal passage of the Compromise of 1850, which included the inflammatory Fugitive Slave Act, and with the publication of Harriet Beecher Stowe's *Uncle Tom's Cabin* in 1852, the long-simmering slavery question was again forcing itself into the open and moving the country ever closer to a fateful, seemingly insoluble, national confrontation. Henry Thoreau published *Walden* in 1854 but initially found few readers. In time, however, its Emersonian embrace of transcendental attitudes toward nature and the infusion of spirit into the material present attracted the attention of intellectuals and religiously minded thinkers. The year 1855 saw publication of a book by yet another Emersonian disciple that would also be slow to gain widespread fame but would exercise significant impact over time: Walt Whitman's slender initial volume of his epoch-making *Leaves of Grass.*

Whitman's work would have enormous impact on the man destined to rival Daniel Burnham as one of Chicago's preeminent architects. On the day before young Daniel celebrated his tenth birthday, one thousand miles to the east of Chicago in Boston's South End, Louis Henry Sullivan was born. Sullivan's father Patrick was an Irish dancing master who had emigrated to the United States in 1847, eventually establishing a dance studio on Washington Street. In Boston Patrick met and married Andrienne List, the daughter of another immigrant family from Switzerland. At the time of their marriage Patrick was thirty-four and Andrienne seventeen.

In 1856 at the age of twenty-one, she gave birth to a son and named him Louis Henri in honor of her father, Henri List, a French language teacher at a local private academy. In *The Autobiography of an Idea,* Sullivan confirmed that his given name at birth was "Louis Henri Sullivan," the *Henri* added "obviously," as Sullivan put it, "to deify Grandpa." But Louis's middle name ultimately settled into the more familiar American spelling of *Henry*, the form used by Louis and his family throughout his adulthood. The Swiss spelling, however, has persisted in various public settings, appearing in numerous publications and on Louis's tombstone.[31]

For the first five years of Louis's life, the Sullivans (Patrick, Andrienne, Louis, and older brother Albert) and the Lists (Henri, Anna, and their two other children Jennie and Julius), would live together in tight but adequate quarters in a house on South Bennet Street.[32] As we have noted, relatively little is known about the day-to-day inner life of Daniel Burnham in the early years of his boyhood—the surviving records are few and uninstructive. We know a great deal about Louis Sullivan's, at least as revealed through Sullivan's own memories, recorded in his autobiography at a remove of some sixty years. Sullivan's recollections had been filtered through a lifetime of reading and reflection and may be more indicative of a romanticized backward look than a precisely accurate account of his feelings, perceptions, and experiences at the time. The autobiography nevertheless sheds a bright light on several key elements and events of Louis's New England childhood, and his recorded memories, however massaged by the passage of time, are as close as we are ever going to get to understanding the boy's internal responses to those elements and events.

Louis admired his father Patrick and observed, "He always was successful. His probity was such that he could always command desirable influence and

Albert Sullivan at age four and Louis Sullivan at age two. (Sullivaniana Collection, Ryerson and Burnham Art and Architecture Archives, Art Institute of Chicago. Digital file # 193101. C33884.)

respect." But he felt some distance from him, writing that "there is nothing in the record to show that he loved others, or that he loved himself."

Louis reserved his most intense feelings and attachments for his mother. He believed that Patrick had fallen in love with Andrienne upon hearing her piano playing at the dance studio—"a jewel without price" and "he lost no time in marrying her as a business asset." In Andrienne's eyes, little Louis was "an angel from Heaven, so great, so illusioning is the Mother-passion." He vividly recalled her dandling him on her foot while grasping his hands and "in great glee and high spirits" singing to him French nursery songs. On one occasion Sullivan crept under the piano while Andrienne played a melancholy but beautiful nocturne. She heard a mysterious sound beneath her and looked around confusedly before discovering it was her son, sobbing and sighing. "Her precious son in her arms," wrote Sullivan, "pressed tight to her bosom; tears, tears, an ecstasy of tears, a turmoil of embraces, the flood gates opened wide, a wonder, a joy, a happiness, an exultation, and exaltation supreme over all the world." To young Louis, this impassioned embrace seemed to open a new "wonder-world within himself" that "awakened a new power within this child of three—a power arising from a fountainhead of all tears."[33]

This intuiting of a mysterious "power within," drawn from this incident and others, was to become a focal point for all of Louis Sullivan's subsequent self-examinations and a potential justification for the career ambitions he would ultimately develop with uncompromising singlemindedness. Sullivan's earliest recollections consistently echoed the romantic rhapsodies of the man who was to become his literary hero, Walt Whitman. In the original edition of *Leaves of Grass*, published just before Sullivan's birth, Whitman outlined the dramatic intensity of a child's world:

> There was a child went forth every day
> And the first object he looked upon and received with wonder or
> pity or love or dread, that object he became,
> And that object became part of him for the day or a certain part of
> the day. . . .
> Or for many years or stretching cycles of years.[34]

By Sullivan's own account, this was very like his experience. Numerous passages in Whitman's poem offer parallels to parts of Sullivan's autobiography. Whitman's intense feeling of oneness with nature, described with remarkable specificity—"The early lilacs became part of this child, and grass, and white and red morningglories [*sic*], and white and red clover, and the song of the phoebe-bird"—closely resembles the intense interior drama Louis Sullivan testified to as, in one of his earliest memories, he described watching snow fall outside of his Boston home:

> Ever at the window pane, he liked to watch the snow, falling gently in large moist flakes and, in the little gusts, swirling and piling here and there, gathering curiously in odd nooks, and crannies, gathering on the window panes across the street, gathering on his own window panes, mantling the trees in a loving way. . . . And the stillness, the muffled stillness, the lovely stillness. He was not satisfied to glance, he must look long, very long and steadily, he must see things move, he must follow the story, he must himself live the drama of dark things slowly changing into white things.[35]

The gently falling snow bedecks objects natural (the trees) and human-made (the windowpanes and nooks and crannies of buildings) "in a loving way," uniting all in a gradual transition of dark to white. The boy himself feels compelled to "live the drama" of the natural and the artificial world merging. Another passage from Whitman's poem explores personal impressions gleaned from the human activities and the structures and objects seen on a busy street: "Men and women crowding fast in the streets . . . The streets themselves, and the facades of houses. . . . the goods in the windows." Whitman's claim that all these can become part of the child, of "him or her that peruses them now," finds corresponding expression in Sullivan: "And then when morning came, the hasty rattle and scoop and sip of the shovels, cleaning the sidewalks, heaping the snow in mountains in the street. Again the song of work, the song of action."[36]

The picture that emerges from Sullivan's account is of a boy unusually sensitive to the sights and sounds of the world around him, one who was intuitively integrating an Emersonian and Thoreauvian attachment to nature into his developing consciousness. It should be noted that there is scant evidence that the mature Sullivan frequently consulted the works of either Emerson or Thoreau for affirmation or inspiration. Some historians have suggested that the extent of his debt to the founders of transcendentalism is open to question. Richard P. Adams, for example, in an examination of several of Sullivan's intellectual influences, made the point that "Sullivan seems not to have read Emerson much, if any."[37] What cannot be questioned, as we have seen, is Sullivan's reverence for and intellectual and artistic debt to the transcendental poetic visions of the Emerson acolyte Whitman. When the adult Sullivan discovered Whitman's *Leaves of Grass* for the first time, it was as if he finally found the poet who could put into words the feelings and intimations that he himself felt with such intensity as a small boy. The line "There was a child went forth every day" was chosen to stand as the organizing epigram for the second chapter of Sullivan's autobiography. In another work, *Kindergarten Chats*, he specifically refers to Whitman, "the good, gray poet," as an unfailing source for understanding the power and value of a child's encounters with nature.[38]

In early 1860 Daniel Burnham was an earnest thirteen-year-old Chicago schoolboy. Little Louis Sullivan was three years old, not yet in school, and his early childhood idyl living with a large and loving extended family in south Boston was nearing an end. The next decade would prove crucial in determining the trajectory of their lives, both professionally and personally.

3

Pathways

1860s

"HE WAS THE HANDSOMEST BOY IN SCHOOL," recalled one high-school classmate of Daniel Burnham, though by some accounts Dan was not the most attentive scholar. As early as 1856, when Burnham was nine and still in elementary school, the only remark his teacher could make on Daniel's report card was, "Too slow about everything. Too sleepy."[1] In Central High's Class of 1865, standout class members like future state's attorney Luther Laflin Mills and business mogul Ferdinand Peck—destined to be the driving force behind Adler and Sullivan's Auditorium Building—were racking up grade averages in the high 90s, while young Dan's "restlessness" led to mediocre scores of between 55 and 81 percent. Even for a popular and outgoing boy, and one of the top athletes in the school, the best young Burnham ever managed was an 88 for "deportment." His interests lay elsewhere.

Most of all, he loved to draw. "He was never without a pencil in his hand," his former classmates told a *Tribune* reporter in 1895, endlessly annoying his teachers by his persistent sketching and doodling during the standard academic classes. He took a casual attitude toward his studies and was repeatedly censured for his negligence, though he managed to escape severe punishment because he "never forgot to be a gentleman in his manners." He visibly yearned for dismissal at the end of each session. However, he achieved prominence in the school before holidays and celebratory events, when "there were boards to be decorated, and he was the only one who could do it. He was then furnished with colored chalks and excused from all class recitations for about a week. This was just what he wanted and he was not selfish about it. He had friends among the boys who looked with longing upon excuse from recitation. He wanted assistants, and his work was deemed of enough importance to yield to this demand."[2]

GARDEN CITY INSTITUTE.

Chicago, January 11th 1856

Weekly Report for Daniel Burnham

RECITATIONS,	5 1/2	Duty requires 7	Excellence in what Study,	
DEPORTMENT,	5 1/2	" " 7	" " Exercise,	Declamation
No. of days absence,	1/2	" " 0	Deficiency in what Study,	
No. of minutes late,	0	" " 0	" " Exercise,	

REMARKS OF TEACHER:

Too slow about everything. too sleepy.

REMARKS OF PARENTS:

Parents please signify reception by signing and returning.

H. O. & O. T. Snow, Principals.

Assistant.

Nine-year-old Daniel Burnham's report card, Garden City Institute, 1856. (Daniel H. Burnham Collection, Ryerson and Burnham Art and Architecture Archives, Art Institute of Chicago. Digital file # 194301.081014-03.)

Lifelong friend Edward Waller was among his helpers in these artistic enterprises. He was less artistically adept than Daniel but more than willing to hold the chalk. The teachers seemed to tolerate the long, desultory talks between the two boys, for the instructors took "great pride in the decorated boards" and somehow intuited "that genius must have its failings."[3]

Louis Sullivan's earliest years spoiled him for the prospect of any alteration or curtailment of his carefree preschool life. The first shock came in 1861, when his beloved grandparents Henri and Anna List purchased four properties and moved to then largely rural South Reading, Massachusetts, some fifteen miles north of the house on South Bennet Street in Boston. Robert Twombly speculates that the move may have been prompted by a change in both families' financial circumstances—likely some form of inheritance—that possibly caused some friction between them but also enabled the move.[4]

More disruptions, some appealing to Louis and some not, would soon follow. In the summer of 1862, just before he entered elementary school in Boston, the Sullivans removed to a rural seaside farm in Gloucester, Massachusetts, and Louis, age five, spent a magical few months exploring the natural delights of Folly Cove on Cape Ann. As intently as he had studied the wonders of a Boston snowfall, Louis immediately embraced with Whitmanian exuberance the pleasures of vast fields, clear skies, and limitless sea. "It seemed natural to him," he recalled in later years, "that there should be flowers, grass, trees, cows, earth underfoot, men, women, children, the great ocean and its rock-bound shore. All these he took at their face value—they all belonged to him." He wandered through the spacious meadows, "picking the sparkling flowers, feeling the lush grass, glorying in the open." The summer even included a memorable fall into a well, with one of the farm's hired hands rushing to Louis's rescue and returning him to the house amid much fuss and bother of the women and the anxious parents.[5]

In the fall it was back to Boston, where Louis began nurturing his lifelong aversion to the regimented miseries of school. From the first, Louis Sullivan's distaste for school went beyond typical schoolboy restlessness. The intense and richly detailed memories of his summer days in Folly Cove gave way to a blank mental slate when he tried to recall his earliest schooldays. Writing as usual in the third person, Sullivan in old age seemed to willfully block out the painful particulars of the experience:

> What a dreary prison the primary school of that day must have been. His recollection of his stay there was but a gray blank. Not one bright spot to recall, not one stimulus to his imagination, not one happiness. These he found only at home. He learned his letters, he followed the routine, that is all. . . . The primary school had, for the moment, dulled his faculties, slackened his frank eagerness, ignored his abundant imagination, his native sympathy.[6]

So intensely negative were Sullivan's reactions that soon his parents packed him (and probably brother Albert) off to South Reading to attend a new school under the less-than-watchful eyes of Louis's maternal grandparents. Henri List did little to curtail Louis's rebellious ways, allowing the boy to explore nearby farms and fields in ways reminiscent of his glorious summer explorations at Folly Cove. As Twombly has noted, "Sporadic attendance during his first school year, coupled with indulgent but responsive adults, and large chunks of nature study, added up to an unusual educational episode, but one that proved to be a precedent, in fact, for an entirely unusual educational career."[7]

❧

In 1861 fourteen-year-old Daniel Burnham, caught up in the patriotic fervor that gripped the country, tried to enlist in the Union army, only to have father Edwin quickly extricate him from that obligation.[8] The boy's relatively undistinguished educational record was of more long-term concern to Edwin and Elizabeth. In 1863 Edwin took Daniel, along with daughters Ellen and Clara, from Chicago to Waltham, Massachusetts, where Dan would embark on a course of studies that he and his anxious parents hoped would result in acceptance to either Harvard or Yale. Then age twenty-six, Ellen kept house while Daniel, seventeen, and Clara, twelve, attended school. In Waltham Burnham first studied under Swedenborgian minister Joseph Worcester in a New Church school. Undoubtedly displaying the genial and engaging nature that would stay with him throughout his life, Daniel commenced a friendship with Worcester that lasted far beyond his brief stay at the school. Two years later Burnham's academic preparation was passed to another Swedenborgian minister, Tilly Brown Hayward in Bridgewater, Massachusetts. A Harvard graduate, Hayward guided Daniel through a period of preparation for college entrance examinations.

In later years, when asked about the boy he knew from this period, Worcester replied with evident fondness, "Dan was the most chivalrous young man I ever knew."[9] The combined efforts of Worcester, Brown, and Burnham's own, however, were not enough to make up for Daniel's previously neglectful academic preparation. He failed the entrance examinations for both Harvard and Yale, apparently a victim of an extreme case of test anxiety. The memory of his Harvard experience was especially painful. He went to Harvard, he said, "with two men not as well prepared as I," both of whom passed with no difficulty while Burnham simply "sat through two or three examinations without being able to write a word."[10]

It may be that his disappointing test performance was affected by other interests and impulses that had drawn his attention during his days in Waltham. It was there that he found time to engage in long discussions with Hayward and Hayward's friend William Pitt Preble Longfellow (nephew of the poet) on the subject of architecture. In Hayward's library, according to Charles Moore, Burnham's love of drawing began to take an architectural turn—an interest that neither Harvard nor Yale could directly satisfy.[11] In the 1860s in the United States, architecture was only beginning to be thought of as a profession distinct enough to require formal academic training. The first school of architecture in the United States would be established at the

Daniel Burnham at age nineteen. (Charles Moore, *Daniel H. Burnham: Architect, Planner of Cities* [Boston: Houghton Mifflin, 1921]. Ryerson and Burnham Libraries Book Collection, Art Institute of Chicago.)

Massachusetts Institute of Technology during the years of Burnham's stay in Waltham. Longfellow would go on to pursue a distinguished architectural career as a professor at MIT, as the first editor of the journal *The American Architect*, and many years later as chairman of the architectural section of the Board of Judges at Chicago's World Columbian Exposition, over which Daniel Burnham would famously preside.

Burnham was also beginning to show interest in young women, and it took no time at all for his thoughts to turn to matrimony. In 1866 he wrote home to his father about his feelings for one Anne Hyde. Friends had encountered Anne at a New Church party and vouched for her beauty. Burnham's report to his parents presented her faults and virtues with almost clinical objectivity and concern for her suitability as a mate: "When I am twenty-one I wish to go to Bridgewater and win her if I can. I believe she is the one best suited to me. . . . I have always had one like Annie in my mind and now know of but one fault which I think she will overcome. She is quick-tempered. But that must give way before her sense of duty. She will do as she thinks right against everything."[12]

Burnham even solicited his parent's judgment once they had a chance to examine the young woman in question. "I would like you to take particular pains when it is in your power to watch her character and I believe my opinion will be yours. She has no *boldness* or roughness, which you so much dislike and which I think is equally detestable to *me*. She has education and cultivation and withal a very engaging address, and impresses every one as being *lovely*."[13] Burnham cited his mentor Joseph Worcester's observation that those who marry from love will marry their ideal. This Swedenborgian sentiment would have appeal for an idealistic young man steeped in New Church concepts of the perfect communion available to right-minded, spiritually oriented couples through "conjugial love" and the institution of marriage.

However strong Burnham's feelings for Anne Hyde at this time, apparently his parents never had a chance to meet her, and mention of her quickly disappears from Dan's correspondence. By the following year he seemed to have shifted his attentions to a new love interest, a young woman whose name he spelled *Lilly*. Back home in Chicago in November of 1867 after his disappointments at Harvard and Yale, Burnham's thoughts turned to this new girl, who apparently had remained behind in Massachusetts. He said he wanted to return, for "more than anything I want to be near Lilly . . . I know she must be lonesome by herself having no intimate associates. It makes me feel desperate sometimes." He said he was determined to go back for her as soon as he could, though of course for a serious young adherent of the faith, he acknowledged that this temporary separation "must be far better so than any other way or He [God] wouldn't allow it." Again, he sought parental approval: "I know very well that the time will come when you not only will like but will love Lilly. For you all love me and when you see her making me a tender, true wife you will take her into your hearts too."[14]

Lilly appears again in another letter Burnham sent to his mother three weeks later. Lilly had complained to Daniel about having been pestered by a "young Wiloughby" at a party held at "Mr. H's," possibly the Reverend Hayward's home. Burnham wished he could have been there to gallantly "stare him out of countenance" as he claimed he once succeeding in doing to a group of people who made his sister Mary similarly uncomfortable at a dinner in Montreal. Burnham even included a sketch of the intimidating stare he claimed to have conjured up on that occasion.[15]

Whatever happened to Burnham's Lilly is unknown. In another letter to his mother, this one written in April of 1868, Daniel mentioned a betrothal party and his having received cheerful and tender letters from Lily (as he

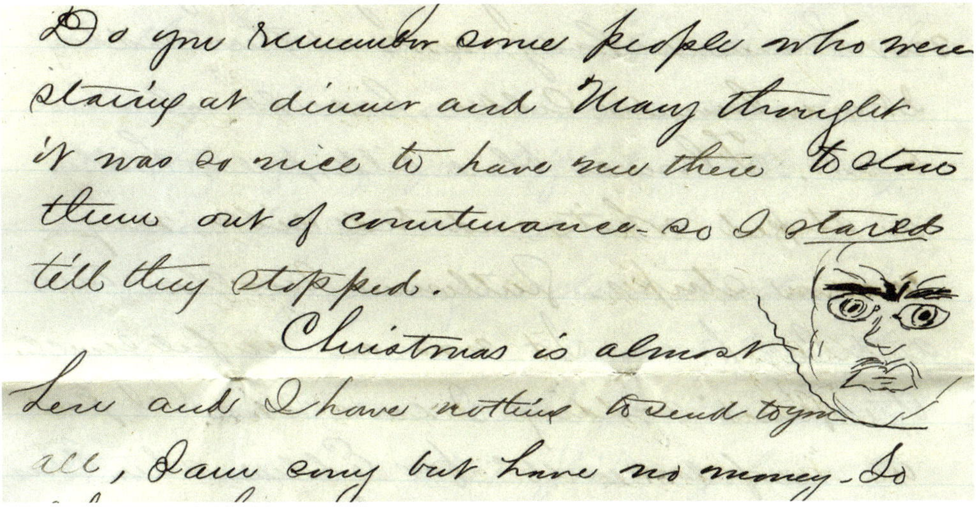
Do you remember some people who were
staring at dinner and Mary thought
it was so nice to have me there to stare
them out of countenance—so I stared
till they stopped.
Christmas is almost
here and I have nothing to send to you
all, I am sorry but have no money—So

In this letter to his mother, twenty-one-year-old Daniel Burnham included a light-hearted and impromptu caricature of himself to illustrate his effort to convince a young love interest that he possessed an intimidating stare sufficient to discourage intrusive strangers, as he claimed to have done on a previous occasion. (Daniel H. Burnham Collection, Ryerson and Burnham Art and Architecture Archives, Art Institute of Chicago. Digital file # 194301_240906-001.)

now spelled her name), but before long this Lily seems to have disappeared from the scene.[16] It would be eight years before Burnham found his true life partner, and even after some years of maturation, the courtship pattern for this young and somewhat impulsively romantic man would repeat itself: the time from initial meeting to intent to marry would prove to be similarly brief.

The written records during this period show an earnest and determined, if anxious, young man, still uncertain of his ultimate destiny but eager to find his way onto the right professional path. Back in Chicago after his college plans fell through, he spent a few unhappy months working in sales for the firm of Day, Allen and Company, wholesale grocers located at 34/36 Randolph Street, in the heart of the downtown business district just south of the river. As would almost always be the case with Burnham's work associates, Burnham's engaging demeanor and the earnestness with which he approached his assigned tasks made him well liked, even as he felt out of his depth in this environment. Early on his bosses could see he was not cut out for their kind of business, but they made allowances and tried to help him find a suitable place. Two fellow employees, S. P. Farrington and

C. Coryell, privately—and separately—told Daniel they planned to leave the firm and would consider taking him with them. One of the owners, W. T. Allen, even offered to fire one of their other employees to find a suitable place for Daniel. "I could get a letter of the very highest value from them if I needed it," Daniel told his mother. "One thing you will be glad to hear, they all spoke to me in the kindest and most gentlemanly way *always* when I was there which was more than they did to most of the men there."[17]

Burnham spoke respectfully of his employers, but the rough-and-tumble world of mercantile Chicago did not agree with him at this time in his life. He claimed to despise "all the evil and deceit I was obliged to witness in my every day life in 'trade' for there is a great deal of evil there." The moral laxity of Chicago businessmen didn't square with his Swedenborgian ideals. Above all, Burnham believed, one must strive to find a calling in accord with "the beautiful and useful laws God has created to govern his material universe." The idea of being *of use* was a special point of emphasis in New Church theology, and Burnham felt convinced that if once he was able to apply God's beautiful and useful laws to his work life, the result would be to "expand [Burnham's] mind and heart towards himself and all mankind," a highly desirable state of affairs.[18]

He knew that his religious convictions set him apart from many of his contemporaries. At the same time, he accepted the sincere skepticism of his mainstream Christian friends with respectful good humor. One day the mother of his good friend Ed Waller raised questions about his adherence to Swedenborgian doctrine. "I have been at the Wallers this afternoon and had quite a pleasant time. Mrs. Waller is greatly exercised about Swedenborg, and we had some lively discussions. But we are the best of friends."[19]

"Now are you sufficiently surprised[?]" Burnham asked his own mother during this period, preparing the way for a bombshell announcement on quite another subject. Having abandoned a career in business, and undoubtedly sensing his mother's anxiety over his future, he assured her that he had finally, at age twenty-one, found his calling. "I am to be an architect," he proudly declared.[20] The architectural interests sparked in Tilly Hayward's library in Waltham, together with his longstanding fascination with drawing, induced Daniel to try his hand as a draftsman in the Chicago architectural firm of Sanford Loring and William Le Baron Jenney.

With classmate Gustave Eiffel, Jenney had studied iron construction and classical architecture in 1850s Paris and subsequently earned a reputation as a skilled engineer for the Union army during the Civil War. He eventually was rewarded with the rank of major, giving him a title that stuck with him throughout his life. In 1867 Jenney embarked on a career that would ultimately make him a legend in the history of Chicago architecture, most notably as one of the key figures in the invention of the skyscraper, utilizing innovative construction methods on the Home Insurance Building of 1885.

But Burnham seemed closest to Sanford Loring, not Jenney, during the early days in the office. The two of them informally conversed about Daniel's prospects. "San said when I first spoke of going into [architecture]," Burnham reported, "'I would advise it by all means if a fellow feels that he has the talent.'"[21] Clearly Burnham felt his natural abilities and long-nurtured artistic interests were now coming together. His fondness for sketching and drawing was finding a logical outlet. When he first entered the Loring and Jenney office, he said, he hardly did "anything but sketch little affairs to see what I could do at draughting." Upon finishing an impromptu effort of a "little Gothic Arch," Jenney—a "sort of partner of San's," Burnham wrote—came by, looked over the sketch, and instantly gave him more work to do, drawings over which Burnham labored for two days. Burnham's conscientious effort paid off: "I did the last stroke Saturday night and coloured them. Jenney was *pleased*, and said so. After a little he broke out—'In one thing you surprised me. It was in making yourself useful when you first came into the office.' He says that students generally require the attention of the architect and are an annoyance, but on the contrary I was of use at first."[22]

At this early stage, the drawing table attracted him and focused his attention. To his mother he expressed eagerness to get back to his recreational drawing outside of the office, saying he looked forward to returning home and doing "some nicer things than I did last summer." As to his draftsmanship in the office, his took his cue from his sister Ellen in resolving to give meticulous attention to every detail:

> The only way is as Ellen says, "to make every stroke as good as I can and the next will be better." Tell her I am much obliged for that little sentence. I never had it put to me in such a practical way before. And since I read her letter it makes my drawing a new thing. I have often thought when I was drawing that I must make the drawings as carefully as I could, but now, Let this stroke be the best and most exact.[23]

To have found a place where his interest in drawing was regarded as useful undoubtedly delighted the youthful Swedenborgian chalkboard artist of Central High. "I am perfectly in love with my profession," exulted Burnham. "I don't feel the most secret doubt now that it is the place for me. I did when thinking of the ministry and when in business, but now that my work has actually commenced, it seems as if I could spend my life almost in the Office." He said he knew the work would be hard and require disciplined study, but he was determined to see it through, even without

RULES OF LIFE,

FROM THE MANUSCRIPT OF

EMANUEL SWEDENBORG.

1. Often to read and meditate on the Word of God.

2. To submit everything to the will of Divine Providence.

3. To observe in everything a propriety of behavior, and to keep the conscience clear.

4. To discharge with fidelity the functions of my employments, and the duties of my office, and to make myself in all things useful to society.

Found among the effects of Daniel Burnham's wife Margaret, this simple distillation of Swedenborgian precepts places special emphasis on self-control, submission, and usefulness in one's working and communal life—principles the entire Burnham family was expected to follow. (Daniel H. Burnham Collection, Ryerson and Burnham Art and Architecture Archives, Art Institute of Chicago. Digital file # 194301_240906-002.)

the benefit of a college education. It must have been a relief for Elizabeth Burnham to read the following sentence from her previously untethered son: "The instant that the thought came into my mind [to become an architect] I knew I had struck the rock and there would be no more drifting for me."[24]

Edwin Burnham was carefully tracking the good reports from the boy's new employers with equal concern. "I think that Dan has made a good impression in the architects' office—But have not been able to see Sandford [*sic*] as he is <u>always out</u> when I call. Shall see him soon. His partner speaks well of Daniel—and I think Daniel is becoming somewhat more earnest and hope he will acquire habits of application. If so he will succeed—he has no lack of capacity."[25]

Young Daniel expanded on his enthusiasm in a letter sent the following week, emphasizing both the spiritual and aesthetic dimensions of his newfound profession:

> The great use and delight of my profession grows in me more and more. It will open the mind more and more to the Great Architect of the Universe the more I study it in simplicity of mind and ask Him to help me. I am going down early tomorrow morning and try to see if I can't make every line I draw perfect and true. And in the evenings I am to study. I shall take John Ruskin's "Stones of Venice." . . . I am also going to study Physiology for that is architecture on the grandest scale which a man can see in this world.[26]

Physiology? John Ruskin? Here we see Daniel Burnham looking to immerse himself in the history of human thought in architecture and to search for his place within it. The idea that the human body represents "architecture on the grandest scale" and can even offer instruction for principles of architectural design goes back at least as far as the Roman writer and critic Vitruvius. That buildings should be "organic" and in some sense resemble the perfection of design in nature appears frequently throughout nineteenth-century thought, not least—as we have seen—among the New England transcendentalists. And the idea that the smoothly functioning and interdependent organs of the human body might bear "correspondences" to larger, beautifully designed structures of the universe, both in heaven and on earth, fits neatly into a Swedenborgian framework. Unsurprising for a young man showing serious interest in young women, Burnham's reading program at this time also included *Conjugial Love*, Swedenborg's well-known and oft-cited treatise on the complex ways love functions in the earthly and spiritual worlds.

It's also not surprising that Burnham expressed interest in John Ruskin, the British critic and architectural historian whose wide-ranging arguments on behalf of Gothic architecture were to have a profound effect on architects of the late nineteenth and early twentieth centuries. Ruskin's insistence that certain elements of the Gothic could be interpreted as in some sense possessing a moral and spiritual dimension likely held special appeal for Burnham. For example, according to Ruskin the curve of a Gothic arch, if properly done by a skilled craftsman, has sufficient strength to oppose the force of gravity in a way that resembles the power of true virtue to oppose worldly temptations.[27] With such high-minded theories as these in the air, Burnham's new career seemed to promise a path where his religious convictions and his earthly ambitions could comfortably coexist and even reinforce each other.

By mid-1868 Burnham's excitement over his new career plan was undiminished, and the scope of his ambition was soaring. "I shall try to become the greatest architect in the city or country," the twenty-one-year-old wrote his mother. "Nothing less will be near the mark I have set for myself." Perhaps even more revealing was the framework within which he was formulating his architectural identity. Major Jenney may have established his reputation as the quintessential engineer/architect, but that was not exactly how Daniel wished to define himself: "I know I shall never feel satisfied with my works. An artist never is."[28]

Concurrently in 1868, Daniel's early mentor Sanford Loring founded the Chicago Terra-Cotta Company, a forerunner of the Northwestern Terra Cotta Company. It would soon become a key Chicago manufacturer of the material that renewed and, in some ways, transformed the face and artistry of the city's commercial architecture.[29]

At roughly the same time that Daniel Burnham was enthusiastically embracing his new profession, in Massachusetts Andrienne Sullivan was pushing her husband toward a fateful decision that would have consequences for the history of Chicago architecture. Repeated bouts with diphtheria convinced her that persistent coastal winds in the Northeast were partly responsible for her illnesses. This prompted her to persuade Patrick to pull up stakes and seek their fortune in the supposedly milder clime of the American Midwest. They arrived in Chicago late in 1868.[30]

Throughout the 1860s Louis remained a restless and sometimes difficult student, whose true passions were reserved for lengthy rambles in the world that existed beyond the schoolroom walls. He had had various opportunities to indulge his love of nature throughout his early boyhood years: first at Folly Cove; then in the seacoast town of Newburyport, Massachusetts; in Halifax, Nova Scotia, where Patrick made a brief and ill-fated effort to open a dancing academy during the winter of 1863–64; and finally back in Boston and South Reading.

Newburyport especially loomed large in memory. Patrick and Andrienne spent several summers there starting in 1863, with Patrick offering his services as a dance instructor to vacationing city-dwellers. Louis, age six, accompanied them only once during that first summer. But the impressions he gathered during that time were impactful, and his summer in Newburyport would later occupy a full chapter of his autobiography. He vividly recalled the train ride up to the northeast coast, during which Louis relentlessly pestered the brakeman in conversation about every aspect of the locomotive and thrilled to every sensation caused by the motion of the train: the "swaying, rattling, banging, clanking, sinking suddenly, rising suddenly, screeching infernally around the curves, amidst smoke and dust and an overpowering roar."[31] The family rented quarters in an unprepossessing hotel for the summer, and Patrick proceeded to impose upon Louis a summer program of vigorous physical exercise. He woke Louis up at 5 a.m., took him by the hand to the town pump for a cup full of cold water, and then coaxed him into a morning run to get the circulation going, culminating in both of them stripping naked and plunging into the sea for demanding lessons in "scientific swimming."

Surprisingly young Louis took to it. He admired his father's skills in the water and found pleasure in the changes he could see in his own body. He appreciated how his father made him "supple and resilient," how Patrick "made of him for his age a competent diver and swimmer, made him vault fences, throw stones at a mark; taught him to walk properly—head up, chin in, chest out; to stride easily from the hip, loose in the shoulders." Of his efforts he later observed, "[T]he child worked with gusto; it became play." The swimming lessons nurtured in Louis a vison of male athleticism that would recur in different forms at various periods of his life: "For he had a new ideal now, an ideal upsprung in a morning's hour—a vision of a company of naked mighty men, with power to do splendid things with their bodies."

Newburyport once again awakened within him the powerful appreciation Louis intuitively felt for the natural world. Patrick and Andrienne were likewise alert to the aesthetic value of Newburyport and spent some of their free time doing sketches and drawings of the local environment. On one memorable day, as his family picnicked on the Merrimack River, Louis indulged his penchant for wandering off, watching the fish jump, and pondering the quiet beauty of the "river so wide, so dark, so silent, so swift in its flow." As he roamed through the woods near the river, "lost in the thought that the world about him was growing so large," he became aware of a looming presence, something "huge, long, and dark," a menacing object in the distance that was barely perceptible through the foliage.

As he moved closer, he slowly became aware that the object was an enormous bridge spanning the river. The "long flat thing" was suspended by chains from two tall stone towers that he briefly mistook for giants, of which he'd heard in fanciful Irish fairy tales from the family's "hired girl" Julia. Sullivan said his father had to explain to him what a bridge was and how the towers and the chains and the roadway all were firmly connected together to safely allow passage for a constant flow of people, wagons, and teams. His fears assuaged, Louis marveled at the mixture of human ingenuity and power that could be harnessed to create such an edifice. He had encountered the "old chain bridge," a historic wrought iron suspension bridge designed by Pennsylvania engineer James Finley and built by John Templeman in 1810. It was truly an imposing and original structure, the first

The Old Chain Bridge of Newburyport, Massachusetts, the first suspension bridge built in the United States. To an impressionable six-year-old Louis Sullivan, the soaring towers at first resembled terrifying giants from Irish fairy tales. Upon learning their true origin and function, he found his "child-mind freed . . . to wonder what men could do" and forced "to adjust itself to the greater world into which it had been suddenly catapulted." (Prints and Photographs Division, Library of Congress. Reproduction # LC-DIG-det-4a07568.

of its kind in the United States, with dramatically sloping peaked towers looming over massive stone piers. Small wonder Louis felt overwhelmed by its size and majesty.

Patrick later took Louis to the shipyards to explore other engineering marvels but also to see if he could find a middle ground between the boy's romantic enthusiasms and the practical realities of a constructed world. Louis had often taken pleasure in observing working men performing their daily tasks in the streets of Boston. His fascination was reawakened by the ship workers, in particular by one man whom he observed expertly working an adze and by others stirring kettles of hot tar, steaming and boring holes in wooden planks, and bolting the planks in place. "The child was in a seventh heaven; here were his beloved strong men, the workers—his idols. What a great world it was into which he had been thrust—the great river, the wonderful bridge, the harbor, the full rigged ships so gallantly moving."

The world of nature would always be the primary source of Sullivan's inspiration, but he saw no contradiction in also admiring the individuals who took the raw materials of the earth and used them to reshape and compose a new and marvelous built environment. Seashore, river, woods, a body-shaping physical regimen, hardworking craftsmen, a mighty bridge, trains, and gallant ships—they were all wrapped up together in the "engulfing splendor of Newburyport" for Louis Sullivan in the summer of 1863.

As always, Louis's summer idyll came to a lamented end, and in the fall he was briefly back in Boston before his father abruptly decided—"for reasons of his own," Louis noted, "whatever they were"—to open another dancing academy in Halifax, Nova Scotia. Louis once again was forced to experience the discomforts of hotel living in a northern environment much harsher than the ones to which he was accustomed. Patrick continued to put his son through rigorous tests of physical endurance, doing such things as marching him out in frigid weather, freezing the boy's cheeks and nose, and then having him wash his face with snow. Andrienne fell ill with diphtheria, and before long it was clear that the whole project was quickly turning into a failed experiment. The family returned to Boston in early spring, and Louis went once again to stay with his grandparents in South Reading until school opened late in 1864.

Fresh from the inspirations of Newburyport and the recurring sight of his idolized working men creating new structures seemingly out of nothing, Sullivan felt himself "developing pride, ambition, and a sense of growing power over material things." Louis maintained his mystical attachment to the open air, characterizing himself as "inarticulate, wondering, believing," but also acknowledged that he would "rather help build a stone wall than listen to a poem." What did not appeal to him was his return to the suffocating confinements of Boston. On returning there to live with his parents, he said, using his characteristic language of organic growth and decay: "The effect was immediately disastrous. As one might move a flourishing plant from the open to a dark cellar and imprison it there, so the miasmas of the big city poisoned a small boy acutely sensitive to his surroundings. He mildewed; and the leaves and buds of ambition fell from him."[32]

Even worse, once the shock of a return to big-city living had begun to recede, Louis suffered the second shock of re-entry to school, that most despised of institutions for this eight-year-old child. The boy spent two years at Brimmer School, then four more years at the Rice Grammar School on Washington Street. Brimmer, he said, was "vile, unspeakably gloomy; a filthy prison for children," in which he yearned for a teacher, a "kindred spirit . . . in whom he might rejoice," but found none. Rice School, he said, had a "deadly philistine air" in which he learned nothing aside from "a sort of mechanical infiltration" of learning that may have somehow managed to seep into his head.[33]

His attitude was partly attributed to the depressing gloom cast by the aging school building itself. A few years later, when the Rice School moved into a brand-new building—a structure designed in "a modern French style" by William Ralph Emerson and Carl Fehmer—the simple change in Louis's physical environment seemed to have an energizing effect on his feelings about traditional academics.[34] He still claimed to learn very little from his teachers, but he began to see schoolbooks as a key to unleashing his dormant intellectual power. As if by magic, he said, "he made a sudden swerve in his course, and became an earnest, almost fanatical student of books, in the light and joy of the new schoolhouse." His grammar book in particular opened his eyes to the power of words. Once he was able to move past the rigid prescriptions of the rules and render them "plastic" in his mind, the grammar book "passed into romance; a dead book became a living thing."[35] Like Sullivan's fond memories of Newburyport, the new light and airy learning environment would later inspire a chapter title in his autobiography, "Boston: The New Rice Grammar School." Such could be the effect of freshly imagined and materialized architecture on the spirit and soul.

More than a century later, when the Rice Grammar School that Sullivan had known was being slated for demolition, the scholar and South End resident Paul Wright expressed hope that locals would see the schoolhouse—the place where Louis Sullivan's educational experience found new life—as a link to historical and literary traditions. Wright was drawn to Boston to study those traditions, a line stretching back through Louis Sullivan to Emerson and Whitman and Perry Miller and the Puritans. He commented wistfully on the neglect of the school's most celebrated graduate: "One would like to report that the school is flourishing—with a portrait of Louis Sullivan, of course, hanging over the stage in the auditorium. But one cannot forget the realities of twentieth-century American life."[36] Efforts to save the school came up short as Paul Wright discovered that city hall had little interest in honoring the name of Louis Sullivan. Though the building was preserved, the school closed in 1981 to make way for conversion of the venerable structure into upscale condos.

Sullivan found other outlets for his outsized imagination beyond grammar books and the walls of his classroom. Like many kids of his time, he dove enthusiastically into Beadle's Dime Novels, the cheap, sensational pulp fiction series that found a ready market among young Americans from the early 1860s well into the twentieth century. "Here at last was Romance!" Sullivan exulted. "Here again were great men doing great deeds." Sullivan cared little for the alluring women characters. Though "always ravishingly beautiful and always eighteen," they barely registered in his mind. He found the villains slightly more interesting, but the manly heroes enthralled him. Like the vigorous laborers whom he saw hard at work every day in the streets of Boston, the larger-than-life male hero of the dime romance was to him that "magnificent man-god" capable of producing a thrill on every page, which he claimed meant more to him than anything he learned in school. Even this form of intellectual escape was tied to one of Louis's characteristic physical impulses: the desire to venture forth for exploration and adventure in the world outside of the stultifying constrictions of ordinary domestic life and the schoolroom. "Here was action in the open," he declared. "He could live these scenes."[37]

Determined to explore every nook and cranny of Boston and the surrounding areas, through several of his elementary-school years Sullivan ranged outward from his home base in the South End to explore as far north as Gloucester and as far south as Jamaica Plain. In his wanderings, he began "to see the city as a power . . . that extended the range and amplified the content of his own child-dream of power as he had seen it manifested in the open within the splendid rhythm of the march of the seasons."

In other words, the city—for all its constrictions and filthiness and crowding—still had latent within it immense power and possibilities for a boy who adored wandering its streets in the open air. However his understanding of that power remained incomplete.

> On one occasion in South Boston, his father took him to a reservoir atop a high hill to see a great view spread before them. The boy at once became exalted with awe at the living presence and expanding power of Mother Earth. . . . As the boy gazed in thrilling wonder, his father called attention, one after another, to special points of beauty in the land and waterscape, finally coming around to the Blue Hills, which indeed were blue and enchanting at the far horizon and its haze.

In the midst of this enchantment, Patrick pointed to two distant hills and asked his son to identify the larger. When Louis pointed to the nearest of the two, his father corrected him and explained the sometimes deceptive effects of visual perspective, which Louis claimed "deeply saddened and perturbed him." He said it made him acutely aware of the "mystery that lay behind appearances, and within appearances, and in front of appearances, a mystery which if penetrated, might explain and clarify all." Louis asked himself whether this mystery could ever be penetrated to find the truth behind appearances and decided that, sooner or later, he would be the one to do it.

His expanding intellectual self-confidence apparently, and perhaps excessively, showed up in his relationships with classmates as well. In the schoolyard Louis managed to incite occasional fistfights by bragging that he could lick any boy his size in the school. He admits he didn't win every time, but he acquitted himself well enough to be included in an unrecorded "Who's Who" among the schoolyard fighters. In his own words, he was "one of the gang and a tough." But he also claimed to have left the good boys alone. He took pride in his toughness, but he was no bully.

Sullivan's aggressive temperament showed itself at home as well. When his mother insisted on giving him piano lessons, the restrictive dullness of the experience soon spurred him into furious rebellion. He reacted similarly to his father's attempts to teach him drawing. His fierce reactions may seem odd in a boy so innately curious about the mysteries of artistic creation and so enamored, from an early age, of music and art. Both of his parents sketched and painted continuously and with considerable amateur skill. Their sketches of Newburyport and other natural scenes still reside in archival collections and show genuine talent and commitment. Sullivan also attested to the pleasure he took in visits to the Boston Music Hall, where the swelling orchestral strains of classical music found him "overwhelmed by the rich volume and splendor of choral harmonies—again a new and revealing world." Sullivan could apply himself diligently to work that interested him, but he could be just as quick to reject any imposition of dull uniformity or repetitive practice, especially if he saw it leading to nothing but recreating something that others could easily do.

Louis Sullivan's Boston ramblings led to an encounter one day in 1868 that brought him one step closer to his professional destiny. At the corner of Boylston and Tremont stood the newly constructed Masonic Temple, a five-story Gothic Revival building that bristled with complex stone tracery, arched windows, a vertical spire and tower, and bold and decorative string courses that seemed to segment the structure into horizontal layers. The architect was Merrill Greene Wheelock, a noted Boston watercolorist who also worked in architectural design.

When twelve-year-old Louis Sullivan first encountered the building, he regarded it as a thing apart from the depressing "conglomerate" of buildings he was accustomed to seeing throughout Boston and to which he assigned

Andrienne Sullivan drawing, *Anemone Japonica, Lyon's Falls*, October 1885. (Louis Henry Sullivan Collection, Drawings and Archives, Avery Architectural and Fine Arts Library, Columbia University.)

distinct personalities. He believed some "said vile things, some said prudent things, some said pompous things, but none said noble things." Boston's State House, with its famous gleaming golden dome, struck him as a mean and stingy old woman, while Park Street Church seemed to stand on guard over its graveyard as it silently monitored the crowds below. Faneuil Hall's simple historic majesty was punctured for him by his grandfather, who one day made a dismissive remark as they stood looking at it.

Wheelock's brand-new gray granite temple was unique—"fresh and full of laughter." The busy and traditional neo-Gothic detailing did not distract Sullivan from the overall effect; in fact, he was thrilled by the complicated web of arches and pinnacles that sprouted from the edifice. But Sullivan was most alive to what he saw as the structure's affinities with his beloved world of nature. The other Boston buildings, he said, denied the "flowers of the field." The Masonic Temple's distinctive corner tower rose from the ground like the stem of a lily, culminating in a "wondrous cluster of flowering pinnacles and a lovely, pointed finial." It was a design feature—an ornate vertical shaft that seemed to burst into intricate designs near the top—that would appear on many of Sullivan's exteriors, including some of the most celebrated tall buildings of his mature years.

The conventional decorative excesses of the Masonic Temple were evident even to critics at the time, and Sullivan came to liken his youthful excitement about the building to a kind of naïve adolescent infatuation. But the intensely personal and emotional attachment to the experience of architecture would remain, and his curiosity about how such buildings could come into being was instantly aroused.

Shortly thereafter Sullivan was struck by the sight of an extraordinarily dignified man in a frock coat and top hat entering a carriage on Commonwealth Avenue and signaling for the coachman to drive away. He asked a workman who the man was. The workman said, "Why he's the archeetec of this building. . . . the man what drawed the plans." Young Louis professed amazement at the idea that a man could have a job that consisted of dreaming up the plans for a building like the Masonic Temple out of his head. He said that before this time he had no idea that architects even existed. "What a great man he must be; what a wonderful man," he thought, to be able to do such things. In his autobiography, he claimed that this was the moment when he determined to become an architect. He relished the prospect of being able to create beautiful buildings, not so much from templates in books, but from his own imagination.

When Mrs. Sullivan's recurrent bouts with diphtheria finally led Louis's parents to make the decision to move to Chicago in 1868, they determined that Louis would stay behind with his grandparents to complete his education in the sparkling new Rice School. That fall the Sullivans, including Louis's older brother Albert, left Massachusetts for good, and twelve-year-old Louis continued his studies and his endless Boston-area rambles. He stayed once again with the Lists in South Reading, a town now in the process of being renamed Wakefield in honor of a wicker-chair manufacturer who had donated a new town hall to the city.

Masonic Temple, Boston, 1860s. To a young Louis Sullivan, this structure seemed to embody a natural freshness and vigor in contrast with the tired respectability of the buildings he encountered in his rambles around Boston. Its prominent corner tower, despite the Gothic detailing, reminded him of a lily stem bursting into flowering pinnacles at the top. By his own account, the building played a significant role in awakening his interest in architecture. (Prints and Photographs Division, Library of Congress. Reproduction # LC-DIG-pga-00388.)

Louis seemed to have few qualms about his parents' abrupt departure. He briefly cried on his mother's shoulder but had less difficulty separating from his father Patrick. For a boy who chafed at all forms of restriction, the absence of his immediate nuclear family—despite the many happy times spent with them in Newburyport and elsewhere—seemed more a liberation than a desertion. The relative laxness of Henri List's oversight would be a welcome, if temporary, change. He was, he said, "much relieved to say to his father: Good-bye! Now he was free!"

❧

As the decade of the 1860s neared its end, both Daniel Burnham and Louis Sullivan seemed to have arrived at similar career goals: to pursue the profession of architect and to become a significant force in the field. Twelve-year-old Louis Sullivan had not yet declared himself determined to achieve preeminent greatness as Burnham had, but Louis's scattershot and inchoate interests and emotions were quickly coalescing around a vision of himself as a creative force that could make a difference in the world. Within him, he said, the decision to pursue architecture represented "a presiding order, a primal impulse . . . governing and shaping him through his own marvel at manifestations of power, his constant wonder at what men could do." For both young men, architecture would become the avenue of choice to achieve great things.

There would still be detours along the way. The most surprising, perhaps, was Daniel Burnham's impulsive decision—just months after assuring his mother of his determination to stick with it until he became the "greatest architect in the city or country"—to join his friend Ed Waller on a mining adventure out West. Louis Sullivan, on the other hand, set aside his habitual distrust of schoolroom oppressors to apply himself to his studies. He saw himself as engaged in a different kind of mining, "digging into the solid vein of knowledge as a solitary miner digs . . . a young prospector grub-staked by an absentee provider [his father] now settled on the shores of a vast Lake far in the West." He stayed the course long enough to earn the only diploma he would ever receive in his lifetime, completing Boston's Rice Grammar School in June of 1870.

4

Apprenticeship

1870s

CHICAGO IN 1870 WAS an engine of activity, energy, and change. The city had literally just risen from the mud, as city fathers largely succeeded in raising the grade of the downtown by four to six feet and more. The process involved hoisting up buildings on hundreds of hydraulic jacks and filling in underneath, sometimes moving entire buildings by several blocks. The Burnham family arrived in Chicago just as the process was beginning, and young Daniel would have spent much of his youth watching the historic process of remaking a central American city unfold.

As part of the same long-term project to purify the city's water supply, in 1870 local officials were in the process of reversing the flow of the Chicago River away from Lake Michigan and down through the state's riverways to the Mississippi. It was considered a significant engineering feat brought to triumphant completion by July of the following year. Over time, however, it became clear that the slow-running water could not prevent sewage from backing up into the lake, and sediment that built up in the river bottom effectively stopped what current there was. The fundamental concept pioneered by Chicago's engineers was nevertheless sound. In the 1890s the Illinois and Michigan Canal was replaced by a wider and deeper Sanitary and Ship Canal, and as the twentieth century dawned, the long-sought desire to reverse the river reached a successful conclusion.

In 1870 the weariness, misery, and carnage of the Civil War were fading, and the Union's revered, victorious General Ulysses S. Grant was in the White House. The pent-up commercial energies of the nation were being unleashed, with railways increasingly converging on the emerging Midwestern metropolis as a trade and transportation center. In 1870 Chicago was the world's busiest railroad junction[1] and was rapidly establishing itself as the grain, lumber, and livestock center of the world.[2] In addition to the existing buildings that had been raised and moved, new ones were constantly going up. As historian Donald Miller has noted, "The legendary building boom the city experienced after the Great Chicago Fire actually began before it, when businessmen, who were fat with war profits, invested in new stores, hotels, and private places. . . . Hotels already large enough to accommodate small armies were made larger and vastly more ornate; and many more of them appeared beside the new five- and six-story brick-and-marble-faced business buildings downtown."[3] Though hardly a typical structure, the newly built water tower north of the central city—famously, and not inaccurately, described by Oscar Wilde as a "castellated monstrosity with pepper boxes stuck all over it"—is a fair representation of the degree of ornate display typical of the time. It was one of the few buildings to survive the fire and can still be visited today on Chicago's Michigan Avenue.

In the 1870s few Chicago architects were being recognized for innovation in design or construction of commercial architecture. Europe's attention tended to focus on what was happening in New York, but the traditional styles and construction methods used there, derived for the most part from European models, were rarely ground-breaking.[4] Twentieth-century critic Lewis Mumford went so far as to call post-Civil War America "autumnal," a period in which drabness and dinginess predominated and where even homes and buildings were characterized by an all-pervading darkness and gloom.

> The nation not merely worked differently after the Civil War: the country looked different—darker, sadder, soberer. The Brown Decades had begun. . . . Brownstone began to be used in New York on public buildings in the early [eighteen-]fifties, and just on the eve of the war it was first used as a facing for brick houses. With this alteration came dark walnut furniture, instead of rosewood and mahogany, somber wall papers and interiors whose dark tones swallowed up the light introduced slightly later by the fashionable bay window. By 1880 brown was the predominant note.

This brooding darkness that characterized the built environment after the death of Lincoln, Mumford asserted, only began to lift when Americans encountered, "like a sun thrusting through the clouds," the bold and glorious golden portal of Louis Sullivan's Transportation Building at the 1893 Chicago World's Fair.[5]

In reviewing Chicago's structures from this time, architect and historian Thomas Tallmadge asked a pointed question and gave a definitive answer. "Are we . . . on dangerous ground in maligning the architecture of Chicago, as practiced from the middle eighteen-fifties to almost 1880? Did they or did they not know what they were doing? And the answer to that is, in my opinion, that they did not." Tallmadge cited the continuing influence of hoary European styles, sometimes well done in New York and Boston but in Chicago "so furiously raged together . . . that the architects imagined a vain thing." He also blamed omnipresent "plan books" that promoted "an extraordinary uniformity from one book to another and are so close to the buildings of the period that one wonders which was the chicken and which the egg."[6]

The cluster of structures that existed in the historical heart of the city in 1870 were diametric opposites of the glistening towers and luxury residences that line that segment of the Chicago River today. Chicago was a city built on business, trade, and manufacturing, and the river was appreciated less for its natural beauty than for its functional efficiency in manufacturing and moving goods. Numerous Illinois Central Railroad lines terminated on the south side of the river, with the array of unappealing sheds and storage facilities that such terminal complexes inevitably bring with them. The north side of the river was dominated by the McCormick Reaper Works. Grain elevators, lumber yards, factories, warehouses, and mercantile establishments large and small lined the shores. Dozens of "swing bridges" that turned horizontally on central piers continuously clogged heavy river traffic and frustrated pedestrians and wagons trying to get across.[7] Things had gotten so bad that, by 1870, department store magnate Potter Palmer was relocating his Lake Street store farther south on State Street so his shoppers could escape the omnipresent dirt and the foul smells emanating from the nearby river.

In 1870 Dan Burnham was twenty-three years old and a world away from the problems and promises of his booming and befouled Midwestern urban home. His declared ambition to become the "greatest architect in the city or country" remained temporarily in abeyance as he had impulsively decided to seek instant riches mining for treasure in regions surrounding Elko, Nevada. He followed a Colonel Cummings ("a very honorable and staunch man") to try his fortune in the Nevada mines. His good friend Edward C. Waller partnered with Burnham on this youthful adventure.

According to Waller, his own involvement was set in motion after a chance meeting on the streets of Chicago with this same Cummings. When Cummings explained that he was carrying a parcel of his wife's silver to pawn, Waller offered to loan him money to avoid the necessity of pawning. Cummings appeared a short time later in Waller's office and said, as a return favor, he would let Waller in on a "good thing" out West, where Cummings had options on several mining claims. Waller then began investing in these claims, eventually to the point of putting his newly founded real-estate business at risk. Apparently Cummings had similar luck in convincing Burnham of the promise of this enterprise and to Nevada Burnham went.[8]

Not much is known of the day-to-day particulars of Burnham's experiences out West. We do know that Burnham ran for the Nevada legislature, an early indicator of Burnham's willingness to take on a leading role in shaping the growth of a newly emerging community. In early October 1870 Burnham spoke at a "rousing meeting" in Eberhardt to a "large and enthusiastic audience." He favored a Democratic platform that, the newspaper noted, sought higher working-class wages in opposition to the cheap-labor practices of "soulless corporations" for whom "cheap labor means continued immigration of Chinese—the more the cheaper and the better."[9]

From Burnham's writings of that period, we can also infer that his time out West left a deep impression. The Art Institute of Chicago preserves several dated and undated manuscripts composed by Burnham, which are set in vividly recalled western and wilderness landscapes. In some cases Burnham described his experiences in straightforward factual detail. In others he appeared to be making youthful forays into the world of literature by semi-fictional or poetic delineations of life in the mountains and mining camps.

In an early letter home to his sisters from White Pine County, Nevada, Burnham acknowledged homesickness and reported on "what a queer sensation it is to live here" with "Indians, Chinamen, Negroes, Irish, Germans, French, Americans & Spaniards all mixed up promiscuously," nearly all of whom were "very poor specimens of their races." The only indicator of any kind of incipient architectural interests appears in one brief note on the condition of Elko's houses, which were "of the most primitive sorts imaginable, built of mud, sticks, logs, [and] canvas." Burnham responded most positively to the natural environment: at sunset, he said, the snow-capped mountains opened up rich vistas of blue "and the most wonderful perspective you can imagine."[10]

A month later Burnham described traveling from Hamilton, Nevada, to Elko and offered his sister Ellen vivid sensory impressions of this brave new world, focusing once again not on buildings or the diverse inhabitants but rather on the natural environment:

> I saw very grand, impressive sights as I came through the mountains. The beautiful neutral tints of the cloud-shadows at one time, and then towards evening, a thunder shower, with the accompanyments [*sic*] of the deep-rolling echoes far away among the hills and valleys. And the air,

each evening, was filled with the melody of a thousand sweet bird-notes, and the dreamy effect, way off in the distance, of the whipoor-will, and the deep, sad note of the raven.[11]

Only nine years earlier, a young Mark Twain had embarked on a similar quest in this same region, filled with similar youthful enthusiasm. Venturing west of Salt Lake City on a trail approaching the Elko region, Twain began the journey thinking, "This was fine—novel—romantic—dramatically adventurous—this, indeed, was worth living for, worth traveling for!" It didn't take long, however, for the realities of the barren surroundings to sink in. "Imagine," wrote Twain, "a vast, waveless ocean stricken dead and turned to ashes; imagine this solemn waste tufted with ash-dusted sagebushes; imagine the lifeless silence and solitude that belong to such a place. . . . This is the reality of it." By the next year, Twain's hopes for instant wealth had vanished in a last-ditch effort to find pockets of gold, but when the "gold gave out in the pan, and we dug down, hoping and longing, we found only emptiness."[12]

In fact the richest veins Twain and others were to explore out West turned out to be literary, not mineral. Bret Harte, Ambrose Bierce, William Wright ("Dan DeQuille"), George Horatio Derby ("John Phoenix"), Louise Clappe ("Dame Shirley"), and Ina Coolbrith were just some of those who achieved notoriety, and in some cases monetary success, by writing fictional and real-life stories and poems of life in the mining camps and boom towns of Nevada and California.[13] And Daniel Burnham, while not openly professing literary ambitions, did take pains during his time in the West to compose writerly descriptions of the exciting and exotic world he briefly inhabited. One wonders if he was in any way inspired by the humorists, journalists, and poets writing about the mining frontier.

Unlike Twain, Burnham seemed not the least put off by the arid barrenness of the Nevada wilderness. He delighted in the "brilliant scarlet of the cactus" and the sight of "many flowers, whose names are unknown to me, and which I never saw before." Young Dan Burnham felt energized by what he regarded as the manly challenges of his western adventure. "I slept now on a bed, now on a floor, with only a blanket—But I am strong and healthy, and slept as soundly and sweetly as any infant." He even took pleasure in what appeared to be a close brush with a reputed outlaw. "I rode for two days with a very pleasant fellow named Kennyon, and slept with him one night. The next day a fellow told me he was a noted horse-thief." Not a problem for Daniel Burnham, western adventurer. "[H]e and I got along very well together, and he was very kind and considerate, and I think many a better man, might be helped by having a little of Kennyon's heart and feeling."[14]

Elko is situated in the arid central high plain of Nevada but is set among mountainous ridges and valleys that fit well with Burnham's poetic personification of a wayward mountain breeze:

> It wanders from valley to valley all unconscious of the death resting in its bosom which now in its tender age only nourishes its gentle flowers, kissing them ever so gently, as it lingers among them, But anon it wanders among the crags, where no tender plant may grow, and suddenly as it turns some high precipice it meets the wild chilling winds of the north, and hesitating a little, it at last becomes charmed with the freedom of its new found companion, and uncontrollably lured on, it hurls itself headlong into the hurricane. . . . The flowers are rooted up and crushed, the old pines bend and groan, the green hill side is torn and scarred by its course. . . . Here under this ledge, where a wild rose grew, there is now no sign remaining to tell the sweet story of its life. . . . Where the clear silver brook wandered down o'er the hillocks, is now only a muddy stream and the dregs of the torrent. The brook may again grow pure, and the wild rose take root, but years must elapse . . . before the seeds of the other can again be planted high up the mountain in the pure air where once they grew.[15]

The self-conscious literary language, the hackneyed romantic imagery, the labored personifications, the disturbing melancholy of the central message—joyful innocence, apparently female, carrying "death resting in its bosom," meeting up with a "new found [male?] companion" that blights its purity and crushes the blooming life around it—all suggest a young man trying to exercise his verbal muscles in florid nineteenth-century prose.

In another piece probably from about this time, Burnham imagines young men yearning to exchange their big city ennui for exciting adventures out West. He invents a fictional alter ego named Jones who arrives in Nevada outfitted in the foppish apparel of the East—a "full hunting costume" of "green velvet coat, skull-cap, knee-pants, and top-boots" who finds himself having to share a stagecoach wedged between a rough-edged passenger in a slouch hat he nicknames "Whiskers" and a gentleman in the black waistcoat of a "gambler-like ensemble." Whiskers assured him that highwaymen rarely attacked stagecoaches in large parties: "only three on each side of the stage" armed with two double-barreled shotguns apiece. The only danger, said the gambler, might come when the robbers fire shots into the coach "just to start up the horses you know."

"'Do they always do that?' asked Jones.

"'Always,' said Whiskers, 'though if you duck your head in time you are all right, but a few buck shot don't amount to any more than swallowing so many grapes.'"[16]

Jones appears again in a story in which, after making a fortune on Wall Street, he convinces his wife to travel with him—not to Paris or the Rhine, as she desperately desires, but to the wilds of Elko, Nevada, where he mixes with ambitious politicians and complains about the exploitative cruelty of the Bank of California in the mining camps.[17]

What to make of these youthful effusions? Clearly Burnham was playing with literary conventions and practices of the day: humorous tales of encounters between genteel Easterners and frontier roughs, earnest evocations of nature in the language of American romanticism, and tales of soaring hope and bitter disappointment. It seems possible that the diatribes against the Bank of California may have had some bearing, directly or indirectly, on the failure of Burnham's and Waller's western dreams.[18]

We know that from an early age Burnham liked to draw. Documentary evidence shows that he also liked to write during this period of his life. In more than one way, he was expressing a personal interest in artistic endeavors and even trying his hand at abortive efforts in descriptive nature writing and frontier storytelling, even if only for his own amusement and that of his family. But as with Mark Twain, Burnham's dreams of wresting a fortune from the ruggedly beautiful western wilderness would end in disappointment. His bid to join the state senate failed. By December of 1870 he was back with his family in Chicago, with no discernible plan for the future.

While twenty-three-year-old Daniel Burnham was writing letters home from the dusty mining camps of Nevada during the summer of 1870, thirteen-year-old Louis Sullivan was embarking on a joyous idyll in upstate New York amid the luxuriant greenery of the farm owned by "Tante Jennie" and Uncle Walter. Sullivan's maternal grandfather, Henri List, had suddenly been seized with the idea to visit the family of his second daughter, Jennie List Whittlesey, and off to Lyons Falls they went, with young Louis excited at the prospect of a new natural landscape to explore. "Grandpa," Sullivan recalled saying to Henri, "I have never seen a waterfall, only in pictures, and they don't roar; I want to live with a *real* waterfall; and I want to see the Berkshire Hills; and the Hudson; you know, Grandpa, pictures don't give you any real idea."[19]

On arrival Louis caught a glimpse of a young woman who was deep into a book and nestled in an easy chair near an open doorway on the veranda. After later touring his aunt's house, he rushed back to the veranda and the girl was still there, still absorbed in reading. When she rose to greet him, he said he saw in her eyes "an endless fund of merriment, of badinage, of joy, of appeal, of kindness, and saturated with an inscrutable depth beyond all of these." In Sullivan's telling, eighteen-year-old Minnie Culver thought to herself, "I'm going to like that boy." In the weeks that followed, Louis would spend endless happy hours with Minnie, exploring the surrounding woodlands, reading Tennyson together, and learning about life from the older and more worldly Minnie. She was his "precious teacher," his "faerie queen," and in some sense his first love, or at least the focus of his first significant relationship with a young girl near his age.[20]

All summer pleasures must end, however, and in the fall Louis found himself back in Boston, taking examinations to enter Boston's English High School, a "single building, rather old and dingy . . . a barnlike repellent structure fronting on a lane as narrow as the prevailing New England mind of its day." To a boy who much preferred the freedom of forest and meadow to the pent-up restrictions of formal education, and who impatiently sought "to advance in the shortest time compatible with sure results," the prospect of yet another year of prescribed drudgery repelled him.[21]

Yet Sullivan encountered one of his first introductions to the pleasures of a life of the mind at English High School. It came in the form of a teacher, Moses Woolson, an inspirational polymath. As Robert Twombly has noted, "Louis came to think of Woolson as a complete and wonderful man, combining the best qualities of teacher, poet, scientist, and naturalist."[22] The lectures that "gripped [me] the hardest," recalled Sullivan, "were those on English literature. Here the master [Woolson] was completely at ease. Here, indeed, he reveled . . . in the careful analysis and lucid exposition of every phase of his subject, copious in quotation, delightfully critical in taking apart a passage, a single line, explaining the value of each word in respect of action, rhythm, color, quality, texture, fitness, then putting these elements together in a renewed recital of the passage which now became a living moving utterance. . . . [He] opened to view a new world, a new land of enchantment." Like Burnham, the youthful Sullivan was awakening to the power, beauty, and complex effects of the written word.[23]

Throughout his life Sullivan combined a highly dismissive critical temperament with an openness to sudden, intense epiphanies and enthusiasms. He would find himself seized by a new and overwhelming encounter or insight, whether engendered by a new discovery in the world of art or music, a moment of transcendent exhilaration in nature, or an admired role model.

Louis Sullivan at age fifteen in 1871. (Sullivaniana Collection, Ryerson and Burnham Art and Architecture Archives, Art Institute of Chicago. Digital file # 193101.C33881.)

Such was the case with Woolson. Sullivan's fascination with literature and writing took firm root in Moses Woolson's classroom. In later years, in his soaring and complex rhetoric, Sullivan often seemed to aspire to the kind of impassioned microanalysis that he had admired years before in Woolson. Speaking of the difficulty of learning architecture solely from books, for example, the adult Sullivan could opine in distinctly Woolsonian terms: "Each word is not the simple thing it appears, but, on the contrary, it is a highly complex organism, carrying in its heart more smiles, more tears, more victories, more downfalls, more bloody sweats, more racial agonies than you can ever dream of."[24]

Something in Woolson's intellect and means of expression spoke deeply to the awakening artist in Sullivan. His second year at the high school offered no such intellectual and emotional stimulation, but he was able to find a new mentor soon enough. The death of his grandmother Anna in April of 1871 hit Louis hard, and before long he had to undergo separation from his grandfather as well, who soon sold his Boston properties and moved to join his son in Philadelphia. Sullivan was left in the care of neighbors, the John A. Tompson family, whom Sullivan had known and whose son George for years had been his playmate. George had induced Louis to take entrance examinations for his own school, the Massachusetts Institute of Technology, commonly referred to by Bostonians of the time as "Boston Tech." Showing what was to become a typical impatience with formal education, Sullivan did not bother finishing high school. After gaining entrance to MIT, he enrolled for the school's architecture program in October 1872. He was just sixteen.

One year earlier, almost to the day, Louis Sullivan's parents had survived the Great Chicago Fire of 1871. Patrick and Andrienne's home and dancing academy, on Twenty-Third Street, was located well south of the O'Leary barn, where the conflagration famously started. Several days of strong winds blew the fire northward, creating a swath of destruction that cut through the central business district, crossed the river, and wrought devastation as far north as Lincoln Park. The toll taken by the fire was enormous, covering some 3.5 square miles, destroying more than 17,000 buildings, claiming the lives approximately 300 inhabitants, and leaving almost 100,000 Chicagoans homeless. Attending English High in Boston at the time, Louis was relieved to receive word that his family had escaped the ravages of the blaze. The Sullivans' abode, like the O'Leary home itself, had been spared due to being on the favorable side of the wind, while the heart of the city lay in smoldering ruins. It did not take long for the city to draw a host of aspiring and seasoned architects and engineers, eager to assist in the immediate rebuilding and rebirth of the great city by the lake. At the very starting point of his architectural training, Louis was not yet among them.

In contrast, Daniel Burnham was in the right place at the right time for a budding architect. He had served a brief stint as an assistant in the offices of John Van Osdel, the legendary Chicago builder and architect. As we have seen, Van Osdel had arrived in the city during the pioneer days of the 1830s. He quickly gained prominence, designing such structures as its city hall and county courthouse, the original Palmer House, and the state governor's Illinois Executive Mansion in Springfield. While several of his buildings had been destroyed by the fire, Van Osdel—now a bewhiskered elder statesman in his sixties—was an active participant in the flurry of immediate rebuilding that took place in Chicago after the fire.

Burnham undoubtedly picked up some useful knowledge during his short stay with Van Osdel and partners, but he soon felt the need to move on. Now back in Chicago after his failed western experiment, he briefly resumed the pursuit of his earlier ambition, setting up a short-lived architectural practice with one Gustave Laureau. Biographer Charles Moore notes that Laureau "disappeared at the time of the Fire," after which Burnham briefly "sold plate glass for a man named Dodge."[25]

With young Daniel still casting about for a worthy entrance into the profession, in 1872 his father Edwin solicited the Chicago firm of Carter, Drake and Wight in a letter addressed to Asher Carter. "Respected & Dear Sir," wrote the senior Burnham from his drug and paint store on Canal Street, "Will you allow me to introduce my son Daniel H. Burnham and to bespeak your kindness, in his behalf." Edwin expressed the hope that Daniel could "render himself useful in obtaining a more perfect knowledge of his profession" by obtaining a position within the firm and signed off with the conventional, and gentlemanly, "Your Obedient Servant, Edwin Burnham." Peter Wight placed the letter in a tin box and kept it for years.[26]

Wight took the young apprentice under his wing and taught him many of the fundamentals of architecture in the heady atmosphere of a city bent on instant resurrection. In 1915 Wight later recalled the challenges and the opportunities that lay before his young apprentice. Burnham's father, said Wight, "was very desirous the Dan should be cured of his roving disposition and continue the study of architecture. He was . . . put under my personal direction as a student. I introduced him to John W[ellborn] Root, who had followed me from New York to Chicago during the winter of 1871–2 and was then head draftsman in our office. We were very busy trying to do our share in rebuilding the burned city."[27] Wight apparently had had no difficulty convincing head draftsman Root to follow him to the burgeoning city whose core lay in ruins. "Chicago wants me," John Root wrote at the time, and westward he went, an event soon to be followed by his fateful first meeting with young Dan Burnham.[28]

Back in Boston at MIT, Louis Sullivan had begun his architectural studies under the established and respected architect William Ware. Louis found him "a gentleman of the old school. . . . His attainments were moderate in scope and soundly cultural as of the day; his judgments were clear and just. The words amiability and quiet common sense sum up his personality." He observed Ware with a mixture of mild affection and condescending amusement. Ware, said Sullivan, "was quite human and in a measure detached. The misfortune was that in his lectures on the history of architecture he never looked his pupils in the eye, but by preference addressed an audience in his beard, in a low and confidential tone, ignoring a game of spitball underway."[29]

To the artistically passionate young Sullivan, Ware possessed a fatal professional defect: "he was not imaginative enough to be ardent." Ware had worked in the offices of the most acclaimed American architect of his day and the first American to have been schooled in Paris's famed École des Beaux-Arts, the New York-based Richard Morris Hunt. Through Hunt, Ware had become fully immersed in the Beaux-Arts' allegiance to French classicism, and in fact later became well-known as the author of an instructional book on how to draw and design the classical orders of architecture.

By an accident of history, we have direct evidence in Louis Sullivan's own hand of Ware's unimpassioned manner and his classical allegiances. In a notebook housed in the Avery Library at Columbia University, we find two pages of an introductory lecture by Ware that Sullivan meticulously recorded, word for word. In the offices of the workaday world, Ware declared, architects acquire experience in the practical side of the trade: the mechanical requirements of plans, contracts, and specifications. In school, he said, the "science" of architecture is studied, and "by critically studying the works of the greatest masters, we endeavor to cultivate a refined taste, and sound judgment." And what did he cite as the beginning basis of sound judgment? It started with the standard three-part division of a classical façade: "An entire architectural order included pedestal, column, and entablature." As to walls, "there are certain kinds of walls and wall cappings which the experience of centuries has proved to be better than any others." Respect for the architectural practices of the past permeated this brief glimpse into the content of Ware's MIT classroom.[30]

The curriculum Sullivan studied was therefore rigorous and traditional but likewise tortuous and uninspiring. He began to feel "a vacancy in himself, the need of something more nutritious to the mind than a play of marionettes. He felt the need and the lack of a red-blooded explanation, of a valiant idea that should bring life to arouse his cemetery of orders and styles." It didn't take Sullivan long to make up his mind to leave the school at the end of the academic year.[31]

His departure, however, did not mean that his time at Boston Tech had been wasted. He had been a diligent student and learned much about the mechanics of architectural work and the physical environment of Boston. He roamed the streets of Boston, identifying buildings that captured his imagination and interest, such as H. H. Richardson's Brattle Square Church, a rough-stoned edifice with wide round Romanesque arches and a soaring tower. He also served with one of MIT's military student battalions sent out to search for looters on Boston's streets after a calamitous fire in November 1872. Coming just one year after similar devastation in Chicago, the event left an indelible impression on young Sullivan and gave him firsthand experience with a destructive urban fire. "What a terror, what a holocaust, what ruin of men, what downfall, what instant collapses of fortune, what a heavy load to meet and bear, what a trial and a test," he wrote. But echoing the aggressive optimism of the Chicago survivors of the previous year, he added, "Yet a proud spirit, the eternal spirit of man, rose to the height of the call of calamity."[32]

Upon leaving MIT and perhaps bearing a letter of introduction from Ware, Sullivan found his way into the New York office of Ware's old mentor, the renowned Richard Morris Hunt. Hunt devoted some time to tell stories and deliver sage advice to the young man and then turned him over to an assistant, who suggested that Louis seek work with another Hunt protégé, Frank Furness, then practicing in Philadelphia. Sullivan shortly reunited with his grandfather and Uncle Julius in Philadelphia and applied to join the firm of Furness and Hewitt.

For this particular architectural apprentice, it was a match made in heaven. Furness was a busy and well-regarded architect. He was also an idiosyncratic character: temperamental, opinionated, independent, and original. By Sullivan's account, Furness's face "was snarled and homely as an English bulldog's," and he looked over the young applicant "half blankly, half enraged, as at another kind of dog that had slipped in through the door." Upon hearing that Sullivan had studied at the Massachusetts Institute of Technology, Furness launched into a verbal explosion that "blew up in fragments all the schools in the land and scattered the professors headless and limbless to the four quarters of the earth and hell." Calling the new hire a fool, "He said Louis was an idiot to have wasted his time in a place where one was filled with sawdust, like a doll, and became a prig, a snob, and an ass." To one who was developing a comparable disregard for the value of formal education and the professors who sought to pour their students into European molds—and whose penchant for strongly held, often acidic, opinions was equal to the boss's—Furness failed to offend. Quite the contrary. "It was here," Sullivan later asserted, that "one could really learn."[33]

And learn he did. Sullivan marveled at Furness's skills in freehand drawing and respected, with somewhat less enthusiasm, the by-the-book productions of Furness's partner George Hewitt. In all things Sullivan sought to apply the demands for speed and precision he had learned at the feet of Moses Woolson. Twombly credits Furness with influencing Sullivan's abilities in elaborate floral ornamentation, multicolored design, and methods of presenting individual elements emerging from strong masses of stone, though as we have seen, Louis had already carefully observed his mother's notable skill in floral design.[34] A quick glance at the complex polychrome patterning of one of Furness's most celebrated works from this period, the

Pennsylvania Academy of the Fine Arts, reveals just how inventive and idiosyncratic Sullivan's boss could be. Under the patient tutelage of Furness's brother William, Sullivan said he became "a draftsman of the upper Crust, and Louis's heart went out to [him] in sheer gratitude."[35]

Furness may also have helped deepen Sullivan's awareness of the philosophical and religious doctrines of the transcendentalists. Furness's father, William Henry Furness, had been a Unitarian minister, a friend of Emerson's, and in Isaiah Ellis's words, "the leader of Philadelphia's Transcendentalist salon." The senior Furness had even been given the opportunity to expand upon transcendentalist ideas as applied to architecture in an address to the American Institute of Architects in November of 1870.[36] William Henry's architect son seems to have applied at least some of his father's principles to his work, going so far as to assert that design solutions could be found in forms observed in nature, an idea that would have appealed to his young assistant Louis Sullivan.

But Sullivan's seedtime in Furness's shop was not to last. On a warm day in 1873, with the office's windows open, Sullivan said he heard a murmur in the streets outside, which soon "became a roar, with wild shouting." The Great Financial Panic of 1873 had begun, and Sullivan would soon hear that "credit had crumbled to dust, that men were ruined, and insane with despair; that this panic would spread like wildfire over the land, leaving ruin in its wake everywhere."[37] The panic was set off when a European stock market crash caused foreign investors to sell off their investments in American enterprises, most notably in American railroads. Consequently many railroads went bankrupt, and the shock waves from these and other failures reverberated throughout the economy. When Jay Cooke and Company, one of the biggest banks in New York, declared bankruptcy, a nationwide run on the banks caused a chain reaction within the banking system, reaching into Pennsylvania and beyond. The resulting depression lasted for most of the remaining decade.

Within a few weeks a chastened Frank Furness approached Sullivan and regretfully delivered the news that business had dried up and Sullivan would have to go. With few options open to him, Sullivan resolved to join his parents in Chicago. He describes his cross-country journey to the rebuilding metropolis in terms of steadily growing excitement. The valley of the Susquehanna River and the majestic Allegheny Mountains opened new vistas to the young man who had known only New England and the East Coast. The wide-open prairies of Indiana amazed and bewildered him. "How could such things be!. . . . Here was power, power greater than the mountains. Soon Louis caught glimpses of a great lake, spreading also like a floor to the far horizon, superbly beautiful in color, under a lucent sky. Here again was power, naked power."[38]

Just how accurate such supercharged recollections were, as described in his autobiography at a remove of almost forty years, is hard to assess. Sullivan always gave himself over to powerful emotions and extravagant expression, and he may well have felt this way as an ambitious and romantic seventeen-year-old on his first trip to what was then considered by many the American hinterland. Or he may have embellished the story of his arrival in the city that was to shape and define his architectural legacy. Did he really, as he claimed in his autobiography, tramp along the platform at the Chicago terminal, look toward the ruined city, look at the sky, stamp his foot, melodramatically raise his hand and declare in full voice, "This is the place for me!"?[39]

We can't know for certain. We do know that Louis joined his parents at their Chicago home for Thanksgiving 1873, and that's when Sullivan's Chicago story begins.

Contrary to some popular conceptions, the influx of ambitious architects in the years immediately following the Great Chicago Fire did not transform the city overnight into an engine of architectural creativity and innovation. Instead, for much of the 1870s, builders and designers—Van Osdel and others of his generation among them—sought to recreate Chicago's downtown and followed well-established and undistinguished architectural designs of the pre-fire days. Within a few years after the fire, as Donald Miller writes, "the rebuilt business core . . . looked much the same as the downtown of 1871 except that it was larger and a few stories higher."[40] The architect Thomas Tallmadge saw the fire as an "episode rather than a turning point in the development of Chicago architecture," since the builders of 1870 to 1880 were simply following European styles that were considered "the *sine qua non* of elegance" at the time.[41]

The construction boom years immediately following the fire clearly benefited the firm of Carter, Drake and Wight. Peter Wight's head draftsman, John Root, was undoubtedly busy at work when a promising new hire named Dan Burnham walked in. Both young men had an appealing physical presence and were instantly drawn to each other. "Mr. Burnham was a trifle taller and heavier than Root," noted Harriet Monroe. "[A]lmost as blonde and slender and supple. Root's skin had that transparent pink-and-white which often goes with reddish hair, and eyes bluer than blue. His eyes always betrayed him; to the last they told the secret of his mood. His instinctive shyness was conquered in a measure by the other's open-hearted fervor, and a comradeship of a score of years began."[42]

Burnham's own description of their earliest encounters matches Monroe's emphasis on the two men's striking physical and personal qualities, perhaps calling to his mind some of the vivid and down-to-earth characters he encountered during his recent western adventures. "I remember how John looked as he stood before a large drawing board with his sleeves rolled up to his elbows," Burnham recalled. "From the first he pleased me; the strength of his muscles, the babyish whiteness of his skin, his frank smile and manner appealed to me, and we became great cronies." Burnham was twenty-five when the two met, Root was twenty-two. Both were ambitious, intelligent, artistically inclined individuals in a rough-edged, rebuilding city that seemed to be bursting with promise and possibility. Little wonder that, as Harriet Monroe put it, "The two young men talked lightly of the coming time when the conditions might justify them in forming a partnership."[43]

The opportunity seemed to come soon enough. By the winter of 1873, Burnham had arranged for several projects for the business partnership he and his new friend envisioned, and the two men felt the time was approaching to take the plunge. As it turned out, the timing could hardly have been worse. The same financial panic that induced wild shouting in the streets of Philadelphia, and which ultimately led to Louis Sullivan's removal to Chicago, also had an immediate impact on the infant enterprise imagined by Burnham and Root. While still with Wight, Burnham started taking on small jobs that he and Root could work on nights in a small room Burnham rented at 90 Washington Street. Burnham described the hardships of those early days of transition at a time of financial uncertainty:

> Root came at night and afterwards for half of each day. We found it difficult to keep enough cash on hand to pay the office expenses and his board. Then Root came permanently, giving all day and half the night to our drawing. . . . I lived with my father and paid no board. The panic of 1873 came and most of the little plants we had hoped to see blossom were blasted. . . . We must have burned a ton and a half of soft coal that winter in order to keep our fingers warm enough to work! Paper we bought a few yards at a time, just enough by the most economical handling to lay out the immediate plan and an elevation or two. Then with a couple of pencils, a piece of rubber, a few boards, two stools, and a dozen thumb tacks we did business.[44]

One client whose building project fell through used $500 worth of credit with his tailor to pay Burnham and Root for the work they had done on his plans. He gave each of them a "suit of dark blue clothes." Thus outfitted, said Burnham, “we were enabled to resume our social duties without the queer feeling that had been growing upon us.” As with many successful individuals who look back upon early struggles, Burnham saw those days through a haze of proud nostalgia: “We were gay and very happy; work gradually came our way, and when it did we used to dive down to the next floor below, burst in on Dr. [William] Woodyatt [whose medical offices shared the same building], a crony of about our age, and tell him about it.”[45]

The “we” in Burnham’s statement was clearly a heartfelt acknowledgment of the mutual respect Burnham and Root felt for one another. The bond between them established instantly in Wight’s office would last without break until Root’s untimely death in 1891. “A very close friendship was cultivated between Burnham and Root from the time they first met,” Wight recalled. Root’s departure deprived Wight of his head draftsman and the man whom he had expected to make his partner after the death of senior partner Asher Carter.[46]

John Wellborn Root’s contemporaries universally recognized him as a young man of exceptional talent. An accomplished musician, he had studied with one of England’s most celebrated organists during the Civil War and returned to the States to study engineering in New York before settling on a career in architecture. Though quiet and reserved in his personal demeanor, Root actively took part in athletics and cultivated a gift for friendship. “I am about the strongest boy in school,” he wrote, “where I have a large number of friends and no enemies,” an assessment borne out by a classmate’s comment: “Every student felt the glow of his bright, genial spirit, while to an inner circle was given a friendship peculiar, original, potent.” In most of these qualities he closely resembled his new friend and the solid anchor of the partnership, Dan Burnham. When the two of them were together, said the wife of one early client, it felt as if one was in the presence of “some strong tree [Burnham] with the lightning [Root] playing around it.”[47]

A sketchbook from August of 1872 shows Burnham trying his hand at copying plates from F. A. Paley’s *A Manual of Gothic Mouldings* along with freehand drawings of horses and other natural forms.[48] Harriet Monroe recorded that in these early days the two partners made careful studies of historical architectural styles and for a time called themselves “Gothicists” for their devotion to elements of medieval Gothic in design. “They would make each other guess the period of details published in architectural publications,” said Monroe, “until at last they could place them within ten years in the nation to which they belonged.”[49]

From the beginning Root thought like an artist immersed in the atmosphere of nineteenth-century American romanticism. At about the time of

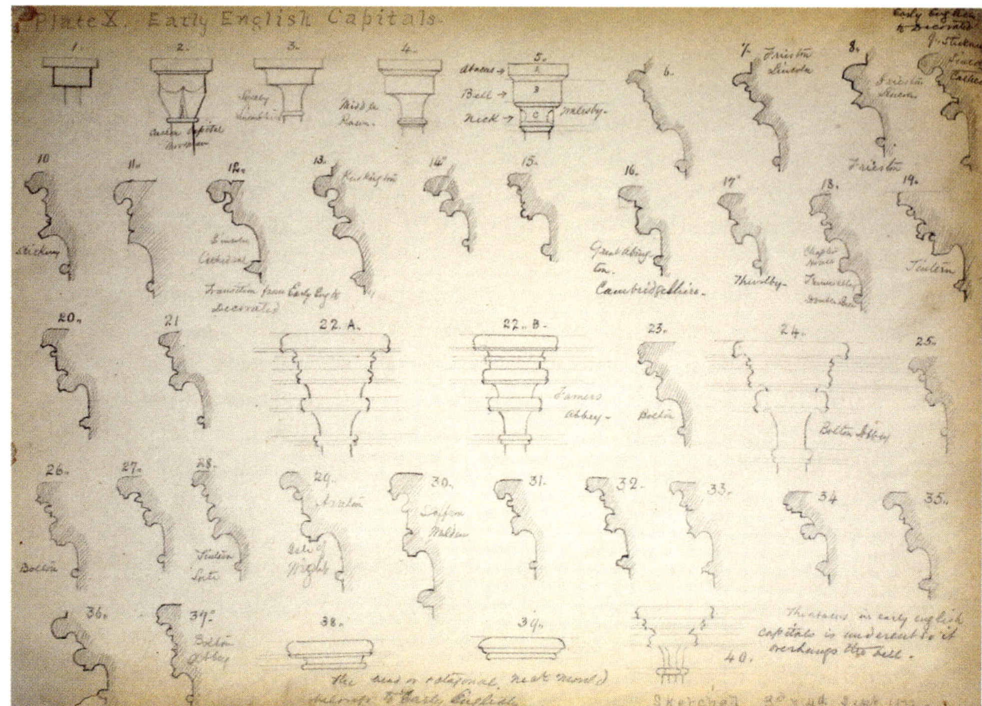

As a young apprentice, Burnham diligently sought to reproduce and master standard historical styles in architecture. He laboriously copied these sketches from Paley's *A Manual of Gothic Mouldings*, which was first published in 1845. (Daniel H. Burnham Collection, Ryerson and Burnham Art and Architecture Archives, Art Institute of Chicago. Digital file # 194301_130124_022.)

his English sojourn, Root spoke of the union of art and nature in positively Emersonian terms:

> Few persons exist, and but few deserve to exist, who have not in their souls that which echoes each strain of Nature's music, and thrills with delight in the perusal of each line of Nature's poetry—poetry written on every leaf, and on every enchanting landscape. There is a certain class of men whom I must exclude from this large number: these are the Hard-fact men,—dry, disagreeable, and as harsh and grating as a file; to whom all poetry is but the manifestation of lunacy out of confinement. Poor wretches![50]

These self-reflections and others demonstrate why Burnham and Root instantly connected as kindred spirits in more than physical appearance and demeanor. The Daniel Burnham who wrote effusively of wandering mountain breezes and of the beautiful neutral tints of cloud shadows would find easy accord with the John Root who saw poetry written on every leaf. Both were devotees of Swedenborgian mysticism. By all accounts, neither of them struck their contemporaries as dry or disagreeable. The differences in temperament that people did notice had more to do with their work habits. Root's "instinctive shyness" led him to prefer attending to his work at the drawing table, while Burnham's "open-hearted fervor" led him to assume the public role of meeting clients and selling them on the work of the firm. According to Harriet Monroe, Burnham had the "initiative, strength of will, and a certain splendor of enthusiasm which captured men and held them, while his partner was amply content to sit in his inner office, aloof from the boresome talkers, and do his work."[51]

Before too long the two partners were on their own, and there was enough business for Burnham and Root to require taking on extra drafting help. William Holabird, "a West Point man, straight as a ramrod," was among the young men who briefly worked in the office and would go on to lead one of the major architectural firms in the city. Burnham noted that Holabird's military manner gave the office a certain dignified look for a time. Root worked at a central table, which he shared with other draftsmen. The office expanded to include additional rooms, with the rent eventually topping $700 dollars a year, which Burnham said "made me lie awake nights." Yet they persevered: "[B]efore seven years were over fortune had smiled on us. We got a real home to build!"[52]

By "a real home" Burnham meant a sprawling mansion for a member of Chicago's business elite. In 1874, a year after setting up shop, Burnham and Root were put in touch with stockyards magnate John B. Sherman. He wished to join his fellow capitalists by building a majestic abode to rival the ostentatious piles then rising on fashionable Prairie Avenue, south of downtown. A friend of John Root's had recommended him to Mr. Sherman, and Sherman somewhat reluctantly agreed to meet and take the measure of the young, largely untested draftsman. Root was out of town when Sherman entered the offices of Burnham and Root, and it was the ebullient senior partner who greeted him. "Perhaps," suggested Burnham's first biographer, "there was method in all this, for already the charm in Mr. Burnham's manner in meeting clients had begun to count."[53] Sherman asked the firm to submit designs for him to consider, and the result was a lucrative commission that pleased the family and brought Burnham and Root to the attention of Chicago's elite business class. The structure was three and a half stories of sheer Victorian excess, with an expansive entry stairway, a solid brick and sandstone exterior, and turrets, dormers, and cupolas sprouting from a Mansard roofline.

Important as this commission was in establishing Burnham's architectural bona fides, it had an even greater impact on his personal life. Sherman's attractive young daughter Margaret, twenty-three-years old and bearing the confident air of a young woman of privilege, was instantly drawn to the talkative and ambitious leader of this unheralded architectural firm. Her good friend Della lived opposite the rising mansion on Prairie Avenue, which Margaret used as a pretext to spend time in the vicinity of the building site. Now twenty-eight, Burnham seems to have rapidly responded to Margaret's obvious interest. In typical Burnham fashion, it did not take long for him to determine to propose, waiting only until the house was nearly complete to finally broach the subject with her and her father. According to Burnham's son Daniel Jr., a small scandal involving Daniel's brother Edwin—caught forging the senior Edwin's name to several checks—led Daniel, with true nineteenth-century punctiliousness, to offer to break off the engagement. He told his prospective father-in-law that, under the circumstances, it would be neither fair nor honorable to pursue his daughter's hand. Margaret remembered her father telling Burnham, "There is a black sheep in every family," and expressing pleasure in the young man's concern for the Sherman family's social position.[54]

Married to a Swedenborgian minister, Daniel's sister Mary sent a congratulatory note to the prospective bridegroom, complete with an expressed desire that he might find in Margaret a true Swedenborgian soulmate. "The truest love for each other," she reminded him, "must be a love for the spiritual and eternal good of each other, rather than a more personal affection centered on things of merely temporal consequence."[55]

Margaret Sherman was, by all accounts, an upright and intelligent young woman, a formidable match for her bright and ambitious fiancé. The early correspondence between them shows conventionally earnest and high-minded mutual affection and respect. As befitted a daughter of a wealthy Chicago businessman who had been surrounded her entire life by prominent and successful men in the growing city, she readily accepted a dutiful wifely role in supporting Daniel's social and financial ambitions. She seemed content, in the words of Charles Moore, to maintain a home "patriarchal in character, abundant in hospitality, and increasingly a refuge and a delight" in subordination to husband and family.[56] The wedding took place on January 20, 1876, and the couple soon moved in with the Sherman family in the grand new Prairie Avenue mansion. They lived there for the remainder of the decade and began to raise a family, beginning with daughter Ethel later that same year.

The trust John Sherman professed to have in his new son-in-law was not unqualified. After Daniel Burnham's death, Margaret revealed to Daniel Jr. that his father "in the early part of their married life was inclined to drink a good deal and that grandfather Sherman was very much afraid that this habit would get too strong for him, in fact he never had implicit confidence in father's judgment or stability at any time." According to Dan Jr., the two men viewed each other warily. They admired the good qualities they saw in each other but never fully reached a point of mutual understanding. So uncertain was Sherman of Burnham's character that he made provisions in his will that, upon his death, all income from his properties would be directed only to daughter Margaret and Margaret's brother John. In an interesting turn of events, when John Sherman later showed evidence of instability in his own character—he abruptly eloped to Europe with another woman—his self-assured and widely respected son-in-law Daniel coaxed Mr. Sherman back into returning to mend the family fences.[57]

Having been introduced into the upper tier of the Chicago elite, Burnham and Root earned other high-profile commissions following the Sherman house, several of them from Sherman's Union Stock Yard and Transit Company associates and almost all of them single-family residences. One notable non-residential exception, designed by the partners and built in 1879, was the stately limestone arched entry to the stockyards. Located on Exchange Avenue near Peoria Street on the South Side, the gate is the only structure from the vast meatpacking complex that remains standing. Designated a National Historic Landmark in 1981, it features the head of John Sherman's prize bull, appropriately and affectionately nicknamed "Sherman."

Only toward the end of the decade would the business climate in the city improve to the point that Burnham and Root felt themselves firmly established, though their business depended almost entirely on residential commissions. The homes they designed largely followed the conventional tastes of their well-to-do clients: Americanized versions of medieval solidity—heavy, rough-cut masonry, jutting cupolas, and expansive entry arches—mixed with fashionable asymmetrical facades and steeply pitched rooflines. In time, however, the company would finally make a widely noted splash in the world of commercial architecture with the 1880 construction of the imposing Grannis Block, a seven-story office building on Dearborn Street.

After Louis Sullivan's 1873 reunion with his parents in Chicago, it did not take him long to connect with yet another famous architect. Always a street wanderer, Sullivan found much to admire in the Portland Block at the corner of Dearborn and Washington and asked who created it. He was told the architect was William Le Baron Jenney, the same Major Jenney under whose direction Daniel Burnham had conceived the ambition to become "the world's greatest architect" a few years earlier. Sullivan sought work in Jenney's office and was taken on partly, Louis thought, because Jenney had also trained at MIT. In fact this was another case of a mistaken remembrance by Sullivan: Jenney had not attended MIT. But Jenney had likely shared periods of schooling with Sullivan's MIT instructor William Ware—at Phillips Academy in Andover, Massachusetts, and Harvard's Lawrence Scientific School—and had also benefited from a stint of architectural training in Paris, a step in a career path that Sullivan would soon follow.[58]

In describing Jenney, Sullivan exhibited the same mixture of heartfelt affection and critical observation he had directed at Frank Furness. Jenney, he said, was "a free and easy cultured gentleman," "a welcome guest anywhere," with a gift for dramatic storytelling in a voice that was "plastic, rich and sweet, and these bits, in sequence and collectively had a warming effect." At the same time Major Jenney was "not an architect except by courtesy of terms." Sullivan saw him, as many did, as an engineer whose expertise lay in the technical aspects of building, whose pragmatic approach to construction over design had been nurtured by his Civil War experiences.[59]

Just as Daniel Burnham found in John Root a partner who was to have a lasting influence on his life and work, in Jenney's office Louis Sullivan encountered a man who left a mark as deep and powerful. That man was John Edelmann, the foreman in Jenney's shop, who was to Sullivan an unforgettable force of nature, a supreme egotist, and "a THINKER, a profound thinker." Sullivan's description conveys an image of the poetic persona that in later years so fascinated him, a kind of youthful Walt Whitman in the flesh. He further characterized Edelmann as follows: "[B]rawny, twenty-four, bearded, unkempt, careless, his voice rich, sonorous, modulant, his vocabulary an overflowing reservoir. A born orator, he must talk or perish. His inveterate formula was, 'I myself' . . . to the sixteenth decimal and the nth power of egoism." Sullivan told Edelmann that John's seeming lack of awareness of his own outsized personality "was remarkable to the point of the fabulous and the legendary, whereupon [we] became fast friends."[60]

Edelmann amused Sullivan with histrionic clowning in the office when Jenney was absent, discoursed at length to Sullivan about politics and psychology and German transcendentalism, explored with him a newfound enthusiasm for the music of Richard Wagner, and dazzled the young and intellectually voracious Sullivan with his theory of "suppressed functions." The word *function* would strike Louis forcefully, the "unexpected explosion of a single word," a word that would later form one half of Sullivan's most famous architectural formula.

In *The Autobiography of an Idea*, Sullivan's explanation of suppressed functions conveys great intellectual excitement but little clarity. By uniting "suppressed" with "function" Sullivan declared that a "new, an immense idea came suddenly into being, and lit up his inner and his outer world," and one could infer that Sullivan intended to celebrate the development and expression of this idea in his autobiography's provocative title. But he never fully delineated how this phrase could "reverse the power of imagination, to cause the veils of the hidden world to rise and reveal."[61] Reveal what, exactly?

Sullivan biographer Robert Twombly argues that the expression, as Sullivan came to apply it to architecture, meant that humanity's creative spirit had been suppressed through the ages by a foolish allegiance to artificial outward forms. Traditional styles—Sullivan would call them "feudal"—served only to bury, rather than express, the true functions of structures under layers of dishonest and derivative forms. The architect as artist had been forced to subordinate his true and unique vision of a structure's underlying function to a false and misleading surface. Twombly is certainly right to suggest that this idea helped lay the groundwork for Sullivan's lifelong devotion to a vision of a "democratic architecture [that] would promote human liberation by directly stating the functions for which it was designed."[62] Timothy Samuelson offers a more positive expression of a related idea, the other side of the "suppressed functions" coin: "For an architect, the Idea was the power to extend the forces of nature and give vibrant life to buildings and their component parts."[63] In other words, once the architect is freed from the paralyzing influence of historical styles and looks to the perfectly designed functions of the natural world for inspiration, then and only then can he or she create something genuinely new and vital and honestly expressive of the functions that lie within.

Whether this was precisely what Edelmann, or even Sullivan, meant by "suppressed functions" is uncertain. But the union of those two words clearly set Louis Sullivan's soul aflame. In describing the effect of Edelmann's theory on him, he even claimed to have anticipated both key elements of his "form ever follows function" dictate by asserting that, shortly after hearing Edelmann reveal this idea to him, "the world of men began to assume a semblance of form, and of function." By "the world of men," did Sullivan mean that human beings themselves buried their inner functions under artificially constructed forms and customs? Much of his later writing would seem to suggest so. Sullivan's caustic views on education and the debilitating power of conventional thinking on a man's independent spirit would certainly fit the concept of stultifying "suppressed functions," whether in buildings or in the artists who were called upon to design them.

Edelmann also introduced Sullivan to another aspect of the "world of men." The idea of manliness had a special significance to young American males of the late nineteenth century. While Sullivan was falling under Edelmann's influence, half a continent away on Long Island, New York, a teenage Theodore Roosevelt—sporting bristly side whiskers and an adventurous, nature-loving spirit like Louis Sullivan—was engaging in an exhausting round of athletic contests of running, jumping, vaulting, wrestling, and boxing. In an earnest and continuing effort to counter the effects of a confined and sickly childhood, Roosevelt kept a sporting calendar, at one point even carefully tracking his personal physical attributes—"Chest 34 in, Waist 26½, Thigh 20"—as if to harden himself into the full manhood and "strenuous life" he would recommend to the nation twenty-four years later as president. "[N]ot the doctrine of ignoble ease," Roosevelt would famously declare, but "the life of toil and effort, of labor and strife [for the] highest form of success . . . comes, not to the man who desires mere easy peace, but to the man who does not shrink from danger, from hardship, or from bitter toil, and who out of these wins the splendid ultimate triumph."[64] Vigorous athletics, like politics and business, was assumed at the time to be the singular province of men, and the adjective "manly" was routinely understood to be a laudatory term, but only when applied to actual boys and men. Participation in athletics was increasingly regarded as a necessary, or at least desirable, rite of passage in a young man's coming of age.

The 1870s marked the birth of organized athletic competition in the United States. The New York Athletic Club had been founded in 1868 and organized the first US championships in boxing, wrestling, swimming, and track and field. Amateur athletic clubs in other cities soon followed suit. The game of "base ball" was popular in loosely regulated forms in parts of the country throughout the century, but the first effort to establish a professional "major league" occurred in 1871.

In 1874 Edelmann persuaded Sullivan to join him on weekends to participate in the newly formed Lotos Club on the banks of the Little Calumet River in Riverdale. The Lotos Club had been founded by William B. (Bill) Curtis, according to Sullivan a "champion all-around athlete" and "a man of brains who never bragged." Sullivan eagerly embraced the opportunity. Sullivan wrote of himself as follows: "Louis was simply wild with joy over this new life. He was now actually a member of a real athletic club. He had never been a member of any club. And these young men, all older than he, were heroes in his eyes, if not demi-gods." Bill Curtis in particular struck Sullivan as a specimen of manly perfection: "He knew his anatomy, and had devised special exercises to develop each separate muscle in his body. So when in the sunlight he walked the pier for a plunge, he was a sight for the Greeks, and Louis was enraptured at the play of light and shade." Like Roosevelt, Curtis devoted himself to athletic excellence to overcome and compensate for a childhood malady, in his case "consumption" (tuberculosis). Sullivan considered Curtis's determination "an exemplar, in the use of the imagination and the will, doggedly to carry out a program."[65] The Rooseveltian impulse was represented even to the extent of tracking the development of members' physiques. On a page of Louis's old MIT notebook, which gained a second life as a sketch book and record book at the Lotos Club, Bill Curtis's bodily measurements were recorded in meticulous detail: "Height 5' 9¼", Weight 176, Chest 41, Fore arm (Curtis' system) 13½, Upper [arm] 14½, Calf 16, Thigh 24, Waist 32½, all . . . taken stripped."[66]

Louis, now seventeen, encouraged his older brother Albert, nineteen, to join the club as well, and the two of them participated whenever circumstances permitted throughout the spring and early summer of 1874. As was characteristic of Sullivan, however, by July he abruptly decided to radically shift direction, and the Lotos Club suddenly lost its youngest and perhaps most enthusiastic member, at least momentarily. Feeling he had apprenticed long enough in Furness's and Jenney's offices, Sullivan decided the time had come to go to "the fountain head of theory," the esteemed École des Beaux-Arts in Paris.

The École had a history dating back to 1648, with roots in the founding of the Académie des Beaux-Arts by the powerful Cardinal Mazarin, the closest adviser and mentor to King Louis XIV. By the time Louis Sullivan enrolled, the architectural program had achieved a reputation for rigorous indoctrination in European principles of design, primarily derived from the long-established traditions of classical Greece and Rome and the Renaissance. Richard Morris Hunt, whom Sullivan had approached for advice the previous year, was the first American to study at the École. The second was Henry Hobson Richardson, whose Brattle Square Church Sullivan had so admired during his student days in Boston and whose Romanesque designs, adapted to American needs and tastes, would soon become a dominant style for prestigious structures throughout the United States. As the reputations of Hunt and Richardson and other École alumni grew, the school took on the aura as *the* place to go for ambitious young Americans seeking top-quality training in the art of architecture.

Seventeen-year-old Louis Sullivan traveled by way of Liverpool and London to Paris and the famed École on the south bank of the Seine. Much of his late summer and fall was spent preparing for the demanding entrance exams, which he completed over several weeks in September and October of 1874. He had taken French in high school, but finding it inadequate to the language of the Paris streets, he hired language tutors, whose lessons he supplemented with careful attention to the "words, locutions, intonations and emphasis" of the locals, snatches of whose conversations he overheard as he roamed the byways of the Latin Quarter. Informed of the extensive nature of the subjects to be covered in the exams—not only architectural drawing and design, but also mathematics, geometry, and history—Sullivan determined to limit his physical exercise to one hour a day and to devote the remainder of his time to study. He also sought the assistance of a mathematics instructor, a M. Clopet.

According to Sullivan, M. Clopet provided yet another life-changing epiphany for the aspiring architect. From Moses Woolson he had learned "discipline and self-reliance . . . in the science and the art of thinking." From John Edelmann he had a model of physical and intellectual vibrancy and a theory of the universal curse of "suppressed functions." And from Clopet he felt transformed by a doctrine of "No exceptions." On his first day with Clopet, this "simple, gracious . . . small dark man" asked to see the descriptive geometry book under Sullivan's arm and, after leafing through some pages, abruptly suggested that he throw it in the wastebasket. The problems and theorems contained therein, said Clopet, included exceptions and special cases. "We shall not need of it here," he remembered Clopet observing, "for here our demonstrations shall be so broad as to admit of NO EXCEPTION." Louis once again reacted to the memorable expression of a key idea of an admired older man as if he had been struck by intellectual lightning. "[He] stood as one whose body had turned to hot stone, while his brain was raging. Instantly the words had flashed, there arose a vision and a fixed resolve. . . . If this can be done in Mathematics, why not in Architecture? The instant answer: It can and it shall be! *No one has, I will!*"[67]

Sullivan spent the following decades passionately explaining his philosophy of architecture, but nowhere in all that strenuous work did he clearly delineate precisely what a "no exceptions" architecture would look like. It is hard to imagine how creatively designed objects made of steel and stone can be analogized to the process of demonstrating universally accepted geometric proofs. Great architecture, almost by definition, is exceptional in some way. One of the core principles of Sullivan's mature writings is that it is the artist/architect's solemn responsibility to *create* exceptions to the received wisdom of the schools and previous ages. It was a concept Frank Lloyd Wright would also take issue with, for almost precisely this reason. Sullivan, he said, was always interested in "the rule so broad as to admit of no exception." But, Wright added, "For the life of me I could not help, then or now, being most interested in the exception proving the rule useful or useless."[68]

Sullivan came to imply that Clopet's "no exceptions" directive simply meant that every problem contains within it a straightforward and discoverable key to its own solution. Thus, as Sullivan put it, "the problem of the tall office building had not been solved, because the solution had not been sought within the problem itself—within its inherent nature."[69] This view that would find expression in his celebrated 1896 essay on tall buildings, wherein he declared such buildings must be "proud and soaring" in a way that emphasizes height and verticality over earthbound stability. Fair enough. But does this really identify a "problem" in need of solution, or is it simply an aesthetic choice based on the architect's or client's unique preferences and beliefs? Surely every architectural problem does not immediately suggest one and only one solution.

Once Sullivan had secured admission to the school, he embarked on the program's rigorous but often self-directed curriculum. Attendance at lectures was not required: students were expected to do most of their work independently under the mentorship of an experienced master in the master's atelier (studio) and to compete with other students for points in a series of architectural competitions and demonstrations of proficiency in academic subjects.

Always the diligent if critically minded student, Louis applied himself to his studies and his drawing exercises but also used his free time to experience Parisian life. A Thanksgiving masquerade ball he attended shows his distinctly non-studious side. It was, he reported, "an enjoyable affair" that went on till 4:30 in the morning, with participants enthusiastically performing the can-can in "outlandish costumes," which he found "appropriate and exceeding amusing," though there was enough of the censorious American in him to add a note of virtuous, if slightly unconvincing, disapproval. "The can-can in costume is as good as a play; but in ordinary clothes it is simply disgusting."[70]

In fact a rigidly moralistic self-discipline was perhaps not characteristic of young Louis during this period. According to Frank Lloyd Wright, Sullivan in his later years admitted that many of the personal habits that Wright felt contributed to the master's decline—smoking, drinking, and whoring—could be traced back to habits of dissipation learned on the streets of Paris. In Wright's words, "habits engendered by his early life in Paris had made havoc with him."[71] We don't have surviving written evidence of such activities from Sullivan's own hand, but he was a young American newly arrived in Paris, and he may well have felt that this was a time to taste the joys of liberation from the strictures of home and family.

With respect to his professional pursuits, the emotional high point of his European adventure did not occur in Paris. In the spring of 1875 Sullivan felt he had to see Rome, a point of origin for the classical style that so dominated the curriculum at the École. There he "came face to face with his first great Adventurer. The first mighty man of Courage. The first man with a Great Voice. . . . The first whose will would not be denied."[72]

That man was Michelangelo. Sullivan spent three days in Rome, but two of them were devoted to deep immersion in the glories of the Sistine Chapel. Once again he had found a mentor—this one long dead—whose influence was instant, intense, soul-shaking. When later looking back on that time, Sullivan could hardly find the words to convey the impact. Michelangelo's artistry had something of nature in it, as glimpsed in part during Sullivan's journey to Chicago ("power as he had seen it in the prairies, in the open sky, in the great lake stretching like a floor toward the horizon"); something of burly, outdoor laboring men Sullivan had grown up watching ("big strong men" who could "build stone walls, hew down trees, drive huge horses"); something of artistic independence ("here was "the free spirit of man striding abroad in the open"); and above all something of sheer exercise of unbridled power ("Here was the living presence of a man who had *done things in the beneficence of power*").[73]

Man's power, yes, but nothing of woman's power. In Sullivan's description the emphasis is strongly framed in images of traditional masculinity: "the man, the man of super-power, the glorified man, of whom he had dreamed in his childhood."[74] Some critics and historians have commented on the masculinized features of Michelangelo's Sistine Chapel female figures—the powerful shoulders, the bulging and well-defined musculature, the thick bodies and legs—and Sullivan could hardly be faulted for seeing the depictions of these figures in largely masculine terms. At the same time, it is clear Sullivan was fascinated by the male body and male musculature. Less than a year before he had marveled at the Greek perfection of the Lotos Club's Bill Curtis's well-muscled form. His nude drawings of the time show equal facility with both male and female models, several of which exhibit the muscular solidity and dramatic postures reminiscent of Michelangelo's figures.[75]

During his time abroad Sullivan had not forgotten his brother and friends in Chicago. Having left Jenney's office to form an architectural partnership with Joseph S. Johnston, John Edelmann enlisted Sullivan's help in creating decorative designs for two Chicago projects: the Sinai Temple and the Moody Tabernacle, which Louis started working on while still in Paris.

Having felt that he had plumbed the breadth and depth of what he could profitably learn from the professors at the École, in May of 1875 Sullivan quickly determined that it was time to go home—another abruptly aborted mission in his growing list of brief educational apprenticeships. He harbored, he said, "the hovering conviction that this Great School, in its perfect flower of technique, lacked the profound animus of a primal inspiration" of the kind he found in Michelangelo's Sistine Chapel. "Solitary" and "heart hungry," convinced that the École possessed "a fatal residuum of artificiality" in thrall to classical traditions, Sullivan returned to the United States to resume his architectural ascent in a city "some three hundred thousand strong . . . beside the shore of a great and very wonderful lake, with a wonderful horizon and wonderful daily moods."[76] Reunited with his admired mentor and friend Edelmann, Sullivan re-engaged with the activities of the Lotos Club and continued preparing freelance drawings for Edelmann's Sinai Temple and Moody Tabernacle projects.

For both Daniel Burnham and Louis Sullivan, the latter half of 1870s was a period of active architectural practice and movement toward the development of their local reputations. Burnham and Root went from one residential commission to the next in relatively rapid succession. Thomas Hines lists twenty-one private homes constructed by the firm between 1875 and 1879, with only one commercial structure, the Union Stock Yard Exchange Building, completed in 1875 as part of John Sherman's immense stockyards complex, and one school, the Washington Heights Female Academy. Hines points out that, after the Sherman house, the firm's residential commissions began gradually to move away from an "eclectic 'Victorianism' toward a newer aesthetic of greater purity and simplicity."[77]

Burnham and Root's early devotion to eclectic styles can easily be seen, as noted, in the Sherman house, with its French Mansard roof, jutting peaked and hipped roof dormers sprouting from the open spaces on the roofline, classical columns and balustrades, Renaissance-inspired curving entrance staircase, expansive octagonal cupola, and dormers topped with exclamatory crosses. The quieter style of later Burnham and Root residences was illustrated by the 1883 A. C. Burnham house of Champaign, Illinois, an equally expansive mansion that presented a simplified exterior featuring minimal ornamentation and one central gable whose pitched roof was echoed in the relatively straightforward porch entry beneath it.

The firm's desired move toward a less derivative architectural style was gradual and probably owed more to Root than to Burnham. But even that movement toward architectural restraint can be overstated. A quick glance at the protruding Dutch gables in the V. C. Turner house of 1888 or the fanciful Richardsonian Romanesque-inspired elaborations of the Edward E. Ayer house of 1885 will suggest that Burnham and Root carried elements of Victorian ornamentation well into the 1880s.[78] In the 1870s in particular, when the firm was new and trying to find its way in a challenging environment, the commissions that came to the partnership from Chicago's elite tended to follow the tastes of the clients and the demands of the age.

Peter Wight outlined the process that structured the two men's working partnership: Burnham would dash off general sketches of the project designed to anticipate and answer whatever problems or needs the client foresaw, sketches that Root would then elaborate into finely detailed plans, with artistic finishes of his own or in collaboration. As Wight noted, "There was a magnetism in both that attracted a large circle of friends. And these friends quickly saw how intimate they were as friends no less than business partners. Hence it was a combination which brought success and was crowned by other successes."[79]

Having returned from his partly disappointing but nonetheless crucial seedtime in Paris and Rome, Louis Sullivan probably devoted as much time and effort to his intellectual and athletic pursuits as to his freelance architectural work. The Lotos Club notebook lists a formidable and wide-ranging collection of books that Sullivan devoured, beginning in Paris with art histories by École professor Hippolyte Taine. Sullivan said he learned three things from Taine: first, that there was such thing as art history; second, that art directly expresses the life of a people; and third, that one must know the life of a people to understand their art.[80] He read prominent American authors as well, popular humorists like Mark Twain and Petroleum V. Nasby (David Ross Locke), and genteel literary lions such as James Russell Lowell. In Chicago he settled down with self-improvement and health books, Charles Darwin's *Descent of Man*, John Tyndall's *Fragments of Science*, and several more ranging from undemanding popular titles to intellectually challenging ones. His list included John Draper's *History of the Intellectual Development of Europe*, which drew a stark contrast between the repressive intellectual culture of medieval feudalism and the Enlightenment's revolutionary and liberating emphasis on science and democracy. Sullivan would subsequently exploit and explain this contrast numerous times as a core tenet of his architectural theory.

Brother Albert's reading list for the same year shows a far less ambitious intellectual agenda: eight books in toto, most focused on health and exercise, including *Wonders of Bodily Strength and Skill* and *Experiments on Digestion*. The one author whom both brothers consulted during the year was the Irish physicist John Tyndall, whose *Forms of Water* Albert read and whose advocacy of scientific thought over religious orthodoxy, *Fragments of*

Science, drew the attention of Louis. Club members were not above poking fun at religion and conventional mores. On one page in what appears to be Louis's handwriting, we find the following definition of matrimony: "That holy state in which they will have a legal right to hate each other as much as they please." Quotation marks placed around the comment suggest that it was a sentiment Sullivan heard or read and whose touch of humorous cynicism held some kind of appeal for the young man.

Louis Sullivan's interest in organic life forms and in artistic drawing appears in the notebook as well. On one page rough sketches of flowering aquatic plants, which Sullivan identifies by their Latin scientific nomenclature, appear under the heading "Analysed by LHS Aug. 6/76." Among his analytical notations are "perfect flowers" and "pistils numerous." Drawings of a specific woman's profile appear several times in the book—Twombly speculates that it may have been of a "Madame Girard" who cooked for the club—as do more finished drawings of grotesque figures similar to sketches done by Sullivan in Paris. Both Sullivan and Edelmann used the book for experiments in freehand drawing along with various ideas for architectural projects in which the two were or hoped to be involved. Among the more charming images presented in the book are two pages, perhaps by Edelmann, showing runners and hurdlers dressed in suitably modest nineteenth-century athletic garb and caps and competing in the kind of contests to which the club was devoted.[81]

As the reading lists suggest, the Lotos Club boasted a library all its own, and after Sullivan's return from Paris, it quickly became again a favorite retreat. John Edelmann and Sullivan's brother Albert both actively engaged and eagerly welcomed Louis back into the brotherhood. The mix of intellectual stimulation, male camaraderie, and athletic competition offered the sorts of challenges young Louis craved. On May 27, 1876, at the "Base Ball Grounds" on the corner of 23rd and State, a series of contests pitted Louis Sullivan, clad in colors of light and dark red, against brother Albert, sporting garnet and blue, and other club members. A reporter noted that the sight of the runners "as they streamed around the course in their many colored costumes" created a "remarkably pretty" scene. Albert defeated his younger brother in the second heat of the 100-yard run and in the shot put, and the athletic Bill Curtis bested Albert by a yard and a half in the final heat of the 100-yard run.[82] A Fourth of July outing recorded in a *New York Sportsman* news item shows brother Albert again excelling in most contests, with Louis and Albert both winning their matches in Greco-Roman wrestling, thus "bringing the brothers Sullivan out ahead," followed by the group's "regular plunge" in the river "and supper, and then to bed none the worse for the exercise, but . . . terribly bitten by mosquitoes."[83]

Louis Sullivan at age twenty. (Sullivaniana Collection, Ryerson and Burnham Art and Architecture Archives, Art Institute of Chicago. Digital file # 193101.LHS_Portrait_1876.)

A little-noticed event in Louis Sullivan's personal history at this time was his participation in the very first football game at Northwestern University in Evanston. The sport of football was then in its infancy. The historic first intercollegiate game had occurred just seven years earlier, with Princeton players traveling to New Brunswick, New Jersey, to compete against Rutgers in a chaotic jumble of young men, twenty-five players on each side, all striving to achieve the primary objective of kicking the ball through goalposts. The game as played on that November day, in Dave Revsine's words, "would appear to a modern spectator to be an amalgam of soccer and rugby, though any resemblances to the latter were coincidental." A touchdown had value primarily because it earned the attacking team the right to kick a single-point "goal" through the uprights. The game itself was as much a social event as an athletic contest. At the inaugural Rutgers game, all the players enjoyed "an amicable 'feed' together," and the Princeton players traveled home "in high spirits, but trusting to beat [Rutgers] next time, if they can."[84]

Louis competed in an equally informal and friendly match on February 22 of 1876. The Lotos Club members traveled north to Evanston, calling themselves the "Chicago Foot-ball Club," and matched their fifteen amateur athletes against the twenty placed on the field by a gaggle of interested Northwestern students. On Campus Meadow (today's Deering Meadow), with ground too hard to anchor either goal posts or line stakes (the goal posts had to be hand-held), the two teams determined "to get along the best way possible under the circumstances" according to a news report. The Chicago club's Augustus Hornsby started things off by kicking to Northwestern, whose players were "evidently at sea in regard to the game, for they let Hornsby follow the ball up, and his next kick took it across the line, enabling him to get a touchdown."[85]

Albert Sullivan and younger brother Louis both played the "forward" positions, and nineteen-year-old Louis, whose architectural destiny remained far in the future, secured a small place in Northwestern University's athletic history by gaining a touchdown after a "good long run." Unfortunately Hornsby failed to secure the point by kicking the ball through the goal posts. After halftime the "original twenty players of the University team increased so alarmingly in number that getting through with the ball was an impossibility, and loose scrimmages took place over the entire field." The Lotos football club ultimately defeated Northwestern three goals to none. The *Tribune* commented that Northwestern will have good material for a competitive team "if they will practice the game under the rules." A day later the student newspaper chimed in as well: "The trial game of foot-ball on Tuesday last enthused the boys so much that they have formed a Foot Ball Association and intend to give those representatives of 'Old Rugby' a hard time to beat them in a 'scrummage' [*sic*] when they come here again."[86] Thus was the sport of football born at Northwestern, with the athletically inclined young Louis Sullivan an active participant.

Sullivan's interest in Lotos Club athletic activities continued through 1876 and with some frequency over the next two years. His involvement with the club was enhanced by a continuing dialog on history, art, and architecture with John Edelmann, who continued in his role as mentor and confidante to his young friend. Sullivan continued to work on a freelance basis on the Johnston and Edelmann firm's projects—Sinai Temple and Moody Institute—while he also, as he put it, "worked briefly, now, at intervals, in the office of this or that architect, until he had nearly covered the field." Sullivan gravitated to the men "mostly of the elder generation," whom he found "very human, and enjoyed their shop-talk, which was that of the graduate carpenter."[87] It seems he valued not so much their artistic creativity as their common-sense, practical knowledge of the principles of construction and the bold solutions they found for the challenges with which they were presented.

During this period his appreciation for master engineers expanded and deepened. He closely followed the development of two new bridges going up in the middle section of the country, the Eads Bridge in St. Louis and the great Cincinnati Southern Railway Bridge that spanned an enormous chasm over the Kentucky River. Both employed innovative construction techniques to create immense, technically sound, and, to Louis's eyes, aesthetically pleasing structures. The Eads Bridge boasted the deepest underwater foundations of its time, pioneering a caisson technology that was used a few years later in the creation of the Brooklyn Bridge. The Kentucky suspension bridge was the highest in the world when built, 286 feet from the base of the rail to the bottom of the foundations.[88] "[I]n these two growing structures Louis's soul became immersed. In them he lived."[89]

For a brief time he was enthralled and dreamed of becoming a great bridge engineer. "The idea of spanning a void appealed to him as masterful in thought and deed." Great engineers represented power, including the power to dominate and create. He spent time with one "caustic joker and a man of brains," the German immigrant Frederick Baumann, whose theory of isolated pier foundations would become recognized as a sound solution for creating structurally stable foundations on marshy Chicago soil. Yet as with the old-timers "of homely make-up, homely ways" whose lore Sullivan eagerly absorbed, even the great engineers did not quite rise to the level of achievement to which Sullivan aspired. His interest in the science of engineering, when supplemented by his wide-ranging reading program, soon led to the conviction that the purely practical applications of science to problems of construction were not enough. Science, he felt, "could not go either fast or far were it not for Imagination's glowing light and warmth." The nature of science was "rigid and prosaic—and Louis noted that the free spirits within its field were men of vision—masters of imagination, men of courage, great adventurers," which was what Louis Sullivan aspired, above all, to be.[90]

In early summer of 1876 reviews began to appear in Chicago newspapers assessing Louis's fresco designs for Johnston and Edelmann's Sinai Temple and the Moody Tabernacle. Viewers were struck by the rich colors and the intricacy of Sullivan's interwoven designs. The *Tribune* writer spoke of a "startling" effect of the ceiling decoration, a "loud and to all appearances utterly inharmonious intermingling of colors" that at first "strike the eye painfully" but after careful study reveals a "simplicity wonderful when compared with the first impression." Ceiling borders had "the appearance of perplexing complications" but were "exquisitely simple and refined." The design contained "a series of botanical forms, connected by a running-root stalk," revealing "a plant of rare beauty unfolding graceful leaves, and supporting a white flower."[91] Sullivan artfully applied his fascination with complex and colorful ornamentation based on intertwining botanical motifs, an interest likely stimulated in childhood by his mother's accomplished floral drawings. And the results elicited generally favorable commentary in the local press.

Sullivan's professional association with Edelmann was relatively short-lived. At about the time the Tabernacle and Temple were completed, Edelmann decamped, first for Cleveland, then for an adventure in rural horse breeding, before returning to the Chicago area in 1879 or 1880, then leaving town for good around 1881.[92] Edelmann's impact—like that of M. Clopet in France, Furness in Philadelphia, and the electrifying example of Michelangelo in Rome—far outlasted the relative brevity of Sullivan's time with him. Sullivan even credited Edelmann with introducing him, in the late 1870s, to the man who would become Sullivan's most significant architectural associate and mentor, the German-born Chicago architect Dankmar Adler.

Elements of Sullivan's recollection of his first meeting with Adler during this period have been questioned.[93] Yet his first visual impression of his soon-to-be partner, whenever and however he actually received it, stands forth as entirely consistent with pictures from the time. Adler, reported Sullivan, "was a heavy-set, short-nosed Jew, well bearded, with a magnificently domed forehead which stopped suddenly at a solid mass of black hair." He had a "broad serious face, and kindly, brown efficient eyes joined in a rich smile of open welcome." Sullivan claimed he could immediately see that "Adler's brain was intensely active and ambitious, his mind open, broad, receptive, and of an unusually high order."[94] Here in Sullivan's memory stood a person not unlike the engineers he admired: a man of vision, courage, and imagination, a great adventurer in the world engaged in the process of creating the modern American cityscape.

By early 1880 Daniel Burnham and Louis Sullivan had established roots in Chicago and were beginning to make notable contributions to the reconstruction of the rebuilding city. Burnham was thirty-three years old,

Sullivan twenty-three. The previous decade began with a young and still largely directionless Dan Burnham unsuccessfully seeking his fortune in the Nevada mining camps and a restless Boston schoolboy exploring the glories of nature under the gentle guidance of a sympathetic young woman. It ended with two committed individuals permanently settled in the great Midwestern metropolis and looking to make names for themselves in a profession just beginning to require formal academic preparation.[95] Their educational backgrounds were spotty and truncated at best. Burnham likely still nursed a secret disappointment at having been denied admission to both Harvard and Yale, while Sullivan held a longer and more impressive, but decidedly incomplete, educational resume. Their brief associations and contacts with important men of the day—Jenney, Van Osdel, Hunt, Ware, Wight, Furness, John B. Sherman, Frederick Baumann—certainly played a role in their long trajectory to recognition. But in the end their talent, initiative, and fortuitous partnerships that were destined to flourish in the next decade—Burnham with Root, Sullivan with Adler—would bring them and their adopted city to the attention of the world.

5

Fruition

1880s

WHEN PEOPLE DESCRIBE Chicago as a "City of Architecture" or as an architectural mecca of some sort, they are really referring to the city's legendary status as an innovative and creative force in architecture that began to emerge in the final two decades of the nineteenth century. Some of the earliest innovations came in response to the problem of constructing large commercial buildings for the bustling metropolis-in-the-making on Chicago's moist and unstable soil.[1]

German-born Frederick Baumann, who arrived in Chicago in 1850 and started his architectural career as a draftsman in John Van Osdel's office, was among the earliest innovators. His "isolated pier" foundation system, first circulated in published form in 1873, was seen as a way to stabilize large masonry buildings. In Baumann's plan, broadly based but isolated stepped pyramids of stone anchored in the soil could be calibrated to evenly support the heavy walls bearing down on them. A disadvantage to Baumann's foundation scheme was that the thick piers tended to take up desired space in the building's basement.

It took a Chicago money man, real-estate attorney Owen Aldis, to see similar inventive potential in the team of Burnham and Root. Just as John Sherman had taken a chance on a young and largely untested Dan Burnham a few years earlier, Aldis was thoroughly convinced of John Root's creative capabilities on first meeting with him. "No other man," said Aldis of that first encounter, "ever impressed me so quickly and so deeply." A chance meeting brought them together at a Chicago reception. In Aldis's account, "We went off into a little room and talked until one o'clock. He did not know I had any special interest in architects, but from that night I knew he was a genius, and the next day I brought him a building."[2]

Aldis harbored interests in literature and the arts, but his professional life was largely devoted to the practical art of getting ahead and finding profits for his clients. His law practice from the beginning focused on promoting the real-estate interests of Eastern power brokers. One of his loyal clients was real-estate investor Peter Brooks, an architecturally astute but cost-conscious Bostonian who, together with brother Shepherd, had an interest in developing business properties in Chicago. Aldis had previously managed for Brooks a Chicago property known as the Portland Block, on the corner on Washington and Dearborn, designed by William Le Baron Jenney. This same commercial building had inspired Louis Sullivan, as he first walked the streets of Chicago in 1873, to seek employment with Major Jenney.

Brooks, like Aldis, would leave a distinctive mark on the face of Chicago, but his attention was more directed to maximizing rental income than to pleasing the artistic sensibilities of wealthy Chicagoans and ambitious architects. In 1880 the Brookses owned the land adjacent to the Portland Block, on which they wished to construct another commercial structure. The result was the Grannis Block, an imposing seven-story structure whose design Aldis entrusted to the relative upstarts Burnham and Root.

The Grannis Block was completed in 1881, and contemporary accounts lauded the building for its straightforward external appearance and thoughtful interior design. A *Tribune* reporter, sounding a bit like a proponent of twentieth-century modernism, praised the Grannis Block for "discarding almost wholly the showier materials of marble, carved stone, etc. and adopting the more durable construction of honest brick and terra cotta." The building's reliance on "the simplest forms"—perhaps in response to Peter Brooks's well-known aversion to excessive and pricey ornamentation—supposedly led to it being "pronounced by all who see it almost without exception 'the handsomest building in the city.'"[3] Burnham concurred. "Here our originality began to show," he declared. "It was a wonder. Everybody went to see it, and the town was proud of it."[4]

As the Grannis Block was going up and marking an advance in his professional life, Daniel Burnham was also experiencing an upward move in his domestic situation. In 1880 his father-in-law, John Sherman, presented his daughter Margaret and Daniel with a new house of their own, located at 43rd Street and Michigan Avenue, only a mile and a half from the stockyards entrance on the South Side. Daniel and Margaret moved in with their four young children—John, Ethel, Hubert, and Margaret (Dan Jr. was yet to be born). It must have been a relief to remove so large a contingent of intimates from the looming presence of a man with whom Burnham never felt fully at ease. Yet the separation hardly represented a radical shift. The site was chosen partly because it was conveniently located for John Sherman—the "old gentlemen," as Dan Jr. called him—to stop by as he made his way back and forth from his office in the stockyards.

Burnham and Root's Montauk Block, a commercial project commissioned in 1881, the year of the Grannis Block's completion, was even more significant. Thomas Tallmadge, who was to begin his distinguished architectural career as an apprentice in Daniel Burnham's office, said the Montauk illustrated "the daring of Burnham and the originality of Root." Admitting to a degree of hyperbolic indulgence, Tallmadge went so far as to declare, "[W]hat Chartres was to the Gothic cathedral, the Montauk was to the high commercial building."[5]

From the outside the building looked impressive and tall but reassuringly familiar to nineteenth-century visitors. At ten stories it was three stories higher than the Grannis Block, a fact that prompted Burnham to assert that the Montauk was the first building to be called a "sky-scraper." Burnham's claim finds some support in a comment by architect Henry Ericsson, who remembered as an eleven-year-old Swedish immigrant in 1882 being told tales of the Montauk—a building "already started that was to rise to the unheard-of height of ten stories, so high that it was being referred to as a 'skyscraper'!"[6]

The completed building displayed enough size and decorative elegance in the exterior treatment to convince customers and passersby that this was the locus of an important business enterprise. At the same time, while the building was perceived as tall, it also seemed to be comfortably anchored to the ground, with its horizontal string courses between floors making it look more like a neatly divided layer cake than a soaring projectile. In an era when tall office buildings were still something of a novelty, and customers didn't entirely trust the safety of elevators or the stability of outsized buildings, the Montauk managed to inspire awe even as it sent implicit messages of reassurance and restraint. It signaled a safe and efficient place to get work done. As Tallmadge put it, "In style it was as functional as Louis Sullivan ever dared advocate and far more functional than any of his work at the time or for some time after."[7]

Burnham's and Ericsson's suggestion that the Montauk Block may have been the first to inspire the application of the word "skyscraper" to tall buildings has added plausibility given that one of the earliest print appearances of the term (perhaps *the* earliest) occurred at about the same time the Montauk was reaching completion.[8] In a column of February 25, 1883, a *Chicago Tribune* correspondent, reporting from New York, headed one section "OUR SKY-SCRAPERS" and marveled at "how radically the new styles of buildings in this country have changed in the last ten years—indeed, nobody else can know it as well by personal observation as the people of Chicago," noting that New York, too, had "picked up on the new mode." The column further explored the many reservations voiced in opposition to such unfamiliar structures. "These buildings would tumble down, they said. They would burn up, and nobody could get out of them. They would breed miasma. They could not be properly ventilated." The reporter's response to these worries? "All nonsense," he insisted. "There are no better or safer buildings in the world than these mammoth structures."[9]

Harper's Weekly writer M. A. Lane would express an equally supportive sentiment, saying that when such buildings were scientifically constructed, no buildings could be safer. But Lane went on to warn, "The most trifling error [of engineering] may well precipitate a disaster calculated to stop once for all the growing use of the Chicago construction; to bring tumbling down into the crowded streets a mass of terra-cotta, brick, beams, joists, and columns, thereby making one of those alarming occurrences that strike the city dumb, and hold the world in awe."[10] Little wonder some of Lane's readers, and others similarly informed, many have felt some hesitation at the prospect of entering novel structures such as these.

The term *skyscraper* was not new; it had been used before in other contexts. Tall sailing ships, high-standing horses, even tall people had been called skyscrapers since at least the late eighteenth century. In Herman Melville's 1849 novel *Redburn,* the title character claims to have heard seamen talk of "sky-scrapers"—small sails mounting even higher than the main "skysail" on a sailing ship—but refuses to believe in their existence since "a skysail seems high enough in all conscience; and the idea of anything higher than that, seems preposterous." With regard to tall buildings, the term was by no means the only metaphor or fanciful image observers reached for in order to describe this architectural novelty that, to many, seemed almost as preposterous as Melville's phantom sail. Six years after the New York correspondent's reference, a *Tribune* headline referred to the latest crop of high-rises, including Burnham and Root's Monadnock Building, as "cloud supporters" and urged readers to "prate no more" of the "sun-kissed summits" of Chicago's water works or the 320-foot clock tower on W. W. Boyington's Board of Trade, "for old Sol is going to find something bigger and better to kiss." The article refers to plans for three new "sky-scrapers" that are still "decidedly castles in the air" but that also stand as harbingers of the Chicago of the future.[11]

A key element that set the Montauk apart architecturally, and another basis for Tallmadge's enthusiasm, was a new foundation system devised

Montauk Block was completed in 1882. Burnham and Root, architects. (Historic Architecture and Landscape Image Collection, Ryerson and Burnham Art and Architecture Archives, Art Institute of Chicago. Digital file # M524649.)

by John Root. The Montauk's ten-story masonry weight was to be carried not by Baumann's separated stacked pyramidal piers but by a vast platform of concrete reinforced by lengthy iron rails. This flat slab extended underground for the entire building's footprint and compensated for the weight of the excavated soil. Root's system did not require penetration into the basement area, thus freeing up much-desired space. For several years this "floating raft" solution was a useful method to address the problem of Chicago's marshy soil until it became technologically feasible to drill vertical caissons all the way down to bedrock. Ralph Peck called Burnham and Root's innovative approach to tall-building foundations evidence of the "genius which led to their undisputed leadership during the next decade."[12] The building was also notable for new fireproofing techniques and for an innovation in Chicago construction practice: by covering the workspace with a canvas tent and heating the space for workers, construction could continue uninterrupted throughout the winter months.[13]

Burnham's status within the growing circle of Midwestern architects received formal recognition when he was chosen to lead the newly formed Western Association of Architects (WAA) at its inaugural convention held in Chicago in November 1884. The group was founded to counter the perceived East Coast bias of the American Institute of Architects and to "lay the foundation of what will soon be a fact rather than a fancy, a distinctive style that will be known as Western Architecture."[14]

Louis Sullivan was also present at these opening sessions and did not hesitate to participate actively in the discussions. The twenty-eight-year-old Louis, who had not yet designed the buildings that would earn his national reputation, did not seem intimidated by the presence of so many distinguished and accomplished elders: Major Jenney (fifty-two), Edward Burling (sixty-five), W. W. Boyington (sixty-six), Frederick Baumann (fifty-eight), and even convention chair Burnham (thirty-eight) and Sullivan's own "big chief' Dankmar Adler (forty). Burnham proposed a resolution committing members to write contracts guaranteeing architects' rights in design competitions. Two proposed conditions were of particular importance to Burnham: one requiring that at the end of the competition each firm's submitted plans be returned by competition sponsors promptly to the architects and another requiring that no distinct design features in the losing plans be incorporated into the winning entry without proper compensation to the originators.

Young Louis Sullivan, true to character, instantly offered a modification that moved in the direction of preserving an individual architect's prerogatives. Such proposals, he cautioned, "must be handled very tenderly." While the resolutions of Burnham and others are "admirably expressed . . . it is rather early for us to bind ourselves to anything. Let us adopt the resolutions . . . first, try them for a year, and see how they will work, each man working on his own responsibility." After a year, if a more binding set of resolutions are seen as needed, the issue may be revisited. Burnham's partner John Root joined Sullivan in advocating for a delay in imposing universal rules for such matters.[15]

When the WAA met again in November the following year, another question arose that sheds some light on the characters of both Burnham and Sullivan. An accomplished woman architect, Louise Bethune, had applied for membership to the organization. Bethune had begun working as an apprentice as early as 1876 and in 1881 entered a professional practice as an architect with her husband, Richard Bethune. By the time of the WAA's second convention, she had substantial professional experience as both businesswoman and architect. Both Burnham and Sullivan had served on the board overseeing the admission of new members, and they put the question directly to the membership. "We would like the decision of the convention, now," said Burnham, "as to whether it desires to admit women." When asked the opinion of the Board of Directors, Burnham replied, "we are very much in favor of it." Sullivan added a clarifying note: "What we desired was a vote of instructions as to the admission of women as a general thing."

The result, after minimal discussion, was a unanimous vote in favor. Later when the discussion turned to the question of how the WAA would define the term *architect* in its constitution, Sullivan even suggested altering a key word in an amendment he had proposed for that purpose, an act that must have been at least partly prompted by the recent acceptance of the group's newest member. The amendment, he said, will now read "person" instead of "man."[16] Not long thereafter, Louise Bethune would serve as one of the vice presidents of the organization.

Throughout this period Burnham and Root's reach had begun to extend beyond Chicago and the Midwest. The firm designed railway stations in Burlington, Iowa, and Galesburg, Illinois, and the Atchison, Topeka and Santa Fe Railway employed the team to create its general office building in Topeka, Kansas. In the fall of 1883 Burnham traveled to the Southwest and to Guaymas, Mexico, to sketch out plans for a resort hotel that was to provide comfortable accommodations at the endpoint of the railway's Sonora system. Burnham's diary of the trip has survived, which allows us to gain some insight into the daily interests and personal characteristics of the increasingly in-demand architect.

On August 19, accompanied by wife Margaret and seven-year-old daughter Ethel, Burnham said goodbye to "Mother Sherman" at the Prairie Avenue mansion and joined railroad executive J. S. Cameron on his private car to commence the journey. The diary is enlivened by Burnham's lifelong habit of including sketches of scenes encountered along the way: a boy catching a fish off the levee in Quincy, Illinois, a cluster of prairie dogs, a jackrabbit. He also tried his hand at working a "photographic machine," including the unwieldy process of trying to change photographic plates in his own improvised dark rooms. In one instance, Burnham wrote, "the ingenuity of the architect came to the front, and we took two trunks—put them 18" apart—covered them with bedclothes—and Yrs truly crawled under partway," and he thought to illustrate the amusing and somewhat undignified anecdote of his amateur photography with another impromptu sketch.

Small misadventures were deemed worth recording. In one entry Burnham relates a humorous account of what seems to have been his first experience with a sauna bath. The family was staying at the recently completed and palatial Montezuma Hotel in Las Vegas, New Mexico.[17] On the eve of leaving Margaret and Ethel behind at the hotel to depart for his solo business trip into Mexico, Burnham took some time to seek out the refreshment of a rejuvenating bath. Adopting the role of passive innocent, Burnham recorded his mock horror at the extreme ordeal he subjected himself to in the local bathhouse. After stripping down to nothing, entering a "sweat hut," and getting sprayed with "125-degree water," a "gentleman in a breech clout" conducted him to a room, and placed him on a marble slab.

> [He] proceeded to dissect me with his thumbs, but finding he could not pull me apart, or run his fingers through me, or squeeze the flesh off—he got mad and commenced to slap me to see how much I could stand. Then he soaped me all over and took a new hold, each of us having recovered from the first round. Then he put me into a scalding shower—and as I stood there he jerked me out and stuck me under an ice cold shower.[18]

Burnham was not above representing himself in self-deprecating and undignified postures, as in this 1883 diary entry, showing him attempting to develop photos—"near dead . . . but determined to go on"—in an improvised dark room between two trunks. (Daniel H. Burnham Collection, Ryerson and Burnham Art and Architecture Archives, Art Institute of Chicago. Digital file # 194301_240906-004.)

"This was enough," declared Burnham, but he then went on to extol the pleasant aftermath. Wrapped in a toga, Burnham noted, he was led to dream away some hours in a deeply padded chair, after which he emerged refreshed and "fine as silk." It was in retrospect the best bath he ever took, and he encouraged Margaret to take one every day he was away.

The diary also records encounters with a range of diverse characters that, in some ways, must have reminded Burnham of the memorable individuals he met during his mining days out West. Ethel was excited to see her first Native Americans but, reported Burnham, "was disappointed that they weren't wearing feathers." A Mexican woman draped in linens "in the Spanish mode of dress" was considered exotic enough to merit a sketch. At one point, to help transport Ethel to an "omnibus" late at night as she slept, "a beautiful black boy" lifted "Ethel up in arms as she was—no hat, no anything but gingham wrap and stockings—[and] carried her to [the] omnibus, and [then] sailed away down the street." In Raton he observed an encampment of US cavalry soldiers who, Burnham was interested to note, "were all colored" but whose presence did not elicit any sign of disparagement or negativity. Near Wallace, New Mexico, Burnham watched a group of Pueblo Indians threshing grain. Adopting the note of condescension that constituted the lens through which many white men perceived native rituals and ceremonies, Burnham saw them as "howling and dancing" as "frantic as their masters and the whole of them . . . yelling, braying, bleating." At the same time he acknowledged the happy efficiency of the Pueblos' method of accomplishing a task. The participants, he added, were "having fun generally & in the meantime business was added to pleasure and the grain threshed." The "pretty" Mexican woman, the "beautiful" Black boy, the pleasurable way the Pueblos had of managing laborious work all speak to Burnham's general tendency to view racial and ethnic "others" in a positive light, albeit from the bemused and lofty perspective of a privileged nineteenth-century white man.

The ostensible reason for the trip—to sketch out plans for a new hotel in Guaymas, Mexico—received only a passing mention in the diary. On September 4, 1883, Burnham wrote that he got a drawing board and T-square and drew up plans for the Guaymas Hotel. "This finishes the business of the trip," he curtly noted. Burnham left Mexico and traveled with the family up the West Coast for a brief stay in San Francisco. On September 14, 1883, they departed for their Evanston home. Shortly thereafter Burnham decided to give away his unwieldy "photographing machine" to "Uncle Joe" Worcester.

As the firm of Burnham and Root moved into the mid-1880s, residential projects continued to account for much of the firm's professional activity, but large-scale commercial commissions began to consume increasing proportions of the two partners' time and attention. According to Hines, twenty-five of the thirty-three projects completed in 1883 remained in the realm of domestic architecture. In 1884 that number declined to sixteen, while major business structures like the Atchison, Topeka, and Santa Fe offices in Topeka, the Counselman and Calumet buildings in Chicago, and the Chicago, Burlington, & Quincy Railroad station in Des Moines comprised about a third of their commissions. In 1885 the commercial share reached over forty percent. Daniel Burnham and John Root were steadily becoming known as premier big-project builders in Chicago and beyond.

In the same year that Burnham made his trip to Mexico to sketch out a plan for a new hotel in Guaymas, Mexico, the Home Insurance Company of New York engaged fellow Chicagoan and WAA member William Le Baron Jenney to design a tall, fireproof Midwestern headquarters at the corner of LaSalle and Adams. No one knew at the time—not Burnham, not Sullivan, not even Jenney himself—that the major was about to take a significant step toward revolutionizing large-scale commercial architecture in America and throughout the world.

In discussing Chicago architecture during the boom times of the early 1880s, Thomas Tallmadge also found it natural to ask, "What was Louis Sullivan doing while Burnham and Root were astonishing the natives and the nation with their tremendous structures and Root was evolving his functional treatment of the high building?"[19] The Borden Block at the northwest corner of Randolph and Dearborn, constructed in 1880–1881, was one of the first major structures that Dankmar Adler and Louis Sullivan worked on together. Sullivan saw it as "our first serious joint undertaking."[20] Adler had dissolved his association with Edward Burling in the late 1870s when he was designing and building the successful Central Music Hall, on which freelancer Sullivan may have done some decorative work.[21] In the late spring of 1881, Adler moved his office into the Borden Block.

The Borden Block seems to have been the project that began to cement the intense working relationship that was to benefit both architects over the next decade and a half. Sullivan credited Adler with several innovations on the project, including a refinement of Baumann's isolated pier foundations, an expansion of surfaces covered in plate glass, and extensive hardwood finishes. Sullivan's design contributions were most visible in the intricate patterns that crowned the top two levels of the building's exterior.

Sullivan consistently marveled at Adler's architectural and engineering skills, especially in his mastery of acoustics in the firm's theater projects.

Consistent with his belief in the power of intuitive genius, Sullivan said Adler's grasp of acoustics sprang not from science or mathematics but from "a feeling, perception, instinct that Mr. Adler had . . . a grasp of the subject . . . which he could not have gained from study, for it was not in books. He must have gotten it by feeling." The earliest evidence of this skill was demonstrated in Adler's Grand Opera House reconstruction of 1880, a project to which Sullivan may have contributed. Although Sullivan was to work on several major theater projects for the firm, including the Adler and Sullivan masterpiece the Auditorium Building, he claimed that he never

Louis Sullivan's interest in music was deep and lifelong. This pencil-on-paper drawing by his mother Andrienne, a skilled amateur artist and musician, shows Louis, in his twenties, fully engaged and perhaps singing at the piano. (Louis Henry Sullivan Collection, Drawings and Archives, Avery Architectural and Fine Arts Library, Columbia University.)

felt any inclination to concern himself much with acoustics, arguing that, in Adler, "the subject was covered."[22]

In Sullivan's retelling, the early years of his partnership with Adler were an almost perfect synchrony of personality and power. After a "mutual sizing up" of each other at close range, Adler supposedly gave Louis a "free hand" to take charge of the office, with the suggestion of a more official partnership in the offing. "It was his [Sullivan's] first fine opportunity," Sullivan recalled. "He used it. He found in Adler a most congenial co-worker, open-minded, generous-minded, quick to perceive, thorough-going, warm in his enthusiasms, opening to Louis every opportunity to go ahead on his own responsibility, posting him on matters of building technique of which he had a complete grasp, and all in all treating Louis as a prize pet, a treasure trove."[23]

Sullivan's account is an odd mix of bold self-assertion and fawning subservience to an elder master. Adler is presented as a "congenial co-worker" who in the earliest days addressed Sullivan on equal terms, even at times giving him free rein to run the office. But in Sullivan's mind Adler also functioned as a revered mentor or father figure offering advice on building technique and treating his young assistant as an unusually gifted pupil. Nonetheless, amid all the self-serving praise, Sullivan's genuine respect and affection for Adler comes through. The combination of feelings and perceptions would strikingly resemble those of the young Frank Lloyd Wright in relation to his own "beloved master" Louis Sullivan.

It is likely that Adler, in these first days, was a warm and encouraging presence but also the boss. As Twombly points out, the Borden Block contained more elements from Adler than Sullivan, with a "mixture of colors, textures, and materials, as well as the horizontal layering" that "were quintessential Adler."[24] The John Borden home, also designed during this period by Adler's firm with contributions from Sullivan, likewise presented the outward appearance of a typical residential mansion of the time, complete with elegant projecting bays, slim, sky-piercing chimneys, and a prominent mansard roof.

Whether Louis was viewed in the early days by Adler as an esteemed equal or a prize pet, it's clear that Adler quickly regarded him as an architect of unusual talent and relentless work habits. At some point in 1881 or 1882, Sullivan was hired as a full-time employee, and in 1883 Louis became a full partner.[25] One commercial structure designed by Adler and Sullivan in the Loop, which remains standing from this period, is the Jewelers Building located at 15–17 Wabash Avenue in the district still known as Jewelers Row. The building is not to be confused with Giaver and Dinkelberg's lavishly decorated neoclassical Jewelers Building, built from 1925 to 1927 at 35 East Wacker Drive.

Standing on Wabash Avenue, if an observer manages to look over, under, or through the elevated railway structure that now bisects the roadway, he or she can see elements of Sullivan's developing aesthetic. The mullions that intersect multiple rows of windows are slim and made of cast iron, not the wider stone divisions typically used at the time. It was a feature perhaps related to Sullivan's boast that he pioneered "slender piers, tending toward a masonry and iron combination, the beginnings of a vertical system" that permitted a much-desired increase of daylight into busy downtown offices." He claimed this "method upset all precedent and led Louis's contemporaries to regard him as an iconoclast, a revolutionary," to which "Louis turned a deaf ear."[26] The claim is exaggerated, since architects had been experimenting with a variety of cast-iron support systems and increased window space for years. One of the experimenters with light, as Sullivan asserted, was his accomplished boss/partner Dankmar Adler. An element reflective of Sullivan's role in designing the building, however, can be seen near the top, where the relative simplicity of the lower levels gives way to twenty-four richly designed panels both within and outside of the broad central arch. Such intertwining, intricate decorative motifs would become so associated with the architect that they are now a key element in what some architectural historians regard as the "Sullivanesque" style.

During the 1880s Sullivan deepened his acquaintance with Burnham and Root, the firm that would quickly vie with Adler and Sullivan for prominence in Chicago's architectural firmament. Sullivan had met Daniel Burnham several years before. Sometime in early 1874, as Sullivan recalled the incident, he happened to be walking around Prairie Avenue and 21st Street on the South Side. There on the southwest corner of the intersection, he encountered the John B. Sherman house, under construction and nearing completion. The house seemed to have "a certain allure or style indicating personality," and, intrigued, he crossed the street for a closer look. When he turned the corner to examine the frontage on the intersecting street, there stood "a fine-looking young man, perhaps [in fact, exactly] ten years his senior, standing in the roadway absorbed in contemplation of the growing work." Sullivan introduced himself, and the man responded with a torrent of friendly insights into his personal associations and ambitions. "Yes; it seems to me I've heard of you."

> Glad to meet you. My name's Burnham: Daniel H. Burnham; my partner, John Root, is a wonder, a great artist; I want you to meet him some

The Jewelers Building (also known as the S. A. Maxwell and Company Store), located at 15–17 Wabash Avenue and completed in 1882, is one of the few still-standing structures from the early days of the Adler and Sullivan collaboration. (Ryerson and Burnham Libraries Book Collection, Art Institute of Chicago. Digital file # 000000_100622-14.)

day; you'll like him. The firm is Burnham & Root. We only started a few years ago. So far we've done mostly residences; we're doing this one for my prospective father-in-law, John Sherman; you know him—he's a big stockyards man—it's the most expensive one yet. But I'm not going to stay satisfied with houses; my idea is to work up a big business, to handle big things, deal with big business men, and to build up a big organization, for you can't handle big things unless you have an organization.[27]

One wonders whether Burnham really said all of this. In the space of a few expansive sentences Sullivan shows us a Burnham who somehow manages to touch on many of the key elements of the unique professional life that was to come, and Sullivan is remembering from the vantage point of a man who, at the time of the writing, had witnessed the full arc of Burnham's career. Burnham's esteem for his partner Root and for architecture as an artistic enterprise, his eagerness to associate with the "leading men" of Chicago, his determination to expand his portfolio well beyond domestic architecture, his intention to create and lead a "big organization" (not the norm at the time for many architects), and his sunny, welcoming openness to an unproven young aspirant all conveniently combine to form a reasonably complete depiction of what was to become the essence of Burnham's legend and legacy.

But whether Sullivan was embellishing or misremembering or conflating fragments of other conversations—or was simply reporting the encounter with journalistic accuracy—the account seems true to the character and temperament and manner of the man he met that day. Sullivan remembered chatting for about an hour and finding Burnham as intellectually alive and generous a soul as his idol John Edelmann. Like Sullivan's most admired mentors, Burnham openly revealed himself to be "a sentimentalist, a dreamer, a man of fixed determination and strong will . . . a wholesome effective presence, a shade pompous, a mystic—a Swedenborgian—a man who readily opened his heart if one were sympathetic." They were now "Louis" and "Dan" to each other, and they enthused together about the "loveliness of nature," the "hidden beauty in the human soul," and the uplifting effects of artistic creation. When they parted Burnham told Sullivan to come round to their offices to meet John Root, whom he identified as a kindred spirit to Sullivan.[28]

In the first half of the 1880s—as he began to make a name for himself alongside Dankmar Adler with buildings like the Jewelers, the Revell, the Troescher, and the Brunswick-Balke-Collender factory—Sullivan eventually accepted Burnham's invitation and developed a relationship with the other half of Burnham and Root. Sullivan's carefully delineated and insightful portraits of the two leading members of the firm during this period make for fascinating reading. Sullivan viewed Root as the dreamer, the witty and debonair man about town whose wide-ranging cultural and intellectual interests and passion for the new both intrigued and animated Sullivan. Root, Sullivan said, was "vain to the limit of the skies," but it was a vanity Root took pains to disguise. Sullivan felt it was hardly an insult to describe John Root as "a man of the world, of the flesh, and considerably of the devil." In fact these were some of the very qualities that made Sullivan think of Root as another "man of power," and he explicitly put him in the same category as his other idols and mentors: Moses Woolson, Michelangelo, and Richard Wagner.

The contrast with Daniel Burnham was evident to Louis. Whereas Root struck him as an extraordinarily talented dilettante, easily distracted by "novelties like a child with new toys," Sullivan saw Burnham as a man of fixed and determined purpose, obsessed with "the largest, the tallest, the most costly and sensational." If thwarted in some way for his quest for the "big," Burnham simply bulldozed his way ahead, doing what he had to do to make his (in Sullivan's word) megalomaniacal dreams come true. Unlike Root, Burnham was not especially susceptible to flattery, but he was willing to shamelessly flatter the businessmen and politicians he relentlessly courted. "Louis saw it done repeatedly, and at first was amazed at Burnham's effrontery, only to be more amazingly amazed at the drooling of the recipient. The method was crude but it worked." Though engaging in unctuous flattery of clients was not Sullivan's strength or inclination, in one respect he also saw Burnham as a kindred soul—and that was in his single-minded pursuit of an architectural vision. "In the dream-imagination" said Sullivan, "lay Burnham's strength and Louis's passion."[29]

Sullivan asserted that in the early 1880s "there came into prominence in the architectural world of Chicago two firms, Burnham & Root, and Adler & Sullivan." Each of these four men performed a different complementary role. Burnham represented Louis's much-admired "man of power," but his power was misdirected toward "the easier way," what Sullivan called a "feudal" vision built on traditional building practices and styles. Root was potentially a man of power, but he risked not realizing that potential under a wayward and undisciplined temperament. Adler was the "sturdy wheel-horse" of the Adler and Sullivan team, the technician, the engineer, the client pleaser. "Louis did the prancing" and brought to the firm the imaginative, creative force that promised to give architectural expression to a liberating new American architecture of "Democratic power."[30]

One of Sullivan's first opportunities to see, in print, his own extended take on his unique architectural vision appeared in Chicago's *Inter-Ocean* newspaper in 1882. Adler and Sullivan had recently completed work on a substantial renovation for Hooley's Theater, and the *Inter-Ocean* interviewer was impressed with their work, even calling Sullivan the "master spirit directing and shaping the creation." At the same time the interviewer managed to sum up young Louis in a single bemused sentence that perhaps remains the most succinct and accurate description of Sullivan's character. Although "Mr. Sullivan is a pleasant gentleman," observed the interviewer, "he is somewhat troubled with large ideas tending to metaphysics, and [harbors] a deprecation of the non-development of the art protoplasm dormant in this city."[31]

In other words, while Sullivan was willing to engage in discourse with the journalist in a courtly, somewhat aloof, manner, he didn't hesitate to display his habitual prickliness and emergent intellectualism. Pushed to define his work, Sullivan mysteriously cited Herbert Spencer's first principles—which in essence hold that all organic and inorganic materials are constantly evolving into more heterogeneous forms—and Darwin's theory of evolution, and he then claimed to "have no words to characterize what you see." Sullivan's design had considerable charm for the reporter but was not unprecedented and failed to contain "any suggestion of Herbert Spencer about it." As for a discussion of art and architecture in Chicago, a city largely devoid of appreciative art criticism, Sullivan declared that "people are not prepared for it."[32]

Such comments and equally critical evaluations of his Chicago rivals and associates portray Sullivan as transparently self-promoting, narcissistic, and unfair. His words of praise, sometimes stated in extravagant terms, for the youthful Root and Burnham and even his own more seasoned partner Adler were usually counterbalanced with devastating critiques or mild equivocations. Yet it is also possible to see in Sullivan's complex, sometimes seemingly contradictory delineations certain qualities in these three remarkable fellow architects that others saw too. Remember Tallmadge's comment that the Montauk Building demonstrated "the daring of Burnham and the originality of Root," which mirrored Sullivan's point that Burnham fearlessly pursued grand visions while Root focused on innovative design details. Harriet Monroe recognized that her brother-in-law Root was "an original force in his profession" but lacked persistence, which Burnham supplied in abundance, "always noting or making opportunities, evolving large projects, which the younger man smiled at—but fulfilled."[33]

Burnham's biographer Thomas Hines dismisses the widespread notion that Burnham served primarily as the public face of the firm while Root possessed the true architectural talent, a misapprehension he partly attributes to Sullivan's "myopic" account of the team's working process. As if to offer a corrective to Sullivan, Hines carefully describes the scope of Burnham's involvement in roughing out the general plans for the team's buildings while collaborating closely with Root throughout the design process.[34] Yet Hines's description is consistent with Sullivan's assertion that Burnham brought a steadfast "dream quality" and "dream imagination" to bear on Root's designs and the discipline to see these dreams through to completion. Sullivan regarded this stellar quality as his personal and artistic link not to Root but rather to Burnham.

Sullivan believed that Dankmar Adler lacked this distinct "dream quality," a particular gift with which he and Burnham were endowed. Adler, he intimated, was a man of great gifts but limited vision, more the capable technician and inventive engineer than the ardent pursuer of artistic ideals. Adler personally contributed to this restricted view of his abilities in the brief autobiographical sketch he composed in the mid-1890s. "Of late years," Adler modestly wrote around the time the partnership broke up, "owing to the preeminence in the artistic field of my partner Mr. Sullivan, I have devoted my efforts to the study and solution of the engineering problems which are so important an incident in the design of modern buildings."[35]

Separating the art from the engineering, especially in the early buildings, is no easy analytical task. Adler was a guiding spirit for the firm of Adler and Sullivan. Even when he entrusted Louis with much of the decorative work, Adler insisted that, in architectural construction, artistic design and structure went hand in hand. In 1891 as the partnership was reaching maturity, he outlined this fundamental principle in no uncertain terms: "You cannot leave the design of the plan of a building to one person, the devising of its structural features to another and its artistic development to still another. To produce even an approximately fine building, there must throughout from foundation to roof, in the arrangement of all the parts, in the design of every line, [be] the imprint of an all pervading influence of one master mind."[36]

It is clearly true that the complex decorative designs that Sullivan became famous for were, over time, left more and more in the creative hands of Adler's junior partner. But the building that Adler always regarded as the "foundation of whatever professional standing I may have acquired" was the Central Music Hall, which opened in late 1879 before Sullivan made any substantive contributions to the firm. And the building was viewed at the time as notable for more than just Adler's structural accomplishments: it provided superior acoustics, solidity, and comfortable seats. The *Tribune* reviewer of the music hall's opening night gala pointed to the "quiet, neutral tints" of the frescoing and to the roof's "very rich and handsome appearance," with "its illuminated skylight, covering an area of 1,000 square feet" and exhibiting "an exquisite combination of pale orange tints relieved by blue, green, deep orange and red." Despite the breathless puffery characteristic of much nineteenth-century journalism, we can discern behind the reporter's comments Adler's desire to pay close attention to the pleasing decorative details that audiences of the time would expect.[37]

A key moment in the history of the two architects' association occurred on May 1, 1883, when Louis Sullivan became a full partner in the firm of Adler and Sullivan, by now united in the firm's offices in the Borden Block.[38] Adler obviously felt the time had come to fully recognize and formalize the team's mutual dependence. And so began an extremely productive partnership that helped change the face of the city over the next dozen years.

The pleasure Sullivan felt in his newfound status in the partnership and the profession must have been dampened somewhat by the declining health of his father. Patrick Sullivan died the following year in June, after which Louis's mother Andrienne closed the dancing academy and left Chicago for good. She stayed for a time with her sister and brother-in-law in upstate New York and eventually established permanent residence out East, where she lived the remainder of her life. Except for his brother Albert, with whom Louis may have briefly shared living quarters during this period, Sullivan was now firmly established as an independent adult living on his own in Chicago and largely freed from the burdens and benefits of close family ties.[39]

Notable projects that engaged the firm of Adler and Sullivan in the mid-1880s include remodeling work for the McVicker's Theater, Haverly's Theater, and the Interstate Exposition Building that stood on the east side of Michigan Avenue on the site of the present-day Art Institute. Designed by W. W. Boyington and originally constructed shortly after the Great Chicago Fire, the cavernous and imposing domed exposition center sheltered, under an arching superstructure of glass and iron, exhibits displaying "the products of every branch of art, including liberal and fine arts; the processes and products of every species of manufacturing, together with collections, models, drawings, etc., illustrative of the sciences."[40]

Adler had long been known for his expertise in theater construction, so it was no surprise that when Dan Burnham's old high school classmate Ferd Peck—now a prominent figure in the business and cultural communities of the city—was looking for architects he turned to the engineering and design skills of Adler and Sullivan. Their assignment: to prepare the north half of the Exposition Building for the newly created Chicago Opera Festival. The opera ultimately kicked off on schedule in April 1885 in a venue that earned almost universal acclaim, both for Sullivan's rich ornamentation and for Adler's superb acoustics. The Interstate Exposition Building renovation would prove to be the trial run for an Adler and Sullivan masterwork, the permanent entertainment structure that would establish the two men's reputations as preeminent architects in the period of Chicago's first architectural renaissance.

On the evening of February 19, 1885, Daniel Burnham was sitting in his office with a client on the sixth floor of the firm's Grannis Building, when he picked up the ominous scent of smoke.

> I passed into our main rooms to investigate, but no smoke could be found there. I arrived at the conclusion that the flames were under the floor of my private office; and after ordering everything thrown into the vaults, I passed out to talk to the elevator-boy. It was then that positive evidence of fire was revealed. A half-dozen sparks flew out of the shaft-ventilator and were drawn down into the elevator hatchway. It was then that the automatic fire-alarm in the attic sounded and brought the fire patrol to the scene.[41]

Burnham's theory of the case was that the fire started in the elevator shaft, where well-oiled wooden guides rubbed up against iron counterweights, unleashing sparks and "creating conditions favorable to combustion." The much-vaunted 1881 ventilation system—which the *Tribune* had four years earlier singled out as an "effective fire stop, making the building much less liable to destruction by fire than most structures of its kind"[42]—turned out to be no match for the wooden elements still embedded in the building's construction. It must have been galling for the increasingly prominent architect to be forced to join a jumble of frightened occupants improvising their ignominious escapes down to the street, only then to witness his own first major commercial project consumed by flames.

The fate of the Grannis Block illustrates just how rapidly construction practices were evolving throughout the decade of the 1880s. New approaches to fireproofing were a constant topic in architectural publications as were ways to improve lighting and ventilation and secure foundations.[43] That the newly built Grannis Block had proved so vulnerable to a foreseeable disaster was just another indicator of the need for positive innovation, especially in commercial structures that were constantly growing in size and in the numbers of people they were expected to accommodate.

Iron had for decades been used in bridges and in large buildings, but in the latter its use was largely restricted to internal support systems—such as those undergirding domes, floors, arcades, and atriums—and to decorative exterior facades. A central article of faith in architectural design, with roots reaching back to ancient Greece and Rome through the Middle Ages and

A *Chicago Tribune* artist captured the devastating effects of the Grannis Block fire, with the remains of Burnham's supposedly fire-resistant building now draped in ice on a cold February day in 1885. (*Chicago Tribune,* February 21, 1885.)

Renaissance and beyond, was that massive buildings required a thick shell of stone to provide the solid external framework, supporting both interior structures and the shell itself. As buildings mounted higher and higher, the thickness of the masonry walls had to steadily increase.

In his 1942 memoir, Swedish-born architect Henry Ericsson—the aforementioned youthful admirer of Burnham's Montauk building—tells a delightful story about the origin of the steel-skeleton frame for big buildings. A key claimant for the honor of the first building to pioneer the use of metal frameworks for Chicago skyscrapers has long been William Le Baron Jenney's Home Insurance Building, which in 1883 was in early stages of construction at LaSalle and Adams in Chicago. The story, claimed Ericsson—who had worked with Jenney during this period—was related to him "as William LeBaron Jenney [himself] told it." A bricklayers' strike had halted progress on this important commission, and as someone accustomed to the rigid discipline of soldiers during his time as a Civil War engineer, Major Jenney was growing frustrated.

> Now a strike of bricklayers is anything but a military problem, and when the men failed to proceed with their work where the stonemasons had left off, Jenney, sick at heart, closed his rolltop desk in the old Lakeside Building and left in the middle of the afternoon for his home in Bittersweet Place. So unusual was this that Mrs. Jenney could only surmise that he must be ill, and as she rose to greet him she found no immediately convenient place to lay the heavy book she was reading. Inadvertently she laid it down on top of a bird cage which stood on a table. At that an inspiration struck Jenney; if so frail a frame of wire would sustain so great a weight without yielding, would not a cage of iron or steel serve as a frame for a building?[44]

The story may exist somewhere on a continuum between highly fanciful and entirely true.

Another theory holds that Jenney's inspiration originated in an early visit to the Philippines, where he was entranced by the capacity of thin bamboo poles to provide the supporting framework for surprisingly resilient native huts. It could be that Jenney was doubly inspired. Ericsson acknowledged that "the metal frame, if somewhat accidental in its first adoption, was a long and quite natural evolution."[45] "Evolution" is right. Architectural historians have argued for decades over whether Jenney's Home Insurance Building of 1885 deserves the title of the world's first skyscraper or whether it can even be considered the first expression of a metal-framed "skeletal" structure. LeRoy Buffington of Minneapolis, a fellow Midwesterner and member of the WAA, had drawn up plans for tall buildings with all-metal frames in the early years of the decade. But he had done so mostly with an eye to obtaining a patent for his process, which he eventually received in 1888. His projected "cloudscrapers" from this period remained unbuilt.

When Jenney's Home Insurance Building was demolished in 1931, a committee headed by architect Thomas Tallmadge concluded that the building was in fact "the first high structure to utilize as its basic principle of its design the method known as skeleton" and thus can serve as "the true father of the modern skyscraper."[46] But in the early 1880s fully steel-framed high-rises whose exteriors expressed their inner skeletal structures were still several years in the future. The Home Insurance Building's base was solid masonry, the metal supports a mix of cast iron, wrought iron, and steel, which was introduced partway through the building process. The party walls were

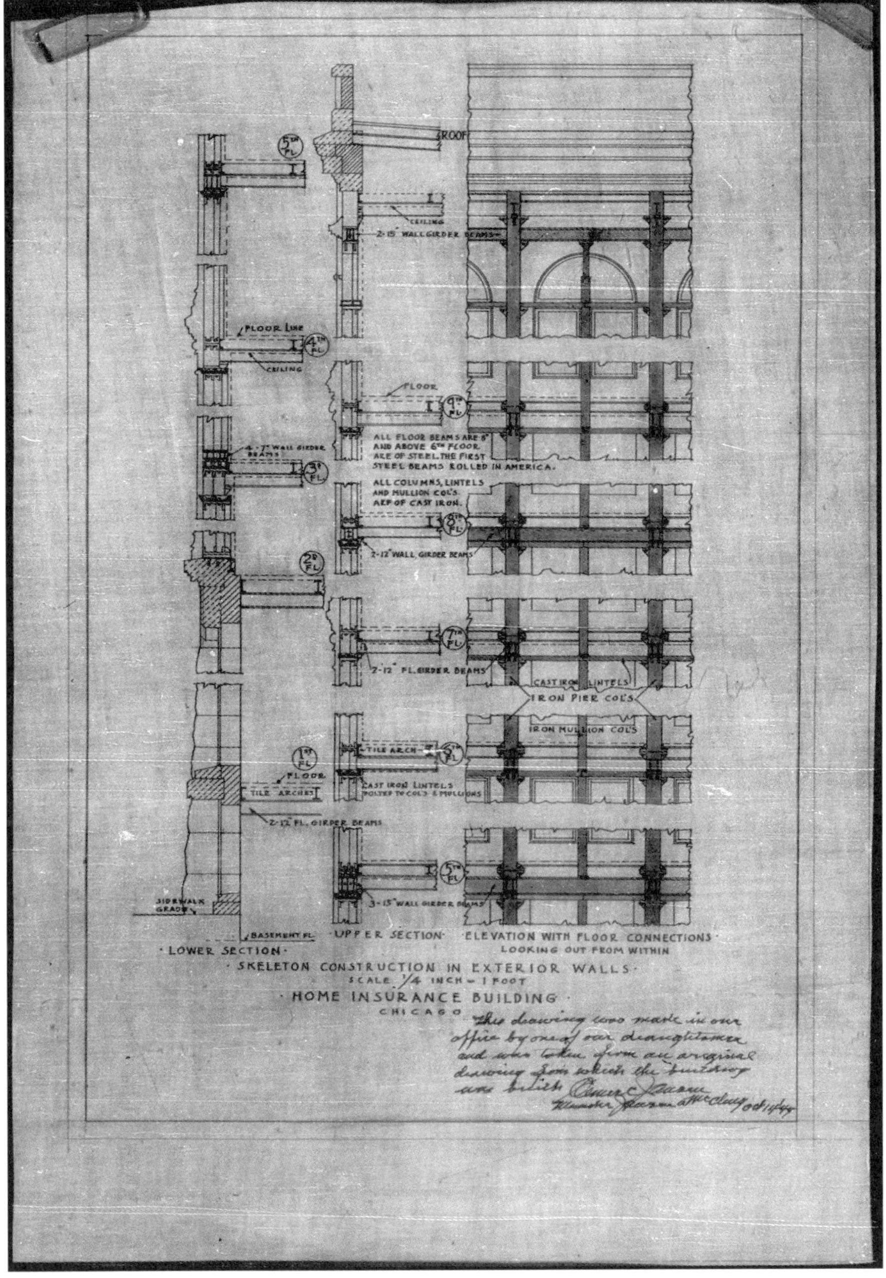

This rendering, redrawn in 1949 from an original document by a draftsman in the architectural offices of Mundie, Jensen and McClurg (now Jensen and Halstead), reveals the details of metallic skeleton construction in William Le Baron Jenney's Home Insurance Building, completed 1885. (Burnham Library–University of Illinois Project to Microfilm Architectural Documentation Records, Ryerson and Burnham Art and Architecture Archives, Art Institute of Chicago. Digital File # 000000_19731_24_004.)

made of brick. The walls facing the street were a mix of brick and iron, not exactly what we have come to know as "curtain walls."[47] From the outside, the building was notably tall for the time, but its exterior appearance differed little from the other tall buildings rising in downtown Chicago.

Ultimately the use of steel for skeletal framing became the game-changer in the movement toward taller and safer buildings. Jenney's decision to take advantage of newly available Bessemer steel to complete the upper half of the building turned out to be a prescient move. Thomas Leslie points out that cast iron supports were strong but brittle, and that wrought iron was weaker but more ductile, that is, less likely to crack or break under pressure. The Bessemer process removed impurities from molten pig iron through the use of blown air. With its adjusted carbon content, steel combined the best features of both materials: strong yet pliable, and in the years to come increasingly capable of forming solid bonds as riveting technology advanced. Only ten years after the completion of the Home Insurance Building, by 1895 *Engineering Record* declared that cast iron was no longer advised for structural purposes. Steel had become the structural metal of choice.[48]

As we have seen, the term *sky-scraper* had already been used for tall masonry buildings. Some critics have noted that the vertical thrust of central cities depended on much more than steel framing alone, including continuous improvements in elevator technology, heating and cooling systems, and lighting. Still, Jenney's structural innovation is uncontested as a significant historical move on the way to the cloud-piercing cityscapes of the twentieth century. This "Chicago Construction" method had a profound effect on other Chicago architects, including Jenney's one-time assistants Daniel Burnham, Louis Sullivan, William Holabird, and Martin Roche. Adler and Sullivan, in buildings such as the Jewelers Building and the Borden Block, had already experimented with exterior composites of brick and iron that use thinner piers and may have seemed to suggest a skeleton-like frame beneath. Burnham and Root, in part influenced by Adler and Sullivan, had similarly sought to condense masonry walls and articulate piers and spandrels.[49] In 1887 construction began on Holabird and Roche's Tacoma Building at the corner of LaSalle and Madison, a tall office building whose frame was entirely of skeleton construction. Burnham and Root's Rand McNally Building, built in 1889 on Adams Street, used an all-steel skeleton frame. Although Adler and Sullivan's innovative Auditorium Building, which opened in 1889, did not make use of Jenney's metal-frame system, by 1890 they were incorporating it into the soaring Wainwright Building in St. Louis, a project sometimes cited as Sullivan's first true skyscraper.

The question of who was first to pioneer skeletal construction was of little consequence to Sullivan. He noted that for some time architects had supported outer spans of floor loads with cast-iron columns beside masonry piers, but since the efforts involved no fixed principle of construction, to Sullivan the "squabblings as to priority are so much piffle." The important part was that "the Chicago architects welcomed the steel frame and did something with it"—himself, presumably, included.[50]

But starting in 1885, it was not the innovative Home Insurance Building that would engage Sullivan's imagination but rather a large commercial masonry structure. In that year merchandising mogul Marshall Field commissioned the renowned Boston architect Henry Hobson Richardson to design his new wholesale warehouse store, a massive project that was to occupy the block encompassed by Quincy, Franklin, Adams, and Wells Streets in the heart of Chicago's business district. Louis's fascination with Richardson reached as far back as his youthful rambles in Boston, when he first came across Richardson's majestic Brattle Square Church.

In his enthusiasm for Richardson's work, he was hardly alone. Even today travelers through older American cities, when they encounter fortress-like edifices of dark, rusticated stone and immense stone arches topped by soaring cupolas and jutting gables, are likely gazing at late nineteenth-century Richardsonian Romanesque structures, either designed by Richardson or by his disciples and admirers. Well-known examples include Trinity Church at Copley Square in Boston, Minneapolis City Hall, the Old Post Office in Washington, DC, Union Depot in Pueblo, Colorado, among many other public, commercial, and religious buildings that still dot the American landscape. It would not be too much to say that Richardson's reputation was dominant among American architects for much of the 1870s into the 1890s, and that his characteristic designs, especially for the public, commercial, and religious buildings, emphasized the heavy, massive solidity of rough-faced stone.

The Marshall Field Wholesale Store opened for business on June 20, 1887. Sullivan watched the rising structure with interest and admiration. In a series of essays written in 1901, Sullivan described Richardson's Chicago store in his characteristically florid, impassioned prose. Addressing a fictional acolyte, Sullivan attempts to correct the young aspirant's dismissal of the Field store as merely "massive, dignified and simple." Oh, no, replies the mentor Sullivan. "It is so much more that I have called it an oasis."

> Four-square and brown, it stands, in physical fact, a monument to trade, to the organized commercial spirit, to the power and progress of the age, to the strength and resource of individuality and force of character; spiritually, it stands as the index of a mind, large enough, courageous enough to cope with these things, master them, absorb them and give them forth again, impressed with the stamp of large and forceful personality; artistically, it stands as the oration of one who knows well how

H. H. Richardson's Marshall Field's Wholesale Store opened in 1887 and occupied a full city block in downtown Chicago. It was demolished in 1930. In Thomas Tallmadge's view, it "combined power and grace to a sensational degree." Louis Sullivan regarded the Romanesque commercial structure as a refreshing oasis among the "barren wastes of meanness and of littleness of soul" that characterized most Chicago architecture, a building wherein "stone and mortar . . . spring into life and are no more material and sordid things." (Historic Architecture and Landscape Image Collection, Ryerson and Burnham Art and Architecture Archives, Art Institute of Chicago. Digital file # 77224.)

> to choose his words, who has somewhat to say and says it—and says it as the outpouring of a copious, direct, large and simple mind.
>
> Therefore have I called it, in a world of barren pettiness, a male: for it sings the song of procreant power. . . . I would place a modest wreath upon the monument of him who stood alone, an august figure in his art, and now, across the bridge invisible made vital by these stones, breathes forth a strain of noble poesy.[51]

It's hard for us, through photographs of the now demolished building, to see Richardson's creation as possessing quite this much supercharged

Captivated by Richardson's simple yet massive and artfully proportioned Wholesale Store, Sullivan sought to give his Auditorium Building's exterior a similarly restrained mixture of monumentality and grace. (Barbara Crane Collection, Ryerson and Burnham Art and Architecture Archives, Art Institute of Chicago. Digital file # 199901_n911.)

meaning, to say nothing of the presumed superiority of male potency that Sullivan assigned to it. But Sullivan was hardly alone in finding the building extraordinarily impressive. Jeffery Karl Ochsner refers to it as "probably the most famous of Richardson's buildings, one that Richardson himself saw as among his most significant."[52] The foremost architectural critic of Sullivan's time, the sometimes acerbic and infrequently effusive Montgomery Schuyler of New York, after pointing to supposed minor defects in the design, spoke of the building in terms like Sullivan's. "The great pile," said Schuyler, "is one of the most interesting as it is one of the most individual examples of American commercial building," with a basement "Cyclopean in scale" and a doorway "Cyclopean in rude strength."[53] Thomas Tallmadge believed the building was "the masterpiece of H. H. Richardson, acclaimed from the day of its completion to the day of its destruction [in 1930] as Chicago's noblest work of architecture."[54]

Proof that Louis Sullivan shared these perceptions is evident not only from his writings but also from the evolution of his design approach to the Auditorium Building. In Sullivan's early designs, beginning in the fall of 1886 when Richardson's structure was rising on the corner of Adams and Wells, he included numerous decorative details on the outside and peaked rooflines and protruding dormers consistent with features and adornments common in other large commercial buildings of the time. When the Auditorium opened on December 9, 1889, many of these elements had disappeared or been reduced. The resemblance of the finished product to the Field store was unmistakable. Dramatic Richardsonian arches graced both the hotel side on Michigan Avenue and the theater entrance on Congress Street (now Ida B. Wells Drive). The external appearance of the building featured a massive, foursquare, masonry palazzo, with rough-faced granite blocks forming the base and paired windows culminating in arches on upper stories. All the peaked roofs and much of the fussy exterior decorative work from earlier designs were gone.

Inspired by Richardson's impressive work, Sullivan was also acutely aware of the pressure to create something remarkable and new in a city filled with more experienced architects. None loomed larger than the Chicago counterpart ten years his senior, Daniel Burnham, who, Sullivan believed, expressed continuing disappointment with Ferdinand Peck's choice of Adler and Sullivan for the Auditorium Building commission. Throughout the long process of designing, reconsidering, and reshaping, Sullivan said, "Burnham's shadow seemed to precede or follow him on all fours with its nose to the ground, as if perturbed."[55] When the project reached completion, the acclaimed result seemed to vindicate Sullivan's design choices. To the day of his death, Sullivan saw the Auditorium as the culminating achievement of his work on masonry buildings and felt special pride in one key departure from the Field store example: the flat-roofed tower over the theater entrance that held "its head in the air, as a tower should."[56]

The confidence that Sullivan was feeling as he embarked on his multi-year Auditorium project was evident in the fall of 1886, when he delivered his first major address to the Western Association of Architects annual convention. This was the third convention that Sullivan had attended as an active and vocal participant, and by now several of his fellow architects would have become acquainted with him through the recently completed Adler and Sullivan projects and through other professional meetings. One can only imagine the astonishment of practical-minded friends and professional associates when Sullivan chose to unleash upon them this extraordinary opening sentence:

> When birds are caroling, and breezes swiftly fly, when large abundant nature greets the eye, clothed in fresh filigree of tender green, when all is animation and endeavor, when days are lengthening, and storm clouds smiling weep, when fresh from every nook springs forth new life,—then does the heart awake in springtime gladness, breezy and melodious as the air, to join the swelling anthem of rejuvenated life, to mate with birds and flowers and breezes, spontaneous and jubilant as the glow of dawn, to pulsate ardently with hope, rich in desire so tremulously keen,—then wondrous joy to simply live,—and question not, to walk into the ample air, to open wide the portals of the winter bounded soul and eagerly to hail the new-born world with voice like mountain torrent quick melted from the heart's accumulated snows,—even so eagerly and so voluminously does the song gush forth and wildly leap, tumultuous as nature's self,—to fall in gentle spray upon the misty valley far below, and there, to live bound up within the very life it sung.[57]

This "Essay on Inspiration" was afterward printed in full in the *Inland Architect and Builder* among more earthbound considerations of "Hardwood and Hardwood Finish," "Wolff's Transparent Paints," and "The Disposal of Sewage of Isolated Country Houses."

For some of the architects present this was probably their first direct encounter with Sullivan's philosophical bent and with his "organic" theory of architecture, which was so dependent on a rapturous and intense personal relationship with the natural world. For those listeners steeped in the currents of nineteenth-century Emersonian Romanticism, as were many Americans of the time, the extravagant language—while arguably out of place in this context—would not have seemed entirely unfamiliar. The young Daniel Burnham, during his brief mining adventure out West, expressed similar sentiments in only slightly less elevated prose. Likewise J. Coleman Hart and Emerson friend William Henry Furness delivered religious and transcendentally themed addresses before many of these same architects at professional gatherings.

In his talk Sullivan did little to guide his audience toward understanding the link between his deeply felt Romanticism and everyday architectural practice. His paean to nature and natural processes of growth, maturity, and decay—themes that would be highlighted again in the murals adorning the Auditorium Theater—didn't stop with the opening lines but continued throughout the long lecture in the same abstruse and often antiquated rhetoric. As the sun hovers over the sea, intoned Sullivan, "so do I o'erhang thee, mighty one, yet where may I find the image of my ardent soul," before he finally arrived at what seemed to be something resembling a central point.

As he launched into his culminating peroration, Sullivan declared "that to arrest and typify in materials the harmoniously interblended rhythms of nature and humanity . . . indicates the deepest inspiration and the most exalted reach of art." In pursuing this artistic inspiration, logic must take a back seat to the intuitive powers of an ardent soul nourished by nature: "The mind speaks in terms of logic, which is conscious and secondary; but . . . the soul speaks in terms of inscrutable intuition, which is involuntary, vital, and primary."[58] In other words, a true architect, after immersing himself (Sullivan's audience would have been overwhelmingly male) in the cyclical glories of nature and natural processes, can give worthy material form to his creations only by trusting more to his spiritual, intuitive self rather than to his rational, logical mind. It would be hard to find a more vivid infusion of an American version of the Romantic movement into nineteenth-century architectural theory.

Sullivan seemed to understand, and even take some impish pleasure in, the burdens his speech placed on its listeners. In his autobiography he acknowledged that at the time the "effusion did not take," the consensus of those present being that Sullivan didn't have any idea of what he was talking about, that he "was plainly crazy, for what had all this flowery stuff to do with architecture anyway."[59] Thinking that the essay might find a kinder reception among those of "higher culture," he sent a printed copy to a University of Michigan Latin professor of his acquaintance and received in return, "The language is beautiful, but what on earth you are talking about I have not the faintest idea." Sullivan came to agree that the piece was "a bit sophomoric and over-exalted" but insisted that the ideas were sound.[60]

Sullivan's rhetorical exuberance in the "Inspiration" essay might be partly explained by his apparent recent discovery, while browsing through a local bookstore, of a copy of Walt Whitman's *Leaves of Grass*. Deeply touched and inspired, Sullivan sat down to write a letter to Whitman in February of 1887. He confessed that the poet had found the words to express precisely the passionate attachment to the natural world and the American landscape that had been stirring in Sullivan since early childhood. He said as soon as his eyes lit on the poem "Elemental Drifts," the lines of the good gray poet "then and there entered my soul, have not departed, and never will depart."[61] The title suggests that the volume Sullivan held in his hands was likely one of the earlier editions, where "Elemental Drifts" introduced the poem that in later editions was identified as "As I Ebb'd with the Ocean of Life." The lines that so impressed Sullivan described the poet walking the shores of Long Island, imagining himself as a bit of seaborne debris, "a little wash'd-up drift, A few sands and dead leaves to gather, Gather, and merge myself as part of the sands and drift." Whitman complicates his pantheistic merge by hearing in the sea wind a more somber message: "the dirge, the voices of men and women wrecked" in which he too, "but a trail of drift and debris," has washed up upon the shore, another of the sea's castaways.[62]

Whitman's language must have recalled to Louis his five-year-old self visiting the shores of Folly Cove, musing "patiently there, inspirited by the salt breeze, listening to the joyous song of the sea as the ground swells reared and dashed upon the rocks with a mighty shouting. . . . It belonged to him." Even the dark undertones of Whitman's poem would have struck a responsive chord in Sullivan, who, after witnessing the near-drowning of his own father in the same sea, claimed to have discovered that "the sea was a monster, a huge monster that would have swallowed up his father, like one of the giants he had told his grandmama about."[63] Little wonder then that Sullivan enclosed a copy of "Inspiration" with his fan letter to Whitman as evidence that he, allied to Whitman in heightened sensitivity to the awe-inspiring and fearsome power of nature, was engaged in an effort to create a "virile indigenous art." To the poet he declared, "it is your opinion of it above all other opinions that I should most highly value."[64]

Lauren Weingarden has argued that Whitman would have a continuing impact on Sullivan's architecture, to the point that she terms several of Sullivan's skyscrapers of the 1890s "Whitmanesque." Weingarden identifies a key impulse in nineteenth-century American thought, "that of integrating material and technological progress with a national identity rooted in the pastoral ideal." Sullivan found in Whitman—in a continuum reaching back to Emerson—a way in which to address that problem. Of particular impact, in this view, was Whitman's insistence that spiritual and democratic values could find expression in urban settings and in "naturalized" technologies of the built environment just as easily as in the actual unspoiled landscapes of America's fields and forests.[65]

Only two months after Sullivan's letter to Whitman, we find his first written reference to another influential writer bearing a mystical/spiritual nature, Emanuel Swedenborg. In April 1887 Sullivan addressed the Illinois State Association of Architects on the subject of "just subordination" of details to mass, in effect a defense of his treasured ornamentation in relation to the solid banality of imposing commercial edifices. Which is more important, he asked: the finely crafted details or the overall impression that the structure instantly makes on the observer? "Candidly," said Sullivan, with the theory of "suppressed functions" perhaps echoing in the back of his mind, "I do not believe in subordination of detail" as it "conveys an idea of caste or rank, with the involved suggestion of a greater force suppressing lesser." Would one ask about a tree, for example, "which is more to us, the leaves or the tree?"[66]

As time went by Sullivan would occasionally present the duality in terms of masculine (rational/mechanical/objective) versus feminine (emotional/intuitive/subjective). The emphasis on masculine power—a feature of Sullivan's thought and rhetoric influenced by Lotos Club athletic competitions and his enthusiasm for heroic artistic figures like Michelangelo and Walt Whitman and H. H. Richardson—remained with him for most of his life. The solid, bold and relatively unadorned mass of Richardson's Marshall Field's Wholesale Store, along with the exterior of Sullivan's own Auditorium, stood on one side of the male/female equation. The finely wrought details that Sullivan would lavish with increasing frequency on his most famous buildings represented the other side. Among his fellow speakers at the 1887 conference, Sullivan singled out O. J. Pierce, whose presentation seemed to embrace this conjunction of masculine and feminine qualities in architecture, an idea that, to Sullivan, seemed "far-reaching in its implied analogies, recalled even the exquisite 'correspondences' of Swedenborg."[67] In this instance Sullivan may have been thinking of the Swedenborgian metaphor wherein man represents "generating wisdom" and woman represents "generating love," a mutually dependent and vital union of seemingly distinct qualities.

Narciso Menocal has presented the most complete consideration of this evolution of Sullivan's designs, ranging from the purportedly "masculine" boldness of the Auditorium's exterior to the more complex "feminine" decorative expressiveness of many of the later works. And Menocal is quite explicit in assigning this evolution to the affinities between Sullivan's beliefs and Swedenborgian thought. That Sullivan knew *of* Swedenborg is clear, but as with Emerson, evidence of direct influence is less certain. The most Menocal can do in establishing a Swedenborgian connection is point to associates like Burnham and John Root as well as friends and family members who may have shown some interest in Swedenborg. At some point, says Menocal, Sullivan's friend John Edelmann "might have been curious to know why transcendentalists were interested in Swedenborg." During this period a number of books and pamphlets on Swedenborg's philosophy and theology would have been available, which Sullivan "might have come across," even though none of Swedenborg's works were listed among the items sold at auction from Sullivan's library in 1909.[68] Yet Sullivan's explicit insistence on the complementary coexistence of masculine and feminine qualities in architecture is consistent with Swedenborg's teachings, and an intellectual connection is possible.

While Sullivan was composing his letter to Whitman, another kindred spirit was unwittingly working his way into the periphery of Sullivan's orbit. A nineteen-year-old Frank Lloyd Wright had just left the University of

Wisconsin—like Sullivan at MIT, without taking a degree—and had set out from his family's home in the leafy, rolling hill-country of western Wisconsin to seek his architectural fortune in Chicago. Wright's memoir tells of days of wandering the city and examining its major buildings, much as Sullivan had done more than a decade earlier, and stopping into the offices of the city's established architects in search of an entry into the profession. He tried names he had heard of and "names that sounded interesting," among them [William B.] Mundie and Jenney, whose Home Insurance Building had recently come to completion. Before long he had landed a position as a draftsman in the offices of J. L. Silsbee, who Wright knew was designing a chapel for his uncle back in his hometown of Spring Green.

Wright quickly grew dissatisfied with his situation at Silsbee's, found work elsewhere, grew disillusioned again, returned to Silsbee, then got a tip on a possible opening with Adler and Sullivan, whose work on the Auditorium was just then getting underway. "I had formed a high idea of Adler and Sullivan," Wright recalled. "Architects foremost in Chicago Radical—going strong on independent lines. Burnham and Root their only rivals." Wright saw Sullivan, now thirty-one years old, as a "small man immaculately dressed in brown" with "amazing big brown eyes." Sullivan looked over the youthful Wright's drawings and, after quizzing him on their originality with a mixture of critical skepticism and grudging admiration, reportedly said, "You've got the right kind of touch, you'll do." Shortly thereafter Wright was put to work on designs for the Auditorium and quickly earned a place in the office as Sullivan's top assistant and sounding board. Always the imperious master, Sullivan gradually developed a personal relationship with young Wright, sometimes holding forth in after-hours sessions at the office, sometimes joining Wright for breakfast at the Congress Hotel. Sullivan would "ask for coffee—pound the table for coffee, his hand shaking, morose until he got coffee," Wright recalled. "Then, soon pleasant, [Sullivan became] expansive mentally as a blooming rose."[69]

Daniel Burnham experienced a consequential uprooting in 1886 after deciding he could no longer bear to live in the city of Chicago. The house on the corner of 43rd Street and South Michigan Avenue no longer seemed the kind of place where he wanted to raise his small children. In what appears to be an abrupt decision that caught several family members off guard, Burnham leased an "old but very good" house, complete with barn and icehouse, near Lake Michigan in the leafy and fashionable suburb of Evanston just north of the city. Burnham and Root had built several Evanston houses beginning in 1879, including some impressive mansions very close to what was to become the Burnham property. In a letter to his mother, Burnham attempted to allay her concerns over the sudden move:

> The decision in the matter of Evanston was entirely mine, and was made against the feelings of Margaret and the loud protests of everyone else. I did it because I can no longer bear to have my children in the streets of Chicago, and because especially I can not stand them being on the South Side, for reasons I will give you when I see you, and which I know beforehand you will most heartily approve.
>
> Now every one has turned and all are enthusiastic in praise of the scheme, even Mr. Sherman who pooh-hood [*sic*] it violently, has taken pains to take me apart and tell me that I have done exactly right, and that he thoroughly approves. . . .
>
> I will say in brief: it is the only place I could go as I have come to feel—and still stay in Chicago.
>
> The place itself is handily situated, on the shore, in the center of the town of Evanston, and is very beautiful.[70]

Burnham packed up his family and promptly took up residence in the spacious sixteen-room home. The site bordered Dempster Street on the north and Forest Avenue on the west, a large expanse of land spanning an entire city block. Dan Jr. recounted a family story that, in his infancy, he was carried into the new house in 1886 "suffering on a pillow just having passed through scarlet fever."[71] The lease included an option to buy, which Burnham eventually exercised, creating what was to become, as he predicted, the family's permanent home to stay in "till the end."[72] The extensive grounds with overarching canopies of shade trees, the proximity to Lake Michigan and to the homes of many of his associates in Chicago's business elite, the increasingly elegant surroundings all made the Burnham home in Evanston a perfect setting for entertaining friends and family over the years, a duty which the Burnhams happily embraced. The natural setting and the lakeshore also furnished Burnham with multiple subjects for the sketches and watercolors that occupied many of his leisure hours. In these early years, Dan Jr. also recalled, there stood an old coal pier that extended out into the lake, where the "family used to go out on hot Summer nights to enjoy the lake breeze."[73]

Just what did Daniel Burnham mean by telling his mother he would give his "reasons [for leaving Chicago] when I see you"? At the time the South Side of Chicago was still viewed as offering highly desirable residential districts for the city's wealthiest families. Prairie Avenue, just south of the downtown business district, was in its heyday as *the* fashionable address for business titans such as farm-implement magnate John J. Glessner, whose

This entrance to Burnham's Evanston estate offers a glimpse into the spacious, richly forested environment available to him and his family on Chicago's increasingly affluent North Shore. (Daniel H. Burnham Collection, Ryerson and Burnham Art and Architecture Archives, Art Institute of Chicago. Digital file # 194301.110204-01.)

remarkable stone mansion by H. H. Richardson was then undergoing construction. Philip Armour, Marshall Field, George Pullman, and Burnham's own father-in-law John Sherman were just a few of the legendary names of Chicago merchant royalty whose resplendent residences lined the street in the mid-1880s. Burnham knew the splendor of Prairie Avenue very well, having lived there with the Shermans in the first years of his marriage. Farther south and nearer the Burnhams' second home stood the resplendent John Cudahy mansion at 33rd and Michigan. In 1893 the area remained fashionable enough for meatpacking magnate Gustavus Swift to build yet another palatial residence for his daughter, two blocks directly south of the Burnhams' Michigan Avenue home, in the district that would later be officially designated the Grand Boulevard Community Area, named after another South Side street lined with eye-popping domiciles of the very rich.

So why did the Burnhams leave? The home the family was now exiting at 4300 South Michigan was less than two miles from Sherman's stock-

Wherever he was, whether on the shores of Lake Michigan at his Evanston home or during his travels across the continent or abroad, Daniel Burnham found time to sketch, draw, and paint. (Daniel H. Burnham Collection, Ryerson and Burnham Art and Architecture Archives, Art Institute of Chicago. Digital file # 194301.090209-01.)

yards. But it doesn't seem that the relative proximity of that immense operation—with the attendant stench and sounds and sprawling industrial squalor—was the operative factor behind Burnham's decision. It is also unlikely that any specific racial animus had a direct role. In time the Grand Boulevard district would become part of a South Side neighborhood dubbed Bronzeville, after the Great Migration of Black laborers from the South. But that historic movement was still some thirty years in the future. Grand Boulevard would ultimately be renamed Martin Luther King Jr. Drive in honor of the famed civil-rights leader.[74] In 1886, however, the residences in the Grand Boulevard area and those just to the west were occupied by a largely white population featuring a mix of working-class and middle-class residents of Irish, English, and Scottish descent alongside German Jews and American-born moneyed elites of the city.[75] The number of African Americans was still relatively small. In the city as a whole, the number of Black citizens had not yet reached 14,000 and represented just over one percent of the total population.

Various forms of social unrest in the city may have factored into Burnham's decision to move. Working conditions for laborers in Chicago—ten- to twelve-hour workdays, six-day weeks, unsafe labor practices, wages that often failed to meet weekly living expenses—fueled furious actions and reactions on the part of workers and worker organizations. These labor conflicts that had begun erupting in the late 1870s and continued into the 1880s and '90s put many Chicagoans in all parts of the city on edge. To many it appeared that periodic outbreaks of labor protest were introducing deadly forms of warfare to the streets of Chicago. "War in Earnest," declared the *Tribune* at the height of the 1877 railroad strike that shocked many Chicagoans, with a "mob . . . of mammoth proportions, numbering fully 1,500, and showing all the elements of extreme viciousness," building "a force of fully 3,000 more of the cut-throats and bandits—the worst scum of [the South Side community of] Bridgeport." At the end of this violent protest, "to get at a list of the killed and wounded was an utter impossibility in the howling wilderness of mob."[76] On Thanksgiving Day 1884 anarchists demonstrated outside of the homes of the Prairie Avenue capitalists and encouraged hoboes, as Donald Miller put it, "to ring the doorbells of the 'robber classes' and demand jobs and bread."[77] That Burnham's father-in-law was a prominent member of this threatened privileged class—a class from which he drew his clients and within which Burnham himself was rapidly securing a place—would not have been lost on this family-centered architect.

The attitudes of most members of the Western Association of Architects toward strikers and militant labor organizers is not hard to determine. In November of 1887 the *Inland Architect and News Record* apologized to its readers for a delay in publication due to a typographical union workers' strike. Thankfully, in the eyes of the paper's editors, their offices were "fast filling up with competent men and we anticipate no further trouble." The pressman's union that refused to honor the typographers' strike, by contrast, was "made up of intelligent, conservative men who believe in the dignity of their trade and in justice and equity rather than brute force."

In the same issue, Chicago architect Irving K. Pond's article "Home" exhibited a similar uneasiness over the current outbreaks of labor agitation. Unlike the brutal inequalities Pond saw in certain aspects of family life in France, England ("where . . . the husband makes a practice of beating his wife, she of beating his children, they of beating each other"), and Germany (where "the husband lives well off the combined labors of his cow and his 'frau' harnessed to the same plow or cart"), the democratic American home ideally fosters an atmosphere in which "wife, mother means sweet sympathy; where husband, father means strong protection; where son and daughter means the perfect image of father and mother." In such a home, extreme sowers of social discord will have no room to grow. The list of evils Pond specifies includes malefactors at the top but is clearly weighted toward the terrifying threats from below.

> Capitalists—oppressors of the poor cannot be reared in this home.
> Agitators—curses of the rich and poor cannot come from such surroundings.
> Anarchy—murderer of the peace, cannot be bred here.
> Revolution is not nurtured here.
> Extreme wealth cannot brighten this home.[78]

The year of Burnham's decision to move, 1886, reached a point of historic intensity in this turbulent period of class conflict. The early months were marked by numerous demonstrations and strikes leading to occasional violent confrontations with police and culminating in the bloody Haymarket Square riot of May 4. Many Chicagoans blamed the influx of immigrant laborers for these increasing outbursts of anger and violence. There is scant evidence that Burnham felt contempt for any specific immigrant group, but a general attitude of concern over, even fear of, activist immigrant populations would have been consistent with that of other members of his social class.

Burnham was very much aware of the social unrest of his time and his city and of the activist movements that sought to remake America's social fabric. In a letter to a friend written some twenty years later, in answer to a question regarding Burnham's opinion on communism, Burnham responded, "I began life very much inclined toward free-trade and communism, but experience has brought wiser counsel." He applied the term "communism" specifically to the Brook Farm experiment of the 1840s, perhaps aware that his parents—proponents of the high idealism of the Swedenborgian faith—had welcomed at least one Brook Farm visitor into their home in Henderson in the years before Daniel's birth. Such experiments in communism, Burnham now said, "will be tried from time to time, . . . but people always find, to their surprise, that instead of getting rid of Old Task, he holds them most strongly in his grip when they depend, not on themselves but upon a community that exacts the performance daily and hourly, of duty from each of its members."[79]

Such systems, he believed, might work if human beings were reliably selfless and as concerned about their fellow citizens as they were about themselves. "Each for all is good when you love your neighbor as yourself, but is hard on you when you do not." In his maturity, his solution was in line with Republican Party progressivism of the early 1900s: let the government impose reasonable restraints to control individual passions, curb the trusts, tax incomes progressively, and "do everything necessary to protect society by law." Lest his correspondent miss the key point, he repeated it twice more. "Enforce law," he wrote. "Enforce law."[80]

It was not just worker unrest that unsettled residents. The big, magnificent houses on the South Side could not shield their occupants from other threatening aspects of life in the teeming, troubled metropolis of Chicago. As Jean F. Block reports, between 1881 and 1889, in nearby Hyde Park crime in all areas increased at an alarming rate. Arrests for disorderly conduct in this period went from 300 to 1,237; for drunk and disorderly conduct, 96 to 127; shooting on Sundays, 9 to 34. On State Street, just two blocks to the west of the Burnhams, working-class families lived and sought refuge from a hardscrabble existence in a string of almost-continuous saloons that stretched from 39th to 59th Streets.[81]

Evanston, by contrast, promised a reassuring suburban refuge from the tumult of city life. The emphasis was on secure and peaceful retreats, places prominent men of affairs could return to after enduring the exhausting give-and-take of daily business battles in the city. One Evanston newspaper from this era put it this way: "Evanston is pre-eminently a city of homes. We make no boast of manufactories, of shops, of foundries, but we are proud of our homes, and justly so."[82] "The people," Burnham assured his mother concerning the move, "are *just* such as you would wish."[83]

The other issue he felt compelled to address with his mother was the effect on his spiritual affiliations. "Now, dear Mother, I feel I can no longer live without a steady religious life—but I do not expect to make the Chicago Society [the primary organization for Chicago Swedenborgians] a permanent home. I do think that just the moment we can[,] we will have our own little church at Evanston, and I have already set on foot a scheme, which if it turns out well, will satisfy even you about church matters."[84]

It is unclear whether Burnham ever realized his scheme to find that "little church at Evanston," but he made up for it in other ways. Thomas Hines reports on an interview he conducted in 1969 with a neighbor, Catherine Wheeler, who grew up knowing the Burnhams and who would ultimately join the family by marrying Daniel's son John. Wheeler recalled being present at Sunday morning religious services that Burnham himself would conduct in the Evanston home, complete with readings from Swedenborg and discourses and discussions on "the mysteries and wonders of life."[85] In 1894 a new Swedenborgian community, comprising both a church and a school, was opened in nearby Glenview, where Burnham played golf and where Burnham's nephew Hugh served as the village's first president while also establishing himself as leading member of the congregation.

The Burnhams often provided entertainment and amusement for friends and associates in carefully orchestrated lawn parties on the family estate. In this lively costume party, Daniel Burnham was the down-and-outer third from the left, and immediately to Burnham's left Margaret Burnham presented herself as a figure of slightly greater elegance. (Daniel H. Burnham Collection, Ryerson and Burnham Art and Architecture Archives, Art Institute of Chicago. Digital file # 194301_110208-39, page 60.)

Daniel Burnham's prominence during this period received another significant boost with the construction of one of the most consequential and beloved of Burnham and Root buildings, the still-standing Rookery Building at the corner of LaSalle and Adams, which was conceived in 1885 and completed in 1888. Financed by the Brooks brothers of Boston and overseen by their Chicago agent Owen Aldis, the Rookery, some have claimed, took its name from a water tower that loomed on the property and that drew flocks of resting birds. Others have suggested that the name was associated with the old City Hall building that had also previously occupied the site, a jerry-built temporary structure that continued to attract birds as well as politicians and political hangers-on who created flurries of constant activity in and about the building. At least one source thought the name came from the dilapidated state of the night room where reporters gathered.[86] Wherever it came from, the name stuck—to the chagrin of the building's backers but to the delight of John Root, who included a pair of

The cackling crows or rooks carved into the entry arch of Burnham and Root's Rookery Building may offer an amusing tribute to the birds (and politicians) that formerly roosted on the site. (Photo by author.)

laughing crows on the grand Richardsonian masonry arch that framed the entrance. Hines credits Burnham with conceptualizing the "large, general plans" that defined the building.[87] Montgomery Schuyler believed that it showed, along with the firm's other recent structures, the unique creativity of its two designers, demonstrating what is "characteristically Chicagoan" in a way that is "not local, but personal," though he attributes most of the individuality in design to Root.[88]

The Rookery is a typical Burnham and Root mix of traditional design elements and architectural innovation. One of its most striking features—in Jay Pridmore's words, "one of the most fascinating and delightful [spaces] ever constructed in Chicago"[89]—is the glass-roofed atrium visitors encounter upon entering the building. To someone standing in the middle of the ground floor, bathed in penetrating daylight and gazing up at the intricate interlacing ironwork above, the space does indeed resemble an extraordinarily elaborate and elegant birdcage. Metal framing, while not used in the

The Rookery's interior atrium, designed by Burnham and Root—lightened and brightened by Frank Lloyd Wright's updates in 1907, renovated with some art deco elements by William Drummond in 1931, and revitalized by Daprato Rigali Studios in 1992—opens the elaborately designed central court to floods of sunlight. "Among historic buildings of Chicago," says Chicago author and journalist Jay Pridmore, "the Rookery . . . reigns as an undisputed favorite." (Photo by Velvet is licensed under CC BY-SA 3.0.)

exterior walls (as Jenney had just pioneered in the Home Insurance Building across the street), provided substantial interior structural and decorative support. As Pridmore points out, the Rookery's use of this feature—along with Root's extensive reliance on new methods in fireproofing, elevators, and plate glass—"introduced many breakthroughs at a time when architecture was on the verge of adopting new technologies."[90] Pridmore's list could also include the grillage "floating raft" foundation that Root had first used in the Montauk Building to address the problem of Chicago's unstable soil and that he now adapted for the Rookery.

Burnham and Root quickly took advantage of the business-friendly accommodations in the new Rookery. In 1888 the firm moved its offices from the Montauk and into the Rookery's top floor. The iconic 1890 photo of the two partners facing each other in stiff nineteenth-century fashion—although Burnham seemingly adopted a relaxed note with hands in pockets and legs casually crossed—was taken in the library of the Rookery.

Daniel Burnham and John Wellborn Root seated in the Rookery library/reception room, circa 1890. (Daniel H. Burnham Collection, Ryerson and Burnham Art and Architecture Archives, Art Institute of Chicago. Digital file # 194301.090706-03.)

In late 1887 Burnham embarked on another western trip, traveling by train through the Rocky Mountains to New Mexico, a journey culminating in a visit to the studio of landscape painter William Keith in San Francisco, a fellow Swedenborgian whom Burnham had gotten to know through the efforts of his minister friend Joseph Worcester. Keith was a successful depicter of mountain scenery of the West, just the kind of subject that would appeal to the Daniel Burnham who, as a young man, rhapsodized about Western landscapes. The trip involved minor mishaps—a brief train derailment, impromptu calls for Burnham to assist fellow passengers as a "squire of dames and babies"—and once again rapturous reactions to the stunning visits and rejuvenating atmosphere of the West.[91]

The western trip ended on a sour note however. In February 1888—while Frank Lloyd Wright was about to join the firm of Adler and Sullivan—the roof of the Midland Hotel, a major Burnham and Root metal-frame project then under construction in Kansas City, suddenly collapsed. It created a gaping hole of fifty to seventy-five feet square, killing one workman and injuring several others. Burnham had to travel to Missouri to address questions about who bore responsibility for the accident.[92] The whole episode, said Burnham, was the most "humiliating and distressing experience I have gone through since my boyhood foolishness in the far West."[93]

The Midland Hotel disaster did little to slow down the demand for Burnham's services in Chicago and elsewhere. During the latter years of this productive decade, Burnham and Root's ever-expanding firm handled dozens of projects for an elite clientele in the Chicago region and beyond: ornate houses, museums, railway stations, schools, apartments, and of course office buildings for Chicago's and America's business titans. In July of 1889 the *Tribune* announced the firm's plans to build "one of the ultimates . . . the highest of the high," the sixteen-story Monadnock Building.[94] Daniel Burnham, who began the decade as a thirty-three-year-old architect on whom Owen Aldis took a chance with the Grannis Block, was now fully established as a reliable chief for whatever massive projects the country's movers and shakers had in mind.

In this heady atmosphere prominent Chicagoan Thomas B. Bryan rose before a US Senate committee in January of 1890 to make the case for a world's fair to be held in the upstart city of Chicago, Illinois. It was the first step in a process that would extend Daniel Burnham's reputation far beyond the boundaries of his region and his home country.

6

Triumph

1890s

AS THE FINAL DECADE of the nineteenth century dawned, the competition to select an American city to host a fair in 1892, in commemoration of the four-hundredth anniversary of Columbus's arrival in the New World, was intensifying. Large fairs had been part of the international scene at least since the trend-setting exhibition of technology and culture at London's Crystal Palace in 1851. Thereafter fairs of varying size occurred in rapid succession in a number of major cities: among them Munich, Paris, Vienna, Sydney, Glasgow, and, in America, Philadelphia in 1876. The 1889 fair held in Paris—where Gustav Eiffel's extraordinary tower demonstrated the structural possibilities of a soaring iron framework—was fresh in the minds of American boosters and added a dash of motivation to out-Eiffel Eiffel.

The primary contenders were New York City, St. Louis, Chicago, and Washington, DC. On January 11, 1890, advocates for the various sites rose before a Senate committee to make their cases. In the morning New York's Chauncey Depew, railroad lawyer and magnate, delivered an impassioned plea on behalf of his home city. Its size, history, architectural distinction, commercial prominence, and seaside location made it seem, to many, the logical choice for an American showcase that would attract a large number of domestic and international (mostly European) visitors.

In the afternoon it fell to Chicago businessman Thomas Bryan to answer Depew's arguments and to paint a more vivid narrative in favor of Chicago. While acknowledging New York's and the other rival cities' legitimate claims to consideration, Bryan did not shy away from notes of humorous aggression against New York in particular. Depew, he conceded, had shown "mental adroitness in sporting over disjointed facts and fallacies" in his presentation, but Depew's very cleverness could not help but call to mind a "squirrel sporting over the top of a ramshackle fence; the agility we admire, but not the fence." Depew, said Bryan, has a "happy faculty of insinuating and driving in the needle so dexterously that no man complains, but it stings just the same." What could begin to bear comparison with Eiffel's magnificent tower? Why, Bryan asserted, obviously Adler and Sullivan's Auditorium, at that time Chicago's newest and grandest architectural marvel.

The fair, Bryan insisted, belonged in the West and in Chicago. "In this matter," he said, "Chicago is for the West in the interest of the entire country, and the West is for Chicago." Doubtless, noted Bryan, some effete Easterners might be afraid of encountering "country bumpkins and mammoth pumpkins" at a Chicago fair, but rather than experiencing the accustomed sight of pampered pets nestling in their masters' laps, wouldn't they prefer "to see the live stock such as Webster loved, and Clay loved, and Grant loved: superb horses, with arched necks, flashing eyes, and faultless forms, snuffling the morning air, and neighing as if in consciousness of nobility of blood, flying like the wind over broad fields under the canopy of heaven"?[1]

The Senate committee referred the question to the House of Representatives, and after much discussion and debate—including last-minute efforts of St. Louis and New York representatives to call into question the extent of Chicago's financial commitment—the exposition was officially awarded to Chicago in April of 1890. Two organizations were given supervisory authority: a National Commission headquartered in Washington and made up of representatives from all the states and territories, and a Chicago-based corporation established by the state of Illinois to provide financing and much of the planning for the fair, subject to the Commission's approval. Familiar figures assumed prominent posts in the corporation's Board of Directors, including Ferd Peck, the driving force behind Adler and Sullivan's Auditorium, and Owen Aldis, the property developer who had taken a chance on the untested young team of Root and Burnham to create their first major commercial structure, the Grannis Block, back in 1880. By the fall of 1890 the corporation settled on its choice to serve as chief of construction: by then a known and trusted figure in architectural circles, Daniel H. Burnham.

The prospect of managing a massive national project of international significance must have disturbed even the capable master organizer and delegator Daniel Burnham. During this time his large and busy firm was in the midst of constructing its largest and most innovative buildings to date, several of which were to secure a lasting place in the history of Chicago architecture.

The ten-story Rand McNally Building, which relied completely on an all-steel frame, was reaching completion on Adams Street. The fourth and fifth floors of the building were quickly commandeered to serve as headquarters for the exposition. Planning and construction were underway for the ground-breaking Monadnock Building, the massive Great Northern Hotel, the twelve-story Woman's Temple, headquarters of Frances Willard's Women's Christian Temperance Union (WCTU), and the even taller (in fact, on completion the world's tallest) Masonic Temple, among other structures large and small. As Thomas Hines put it, for Burnham and Root during this period, "[L]ife seemed good. They were building their greatest buildings, from houses to skyscrapers, and they were soon to embark on what promised to be their greatest collaborative effort—the building of the World's Columbian Exposition."[2]

Of the above-mentioned structures, the Monadnock—the only one still standing in downtown Chicago—is perhaps of the greatest significance.

Published May 25, 1892, this cartoon from the humor magazine *Puck* captures the feeling of many at the time. To those whose concept of urban architecture had been conditioned by the example of Old Europe, the New York ventures in skyscraper design were new and notable. But Chicago epitomized the marvel of previously unheard-of heights in tall-building construction. (Courtesy of the Newberry Library, Chicago.)

Chicagoans of the time marveled at the sheer number of workers who entered and exited every day. A cartoon printed in the *Tribune* offered a humorous take on how it might look if all six thousand people in the building tried to leave at one time, depicting an immense cube of people stacked on each other's shoulders ten rows high and clogging the entire width of Dearborn Street.

The building's most striking aesthetic departure from other large commercial structures of the era is the relatively unadorned simplicity of the exterior. The add-on decorations and horizontal stringcourses of the time are largely gone. Instead the observer sees vertical lines of bay windows pulling the eye directly and uninterruptedly skyward. Joanna Merwood-Salisbury meticulously describes the slow evolution of John Root's design from customary historical reference elements to this new straightforwardness and simplicity.[3] The driving forces behind this streamlined design were likely the developers, Peter and Shepherd Brooks of Boston, who insisted on commercial structures light on ornament and heavy on what they saw as the bedrock commercial values of solidity and strength, ideas that Root himself often claimed to share. Root's original and more conventional sketch of 1885 shows at the north end a flat façade divided horizontally by stringcourses and vertically by four decorative pilasters that culminated in capitals of sculpted Egyptian lotus blossoms. The concept was reworked over time and metamorphosed in 1889 into the restrained exterior of the finished product.

This simplification, however, did not mean Burnham and Root skimped on careful attention to design details. They kept a quiet suggestion of an Egyptian column motif by creating an inward-slanting base rising to a gentle outward curve in the cornice at the top. The bay-window verticals do not bottom out in straight horizontal cantilevers but appear to emerge from the exterior wall in rounded brickwork at the third-floor level. At the corners standard sharp-edged bricks gradually transition to increasingly rounded edges as the eye ascends, culminating in a fully rounded corner at the top.

On the design of the Monadnock, as on several other structures, it is impossible to know precisely where the hand of Burnham left off and the hand of Root took over. It is widely accepted that on most of their projects Burnham would sketch out the general concepts and layouts, and then Root would focus on bringing the buildings to life with carefully crafted detail. But that is a bit of an oversimplification; the two partners were constant collaborators throughout the design and construction process. Burnham's "judgment and taste were good," said Harriet Monroe, "and as a critic he was very suggestive." Monroe cites a long-time employee who provides a clarifying depiction of the two friends at work:

The northern portion of the Monadnock Building was the last all-masonry skyscraper built by the firm of Burnham and Root. Its relatively clean, unornamented exterior is regarded by some as a precursor to a modernist aesthetic in tall-building design. This photograph shows the sharp corners of brickwork at the base gradually yielding to more rounded corners and culminating in the fully rounded cornice at the top. The exceptional number of workers such a building could hold was a subject of constant comment. In 1900 the *Chicago Tribune* printed a full-page tribute to "The Most Remarkable Postal District in the World," wherein four mail carriers could complete their rounds without ever leaving the building. (Richard Nickel Archive, Ryerson and Burnham Art and Architecture Archives, Art Institute of Chicago. Digital file # 201006_120221-020.)

> [Burnham] would lean over John's drawing board . . . and say, "John, I don't like that very well." "Well, what's the matter with it?" John would say. And then Dan would point out something: tell him to fix up that corner, or change the grouping of those windows, or strengthen the sky-line, or do something else with the drawing. And John would reply that he thought it was pretty good as it was. But invariably after Dan had left he would fall to studying over the drawing, and would end by strengthening the weak places as Dan had suggested.[4]

Monroe goes on to assert that, while on some buildings Burnham's influence was relatively slight, on the Monadnock that was not the case—his ideas were very much reflected in the final design.

The atmosphere in the offices of Burnham and Root was exceptionally humane for late nineteenth-century office culture. One unnamed draftsman commented on the unusual gentility of the work environment: "No fault was ever found with our work by either Mr. Burnham or Mr. Root. I cannot imagine how they accomplished it. They must have gone into a closet for a private swear now and then. The men were treated invariably like gentlemen."[5] Paul Starrett, who began working as a draftsman's helper in the firm in the late 1880s, recalled the heavy workload that Burnham somehow managed to combine with these relatively free and easy working conditions. Burnham dominated, both by his sheer physical presence ("one of the handsomest men I ever saw," said Starrett) and by a magnetic personality that "combined with his magnificent physique, was a big factor in his success." But he also made time in the workday for physical exercise, including occasional noontime excursions to play handball or give lessons in fencing to his young employees. At one point Root brought a piano into the office and proceeded to offer an impromptu concert for the staff.[6]

One of the more revealing anecdotes from Starrett's time with Burnham shows how Burnham came to earn the sobriquet "Uncle Dan" among his associates. Starrett had been disappointed by the low pay offered him when Burnham had first approached him with an offer for a steady three-year contract. Eager to stay with the firm and overwhelmed by the presence of Burnham, he nonetheless accepted on the spot. Young Starrett, at that point in his life, had grown somewhat accustomed to the harsh "take it or leave it" attitudes of many employers of the time. Working for a hardware store for $4 a week some time earlier, he had had the temerity to approach the manager for a raise only to receive a typical rebuff: "Why, Paul, you don't know how lucky you are. When I was your age, I got down to the store at six, not seven, I opened it up, scrubbed the floors, cleaned out the spittoons, and look at me now!" He got a similar response when he tried the same thing as an agent struggling to make a living selling insurance on commission. Imagine the pleasant surprise in store for Starrett when he finally mustered the courage to approach Burnham with the same request.

> After I had worked two years on my contract with Burnham and was starting on a third, I got up my nerve one day and said: "Mr. Burnham, I think I'm worth more that twelve-fifty a week."
>
> Burnham looked at me, stroking his handsome mustache. I wondered whether he was going to give me the same answer as the hardware and the commission merchant when I struck them for a raise.
>
> "What do you think you are worth?" asked Burnham.
>
> "At least twice what I'm getting—twenty-five a week!"
>
> "Well, I think you're right. I'll tell the bookkeeper."[7]

In the first days of 1891 the firm of Burnham and Root seemed poised to continue its triumphant trajectory—now set to include the internationally significant World's Fair—with no end in sight. Not only was Burnham energetically assuming his supervisory duties for the fair, but John Root had also been designated as consulting architect and had already begun preparing plans for the fair's building program. In October 1890 Root had attended the annual convention of the American Institute of Architects and was actively performing his duties as secretary of the organization. In December Burnham had invited an assemblage of architects involved with the fair to Chicago to acquaint them with the chosen site and to discuss preliminary plans.

On a cold January day Burnham took his fellow architects on an excursion to Jackson Park on the far South Side to look over the grounds. John Root stayed behind at the office to nurse what he thought was a mild cold. On Sunday, January 11, Root spent the day pursuing his normal round of duties and pleasures—visiting a sculptor's studio in the morning, getting in a couple of hours work at the office, singing with his children—and ending with him and his wife entertaining the visiting architects at their North Side home in Evanston. At the end of the visit Root accompanied his guests down the steps of his house and into the winter cold, neglecting to don an overcoat to protect himself from the elements. The next day Root was diagnosed with pneumonia.

As soon as the seriousness of his partner's condition became clear, Burnham determined to stay with his friend at the Roots' house on Astor Street. Root was reportedly at first "incredulous at his illness" and sent for a drawing board to be brought home so he could work from his sickbed. He joked with his nurses in a way that suggested a lighthearted unconcern for his condition. Harriet Monroe's account of his rapid decline contains a typically Victorian emphasis, perhaps exaggerated, on the poignant drama of his final hours and last words. She includes in her telling Root's well-known love for color in architecture as well as his lifelong devotion to music—with an added strong dash of something like Swedenborgian hope. The "mighty change" from life to death seemed to him, wrote Monroe,

> a mere transition from a world of incomplete conditions to one fit for the gradual purification and fulfillment of the soul's desire and energy. . . . In the last hours sweet illusions assailed his brain, and he talked of them to the women around him, "isn't it beautiful—all white and gold!" As the early night came on, he whispered huskily, "Do you hear that music?" And when they assured him it was lovely, his fingers played the celestial air, and his voice grew rich and deep once more for the last large words—"That's what I call music—grand."[8]

Burnham was deeply attentive to Root's needs in the days he spent with him. On Root's last day, Burnham recalled, "When I went in John was breathing very rapidly and said, 'You won't leave me again, will you?' I said, 'No, John, I will stay.' I went in to see his wife, who was very ill. His aunt [Nellie Mitchell] came into the wife's room and told me that he was dead."[9]

Burnham was, of course, unprepared for and devastated by the loss of his partner. The two had liked and respected each other from their earliest days in Peter Wight's office, had endured the hard times of the 1870s in their struggling young firm, and emerged in the 1880s as major figures in the city's architectural community. Much of the January 1891 issue of *Inland Architect*, which still listed Root as a key officer, was devoted to expressions of shock and sorrow over Root's death. Those who signed the resolution of condolence include a who's who of American architecture at the time: Richard Morris Hunt; McKim, Mead and White; George Post; William Le Baron Jenney; Henry Ives Cobb; and for the firm of Adler and Sullivan, Louis H. Sullivan.

The evidence suggests that, had Root lived, the visual character of the Chicago World's Fair—and given the fair's subsequent influence, perhaps much public architecture in following decades—might have taken a somewhat different stylistic turn. Early on *The Inland Architect* noted that Burnham and Root expected the fair to highlight American styles of architecture, which at the time were widely understood to draw from distinctly European sources. Root's preliminary designs for key structures did fit within accepted historical guidelines but also leaned "idly and in a desultory way," as Burnham put it, toward greater variety in style and color, in contrast to the tightly controlled, all-white Beaux-Arts classicism that was to emerge later.[10] Root's canal portal, for instance, was likely intended to be red, not white, in color.

Root had long advocated for an architecture enlivened by a varied palate of colors. Some seven years earlier, citing a theory of the evolution of colors in the plant and animal world in terms that Louis Sullivan would have applauded, Root made a case for a more color-conscious architecture, especially as expressed through materials newly available to architects on a large and affordable scale: "Think for a moment what our streets might become, if to the somber grays of stone or reds of brick were added the full unfading bloom of [stained] glass, marble or tiles." If his friends and colleagues were to embrace such an approach, he predicted that "in a few years there will be everywhere, as in a lovely symphony, the full verdure of woods, the warm blue of summer sky, the eternal joyousness of blooming flowers, crystallized into unfading colors, and greeting us in our daily avocations." There was, he believed, "no limit to what may be done when we have artists educated to a nice sense of blended and complementary colors." As Joanna Merwood-Salisbury points out, Root felt that vivid colors were imbued with Swedenborgian significance, mediating between the world of ordinary life and higher spiritual realms.[11]

Root's sister-in-law Harriet Monroe was among those entirely convinced that, had Root lived, the outward appearance of the fair would have been much different: "a City of Color, a queen arrayed in robes not saintly, as for a bridal, but gorgeous, for a festival," not structures suggesting the "false illusion of weight and permanence" but something "lighter, gayer, more decorative than the solid structures along our streets."[12] Just how strongly Burnham would have been wedded to his partner's supposed vision is unclear. He later acknowledged that under Root's artistic supervision, the fair "would have been modified and stamped with something of his great individuality."[13] We do know that the ideas for a stately, heavily classical theme emerged when the New York architects, headed by the esteemed Richard Morris Hunt, gathered together in Chicago shortly after Root's death and pushed for variants of the Beaux-Arts building styles for which they were trained and in which they specialized. Burnham had said that each architect selected to design the fair would be asked to create "such work as would be most nearly parallel with his best achievements," an approach that almost assured a traditionalist approach to several of the most important structures at the fair.

Burnham's conception of the fair's design did not go unquestioned. The man first named as director of decorations, the English artist William

Pretyman, resigned within a matter of months, by Burnham's account over a dispute concerning the color scheme for the fair. "I was urging every one [*sic*] on," Burnham recalled,

> knowing it was an awful fight against time. We talked about colors, and finally the thought came, "Let us make it all perfectly white." I don't recall who made the suggestion. It might have been one of those things that occurred to all minds at once, as so often happens. At any rate, the decision was mine. At the time, Prettyman [*sic*] was in the East, and I had Beeman's [*sic*] building [probably the Mines and Mining Building] made cream white. When Prettyman came back he was outraged. He said that so long as he was in charge I must not interfere. I told him that I did not see it that way; that I had the decision. He then said he would get out; and he did.[14]

The person who first suggested to paint the buildings a glowing white may have been Pretyman's successor, Massachusetts native and Art Institute instructor Francis Millet. We know Millet was advocating for this choice by December of 1892. However the group of architects and designers ultimately came to the decision on color, Burnham's recollection underscores two seemingly contradictory elements of his managerial approach: his inclination to accept collective decision-making and his willingness to assert his own authority when challenged.

One wonders, along with Harriet Monroe, just how different the fair might have looked had Burnham and Root, the two friends and partners bonded together with years of experience and deep mutual trust, been able to collaborate throughout the process. Would Burnham have stood up for Root's visions as decisively as he shut down Pretyman's? Or would he have yielded to the consensus opinions of the larger group and urged his partner to go along? The architect selected to take over Root's role as consulting architect, Charles Atwood of Boston and New York, had no difficulty accepting the agreed-upon color scheme and working in the standard classical modes, and after Root's untimely death neither did Daniel Burnham.

The story of the struggle to create the magical White City in Chicago's Jackson Park, of the World Fair's international significance and great domestic success, and of Daniel Burnham's professional role in the entire process, has been well told in a treasure trove of books, articles, and films.[15] The most notable personal aspect of Burnham's role centers on his decision to routinely forgo the comfortable domestic life he enjoyed with his family in his Evanston home to rough it night after night with fellow architects, painters, and sculptors living in a primitive but reasonably spacious log cabin in Jackson Park while the construction work was underway. The self-

BURNHAM AND ATWOOD IN THE WORLD'S FAIR DRAUGHTING-ROOM
From a drawing by Thulstrup

Burnham and his army of assistants at work on design projects for the World's Fair. The person at the drafting table next to Burnham is Charles Atwood, the Boston architect called in to replace John Root after Root's untimely death. (Charles Moore, *Daniel H. Burnham: Architect, Planner of Cities* [Boston: Houghton Mifflin, 1921]. Ryerson and Burnham Art and Architecture Archives, Art Institute of Chicago.)

imposed hardship is not entirely surprising, perhaps, in a man who had briefly embraced the rough and tumble lifestyle of a mining adventure in the wild West.

Charles Moore describes a "fluctuating household" of associates who would join Burnham in the rustic retreat on the Wooded Isle for intensive planning and supervisory sessions. Architectural and artistic royalty such as Richard Morris Hunt, George Post, Augustus Saint-Gaudens, and Daniel Chester French were among those who would, on occasion, sleep on the cots spread out in Burnham's shanty, to awaken early the next day and head out to inspect progress on their respective projects. On their return, the planners and designers would seat themselves around a long table to engage in endless discussions about the problems they encountered and the challenges that lay ahead.

The inevitable tensions of their situation were alleviated by "jests and stories and practical jokes" and music on Sunday evenings with a small band selected from Theodore Thomas's symphony orchestra, with Thomas himself conducting. The amusements sometimes verged on the irreverent and bawdy, with Richard Hunt, "no respecter of personages," letting fly with ego-puncturing shafts of wit, artists Robert Reid and Edward Simmons offering up caricatures of participants at once "grotesque" and "satirical," and the cosmopolitan Frank Millet attempting to keep the "fires of friendship brightly burning with his racy stories." Among the less frequent guests to attend this strenuous exercise in male bonding and fair planning was a game, though likely wary, Louis Sullivan.[16]

The result of this monumental and massive effort is well known to history. Much of the ragged, neglected parkland chosen as the site of the Chicago World's Fair was transformed by Frederick Law Olmsted into what still stands today as an elegantly designed Jackson Park, with much of the park, including Olmsted's cherished Wooded Island, remaining a permanent feature of Chicago's park system. The fair took up 633 acres of land on Chicago's South Side, including an 80-acre strip of greenspace known as the Midway Plaisance. Olmsted and his partner Calvert Vaux had envisioned this "pleasure drive" twenty years earlier as part of a South Parks proposal to link Jackson Park to Washington Park. By comparison, California's Disneyland presently covers eighty-five acres, and three of the four major theme parks in Florida's Walt Disney World (the Magic Kingdom, EPCOT, and Disney's Hollywood Studios) cover a total of 547 acres, all of which were built to draw crowds for decades, not for the brief interlude of one evanescent summer. Almost two hundred buildings were constructed for Burnham's Fair, all designed to be dismantled or destroyed at the end of the summer. They were made using a combination of interior steel sup-

This playful Edward Emerson Simmons caricature of Burnham aide Ernest Graham was one of dozens of similarly humorous depictions of friends and associates created by Simmons, Robert Reid, and Charles Turner during the planning and construction of the 1893 Columbian Exposition. (Daniel H. Burnham Collection, Ryerson and Burnham Art and Architecture Archives, Art Institute of Chicago. Digital file # 194301_110718-019.)

ports, wood, and exteriors composed of a material called "staff," a mixture of plaster, cement, and hemp fiber. Over 40,000 skilled workers were employed to construct the fair, many of whom caused headaches to Burnham and the other supervisors by engaging in disputes over union participation, wages, and the extreme working conditions on site. By one account more than two dozen strikes occurred both before and during the fair.[17]

Labor issues comprised only one subset of the daily challenges Burnham, his Board of Directors, and other officials faced. Trying to balance the interests and demands of the National Commission in Washington, DC, with those of the Chicago-based corporation was a source of persistent tensions

The architects of the Chicago World's Fair shown here represent a veritable who's who of American architects of the late nineteenth century. At far left is William Le Baron Jenney, whose Home Insurance Building helped pave the way for all tall building innovations. New York architect Charles McKim, Burnham's good friend and close associate, is second from right, holding the pointer. Louis Sullivan is the dark-haired, dark-bearded figure near the center sitting at the table examining documents. The standing figure bending and looking down toward Sullivan is the fair's Director of Works, Daniel Burnham. (Daniel H. Burnham Collection, Ryerson and Burnham Art and Architecture Archives, Art Institute of Chicago. Digital file # 194301_081014-01.)

and delays. And there was the matter of deciding who would be slated for inclusion in the exhibits and attractions and who would be excluded. Buffalo Bill's Wild West Show, for example, was not allowed a place within the grounds of the fair, though William Cody still managed to rent a spot between 61st and 63rd Streets to set up his popular entertainments.

Several prominent African American leaders—among them Ida B. Wells and Frederick Douglass—published a pamphlet entitled *The Reason Why the Colored American Is Not in the World's Columbian Exposition.* Douglass was now in his late seventies, a widely revered elder statesman in the cause of racial justice, with experience from having served in the Republican administration of Benjamin Harrison as consul-general to the Republic of Haiti. The piece was a scathing indictment of the hiring practices, lack of Black representation in administrative and supervisory positions, and demeaning representations of colored persons at the fair. The creation of a special Colored American Day on August 25, 1893, was seen by some (including Wells) as an insufficient effort to repair the damage, though Douglass and other Black leaders decided to participate. They used the occasion to celebrate Black achievements and to issue a public call for more aggressive action toward equal rights for all citizens. Several exhibits on the Midway in particular, though well-intended by some of the planners to introduce visitors to the lifeways of exotic cultures from around the world, were seen by many, then and now, as exploitative. They provided titillating glimpses into the built environments of "primitive" peoples in obvious contrast to the more advanced civilized structures represented in the elegant (and Europeanized) Court of Honor.[18] In an 1895 speech to the Chicago Literary Club, Burnham spoke of world's fairs as important ways to reach "the individual barbarian or savage," who can then go back and offer uplift and inspiration to his tribe.[19]

Women did receive an honored place in the design of the fair, but their representation was primarily concentrated in a single structure, the Woman's Building located just off the lagoon surrounding the Wooded Island, not far from the Court of Honor. The building had been designed by a recent female MIT architectural graduate, Sophia G. Hayden, and the entire enterprise was overseen by a Board of Lady Managers headed by Bertha Palmer, Chicago socialite and wife of hotel mogul Potter Palmer. The purpose of the exhibits was to showcase examples of traditional women's work in domestic life as well as their contributions in the arts, sciences, literature, industry, and politics. Bertha Palmer somewhat pointedly insisted that it was time for women to step down from the pedestal and actively participate in practical affairs and archly noted, at the dedication ceremonies for the fair, that "even more important than the discovery of Columbus is the fact that the general government has just discovered women."[20] At the same time, in keeping with the fair's emphasis on the perceived ever-upward movement toward higher forms of civilization, women from native cultures were presented in less-than-respectful terms. Visitors were greeted with expansive murals depicting "Primitive Woman" by Mary Fairchild MacMonnies and "Modern Woman" by Mary Cassatt and exhibits featuring the handicrafts of Black, Polynesian, and Native American women under the demeaning heading of "Woman's Work in Savagery."

Despite the logistical challenges, controversies, labor disputes, and misguided attempts to construct a satisfactory message on civilization and

The massive expanses and artfully curated design of the 1893 Columbian Exposition are evident in this bird's-eye view. The Manufactures and Liberal Arts Building, designed by New York's George B. Post, dominates the center of the spread. Its south end (left side of the building as shown here) fronts the magisterial Court of Honor, whose T-shaped basin contains Daniel Chester French's Statue of the Republic and Frederick MacMonnies's Columbian Fountain. Louis Sullivan's Transportation Building, with the famous "Golden Door," is the elongated, red-roofed building near the top and left of center (bisected by the crease). The other red-roofed building, just to the upper right of center and facing the Wooded Island, is Sophia Hayden's Woman's Building. (World's Columbian Exposition Collection, Ryerson and Burnham Art and Architecture Archives, Art Institute of Chicago. Digital file # 000012_WCE_birdseye_color_1.)

"savagery," what had seemed impossible to many observers at the beginning of the process did, in fact, come to pass. The Chicago World's Fair opened on time and with most exhibits and attractions in place. As the immense project neared completion, on March 25, 1893, several hundred of Burnham's associates and admirers gathered in Madison Square Concert Hall in New York to congratulate Chicago's now preeminent architect on his spectacular achievement. In his remarks Burnham offered his appreciative summation

COLUMBIAN EXPOSITION, CHICAGO, 1893.

of how the project came to fruition and thanked the many contributors "who wrought with me" through those consequential months.[21] Among those he thanked by name was Louis Sullivan, whom he mentioned without reference to Louis's partner Dankmar Adler, though Adler, not Sullivan, wrote one of the effusive congratulatory letters read aloud at the event. Burnham's omission should hardly be viewed as an intentional slight. Rather it suggests that, in the matter of design and artistry (always of deep concern to Burnham), he most associated Sullivan with the success of Adler and Sullivan's contribution to the fair, the remarkable Transportation Building.

Some three years earlier, on December 9, 1889, Adler and Sullivan's Auditorium Building had opened to the public, with President Benjamin Harrison performing the official dedication and Italian-born international opera star Adelina Patti singing "Home, Sweet Home" to an enthralled audience. The program ended with a stirring rendition of Handel's *Messiah.* To say the evening was a thunderous success would be an understatement. Newspapers devoted entire front pages to the coverage. Chicago's *Daily Inter Ocean* made no effort to restrain its enthusiasm for "a gathering and a building the like of which are rarely seen."[22] Adler's incomparable acoustics and Sullivan's brilliant bands of electric lights that spanned the ceiling drew rapturous commentary. The *Chicago Tribune* noted, "instead of rafters, the hall was roofed with ivory and gold and starred with electricity," you "could hear every word or note uttered on stage," the whole effect being at once "sumptuous and chaste."[23]

When Mayor DeWitt Cregier rose to speak at the Auditorium gala, he could not help but link Adler and Sullivan's great building to the proposed fair. The Auditorium, he said, now stands alone in the great city and needs a mate. "The bride is a little timid yet," said the mayor, but hoped a wedding would take place in the years ahead, when a great fair will rise on the shores of Lake Michigan to serve as worthy companion to Adler and Sullivan's masterpiece.[24] But the deal was not yet done. Just one month later Cregier would appear before Congress to plead on behalf of Chicago's bid for the fair.

Louis Sullivan was there on the Auditorium's opening night, but records suggest that the ceremonies made little mention of either Adler or Sullivan. One of the contractors on the project complained anonymously of the oversight to the *Tribune.* "Workmen employed upon the building know that Mr. Sullivan was the guiding spirit, everywhere and all over, attending to the smallest details, giving up a great deal more time than his health warranted, until, in fact, his nervous force gave way, and he was some weeks in recovering."[25]

Sullivan, now thirty-three years old and entering his architectural maturity, readily acknowledged the toll the Auditorium had taken upon him physically and emotionally. Shortly after overseeing the finishing touches the building required, in the early months of 1890, he traveled to California to rest and recover. From there he went on to New Orleans, where he happened to meet friends he had known in Chicago, James and Helen Charnley. Neither California nor New Orleans had done much to raise his spirits, as he found California's climate irritating and New Orleans "filthy." The Charnleys induced him to spend some time with them on a vacation getaway to Ocean Springs, Mississippi, a small town on the eastern shore of Biloxi Bay.

The place enchanted him from the start. Years earlier his first sight of Chicago had awakened in him an almost overwhelming feeling of excitement and a jolt of creative energy, an eagerness to help reconstruct a broken city. His high ambition had recently culminated in two things: the triumphant success of the Auditorium and a state of nervous exhaustion. Ocean Springs offered relief and respite. It was a world away from Chicago: in Sullivan's words, it offered "no 'enterprise,' no 'progress,' no booming for a 'Greater Ocean Springs,' no factories, no anxious faces, no glare of the dollar hunter," but instead, "peace, peace, and the joy of comrades, the lovely nights of sea breeze, black pool of the sky oversprinkled with stars brilliant and uncountable."[26]

The Charnleys were equally enchanted and immediately bought a parcel of beachfront land from a Michigan millionaire. Sullivan then purchased property adjacent to the Charnleys and a few days later acquired five additional acres from them on the understanding that he would design a house for them. As Sullivan later recalled, "He knew what he could do. He planned for two shacks or bungalows, 300 feet apart, with stables far back; also a system of development requiring years for fulfillment."[27]

The Ocean Springs getaway became a labor of love for Sullivan, who did in fact make it into a long-term development project, a place he returned to frequently for rest and regeneration over the next twenty years. At completion the complex contained rose gardens, walking pathways, pools, fountains, servants' quarters, an abundance of towering trees, curved roadways, chicken yards, arbors, flower beds, vegetable gardens, and other amenities suited to a curated natural setting. The living quarters were thoughtfully constructed in something resembling the horizontal Prairie Style later made famous by Frank Lloyd Wright. Then working in the Adler and Sullivan office, Wright later claimed to have been responsible for much of the design work on the two cottages.[28] One of the most frequently published pictures of Louis Sullivan in his maturity shows the architect adopting a relaxed confident stance as he surveys his much-loved semi-tropical southern retreat. It was here, Sullivan insisted, "that he did his finest, purest thinking. 'Twas here that he saw the flow of life, that all life became a flowing for him, and so the thoughts the works of man."[29]

Returning to Chicago after his initial visit to Ocean Springs, Sullivan plunged back into the increasingly heavy demands of Adler and Sullivan's design work. Several major projects were either underway or in the planning stages in the first years of the 1890s. Some of these clearly reflected the firm's established expertise in theater construction and renovation, but other, smaller projects occupied them as well, including the second of Sullivan's tombs designed for Chicago's Graceland Cemetery, the imposing but delicately ornamented Carrie Eliza Getty tomb.

In retrospect Sullivan's artistic sensibility was then most fully engaged in a high-rise office building in St. Louis, the Wainwright. Many have seen the Wainwright Building as a landmark in the history of skyscraper design. The building is tall for its time, standing ten stories above the street, and Sullivan's design emphasizes verticality in the unbroken piers that project from above the base to just below the decorative frieze at the top. Several

Louis Sullivan, in his early forties, at his cottage in Ocean Springs, Mississippi. (Richard Nickel Archive, Ryerson and Burnham Art and Architecture Archives, Art Institute of Chicago. Digital file # 193101. C33914.)

other structures built prior to this also had strong claims to the skyscraper designation and were just as tall or taller. Burnham and Root's Monadnock Building was also rising at about the same time, with vertical bands of oriel windows rising straight to the top with no disruptive horizontal courses. Even Adler and Sullivan's own Troescher Building from 1884 had smooth pilaster-like verticals projecting out from the midsection of the building for several stories. For Sullivan, though, the Wainwright marked

The Wainwright Building, St. Louis, 1890. Adler and Sullivan, architects. (Richard Nickel Archive, Ryerson and Burnham Art and Architecture Archives, Art Institute of Chicago. Digital file # 201006_120301-002.)

a significant departure: he viewed it as a game-changing skyscraper with soaring verticals and an exterior that was the first to authentically express its structural metal frame.[30] In fact, he said, it was the first of such buildings to really interest him.[31]

He followed the Wainwright with several tall buildings that similarly sought to combine strong vertical patterns with his signature complex nature-based ornamentation, including the thirteen-story Chicago Stock Exchange Building at LaSalle and Washington, the eye-popping Schiller (later Garrick) Theater, and the highly ornamented Guaranty Building in Buffalo, New York. Adler and Sullivan's designs for the unbuilt thirty-six-story Odd Fellows Temple imagined a building that would have reached heights previously unheard-of and would have featured a series of dramatic setbacks to a degree previously unseen in skyscraper design.

But the Sullivan creation that received the most widespread attention during this first half of the decade was not a skyscraper. It was the Transportation Building he designed for Burnham's Columbian Exposition. After Adler and Sullivan initially objected to the projects Burnham had suggested to them, Sullivan eventually agreed to design an immense, cavernous building (960 feet long, 260 feet wide) housing outsized exhibits of historical modes of, and recent advances in, transportation. In a letter to Burnham written after the fair had closed, Sullivan recalled the ideas that had guided his vision for the structure. He told Burnham the building was meant to represent not historical styles as commonly understood but an independent way of thinking about architecture. He did not directly question the gentlemen's agreement among the Court of Honor architects to adhere to a uniform classical motif with whitewashed buildings and a consistent cornice height, but some of the items he listed as intentional attributes clearly departed from the accepted formulas for the Court of Honor and some of the other major buildings at the World's Fair.

For one thing, Sullivan's Transportation Building was awash in color, perhaps exceeding anything even John Root would have envisioned. The structure, he said, was meant to display "the use of colored decorations to show the possibility of sequence, combination, and repetition when a great many colors are used—hence the true nature of polychrome." It would show how "large simple masses" could nonetheless "carry elaborately and minutely worked out ornamentation" and that through a process of "systematic subdivision" the total effect would be that of a "quieter and more dignified" whole.[32] The centerpiece of the building and the central focus of public attention was the magnificent, expansive, and multilayered arched golden doorway, which in daylight must have glittered as brightly and memorably as the electrically illuminated Court of Honor did at night. A typical contemporary account stressed the uniqueness of Sullivan's design in an otherwise tightly controlled architectural setting. It was, said this observer, "a complete departure in style and hue from the great mass of structures which gave the White City its name, and its greatest entrance was its most novel and beautiful part. . . . Not merely because of its richness and originality but because of the lesson it taught by comparison with less florid but grander styles the Golden Doorway was certainly among the most notable architectural features shown."[33]

The Transportation Building particularly attracted the attention of a French delegation to the fair. The result was official recognition from the French government and the opening in 1895 of a specially designated "Louis H. Sullivan Section" of the Musée des Arts Décoratifs in Paris, a museum in the northwestern wing of the Louvre. The section displayed models of his Transportation Building decoration as well as replicas of the bronze doors from the Getty tomb and another remarkable tomb Sullivan had designed in honor of Charlotte Dickson Wainwright, the deceased wife of his St. Louis client Ellis Wainwright.[34]

Louis Sullivan's "Golden Door" was a memorable feature of the Transportation Building, World's Columbian Exposition, 1893. (Historic Architecture and Landscape Image Collection, Ryerson and Burnham Art and Architecture Archives, Art Institute of Chicago. Digital file # L049953.)

The Transportation Building was positioned just northwest of the Court of Honor near the Wooded Island and the Woman's Building and so did not directly confront the uniformity of design that characterized the cluster of buildings surrounding the Grand Basin. Daniel Burnham apparently did not voice serious objections to Sullivan's original creation, and Sullivan's relationship with Burnham seems to have remained respectful and friendly on both sides for the duration of the fair. In fact it was Burnham, not Sullivan or Louis's mentor Adler, who originally thought to position the soon-to-be-famous portal as a central focal point for the structure. In a letter to Sullivan written in February 1891, Burnham's approach strikingly resembled the firm but gentle direction he had practiced with his late partner John Root, and he diplomatically advised the following: "My dear Louis . . . Looking over the plat this morning with another gentleman, it was suggested that the best possible method . . . will be for you to have one grand entrance toward the east. . . . Am sure that the effect of your building will be much finer than the old method of two entrances on this side."[35] Sullivan seems to have easily accepted the suggestion, with a result memorable to many fairgoers and critics. Sullivan ended his post-fair letter to Burnham by expressing admiration for his leadership. "[W]ithout your great fostering care," Sullivan told him, "the Exposition Buildings as they stood through the summer of 1893, could not have been a realization."[36]

The seemingly inevitable upward trajectory of Sullivan's career at this time was soon to be short-circuited by a combination of deteriorating economic conditions and Sullivan's own imperious, quicksilver temperament. In 1893, the year of Sullivan's great success with the Transportation Building, he angrily confronted his stellar young protégé Frank Lloyd Wright for designing houses on a freelance basis outside of regular office hours. Citing a violation of Wright's contract with the firm, Sullivan refused to issue the deed for the Oak Park house he had helped Wright finance several years earlier. Brendan Gill suggests that "it is fairly certain that Sullivan and Wright were equally eager to set themselves free, each from the other," in Sullivan's case out of jealousy for his apprentice's rising reputation, on Wright's part to bring that reputation out from under the long shadow cast by Sullivan.[37] Whatever private motivations or simmering animosities may have figured in the split, Wright did abruptly leave the firm, thus depriving the "master" of sharing some of the glory that would eventually accrue to his most illustrious pupil.

Even more devastating to Sullivan, just two years later he was to lose the partnership with the "big chief," Dankmar Adler. As the World's Fair was winding down, another massive banking panic hit the United States, and plum architectural assignments started to dry up. Twenty years earlier the newly formed team of Burnham and Root struggled to survive through a similar economic crash, and a young Louis Sullivan heard despairing shouts in the streets of Philadelphia, signaling the beginning of the end of his association with Frank Furness. No longer the powerless apprentice, Sullivan was now in a position to see his major projects through to completion, as he did with the Chicago Stock Exchange Building in 1894 and Buffalo's Guaranty Building in 1895. But financial conditions remained poor through the middle years of the decade. The situation grew so serious that in 1895 Dankmar Adler, a man with a family of five to support, felt compelled to accept a salaried position with his friend Richard Crane's elevator company, leaving Sullivan in sole charge of the architectural firm. The break must have been especially shocking given the relatively close relationship Sullivan had established with Adler's family. Robert Twombly reports on an interview conducted in 1961 with Adler's daughter Sarah, in which she recalled Sullivan's numerous visits to the Adler family home, complete with elaborate gift-giving on Sullivan's part and active participation in family activities.[38]

When Adler concluded that he had made a mistake and determined to take up architecture again at the end of 1895, Sullivan, now fully in charge of the office, showed no interest in inviting his old partner back into the fold. Adler, for his part nursing a grudge after Sullivan had downplayed Adler's role in the construction of the Guaranty Building in Buffalo, opened his own office in the Auditorium Building but apart from the tower where Louis Sullivan still sought to keep a struggling practice alive in the face of ever-elusive commissions.

What was the trajectory of Daniel Burnham's life after the Chicago World's Fair? He had already earned a reputation, in Chicago and elsewhere, as an architect and skilled manager of a large architectural firm. But his contributions to the fair proved he could manage and design not just individual buildings but also large urban spaces—a crucial step toward his second identity as an expert in city planning. The accolades that accrued to him in 1894—including honorary degrees from Harvard and Yale, both of which had denied him undergraduate admission, and from nearby Northwestern University—directly resulted from his success with the Columbian Exposition. So did his election to the presidency of the American Institute of Architects, which occurred in the same year and which led to lengthy involvement in a battle with the federal government to reform the architectural practices of the US Treasury Department's Office of the Supervising Architect.[39] But as flattering as these honors were, Burnham and his chief designer, John Root's replacement Charles Atwood, quickly turned their attention to a new city-wide civic improvement project: the preservation and expansion of Chicago's park system.

Burnham had long been a believer in the moral and physical benefits of exposure to the world of nature. Some of this had been evident in the days of his western travels, as when he remarked on the "brilliant and fairly sparkling air" just west of Topeka ("It is life to be here") or, in the same trip near Mexico, when he compared breathing in the atmosphere of the Southwest to imbibing drafts of champagne, "a pure unadulterated gift to man."[40] The depth of Burnham's faith in the almost mystical power of nature to heal and inspire could be compared to that of Louis Sullivan.[41] Olmsted's revitalized Jackson Park, he believed, should remain largely intact after the fair to offer the benefits of peaceful repose and beauty to the residents of Chicago's South Side, and more open space could be created in the downtown area extending past the Illinois Central train lines and into Lake Michigan.

Burnham and Atwood outlined their proposals in the City Council chambers on June 3, 1895, before a group of power brokers and businessmen, most of whom had worked with Burnham on the fair. The new lakefront would essentially be an attempt to recreate many elements of the fair on public land downtown. It would contain expanses of greenspace, to be sure, but also an elaborate complex of buildings, statuary, walkways, and fountains. In the words of the *Chicago Chronicle*, these "public spirited citizens" were hoping "to build another white city, not of staff, but of marble and bronze, not for a summer's festival, but for all the children of all the time to come."[42] The novelist Henry Blake Fuller, in a book published that same year, presented a character envisioning how the model of Burnham's White City could be used to "hover as an enlightenment" over the present-day "Black City" that "sprawled and coiled about . . . like a hideous monster."[43] It was a vision that Burnham clearly shared.

In Burnham's view, encounters with such a carefully designed natural and built environment would not just offer the people passing moments of refreshment and spiritual uplift. They would also have the potential to create a stronger communal bond of responsible citizenship. In an 1887 speech delivered to the Merchants Club, Burnham declared, "When a citizen is made to feel the beauty of nature, when he is lifted up by her to any degree above the usual life of his thoughts and feelings, the state of which he is a part is benefitted thereby." These beautiful spaces and sensations open to all would help the effort toward "cementing together the heterogeneous elements of our population, and towards assimilating the million and a half of people who are here now, but who were not here some fifteen years ago."[44] The unspoken hope suggested here is that these "heterogeneous" populations so assimilated would include immigrants, those persons of color who had long been denied entry into the middle or upper classes, factory workers struggling to gain an economic foothold—all those members of the urban underclass who had sometimes shown themselves to be receptive to the socially disruptive messages of agitators, anarchists, and labor organizers.

Burnham was a man of his time and social stratum, and he saw no contradiction in striving to accomplish this high-minded democratizing beautification while also inviting the wealthy Chicago business class to participate. Without deep-pocketed movers and shakers, Burnham noted, his plan could not be realized. With their contributions beauty can be created all along the lakefront, and beauty, he noted, "has always paid better than any other commodity and always will." Why do people of means, asked Burnham, seek their pleasures elsewhere—in Paris, or the Riviera, or Cairo, or Vienna? It is because "life at home is not so pleasant as in these fashionable centres."[45] If Chicago could be made as beautiful as Baron Haussmann made Paris or as New York architects, millionaires, landscapers, and others made key parts of their city, pleasure-seekers from around the world would come to Chicago and bring in much-needed wealth. And if well-to-do Chicagoans could be induced to build elegant residences on a strip of land two hundred to three hundred feet wide between the South Shore boulevard and the lagoon, their presence would help pay for this otherwise unaffordable expansion and would create more beautiful and inspiring effects than any single designer could produce.

Perhaps thinking of his own lakeside estate in Evanston, Burnham pictured—in addition to the park's intersecting walkways, decorative sculptures and vases, clinging vines, and bicycle and equestrian courses—rows of palatial mansions, with wide terraces and magnificent gardens and stairways extending down to the lakeshore, offering pleasing vistas to all parkland visitors. "The very beauty that attracts him who has money," he would say more than a decade later in the *Plan of Chicago*, "makes pleasant the life of those among whom he lives."[46]

As Burnham began involving himself in civic-minded projects such as these, his firm, now called D. H. Burnham and Company, continued its string of successes with individual buildings, among them the historically significant and still-standing Reliance Building in downtown Chicago. The Reliance project was begun under the design direction of John Root and then completed by Burnham's new partner Charles Atwood. It was a unique construction for several reasons. First, the proposed site on the corner of Washington and State was already occupied by a four-story building with tenants whose leases would not lapse until well after the time when the client, William Hale, desired to construct his new fourteen-story commercial structure. Root's solution? Put the second, third, and fourth floors effectively on stilts with exterior access for tenants while construction commenced on the basement and ground floor. After Root's death and after all leases had expired, Atwood oversaw the rest of the construction, which involved extra-large plate-glass windows to let in abundant daylight and sparkling, newly developed white glazed terra-cotta cladding on the exterior that the builders thought would be self-cleaning as recurrent rain water washed away the dirt. The self-washing feature was not to function as envisioned. By the 1990s the Reliance had accumulated decades of caked-on detritus on deteriorating terra-cotta that gave it a dingy appearance and required a full-scale effort at rehabilitation, including a thorough renovation of the exterior.

Architectural historians have sometimes cited the Reliance as a kind of proto-modernist structure for its slim vertical profile, its relatively light terra-cotta façade draped over a steel frame, and its use of large expanses of glass. The *Chicago Tribune* anticipated this take at the time by noting its "cleanly and attractive appearance," which made it seem "more modern than any of the large office buildings of the city, an effort in this direction having activated both the owner and architect."[47] Siegfried Giedion's widely influential *Space, Time and Architecture* went so far as to suggest that structures such as the Reliance may have inspired Mies Van Der Rohe's prescient 1921 design for a soaring glass office tower, the unrealized Friedrichstrasse Skyscraper.[48] Such characterizations have been vigorously debated and disputed. Terra-cotta cladding, for example, was hardly new to Chicago architecture and on the Reliance was complemented with bright-white ornamental detailing that would not have seemed out of place in Charles Atwood's classical designs for the World's Fair. As Joanna Merwood put it, the outer surface of the Reliance Building "exists within a discourse of continually changing reception and criticism, and the mutable interpretations to which it is subject have the ability to alter our perception of its material presence."[49] What can't be disputed is that the Reliance of the mid-1890s, like a handful of earlier buildings such as the Rookery and the Monadnock, has secured a lasting and honored place in the Burnham company's architectural legacy in Chicago.

A major disruption unsettled the firm in December 1895 when Burnham's creative designer Charles Atwood resigned, likely under pressure from Burnham. Atwood had scored numerous successes as Root's replacement for the World's Fair and as Burnham's right-hand man in the heady years that followed. But he had also proven to be a more erratic partner than Root, with occasional mysterious absences and faltering physical stamina that made it increasingly difficult for him to adjust to the pace of the work at

Burnham and Company.[50] Burnham later confided to Charles Moore that Atwood had also "got himself into difficulty" through drug use, adding, "(I did not know it [at the time], none of us did)."[51]

Burnham publicly attested to Atwood's personal charm and accomplishments. Atwood cut an "elegant figure," said Burnham, and "his presence was grateful to one's love of grace and dignity." His designs, Burnham declared, were those of a true architectural master, and as a draftsman he had no equals. But amid Burnham's kind remarks in an open forum could be found notes of disappointment and distrust. For the last couple of years, he said, Atwood's deteriorating health had prevented him from adhering to a steady work regimen. Like many great artists, Atwood "was a mere child in the practical things of life."[52] Burnham was perhaps unsurprised when he received on December 19—only nine days after his number-one lieutenant departed the firm—a telegraph message saying that Charles Atwood, at the age of forty-six, was dead.

The work of the firm went on, however. Burnham's trusted associates, Ernest Graham and engineer Edward Shankland among others, continued to provide a solid foundation of competence and expertise within the company. Shortly after Atwood's death, Graham accompanied Burnham to review progress on a Buffalo, New York, project, and in the coming years Graham would be sent to represent Burnham on a number of other out-of-town site visits.

All the business travel did nothing to dampen Burnham's interest in travel for pleasure. Just one month after Atwood's death, Burnham, wife Margaret, and Margaret's parents embarked on a voyage to the Mediterranean, marking Burnham's first trip to Europe. European architectural styles and practices had long been an inspirational presence in Burnham's life. He and John Root would while away the idle hours in their struggling new practice testing each other on their knowledge of Gothic terms and time periods, and those historic influences were obvious in the famously Greco-Roman-themed World's Fair.

Burnham's detailed 1896 diary of the trip shows an eager student of European cities and structures and an enraptured, enthusiastic first-time visitor to the Old World. Having passed through the Strait of Gibraltar and feasted his eyes on the coast of North Africa, Burnham imagined himself an "Arian [*sic*] son returning to the gateway of the east through which your fathers came," and his excitement was palpable: "Oh! day! never to be forgotten, you bring glory to the eyes who never saw it except in dreams, and dreams hereafter shall be wider & richer because of you."[53] Throughout the trip Burnham rhapsodized with undiminished enthusiasm. On Rome: "To be in it, to wake up in it, what a delight." On Greece: "[O]nce and forever stamped in my soul. It is the blue flower; the rest of life *must* be the dream and this land of Greece the reality for me in which I am really to live."

Burnham viewed many of these new scenes and experiences as an interested outsider observing a passing show that struck him as alternately picturesque, inspiring, beautiful, and on occasion repellent. Unlike most wide-eyed tourists, however, Burnham recognized the aesthetic qualities of the scenes before him. He was especially receptive to the vivid range of colors he perceived in the ever-shifting panorama of people and places. Almost everywhere he went, he commented on the variety of colors encountered with the precision and sensitivity of a practicing artist. Among Portugal's Madeira islands he looked back at the mountains and saw "superb seal-browns and rich greens, all laid over an undercover of red ochre, mingled with the deep blue sea and the sky." Impressed by the scene he noted, "If Europe can beat this, it will be too much for me." In Funchal he was struck by the "rich colored headgear" of the women. In Algiers he remarked on the narrow streets and colored courts, one of them "whitewashed a strong blue, and from the doorways in it, girls looked down at us, and they were dressed in very brilliant but very tender colors. The *tout ensemble* was entrancing."

With amateur but artistic flourish Burnham recorded his colorful sights and impressions in vivid watercolors and impromptu drawings on the pages of his diary. These were the days, after all, before personal photography was an easy, or even realistic, option for most travelers and rendering colors through photographs was out of the question. Burnham described his daily schedule aboard ship as follows (emphasis his): "The mornings belong to *art*, the evenings to whist." His paintings, even those he inserted on the pages of the diary, are carefully crafted, with close attention paid not only to color but also to depth, perspective, facial expression, and the flowing drapery of native dress. For instance the colored courts near the fish market in Algiers show receding streets complete with deepening shadows, figures in those shadows reduced in size to establish proper spatial relationships with each other and with the dominant figure in the foreground, and gradations of blue suggesting shadows against the white city walls. Burnham also included pencil sketches of various individuals he encountered, again with considerable amateur skill. His depiction of an Egyptian runner or soldier in motion presented careful delineations of the man's erect carriage and flowing garb, in contrast to the childlike sketches of camels and what appear to be robed women hastily inscribed above on the same page.

Burnham understood these pictures were meant for family eyes only and occasionally commented in self-deprecating terms on the quality of his artwork. On completing a large watercolor of the Greek island of Rhodes, Burnham noted, "poor as usual." On Madeira Island, he offered an excuse

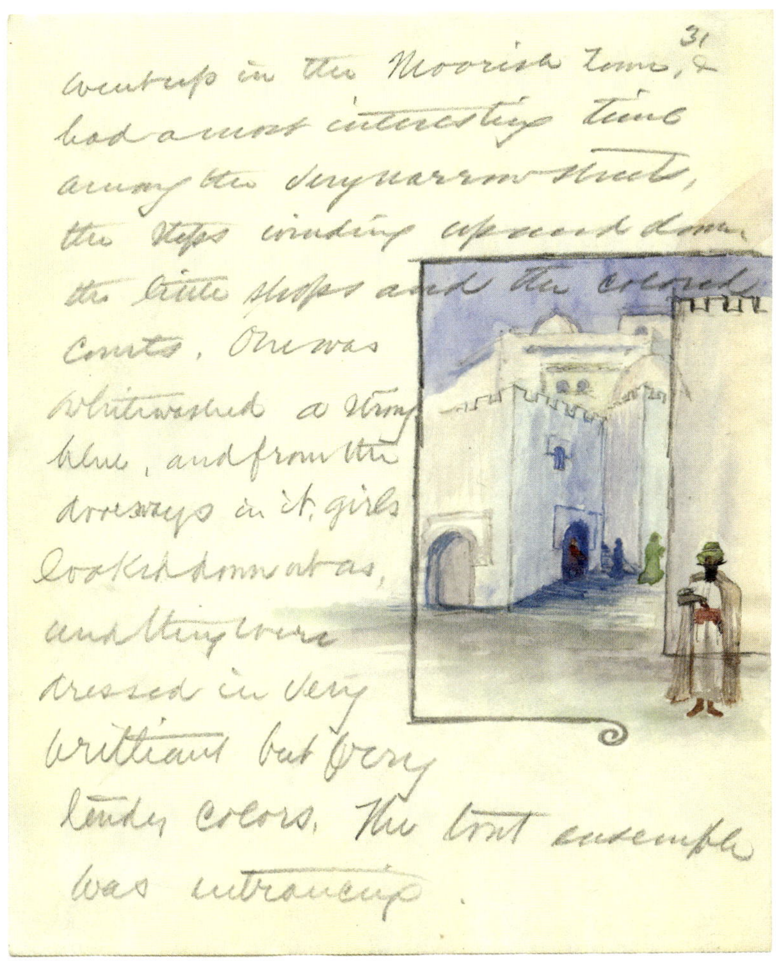

31

went up in the Moorish town, & had a most interesting time among the very narrow streets, the steps winding up and down, the little shops and the colored courts. One was whitewashed a strong blue, and from the doorways in it, girls looked down at us, and they were dressed in very brilliant but very loudy colors. The tout ensemble was entrancing.

Burnham's propensity for enhancing diary entries with sometimes rough, sometimes carefully rendered sketches and watercolors is shown in his detailed representation of a street scene in Algiers, 1896. (Daniel H. Burnham Collection, Ryerson and Burnham Art and Architecture Archives, Art Institute of Chicago. Digital file # 194301_240906-005.)

of sorts for falling short artistically: "There I made the attached bad water color. If people would only keep away when one is sketching he might do better. I am going to tell them so hereafter." Burnham was seriously devoted to the art and craft of drawing. In a speech to Armour Institute students delivered in 1897, he insisted that architects needed to sketch every day and master the techniques of perspective. "One should cultivate the power of dreaming vividly," he said to them, "and the power of making others see what he dreams."[54]

At times the present-day scenes he was so eager to represent seemed to melt away, and Burnham imagined, in standard tourist fashion, the great names from the classical past inhabiting these same spaces. At other times his encounters put him in mind of familiar places burned into his memory from back home. The shoreline of Alexandria recalled the sandy Lake Michigan beachfront of his beloved Evanston home. Athens did not seem as strange and exotic as many of the other, more dreamlike settings Burnham encountered. "It has all seemed very familiar," he said, "the great amphitheater in which Athens lies, the Acropolis, the view from it, the shapes of the hills, and the colorings of everything. I imagine this is due to my old residence in the mountains of Nevada, . . . at times I have felt sure that I was here before." So at least in this instance, some twenty-six years after his brief mining adventure in the American West, it was not the classical styles of ancient Greece that he had studied for so many years and that were so prominently on display in the great Chicago World's Fair that came instantly to mind but rather visions of the colorful mountainscapes of Nevada.

Charles Moore's 1921 biography of Burnham devotes an entire chapter to this 1896 excursion and does so by seeming to reproduce the diary in toto. In fact Moore's printed version stitches together selected excerpts from the handwritten original and contains numerous unacknowledged emendations, edits, and deletions. Some of Burnham's observations on the native populations he encountered are among the missing pieces. Arriving in Funchal, Burnham and his companions were amused by "little fellows" in a rowboat who would approach the ship, gesticulate wildly for the travelers to throw coins into the water, then dive in to catch the sinking coins, and toss them into their boat. He was comfortable expressing opinions and negative prejudices that would have been typical of many of his countrymen at the time, particularly those white men of his social class who inhabited comparable positions of power and privilege.

The people of Beirut, Lebanon, struck Burnham as dull, apathetic, and uninteresting, which he partly attributed to the oppressive effects of their Turkish overlords. "They don't seem to have any energy or any hope, but just let the fleas bite them, and they don't even seem to resent the operation enough to scratch." A group of Coptic boatmen in Alexandria, he said, approached the ship "chattering like monkies [*sic*]" and fighting with one another. His complaint about another group of boatmen—again in Beirut—who tried to extort additional money for rowing him ashore was perhaps more troubling. Burnham said he "showed fight" and refused to pay, proposing that "They need masters, white men, all of them." Moore did not include this last unflattering notation, like others cited above, in his rendering of the architect.

Yet Burnham could also write admiringly of the openness and energy of the native peoples he encountered. In Egypt, while Margaret and a companion went off to talk to the "royal ladies" in the palaces of three princes, Burnham said he "cooled [his] heels in the reception-rooms, drank coffee, smoked cigarettes, & talked with the attendants." He could marvel at the "winding roads" leading from the great pyramids to Cairo among "the palaces and palms and swarms of people and camels carrying loads" and enjoy watching the "picturesque" dragomans standing in groups before the hotel. The dress and demeanor of the hotel guests together with the street scenes of lively running criers all formed "a whole[,] the animation and joyousness of which was delightful."

The pleasure he took in observing native peoples was complemented by occasional encounters with familiar faces and new acquaintances from back home. In Rome he was delighted to find his good friend and fellow architect Charles McKim and carried on a long conversation till one o'clock in the morning with University of Chicago classicist William Gardner Hale. In Athens he met with Rufus Richardson, the head of the American School of Classical Studies. In Egypt he spent time with McKim again along with timber magnate and former Chicago client Edward Ayer and his wife, the president of the Pennsylvania Railroad Alexander Cassatt, and Cassatt's sister, the painter Mary Cassatt, a contributor to the Woman's Building at the World's Fair.

Yet most of his recorded observations focused not on fellow American travelers or the abundant humanity that filled the streets and houses and ship cabins of this lively Mediterranean world but rather on the physical environments he saw all around him: the natural settings and the remarkable human-made structures of Old Europe. He wrote at length on the structural elements of architectural practice in passages about the pyramids. He complimented the designer (and the "King who let him do it") for choosing a high shelf of sand in the desert for the monumental structures' base, even if it meant hauling stone fifteen miles from the quarry site. It also meant the great pyramids would not "be in competition" aesthetically with nearby mountains. The result has "enabled men forever to feel the greatness of their conception and execution. Would that moderns could follow their example!"

As Thomas Hines has written, "The trip . . . opened new worlds to Burnham and made real for him what had formerly only existed in a world of dreams and picture books."[55] In the Columbian Exposition Burnham had

Daniel Burnham memorialized his encounter with the pyramids of Giza, Egypt, in this stand-alone 1896 watercolor. Burnham praised the ancient Egyptians for placing these iconic monuments in settings that would enable viewers to "forever to feel the greatness of their conception and execution." (Daniel H. Burnham Collection, Ryerson and Burnham Art and Architecture Archives, Art Institute of Chicago. Digital file # 194301.081208-03.)

helped construct a grand plan for grafting Old World monumental architecture onto a highly controlled and uniform vision for a new American city, much of it as filtered through the imaginations and design assumptions of his esteemed friends and colleagues. It seems fair to say that, in Burnham's conception, the White City had offered a physical approximation of a kind of Swedenborgian heaven—a material reality of walls and fountains and plazas and exhibits that also had the power to offer spiritual uplift to all who fully experienced it.

Not long after the fair had closed, Burnham asserted in 1895 that the "souls" of those who had worked on the fair had been "played upon by a higher hand, and the outward forms we built were expressions of enduring, everlasting law—they were beautiful because of this."[56] The sentiment calls to mind the scriptural passage ("Oh, how love I thy law") that graced his father-in-law Holland Weeks's gravestone. And the celestial comparisons were not Burnham's alone. One artist was heard to comment hyperbolically that after visiting the fair the very streets of heaven would look tawdry by comparison. So much so, he declared, that "I've relinquished my ticket [to heaven] and I'm staying at the fair."[57]

Burnham's firsthand encounter with Europe surely confirmed his essential faith in the power of these architectural styles, in beautiful natural settings, to enrich the human soul. Like the raucous, sensually stimulating entertainments of the fair's Midway that offered visitors an array of less high-minded pleasures, so too did Europe present sensual delights and examples of flawed humanity openly engaging in less high-minded pursuits.

His final diary entry combined a complimentary—if hard to visualize—simile ("We saw Gibraltar like a swan on the waters") with a last appreciative comment on the striking array of colors ("the last view of Europe being pink and blue") that had so impressed him throughout the trip. Wrote Burnham, "It was a lovely farewell."

As Daniel Burnham was excitedly immersing himself in the glories of the ancient Mediterranean world in March 1896, an article appeared in *Lippincott's Magazine* that was destined to become Louis Sullivan's most read, and most influential, literary effort. The piece, titled "The Tall Building Artistically Considered," was shortly republished in *The Inland Architect and News Record* alongside an entire supplement devoted to D. H. Burnham and Company's "building without walls," Chicago's Fisher Building. It later enjoyed an extended life in such publications such as *The Craftsman* (1905) and *Western Architect* (1922), not to mention occasional reprintings and citations in the architectural literature of the twentieth century.

Sullivan's essay is the first to formulate the memorable phrase "form ever follows function," which in later iterations naturally condensed into the more crisply alliterative "form follows function." The article was also one element of the Sullivan legacy that, along with the completed Wainwright and Guaranty buildings, prompted many admirers to designate Louis Sullivan the "Father of the Skyscraper." His rhetoric offered ample reason for the article's lasting influence, and many lines practically cried out for frequent quotation. Of the modern tall office building, he said, "The force and power of altitude must be in it, the glory and pride of exultation must be in it. It must be every inch a proud and soaring thing, rising in sheer exultation . . . from bottom to top . . . a unit without a single dissenting line."

Beneath the grand language lay an argument that attempted to marry pragmatic architectural and economic considerations to an ambitious artistic agenda, but his proposition did not actually require disruptive departures from the architectural practices of many of his contemporaries. First, Sullivan asserted, the problem of the tall office building will instantly and clearly contain within it the key to its own solution. M. Clopet's idea of "no exceptions" from Sullivan's Paris days seemed to suggest that an architectural "problem" could be solved by a clear and unambiguous rule applicable in all cases. Similarly the practical and artistic needs of a tall office building could be easily and logically determined if one simply proceeds "step by step from general to special aspects, from coarser to finer considerations."[58] Sullivan then suggested that tall buildings should openly display their functions in ways that years, even centuries, of static architectural traditions had kept from full expression. In effect this would involve opening up the "suppressed functions" that John Edelmann talked about in those long-ago conversations.

Furthermore, this new approach could only be brought to fruition by an architect who, like Michelangelo, will recognize his own unique creative power and who will uncompromisingly use this power to guide the tall building to find its natural form. Only, said Sullivan, "when the known law, the respected law, shall be that form ever follows function; when our architects shall cease strutting and prattling handcuffed and vainglorious in the asylum of a foreign school . . . [and when] each and every architect might, under the benign influence of this law, express in the simplest, most modest, most natural way that which is in him to say . . . then it may be proclaimed that we are on the high road to a natural and satisfying art."[59]

Sullivan identified several arguments of "theorists" of architecture, most of whose theories accepted the notion that the vertical expression of a tall building should be divided into three major parts. For the classicists, the model was the classical column, with its base, shaft, and capital. For those of a mystical slant, said Sullivan, the number three had special significance in the world around us, as represented by the three divisions of the day (morning, afternoon, evening) or the three parts of animal bodies (limbs, thorax, and head). Others reasoned from another kind of "organic" model. Just as plants often have clusters of leaves at ground level, stems that reach seamlessly upward, culminating in expansive blooms at the top, so too will tall buildings begin with a clearly defined base, rise in continuous uniformity upward, and terminate in a kind of foliated decorative crown, with each segment performing its "natural" function. Even those who purported to resist any such strictures, he said, and conceived of their designs as a holistic unit with a "sense of singleness and repose" nonetheless "accepted the notion of a triple division as permissible and welcome, but nonessential."

Sullivan claimed to reject all these theorists and critics, saying their prescriptions were all secondary, though his writings, here and elsewhere, aligned very closely with the organic view. In any case, he acknowledged that even tall buildings, as they soar vertically "without a single dissenting line," must also honestly reveal their functional divisions on the exterior. The base, the first division, will necessarily have a basement containing mechanical units, supporting a ground floor and a second floor requiring special spatial and decorative elements to attract and accommodate clients and customers. The upper floors will consist of multiple stories of identical office spaces rising to the top, where the building will terminate in another largely functional segment housing additional mechanical systems linked to the physical plant below.[60] So the tripartite pattern holds, not from any misguided adherence to ancient precepts or formulas but by letting a simple and obvious solution to the tall office building "problem" reveal itself in a natural progression to the mind of an architect of power. Sullivan's concept of a three-part external design for tall buildings, it should be emphasized, was hardly new to nineteenth-century architects, nor did it become anything like a widely accepted template for Miesian-style modernism.

As documents composed in parallel during 1896, Burnham's travel diaries and Sullivan's most influential essay provide clear signs that the architects were moving away from each other in matters of architectural theory and practice, a bifurcation that had been building for some time. Burnham's first direct encounter with Europe strengthened his respect for and devotion to historical models as an inspirational basis for grand structures in a new American cityscape. For Sullivan, whose Transportation Building at the Chicago Fair had already highlighted some dissenting features from traditional or accepted formulas, tall buildings offered opportunities to find new avenues of structural and artistic expression.

"The Tall Building Artistically Considered" can be viewed as marking a literary and reputational high point in Sullivan's career. His fellow architects were aware of his accomplishments and his innovative design ideas, and he still maintained good relations with many of them. But like Burnham in the early and middle part of the 1890s, he also had to deal with sudden disruptions both personal and professional. Adler's departure for a secure position with an elevator company was one such event and the break with Frank Lloyd Wright another.

Louis's estrangement from his brother Albert proved even more serious. Not so many years before, Albert had happily competed along with Louis at their Chicago athletic club; had worked with him on building projects for the Illinois Central Railroad, a company in which Albert was steadily advancing through positions of increased responsibility; and had even recently provided financing for a Louis-designed home in Chicago for their aging mother Andrienne. In fact it was this modest home on Lake Park Avenue that created the initial rupture. Andrienne died in 1892, leaving the house open for occupancy by Louis Sullivan and I. Giles Lewis and his wife, a couple with whom Louis had previously cohabited. When Albert's wife Mary gave birth to a daughter, also named Andrienne, in early 1896, the couple decided their needs would be better served in the house for which Albert had paid, forcing removal of Louis and the Lewises from the premises. In addition, rumors of a questionable relationship between Louis and the wife of a University of Chicago professor, which Willard Connely asserts may have been no more than a harmless flirtation, was viewed as improper by Mary, and this seems to have contributed to the final break. After 1896 the brothers' close relationship was effectively ended.[61]

One positive turn of events materialized for Sullivan in 1897, a new opportunity to realize the ideas of his tall-building essay in stone and steel in New York City, the showcase metropolis of America's eastern seaboard. Though not the only New York project for which Sullivan was considered, the Bayard Building at 65 Bleecker Street was destined to remain Sullivan's sole contribution to the cityscape. Like the Wainwright in St. Louis, the Bayard featured a vertical emphasis in the multistory central portion, with four prominent fluted columns rising skyward in contrast to noticeably recessed, though wide and heavily ornamented, horizontal spandrels. Also, in true Louis Sullivan fashion, the columns ended in arches that expanded over the two-window bays and floated among a riot of richly ornate decorative designs all along the upper frieze. Directly above the columns, carved angels with wings outspread and projecting cornices completed the elaborate crown of the building. After many design revisions the Bayard-Condict Building—so named because the Condict family had in the course of construction acquired a half-interest in the project—opened in 1899 to great acclaim.

A similar Sullivanesque treatment of a building façade appeared in the same year on the third of three adjoining buildings on Chicago's Michigan Avenue, known collectively as the Gage Group Buildings. Although the cluster of three buildings was developed by the firm of Holabird and Roche, the Gage Brothers insisted on a special artistic contribution by Louis Sullivan. Again we see emphatic fluted verticals culminating in complex vegetative blooms at the roofline and decorative elements in the recessed spandrels between floors. Bayard-Condict and the Gage Group, particularly in its northernmost façade, remain standing as admired examples of Sullivan's late-1890s art.

The Gage Group Buildings, 18–30 South Michigan Avenue, 1899. The two buildings of simplified design on the left were products of the Holabird and Roche firm. For the tallest structure of the three, the Gage brothers sought the artistic flourishes of Louis Sullivan, who was hired to design the façade. (Richard Nickel Archive, Ryerson and Burnham Art and Architecture Archives, Art Institute of Chicago. Digital file # 201006_171A.33.)

During the planning for Sullivan's Gage façade, Louis reportedly responded in characteristic fashion to his clients' expressed concern over a feature in the architectural design. A question arose over the expanse of ornamentation Sullivan had determined to place over the topmost row of windows. Would not that space be better used for taller windows, thus allowing in additional natural light? Sullivan's response to his milliner client? "If I came to you for a hat, I'd use your judgment."[62] In effect, Sullivan was telling the Gage Brothers to stick to the business they knew and leave the architecture to him.

Unfortunately, in the years immediately following "The Tall Office Building Artistically Considered" and his involvement in these two singular projects, Sullivan's chances for building tall steadily diminished. The prolonged economic downturn and recession in the years following the World's Fair was one factor. The absence of the client-friendly, socially connected engineering expert Dankmar Adler was another. Fortunately for Sullivan, Chicago dry-goods merchants Leopold Schlesinger and David Mayer had used Adler and Sullivan on various renovation projects beginning in the 1880s, and a commission for a new ten-story edifice in mid-1896 fell not to Adler but rather to his erstwhile partner. This marked the beginning of a long process that moved through several stages, culminating in the massive Schlesinger and Mayer department store that wrapped around the southeast corner of State and Madison streets in the heart of downtown Chicago. One of the early plans showed a slim two-bay building that, despite its narrow profile, did not really appear to soar vertically but instead allowed strong visual emphasis on the horizontal.[63] That emphasis continued in Sullivan's later iterations of the building as most of its expansion occurred not vertically but horizontally. When time came to add more bays on State Street, they turned to Burnham and Company for the construction of an architecturally compatible extension, which only served to accentuate the building's horizontal thrust.

The structure that has come down to us, now known as the Sullivan Center, is considered one of Sullivan's signature works—though contemporary eyes will not regard it as a soaring skyscraper. The relative plainness of the upper stories and the absence of seamless verticals on the longest expanses may seem surprising when compared to the ornamental extravagance and central upward thrust of buildings like the Wainwright, the Bayard-Condict, and the Gage Group façade. But Sullivan and the building's tenants had other aesthetic values in mind for Schlesinger and Mayer.

The horizontal and vertical panels would present a simple expression of the straightforward steel frame beneath. The first two floors, by contrast, would be adorned with cast-iron decoration of intricate complexity that would frame wide plate glass show windows to attract shoppers, in particular the affluent women to whom the store owners hoped to appeal. Sullivan's contemporary, Lyndon Smith, anticipating the masculine/feminine analysis of architectural historian Narciso Menocal, described the store as an example of Sullivan's emphasis on the "feminine" element in architecture. The ornamental detail surrounding the entrance and lower-level windows, Smith said, was designed to attract women's attention because it was "sensitive to a high degree, delicately pleasing to the sympathetic eye and with fine feeling and movement permeating its most incidental ramification."[64]

For this crucial aspect of the project, Sullivan would depend heavily on the design and drafting skills of his lead assistant George Elmslie, who had

Carson, Pirie, Scott, and Company department store, corner of State and Madison, Chicago. Originally designed by Louis Sullivan as the Schlesinger and Mayer store, the property was occupied by Carson, Pirie, Scott for over a hundred years. It is now known as the Sullivan Center. Daniel Burnham and Company completed an extension along State Street in 1906. (Historic American Buildings Survey, Prints and Photographs Division, Library of Congress. Reproduction # HABS ILL,16-CHIG,65-1.)

become adept at working in the artistic idiom of Louis Sullivan. Display windows and an entrance of unrivaled elegance would draw the desired clientele into a vast, well-lighted interior filled with merchandise of superior quality. Today's visitor to the Sullivan Center can still bear witness to the powerful effect of Sullivan's and Elmslie's lavish ornamental design, which in Sullivan's own words remains "exceedingly rich and delicate."[65] A close inspection will also reveal, woven into the floral intersections, Sullivan's initialed signature, "LHS."

Sullivan's design was just the kind of commercial magnet that Theodore Dreiser vividly described in his Chicago-based novel of 1900, *Sister Carrie*. The book tells the story of Carrie Meeber, who at age eighteen arrives in Chicago from a small Wisconsin town, "bright, timid, and full of the illusions of ignorance and youth." The year is 1889. Adler and Sullivan's Auditorium is moving toward its grand opening, and large department stores have now become familiar, but still striking, features of the downtown area. Searching for work as a shop girl in the intimidating environment of a crowded American city, Carrie is struck by the wide expanses of plate glass, which allowed causal passersby to marvel at the sight of busy clerks and businessmen hard at work or lounging about within. A policeman directs her to the discount department store called The Fair, and Carrie enters, "much affected by the remarkable displays of trinkets, dress goods, stationery, and jewelry" as she drifts among the extensive labyrinth of aisles. The presence of so much glittering material abundance, of exactly the kind she longs to possess but knows she can't afford, has an almost physical effect on her. She feels misery at her own lowly situation and deep pangs of envy for the affluent women who push her aside as she realizes "how much the city held—wealth, fashion, ease—every adornment for women, and she longed for dress and beauty with a whole heart." A few days later Carrie, now having become acquainted with a traveling salesman named Charles Drouet, enters the Schlesinger and Mayer store on Madison, where "the shine and rustle of new things" enthralls her, and where Drouet insists on buying her a jacket like one she had admired at The Fair.[66]

The Schlesinger and Mayer store Dreiser places Carrie in was not the building Louis Sullivan designed in the latter half of the 1890s, nor was Carrie Meeber fictively moving through spaces Adler and Sullivan had renovated for Schlesinger and Mayer several years before that. Carrie's store, in fact, would have been the conventional commercial structure designed by W. W. Boyington before either Adler or Sullivan became engaged in the project. But Sullivan's 1899 design for the new Schlesinger and Mayer store was precisely conceived for the functional and commercial purpose that Dreiser understood so well: to inspire the "drag of desire" in the hearts and minds of shoppers, in particular women shoppers with money to spend. Sullivan's ornamental ironwork at ground level created a framework of unsurpassed intricacy and elegance for what the store owners claimed were the "largest and finest display windows in the world."[67] The combination of long expanses of plate glass and the rich floral complexity and subtle color treatments in the surrounding metal ornament was meant to create, in Joseph Siry's words, "a special event in the eyes of passing pedestrians along State Street" of a kind that couldn't be replicated in any other large department store in the downtown district.[68]

As Sullivan was beginning his deep professional engagement with the Schlesinger and Mayer project, in his personal life he decided to embark on another kind of engagement, one that must have surprised his friends and associates. On the first of July in 1899 he married a divorcee named Margaret (born Mary) Hattabaugh at St. Paul's Reformed Episcopal Church.[69] The story of their meeting, as told by Sullivan biographer Willard Connely, has Louis Sullivan walking down Michigan Avenue one day and happening to encounter a "fairly tall woman, with dark brown eyes and hair" walking her dog. Sullivan supposedly exchanged casual inquiries about the pet, was struck by this "matured Gibson girl"—a composite feminine ideal of the period, drawn by artist Charles Dana Gibson—with a "figure something voluptuous," and determined to meet the woman again.[70]

Although Louis Sullivan wrote and spoke voluminously and passionately about nature, architecture, philosophy, poetry, and any number of esoteric intellectual and artistic preoccupations, he left scant record of his romantic or sexual interests. His biographers have been left to conjecture, mostly from the second-hand accounts of associates. Frank Lloyd Wright recounted a late-night conversation wherein Sullivan suddenly turned to him and asked him about how many women young Wright had "had." "Why, Mr. Sullivan," Wright self-righteously replied. "I never thought of women in those terms." Walking to the window in the Auditorium Building and stretching out his arms toward the street, Sullivan then boasted, "If you took all the women I've had and laid them end to end, they'd stretch from here to Milwaukee!" Sullivan's habit of seeking out prostitutes apparently stretched back as far as his student days in Paris and lasted well into his old age. After Sullivan's death, his trusted associate George Elmslie may have helped hide written evidence of Sullivan's sexual adventures by destroying many of the personal diaries that had come into his possession, some of which purportedly listed meetings with various mistresses, by each of whose names Sullivan had inscribed "a curious symbol—an algebraic formula."[71]

The pride Sullivan seemingly felt about his sexual prowess—extending even to the disturbing practice of keeping some kind of numerical record of his conquests—fits the man who, as we have seen, worshipped from a very young age what he perceived to be expressions of manly power. However it seems at odds with Robert Twombly's suggestion in his 1986 biography that Sullivan's "romantic interest in women was sporadic enough to be virtually nonexistent." Twombly further conjectures that Sullivan may have spent his adult life as a closeted gay man, whose true sexual orientation may have been "so repressed that he may not have known it himself."[72] Sullivan's late and surprising marriage, his long-standing artistic interest in the male physique, and his often rapturous effusions about manliness and the physical characteristics of the young men he knew at places like the Lotos Club—men like Bill Curtis and John Edelmann, "heroes in his eyes, if not demi-gods"—could be viewed as offering a degree of support for Twombly's conjecture. Some members of the LGBTQ community, following Twombly's lead, continue to regard Sullivan as one in the long line of artists, intellectuals, and other notable historic figures who may be counted among their number.

But Sullivan scholar Paul Sprague has explored the question of Sullivan's supposedly repressed homosexuality with meticulous care and concludes that there is no evidence from the historical record to justify Twombly's conjecture. Sprague observes that all the tales of close associates testifying to Sullivan's sexual activities "support the conclusion that Sullivan was heterosexual," and, Sprague implies, exclusively so.[73] Of course multiple experiences with women would not preclude the possibility of a bisexual orientation, with Sullivan either hiding or repressing a side of him that was physically attracted to men. In any case we currently have no conclusive written or testimonial evidence of a same-sex orientation, which is hardly surprising given the cultural mores of late nineteenth- and early twentieth-century America. We can say with some confidence that the dominant impression among those closest to him was that Louis Sullivan's sexual interests appeared to have been directed toward women.

Sullivan's marriage to Margaret may offer confirmation that, at age forty-two, Sullivan had a genuine interest in a permanent romantic relationship as well as intellectual companionship with a woman. Twombly professed puzzlement over the disparity between Margaret's reported age on the marriage license (twenty-seven) and the photograph of her taken at about that time, wherein Margaret "looks even older than her alleged years."[74] The clarifying answer, once again thanks to Paul Sprague's extensive archival work, is that Margaret had a habit of misrepresenting her age about as often as she changed her name. Her actual birthdate was May 29, 1858, which would make her at the time of her marriage to Louis not twenty-seven but forty-one.[75] As Twombly suspected, her age on the marriage license was indeed "alleged." She was near Sullivan in age and presumably combined, in Connely's words, a "voluptuous figure" with a degree of life experience and cultural and intellectual maturity, including literary ambitions, that Sullivan would find appealing.

And while it's true their marriage ultimately failed, there is reason to believe that the couple enjoyed a satisfactory time together. Biographers have wondered about the odd choice Sullivan made to spend much of his wedding day working on one of his writing projects and then, in the days following, returning with customary single-mindedness to the office, with no honeymoon in sight. But this would hardly seem inconsistent

Margaret Sullivan on the porch of the Ocean Springs cottage, holding a rose picked from the Sullivan garden. (Sullivaniana Collection, Ryerson and Burnham Art and Architecture Archives, Art Institute of Chicago. Digital file # 193101.Margaret_Portrait.)

with Sullivan's well established personal predilections and eccentricities, including his intense work habits and his passion for putting poetic and philosophical reflections in writing. We know how much Sullivan treasured his time in his Mississippi cottage, and one would think he would have been eager to show the property to his new bride. But as Twombly points out, Ocean Springs is hot in July, and a fall honeymoon there would make for a more agreeable choice for a marital getaway, which is apparently what the couple ultimately decided upon. The newlyweds enjoyed an extended stay in Ocean Springs from the end of November through the following March. As Sprague notes, there may have been another compelling reason for so long a sojourn: it appeared a child was on the way.[76]

Daniel Burnham's Mediterranean trip of 1896 can be seen as marking a new phase in the career of a man who then occupied a significant place on the international stage. He had traveled extensively within North America before, and trains and ships were becoming something of second homes as he traveled to inspect project sites within the United States and increasingly abroad. The daily diaries he kept between 1895 and 1912 show a man in constant motion, busily trying to juggle an active social and family life with an endless stream of demanding professional commitments. In 1896, shortly after getting back from his Mediterranean voyage, he attended a Columbian Exposition Directors' Association dinner and that same night left for Buffalo to inspect the company's Ellicott Square project. In May he was in New York enjoying dinner at the home of his good friend Charles McKim. August found him back home, painting watercolors of two big trees on his estate and later spending a full day painting alongside Eda Hurd Lord, a wealthy art collector and Evanston neighbor. In September he camped out at Island Lake, Wisconsin. In November he traveled to Toronto, Canada, and a few days later was back home nursing a case of cholera. And all this while Burnham involved himself deeply in plans for a new Field Museum, a reshaped lakefront, and a plan for a South Shore Drive, which he actively promoted by presentations before several local boosters and community groups.

On numerous occasions when returning from long trips, Burnham took the overnight train and then went straight to his Chicago office, with no time for even a brief respite at his Evanston home. On one such trip he stopped for meetings, first in Pittsburgh, then in Washington with President McKinley and members of Congress, and then hurried back to Chicago, arrived at 8:20 a.m., breakfasted at the Grand Pacific Hotel, and was in his office by 9:20. Five days later he headed east again, arriving in Cincinnati at 7 a.m., the next morning returning to Chicago at 7:45 am. By 8:30 he was back at work in the Rookery.[77]

We can get glimpses of the constant traveler's day-to-day experiences and impressions in letters to wife Margaret during this period, wherein Burnham mixed references to his frenetic schedule with expressions of yearning for home, worries about the children, and observations on his many encounters

Portrait of Daniel H. Burnham by Anders Zorn, 1899. (Daniel H. Burnham Collection, Ryerson and Burnham Art and Architecture Archives, Art Institute of Chicago. Digital file # 194301_110614-022.)

with friends, associates, and new acquaintances. In a typical example from late 1895, Burnham wrote from New York, "I expected to be home tonight. I must however go to Pittsburgh, then to Buffalo, and then return here for Friday and Saturday, and arrive home Sunday." The reason? He needed to attend to a project on lower Broadway, and the company officers would not be in till the end of the week. With customary Burnham brio, he declared, "I am determined, this time, to bring the matter to a head, or else drop it, and I think I can do the former." Also characteristic was an expressed hope for an end to the rush of business affairs and more time to relax at home with his family. Success with this project, he said, would mean "a comfortable income for us, and I can look forward to a quiet life at home, and enough money to carry us along."[78]

The latter half of the 1890s saw several Burnham and Company structures rise in Chicago and nearby Illinois communities and also in Cleveland; Detroit; Philadelphia; Youngstown, Ohio; Connecticut; and Pittsburgh. Few of these buildings are seen today as architecturally significant, but one completed in 1896, the Fisher Building at 343 South Dearborn Street in Chicago, has achieved landmark status and continues to pique the interest of architectural historians. Thomas Leslie makes the case that the Fisher, more than Jenney's Home Insurance Building or Burnham's Reliance, represents a true "first skyscraper," since it has all the key elements of twentieth-century skyscrapers: it "is skeletal rather than massive . . . it divorces the structural frame from the cladding, and . . . it relies on assemblies of specialized components for its skins, rather than on the skill of masons in laying identical units into various forms."[79] With Edward Shankland's engineering refinements, writes Leslie, "the metal frame lost its experimental status and became a ubiquitous feature in all North American buildings."[80] The Fisher remains a visible and charming presence in the southern portion of the downtown area. Its striking salmon-colored terra-cotta exterior, along with the usual rich ornamental extrusions, showcases fishes and other marine creatures, a move reminiscent of the whimsical inclusion of the sculpted birds who seem to caw at each other in amusement as they observe the visitors who enter John Root's Rookery.

When the 1890s began Daniel Burnham and Louis Sullivan were well-established in their professions but not household names. They had, to be sure, achieved notable recognition within the architectural community and among the city's elites, and Chicagoans were acutely aware of the remarkable new buildings that had risen and still were rising in their midst. But most casual pedestrians or office workers—the Sister Carries of the world—

marveled first and foremost at these new physical wonders without giving much thought to who created them.

Expressions of wonderment took many forms, but speed of construction, volume, and height were the most common subjects of commentary. In a novel suggestively titled *The Cliff-Dwellers*, Henry Blake Fuller imagined a fictional "modern monster," a building named the Clifton that he compared to Burnham and Root's Monadnock, to illustrate how radically the new multipurpose high rises were changing the face of Chicago and the conditions under which people worked. The Clifton, he wrote,

> stands full eighteen stories tall. Its hundreds of windows glitter with multitudinous letterings in gold and in silver, and on summer afternoons its awnings flutter score on score in the tepid breezes that sometimes come up from Indiana. Four ladder-like constructions which rise sky-ward stage by stage promote the agility of the clambering hordes that swarm within it, and ten elevators—devices unknown to the real, aboriginal inhabitants—ameliorate the daily cliff-climbing for the frail of physique and the pressed for time.[81]

Chicago, wrote George Ade, is a "town [that] is never satisfied with itself," a place which no sooner creates a street of tidy downtown storefronts "before a vandal army wrenches a building to pieces, puts a rough wooden shed over the sidewalk and begins the clamorous work of driving the earth full of enormous piles, on which is to rest the towering structure of bolted steel."[82]

At the century's turn, Sullivan and Burnham were widely known to be responsible for these behemoths and the immense structural changes taking place in the city and the country. Daniel Burnham was the recognized maestro who had orchestrated the stunningly successful World's Fair and who had guided to completion several of the city's tallest buildings. Louis Sullivan had given the public the internationally recognized Transportation Building with its glorious Golden Door and the dazzlingly complex designs for the Auditorium, the Stock Exchange, the Schiller Theater, the first section of the Schlesinger and Mayer store, in addition to major buildings outside of Chicago. But by January of 1900 their accomplishments, their personalities, and their principles were leading in two different directions. Daniel Burnham's world was ever expanding; Sullivan's was continuing to shrink.

7

Divergence

1900s

ON JUNE 9, 1900, Louis Sullivan rose in the ballroom of the Adler and Sullivan-designed Auditorium Hotel to address the attendees of the newly formed Architectural League of America. The league had only come into existence the previous year, for much the same reason the Western Association of Architects had been founded sixteen years before: to create a new organization distinct from what Sullivan and like-minded architectural rebels perceived as the oppressively conservative, old-boy, and still East Coast-dominated American Institute of Architects. Sullivan was greeted as a prophet and hero, and his speech picked up and expanded on themes he had been developing in over a decade and a half of public pronouncements on the state of American architecture. The toastmaster for the event? Louis's friend, rival, defender of Beaux-Arts classicism, and recent president of the AIA, Daniel Burnham.[1]

The younger Louis Sullivan who had willingly, if warily, collaborated on mostly congenial terms with Daniel Burnham and his prominent East Coast friends on the Columbian Exposition was nowhere in evidence. This was a different man: Louis the firebrand. Entitled "The Young Man in Architecture," the speech clearly outlined Sullivan's ambition to become a spokesperson for the emerging generation in architecture. It was a call to action for young, unspoiled practitioners. He accused his own generation of "American malpractice of the architectural art," "blind" to color, "deaf to discuss harmonics," "dry of heart," and "mentally crippled." Among the cultural noises contributing to the "prevailing cacophony" in architecture he included, unsurprisingly, "the purring of the select company of the [medievalist] Ruskinites." Somewhat more surprisingly he also excoriated the pronouncements of those who professed to follow two of Sullivan's intellectual forebears, scornfully rejecting "the gasping of the Emersonites" and "the rasping of the Spencerites."[2]

The only hope for the future, Sullivan assured them, lay with "the good, the true, the beautiful and the young." And one of the first things young architects must do was to forget just about everything they learned in school. At age forty-three Louis Sullivan was just as vehement in his revulsion against the stultifying effects of formal education as he was when he had suffered through long tedious days at the Rice and Brimmer elementary schools in Boston. Sullivan warned his audience that "books, photographs, and plates" cannot give even a "remote conception of what constitutes the real, the living, architectural art." Instead the academic approach to architecture had produced "for generations upon generations . . . one unvarying result: dreary, miserable failure."[3] Although Sullivan didn't directly mention Burnham or the World's Fair, the entire speech can be read as a kind of screed against historicist reverence for the antique "styles" that the toastmaster's World's Fair so famously showcased and that was finding a new life in a host of building projects, influenced by the City Beautiful movement, going up across the nation.

Sullivan's desire to associate himself with a new generation of architects may have been hastened by an increasing awareness that many members of the nineteenth-century architectural old guard in America were beginning to pass from the scene. Chicago pioneer architect John Van Osdel and Sullivan's old friend John Root were now long gone, both having died in 1891. Richard Morris Hunt, one of the leading figures in historicist architecture, the designer of the prominent Beaux-Arts Administration Building for the World's Fair, and the man from whom Sullivan briefly sought advice in the earliest days of his career, had died in 1895.

Most significant for Sullivan and the most recent loss that must have been on his mind as he addressed the young architects, his former "big chief" Dankmar Adler had died in April of 1900 of complications from a stroke. Adler was only fifty-five years old. Sullivan was asked to serve as a pallbearer for the funeral, which was performed in the very synagogue the two of them had designed together just as the firm of Adler and Sullivan was rising to prominence. As Twombly poignantly notes, "What could [Sullivan] have thought as he entered their home again under such circumstances, probably for the first time in years?"[4] On joining the family to pay his respects at the Adler home, might he have been thinking of the days, not many years past, when he was a frequent visitor and showered Adler's wife and other family members with expensive gifts, as Adler's daughter Sarah fondly recalled?[5] For the May issue of *Inland Architect* Sullivan provided an elegant, rectangular border for the journal's memorial portrait, with Sullivanesque vinelike clusters surrounding Adler's name and birth and death dates at the base. The formal, elaborate design stood in contrast to the exuberant framing of circles and ascending swirls he had used to highlight both their names on the office door when the partnership was new in 1883.

The pleasure Sullivan apparently took in spending time with Adler's children during the period of their partnership seems not to have resulted in a desire to raise children of his own once marriage afforded him that opportunity. Paul Sprague determined that historical records indicate a strong likelihood that a son, named Lester, entered the couple's lives in April of 1900 approximately nine months after Sullivan's marriage to Margaret and shortly before his stirring address in the Auditorium. Sprague further suggests that Louis and Margaret put the boy up for adoption not long after the birth, with the process reaching completion between June 1900 and August of 1901, when Lester was permanently given over to the care of a couple named Pigott. Details concerning whatever feelings Sullivan may have harbored toward, or about, his son are nonexistent. It is not even certain that the Lester Sullivan listed in census records was in fact Louis's son or that Margaret was the mother, though the evidence points that way in both cases. Until Sprague's discoveries, in the absence of contrary evidence, it was widely assumed that the Sullivan marriage was childless.

Why the decision to seek adoption? Why the secrecy? The possibility that the child may have been borne not by Margaret but by one of Sullivan's mistresses may have been a major reason. As Sprague points out this may be indicated by the couple's apparently successful efforts to hide the existence of the child from their friends and associates. The economics of childrearing may have played a role since the Sullivans' financial situation was by no means settled and dependable. Sullivan's singular dedication to his working life may have contributed to the decision, as could Margaret's own personal ambitions. In any case all we do know of Sullivan's son, based on Sprague's detective work, is that this Lester Sullivan—a name he kept throughout his life—grew to young manhood and worked for a time as a clerk in the Postal Telegraph Company (a Western Union competitor) and that Louis and Margaret did not openly acknowledge a relationship with him.[6]

However troubling or time-consuming Sullivan may have found this personal circumstance, it does not seem to have slowed him in the pursuit of his professional ambitions. Buoyed by the enthusiastic reception of his young audience at the league meeting, Sullivan was quick to accept an offer to compose a series of articles outlining his vision for a new approach to American architecture. A newly founded professional publication, the *Interstate Architect and Builder,* offered Sullivan an opportunity to expand on his "Young Man in Architecture" speech in fifty-two articles to be published weekly for an entire year. Sullivan immediately got to work producing installments. Here was a chance to expound upon his deeply personal and long evolving convictions on the art of architecture. For several years he had been offering his sometimes contrarian thoughts and opinions in short essays and speeches. With this offer of the supportive *Interstate Architect,* he now had significant space within which to explore his theories and ideas. The result was ultimately revised and published in book form as *Kindergarten Chats,* a compendium of the individual pieces that ran in the journal from February 1901 to February of the following year.

In *Kindergarten Chats* Sullivan adopts the role of a master architect introducing a young unnamed neophyte to the proper role of an architect in the creation of a new American architecture. Given the expansive format, it's no surprise that Louis Sullivan used the opportunity to let loose. The range of writing habits from good to bad, which he had been practicing since producing his startling prose-poem "Inspiration" in 1886, is on full display—the linguistic excesses and obscurities as well as occasional bursts of eloquence and trenchant criticism. Frank Lloyd Wright's widely cited remark concerning the difference between Sullivan's skill as a designer versus his rhetorical surfeit as a writer—"miraculous when he drew" but "ridiculous when he wrote"—may strike even some Sullivan admirers as applicable to more than a few passages in *Kindergarten Chats.*

Sullivan contended that the contents were nothing more than a lucid exposition of obvious truths. In the foreword to his proposed 1918 edition, he explained the title as an answer to critics who might question his flamboyant and sometimes mystifying rhetorical style: "The ideas underlying the work are simple and elementary: hence the title 'Kindergarten Chats.'"[7] He returned to this point in a later section of the text, where he contrasted the advanced and nourishing techniques now being practiced by teachers of the very young—"animated in their work by enthusiasm, by devotion, by love"—to the antiquated and repressive atmospheres of the architectural schools. Apparently Sullivan believed primary-school education had much improved since his own unhappy schooldays in Boston. The modern kindergarten, he asserted, "has brought bloom to the mind of many a child. . . . But there is, alas! No *architectural kindergarten*—a garden of the heart wherein the simple, obvious truths, the truths that any child might consent to, are brought fresh to the faculties and are held to be good because they are true and real."[8]

These supposedly simple truths laboriously elaborated in *Kindergarten Chats* cannot be fully captured in a brief synopsis, but most of them tend to fall under four general concepts: the need to infuse architecture with

1) organicism, 2) democratic values, 3) individual creative power, and 4) the nearly total rejection of forms and theories imposed by the past and by corrupt educational institutions. The term *organic architecture* has become commonplace in discussions of the building arts, though the exact meaning of the term remains unclear. Finding a satisfactory definition has sometimes not been helped by many of its practitioners and interpreters—chief among them Frank Lloyd Wright. As Stuart Graff, CEO of the Frank Lloyd Wright Foundation, has written, it is "the most elusive concept in all of Frank Lloyd Wright's work," one which Wright himself "struggled to define (and redefine) throughout his life." To many, Graff suggests, it may mean simply looking to nature's forms and principles for inspiration. To others the concept can include reliance on natural materials such as wood and stone; fluid, open connections between exterior and interior and the use of "abstracted plant geometries"; or "interpenetrating volumes and contrasts" that make movement through a building resemble a walk through the natural environment. According to Graff, Wright's way of unifying these disparate views was through the idea of sustainability.[9]

David Pearson's Gaia Charter, promulgated as recently as 2001, attempted to isolate eight rules for modern architectural design in an organic mode. To be considered truly "organic," said Pearson, a building should

1. be inspired by nature and be sustainable, healthy, conserving, and diverse.
2. unfold, like an organism, from the seed within.
3. exist in the "continuous present" and "begin again and again."
4. follow the flows and be flexible and adaptable.
5. satisfy social, physical, and spiritual needs.
6. "grow out of the site" and be unique.
7. celebrate the spirit of youth, play, and surprise.
8. express the rhythm of music and the power of dance.[10]

Several of the characteristics identified by Pearson and Graff would seem to apply to Louis Sullivan's definitions of organicism as outlined in *Kindergarten Chats* and elsewhere. Sullivan's central conviction that architects should look to nature for inspiration was present from the very beginning of his career and permeates *Kindergarten Chats.* That a building should "unfold . . . from a seed within" is repeated more than once in Sullivan's finished text and represented in his favorite image of an acorn realizing itself in an oak tree: "If you put an acorn in the ground, that acorn, containing the function oak, will seek the form oak, and in process of time, will become an oak-tree."[11] Pearson's "continuous present" and perpetual renewal cycles could be applied to Sullivan's categorical rejection of historical styles, as could his insistence on fluidity, flexibility, and adaptability in design, though Pearson adds to this an openness to curvilinear forms over the traditional restrictiveness of straight lines. The concept of "sustainability" or reducing a building's carbon footprint, ideas that have gained greater urgency in the twenty-first century, may not have been top of mind for nineteenth- and early twentieth-century architects, but many were acutely conscious of the related imperative to manage materials and resources for maximum efficiency and economy.

Certainly Sullivan's definition of functionalism included addressing the social and physical needs of the people, and he connected those explicitly to spiritual needs as well. He declared that "for Man there is nothing but the physical; what he calls his spirituality is but the most exalted reach of his animalism." There is "form in everything and anything, everywhere and at every instant," and all forms "stand for relationships between the immaterial and the material," which he envisioned as unbreakable bridges between the subjective and the objective, between the inner world of consciousness, emotion, and spirituality and the outer world of physical things.[12] Sullivan's philosophy resembles Burnham's Swedenborgianism, wherein the spiritual and the physical exist as two indivisible elements along a single continuum. For both architects, material objects—and specifically the buildings they constructed—had spiritual meaning and the capacity to express and inspire what Sullivan called the Infinite Creative Spirit of humankind.

The idea that buildings should "grow out of the site"—in Wright's memorable phrase, be "of the hill," not "on the hill"—and in some sense, as Pearson contends, express youthful exuberance and the harmonies of music and dance, however abstract those parallels may seem, did not seem strange to Sullivan, the Wagner and Beethoven enthusiast who also likened architecture to poetry and song. For function and form, he said, "the fragrance of them is rhythm, the language of them is rhythm; for rhythm is the very wedding-march and ceremonial that quickens into song."[13] And opening up interior spaces to the outside, as Wright was to do, would likely have struck him as a legitimate union of function and form, of nature and art.

But for some professionals the term "organic architecture" remains problematic.[14] Consider a few simple truths. Buildings aren't plants. With rare exceptions they don't resemble plants or any other living organisms. They don't grow from seeds in anything but a metaphorical sense. They are not nourished by water and sunlight, and in most instances it's quite the opposite: they are designed to keep out rain and to control heat and other effects of the sun. In Sullivan's time and place in particular, moisture in the soil was not a friendly condition for architects but rather a problem with which to contend. Sullivan's contemporary Henry Ericsson characterized the natural forces such as fire and gravity as examples of "imperious teachers in the hard School of Building which Nature keeps."[15]

The three-part structure that, Sullivan noted, some "theorists" found in plant life is anything but universal. Many plants—blades of grass, for instance—do not display a base, stem, and bloom. During Sullivan's lifetime large commercial buildings, including his own, were almost uniformly rectilinear in design, square or rectangular boxes whose straight lines were relieved only by decorative flourishes or Roman-style arches and domes. They did not project anything like branches or leaves or petals that swayed in the breeze, nor did they interact with counterparts, other than perhaps visually, in a larger interdependent ecosystem. Extravagantly curvilinear designs such as Frank Lloyd Wright would utilize in New York's Guggenheim Museum and other buildings found no expression in Sullivan early or late.

Most crucially the incipient form of a building, which Sullivan equated with the interior blueprint inside an acorn, must originate and emerge through conscious, considered thought in the mind of an architect and in consultation with a client, not in a spontaneous process involving atoms, molecules, and organic matter evolving naturally and by chance over eons. In other words any "seed germ" of a building's design must originate in the abstract and structured thought processes of the architect. In the "Young Man in Architecture" speech Sullivan insisted that the architectural process must begin with analysis before it can move to synthesis, presumably to determine the proper form for the building's function. He exhorted young architects to look to how a plant grows to see how it exhibits "in its highest form the unity and quality of analysis and synthesis," but he didn't explain how plants analyze or synthesize.[16]

Many people, of course, see the hand of a designer God in the complex patterns around us in the natural world. In this sense a young architect could look to God the creator as an inspiration and source of instructive models in nature. But Sullivan showed little interest in invoking the traditional Judeo-Christian God as the conscious source of design in organic life. He did often write of the Infinite Creative Impulse or Divine Creative Energy or Mysterious Power at work in the architectural process in terms reminiscent of the vague, non-sectarian, and not uniquely Christian formulations of the transcendentalists.[17] But if Sullivan regarded an anthropomorphized God as the supreme architect whose organic designs perfectly united form and function in ways instructive to human architects, he rarely if ever said so directly. With his sense of the spiritual firmly grounded in things of this world ("never came [to me] the sense of immortality," Sullivan once remarked), one can easily agree with Hugh Dalziel Duncan's characterization of Sullivan's central religious conviction: "The God Sullivan found within him was the artist."[18]

Whatever limitations the idea of an organic architecture may have, the concept continues to inspire architectural theory and practice. Some of the parallels between our constructed environment and the world of nature have obvious merit. Buildings, like living things, have life spans. They are born, age, and with very few exceptions eventually reach an end to their useful life. They have circulatory mechanical systems and contain teeming life and motion within. They require careful maintenance to stay healthy and strong. They can exhibit geometric patterns resembling those as elaborate and precise as any found in crystalline formations of ice or minerals. They can be built of natural materials taken from local forests and quarries. They may be designed, in some sense, to fit the landscape or site, just as Frank Lloyd Wright's Fallingwater seems to mimic the presence of horizontal limestone ledges over a cascading river. The most visible sign of Sullivan's inspiration from nature repeatedly appears in his rigidly controlled botanic detailing and colorful stenciling that match the complexity of interweaving floral patterns found in medieval illuminated manuscripts. While his foursquare buildings don't appear to grow from the ground up and don't foreshadow the immense swooping curves of some twenty-first-century organic architects, they do exhibit an abundance of fluid natural patterns in their ornamentation, creating a signature style that clearly reflects the natural world.

We do not know how many colleagues present at his "Young Man in Architecture" speech or how many readers of *Kindergarten Chats* came to think of themselves as Sullivan disciples, but we do know that Sullivan's example and words became sources of lifelong inspiration to several successful and influential architects. The most famous of those, of course, was Frank Lloyd Wright, who is now often seen as the father and chief theorist of the modern organic-architecture movement. But there have been others. George Elmslie, who like Wright spent his formative years apprenticing under Sullivan and was ultimately named executor of "the master's" will, was a lifelong devotee of Sullivan's philosophy. William Gray Purcell worked briefly in the Sullivan office and later partnered with Elmslie to create several designs in the organic mode. The architect Bruce Goff, who at the start of his career sought professional advice from both Sullivan and Wright, developed a theory of "beginning again and again," of creating each building as "the first and last" of its kind, an approach Sullivan would have applauded. Architect, author, and stage designer Claude Bragdon recounted how he eagerly awaited each issue of *Interstate Architect and Builder* to absorb the concepts that would destroy "for many young men—I was one of them—the world of ideas into which they had been educated, but only to create another and a better world of ideas in their stead."[19] In fact almost all practitioners of what came to be called the Prairie School of architecture were touched, directly or indirectly, by the life and thought of Louis Sullivan.

And it wasn't only the organic emphasis that influenced them. Goff had been talked out of pursuing further study in higher education by Sullivan's and Wright's insistence that formal architectural instruction would stifle his creativity. The notion that a new architecture could and should express American democracy became a common operating principle among a number of Sullivan's admirers. Wright regarded his Usonian houses—simple, affordable structures largely devoid of any reference to historical or European styles— as representative of a native, everyman-based style for "Usonia," his adopted name for the United States of America that Wright thought removed the taint of Old World naming practices. Sullivan's impassioned insistence on the need for creative independence would predictably resonate with a generation of young architects seeking to distinguish themselves in a competitive profession that often placed obstacles in the way of stylistic innovation.

After Sullivan's bold and bracing call to arms at the Architectural League of America's 1900 convention, it is perhaps surprising that he declined to attend their next two national meetings. It may also seem a little odd that the self-styled architectural revolutionary accepted a term on the board of directors for the conservative Municipal Art League, sitting alongside his supposed bête noire Daniel Burnham and the now sixty-two-year-old historicist architect Peter Wight.[20] But such associations may not be surprising at all. Sullivan was active in professional organizations for many years and had always showed a willingness to join architectural and artistic committees and subcommittees and to seek professional connections, whether with the old guard or young Turks. But he also had a new wife, a business to run, manifestos to write, and economic challenges to face. As for his attitude toward Burnham, in some ways Sullivan still viewed him as "Uncle Dan," the "man of power" who led the international success of the World's Fair and put Chicago architects and architecture on the map. Sullivan's polemics notwithstanding, the two men still maintained a respectful personal relationship.

The financial side of Sullivan's life, not the personal or the theoretical, was demanding most of his attention during this period. New commissions continued to dwindle in number and quality. He spent much of his time in the early 1900s overseeing the Schlesinger and Mayer completion and designing a woman's dormitory for a Tennessee college, a women's pavilion for a hospital that was never built, and a handful of private residences, small offices and factory facilities.

A renewed interest in rigorous physical activity provided one outlet for the various stressors impacting his life. Always an enthusiast for competitive athleticism, Sullivan was finding release and respite at the Chicago Athletic Association in what was then considered among the most "manly" of sporting activities: boxing. In October of 1901 Sullivan wrote to New York architect Lyndon P. Smith, "Business still dull, but with some promise in the air. . . . Have gone back to [boxing instructor] Geo. Dawson and am boxing for dear life 3 times a week—nothing like it."[21] For the sake of the exercise, Sullivan was probably willing to walk into the gym while concealing his contempt for the historical design elements of the athletic club on Michigan Avenue. Its elaborate Venetian Gothic façade had been designed by Henry Ives Cobb for the purpose of attracting the attention of visitors to the Chicago World's Fair.

By 1903, his practice clearly struggling, he began actively soliciting potential clients in an increasingly desperate effort to drum up business. Sullivan's practice completed only two minor building projects that year. Meanwhile D. H. Burnham and Company brought twenty-eight projects to completion.[22] In late 1905 Sullivan took the extraordinary step of writing the president of the University of Michigan to inquire about a teaching position after hearing of the school's recently announced plans to found a school of architecture. For the proud and unrelentingly fierce critic of formal education in architecture, having to seek a professorship, of all things, must have seemed a bitter pill.[23]

In the early 1900s the idea that cities could be subject to comprehensive planning was not exactly new. Over a hundred years earlier an unpromising mix of swamp, humidity, and mosquitoes on the East Coast had been chosen as the site for the nation's capital, and a foreign-born architect had been invited to design a new city from scratch. The city, soon to be called Washington, was to be placed within a special federal district carved out of Maryland and Virginia on banks of the Potomac River. The Potomac was navigable and was chosen partly for its promise as a gateway to the economic engine of an inland canal. The architect, Pierre L'Enfant, was skilled in both the fine arts and engineering, and the comprehensive plan he came up with presented ordered streets and grand radiating diagonal thoroughfares similar to the templates he knew in the Versailles and Paris of his youth. It wouldn't be the last time France served as an inspirational model for urban planning in the United States.

Daniel Burnham's reliance on European architectural precedents in his persistent efforts to beautify the befouled industrial city of Chicago is emphasized in this 1901 newspaper cartoon. (Charles Moore Collection, Manuscript Division, Library of Congress.)

Even the famously untrammeled and explosive growth of Chicago began with a plan of sorts. Throughout the nineteenth century city officials and builders generally constructed the city along extensions of the central grid lines initially laid out in 1830 by James Thompson, who had carefully observed guidelines established by the national Land Ordinance of 1785. Thompson, and the Illinois and Michigan Canal commissioners who hired him, felt confident the town's geographic location on the Chicago River meant the area was slated for rapid growth. They could easily foresee quick sales of the rigidly rectangular lots projected in the map, many of which remained, like Washington, DC, prior to development, simply unoccupied stretches of unappealing swampland.

By 1900 both Washington, DC, and Chicago had grown into major urban centers, with all the attendant ills and challenges of rapid, sometimes hard-to-control growth. L'Enfant's vision for Washington, DC, provided some guidance through the first few presidential administrations. But as one historical account put it, "after the passing of John Quincy Adams, the authority of the plan, never strong, had dwindled into vague suggestion."[24] Several liberties had been taken with the National Mall, the most intrusive of which was a railroad and railway station that invaded the mall just at the point where the gardens of the West Front of the Capitol ended. The open vista that now stretches from the Capitol to the Lincoln Memorial was essentially a haphazard mix of buildings, trees, gardens, and railroad tracks, and what "was to have been the grand avenue connecting [the White House to the Capitol] had become a common pasture, watered by a canal lined with wood-yards."[25]

A senator from Michigan, James McMillan, assumed a leading role in advocating for large-scale improvements in the National Mall and the surrounding public spaces. McMillan's personal secretary was Charles Moore, a Harvard graduate who began his career as a journalist in Detroit, where he became acquainted with McMillan and followed him to Washington on McMillan's election to the Senate in 1889. At festivities in late December 1900 celebrating the one-hundredth anniversary of US capital's move from Philadelphia to the new federal district in Washington, President McKinley and assembled members of Congress and other dignitaries heard plans for enlarging the White House and improving the mall. The observance set in motion a renewed determination, led by McMillan, to finally take action in reshaping and refining much of the physical environment at the heart of the national government. In February 1901 the Chicago-based *Inland Architect and News Record* chimed in with a recommendation to beautify Washington along the lines of Burnham's 1893 World's Fair, which demonstrated "the benefit to be derived through a small number of professional men working together."[26]

Charles Moore would play a key role in not only in the Washington, DC, improvement plan but also in the life and legacy of Daniel Burnham. He would go on to edit Burnham's and Edward Bennett's famous Chicago plan of 1909 and to ultimately write the first comprehensive biography of Daniel Burnham. Based on his extensive and first-hand knowledge, Moore devoted the better part of nine chapters to Burnham's work on a variety of urban planning projects, beginning with that of Washington. Altogether these projects consumed roughly ten years, or one-quarter, of Burnham's working life, while these same projects took up almost two-thirds of Moore's two-volume narrative. The wealth of credible, closely observed detail that Moore was able to convey about these years is of great benefit to students of Burnham, though Moore's close relationship to Burnham, and his deep admiration for his subject, also colored his presentation.

According to Moore, William E. Curtis, a *Chicago Herald* columnist who had worked on publicity for the World's Fair, played an important role in bringing Burnham to Washington.[27] When plans to enlarge the White House were proposed, Curtis immediately thought of the maestro of the Columbian Exposition and suggested Burnham's name to the Washington power brokers. Moore took credit for recommending Burnham to McMillan in relation to the redevelopment of Washington's park system. On March 26, 1901, Burnham sent a letter to Margaret expressing surprise at having received the appointment: "I arrived in Washington all right and found they desired me to have part in planning the improvements of the entire city of Washington."[28] He was delighted to report that working alongside him would be his old friend Charles McKim and young Frederick Law Olmsted Jr., known to his friends and associates as "Rick." The elder Olmsted, designer of Central Park in New York City and landscape architect for the Columbian Exposition, had retired at age seventy-three not long after the fair closed.

In short order the acclaimed sculptor Augustus St. Gaudens, another veteran contributor to the World's Fair, joined Burnham, McKim, and Rick Olmsted on the project. All four volunteered their services, requiring compensation only for expenses. Moore would serve as the commission secretary and special assistant, and at their first planning meeting on April 6, he got a glimpse of what he was in for. After spending the better part of an afternoon listening to Burnham and the others discourse on one of McKim's domestic projects rather than focus on the task at hand, Moore expressed mock frustration mixed with admiration as he resigned himself to similar long days ahead with a group so aesthetically inclined. "With artists," he remarked wistfully, "the longest way around is usually the shortest way home."[29]

Almost immediately the idea was floated for Burnham and his fellow commission members to travel to Europe to inspect firsthand the landscape configurations of venerable European cities. Burnham hesitated, in part because he was not entirely sure of his travelling companions. Would his relationship with his old friend McKim come under strain? "McKim is a very nervous man," he confided to Margaret on April 1, "and I shall feel quite different if I am to go with him from what will be the case if I go by myself."[30] By April 10 he seemed to have overcome any qualms, as he wrote to McKim urging his good friend to consider the need to "refresh our minds" in order to "properly do this enormously important work which has been entrusted to our hands."[31] Before long members of the group agreed to the excursion, beginning with visits to several famous estates on American's Eastern seaboard.

They departed for Europe on June 13, returning to New York on August 1. Burnham's promise for a "swift run" over many countries was fulfilled: the itinerary included Paris, Versailles, Rome, Venice, Budapest, Vienna, and London, with side trips by Burnham to Frankfort am Main and Berlin. No major disruptions or disputes among the four commissioners occurred during the journey, and the days were filled with feverish sketching and long discussions over, as Burnham put it, "parks in their relation to public buildings." The project was all-consuming: "That is our problem . . . in Washington and we must have weeks when we are thinking of nothing else."[32] Whatever his initial reservations, Burnham viewed the trip abroad as a chance to reconnect personally and professionally with old friends and to deepen his association with the son of another esteemed colleague from the days of the World's Fair. It was also an opportunity to immerse himself more deeply in the architectural glories of the Old World, which could only have the effect of strengthening his attachment to the architectural traditionalism that had proven so popular among members of the fair-going public in 1893.

A key event in the journey, which Charles Moore called "momentous," occurred during a meeting Burnham held in London with Alexander Cassatt, the president of the Pennsylvania Railroad, with whom he had spent many happy hours in Egypt in 1896. Cassatt's company had been involved in plans to develop and renovate the rail terminus in the National Mall for some time, with Burnham's company and others under consideration for the job. But Cassatt had resisted moving his terminal out of its advantageous position on the mall directly in front of the Capitol building. In London, however, Cassatt informed Burnham that his company had recently bought control of its chief competitor, the Baltimore and Ohio Railroad, and was now willing to consider moving the station, if Congress would provide partial funding for a tunnel under Capitol Hill to facilitate rail connections to the South.[33] At one point as the plans went forward, Burnham expressed concern that an enormous new rail station might diminish the visual prominence of the Capitol building. "After another fit of fear and trembling," he confided to Charles McKim, "I asked Mr. Cassatt to let me lower the depot twenty-odd feet" to lessen the appearance of "competition of the two structures." To his relief, "Mr. Cassatt not only agreed, but gave us praise for a more sensible railway solution."[34]

The ultimate result was Washington's still vibrant Union Station, built over a period of five years from 1903 to the official opening in 1908. Burnham remained actively involved in the process throughout the entire period, reacting to and advising on numerous setbacks, not least of which was strong community opposition and continuing resistance to the whole project from a powerful member of the House of Representatives, Illinois' Joe Cannon. Designed in large part by Burnham's trusted assistant William Peirce Anderson, the station remains an impressive example of neoclassical, post-Columbian Exposition architecture. It's an imposing presence in a city known for monumental structures, but its position on Massachusetts Avenue offers a convenient and memorable entry point to the city while remaining architecturally subordinate to many of the grand buildings of central Washington.

Burnham's Senate Park Commission contributed to other improvements in the city as well. The Washington Monument, long in the making but finally completed in 1876, had been located slightly off center of the L'Enfant axis. To rectify this anomaly the commission drew a line from the Capitol to the monument, thereby reorienting the axis of the mall, along which all future buildings would be placed. Columns of elm trees would frame the central open space, which Burnham contended should remain parklike, presenting an expansive 300-foot-wide carpet of grass as an architectural feature. President Theodore Roosevelt ordered construction to stop on a Department of Agriculture building, and it was repositioned to conform to the new axis. Provision was made for a memorial to Abraham Lincoln to be placed at the far west extension of the mall on land reclaimed from what many, including the reliably antagonistic Joe Cannon, had viewed as unpromising marshland. Several of these changes met with resistance and controversy along the way, and the commission's plan was not always followed as devised. But it's fair to say the numerous alterations to the governmental center of Washington, DC, since Burnham's time have been based on, and generally followed, some of the design concepts outlined in the Senate Park Commission's refined and reimagined version of L'Enfant's original template.

Burnham showed devotion to the project that lasted many years. In this and other matters of federal architecture and planning, he remained intermittently involved to the end of his life. The Washington project was, perhaps, second only to the Columbian Exposition in cementing his international reputation in the field of public architecture. And it led almost inevitably to other invitations for city planning on a large scale. The progressive mayor of Cleveland, Ohio, Tom Johnson, quickly enlisted Burnham in the cause of beautifying his city's center. Burnham was appointed head of a commission to come up with a plan. He was joined in the project by two distinguished New York architects, John Carrère and Arnold W. Brunner, both of whom shared educational pedigrees with Louis Sullivan—Carrère at the École des Beaux-Arts in Paris, Brunner at MIT under William Ware. Unlike Sullivan both architects were perfectly comfortable working in the traditional styles of the nascent City Beautiful movement inspired by Burnham and the World's Fair. After a period of intensive study and much back and forth, the group issued its report in August of 1903.

Burnham was actively involved throughout the process, not just in managing the politics and lending the prestige of his name and reputation but also in contributing to the hands-on work product. Arnold Brunner's description of Burnham's role in the project reminds one of the working relationship he had established many years earlier with John Root: "For over a year we worked at the drawings and constantly conferred about the details of the plan, Mr. Burnham always adding fresh inspiration and proving himself to be a designer as well as a more than intelligent critic. In writing the reports, which contained reproductions of our drawings, Mr. Burnham contributed largely to its presentation."[35]

The mayor and many in the political class and the press greeted the Cleveland report enthusiastically, and in the years that followed several grand neoclassical buildings came to completion clustered around a central mall unsurprisingly similar to the one Burnham's team had just designed for Washington, DC. As with all of Burnham's planning efforts, some of the group's suggestions were rejected by city leaders. For example, the railway terminal that the commission had hoped would bring new vitality to the civic center was never built, much to the regret of Burnham and his associates.[36] Nonetheless a historical marker on the site of the mall commemorates Burnham's 1903 plan for the city and contends that the mall, "as built, was the most completely realized of Burnham's city planning efforts . . . an enduring and vital element of Cleveland's civic culture."

San Francisco was the next city to enlist Burnham on behalf of beautification. Burnham had made previous visits there, and his company had a representative in residence, West Coast architect Willis Polk. As early as 1902 Burnham was made aware of the desire of the progressive former mayor James Phelan and various associates to formulate a new plan for the city. Burnham embraced the opportunity as the "most delightful occupation possible" and a "labor of love." And as with Washington and Cleveland, he volunteered to donate his time, with payment only for expenses.[37]

By 1904 he had established himself in a newly built house that Polk had been instructed to build on the centrally located promontory Twin Peaks, and with his trusted assistant Edward Bennett, he set immediately to work. Burnham considered the small Twin Peaks bungalow a 'shanty" or "shack," and the days and nights he spent there must have reminded him of the primitive quarters in Jackson Park during the exhausting but exhilarating days of building the Chicago Fair. The site had the additional value of offering him a panoramic view of the city and surrounding areas. "Being up there," he told Polk, "we can constantly see the city and everything else . . . where the influence about me shall stimulate Golden Gate Thoughts."[38]

As was sometimes the case with Burnham, the practical challenge of re-envisioning San Francisco was accompanied with reflections on how so purely physical a task could be viewed in the context of Swedenborgian transcendentalism. In San Francisco Burnham had the pleasure of visiting with his old friend and religious mentor Joseph Worcester, who now lived in the city. Edward Bennett reported that during this stay, "the laws of spiritual correspondence were often in his [Burnham's] mind, and one evening at the bungalow on Twin Peaks he interested himself in tracing the correspondence of spiritual powers and the municipal powers as indicated in the physical lay-out of the centre of the city." Burnham added that he had figured out a way to demonstrate the certainty of life after death based on a necessary "belief in an absolute and universal power," that is, God—the exact opposite of the religious conclusion Sullivan said he had long ago arrived at on the question.[39]

During this same period Burnham agreed to take on other formidable tasks that would require both deep attention and extended periods of time away from home. Burnham's connections to the highest officials of the federal government and influential members of politically powerful elites were now firmly established. As early as 1902—just as Burnham was immersing himself in the details of the Washington Plan—Secretary of War Elihu Root asked Burnham to enter a competition for a redesign of key buildings at the nation's military academy at West Point, this time for compensation. Burnham initially resisted, citing the lack of architectural control the competition required and inadequate payment for the work performed. Secretary Root attempted to allay those concerns, and Burnham ultimately consented. Once he examined closely the problem at hand, Burnham concluded that only a comprehensive overhaul would do. His bold visionary stand, however, did not result in getting the commission, which went to the Boston firm of Cram, Goodhue and Ferguson.

Despite that minor setback, Burnham's reputation among the power brokers of Washington remained high. On April 2, 1903, Burnham played a key role in President Roosevelt's visit to Evanston to deliver a speech at Northwestern University, just a few blocks from Burnham's home. Burnham's diary notes that he met the president at a reception in the morning and rode with other dignitaries in a carriage to the site of the speech. In the evening Burnham joined other prominent guests to dine with the president in the magnificent banquet hall of Adler and Sullivan's Auditorium.[40]

In 1904 Roosevelt had a new project for which Burnham's name came to the forefront. The War Department, now under the leadership of William Howard Taft, had overseen the redevelopment of Washington, DC, and the West Point competition. It also had responsibilities for the country's colonial interests, the most recent of which involved the United States' occupation of the Philippines following victory over Spain in the Spanish-American War. The government's plans for this new territory included improvements to the capital city of Manila and the creation of a new city, Baguio, to be placed at a more temperate point on the islands, some 4,800 feet above sea level, to serve as the nation's capital in summer. Founded by the United States in 1900 as a "hill station"—essentially a high-elevation refuge for colonists unaccustomed to the intense heat of valleys and plains—Baguio was soon identified as a likely site for a major city, to be mapped out and built under the auspices of the American government. The project would transform the existing village of Kafagway, land then inhabited by a native farming people, the Ibaloi. Many in Washington viewed such an enterprise as an act of generosity, an effort to bring the benefits of civilization to an oppressed and backward population.[41]

To take a leading role in overseeing elements of this project, President Roosevelt selected the ambitious son of an established and wealthy New England family, W. Cameron Forbes. Burnham was something of a mentor and benefactor to Forbes, having earlier recommended the thirty-three-year-old for a government position in Panama. In return Forbes sent Burnham, as a gift, a biography of his renowned maternal grandfather, Ralph Waldo Emerson. Burnham was pleased with the gift, given Emerson's interest in the transcendental mysticism of Emanuel Swedenborg. "I am reading it and am halfway through the first volume," Burnham wrote to Forbes. "What a wonderful man [Emerson] was! Everything he did interests me."[42]

When the time came to select a man to spearhead planning for the Philippines mission, Forbes's first thought went not to Burnham but to Rick Olmsted. The junior Olmsted's reputation in landscape architecture was growing, enhanced by his work on the Washington project. Olmsted was not available, and Burnham's other partner on the Senate Park Commission, Charles McKim, was consulted next. After Burnham dropped hints that he himself might be interested, Taft was quick to direct the job offer to him. When McKim later indicated he would like to join his friend Burnham on the project, Forbes understandably felt he had stumbled upon "an embarrassment of riches." And despite his continuing involvement in other city-planning ventures during this period, Burnham readily accepted.[43]

All the while that Burnham was volunteering his time for city planning projects, Burnham and Company was continuing to create significant new buildings for profit in Chicago and across the nation: in Pittsburgh, New York, Cincinnati, Milwaukee, New Orleans, Indianapolis, San Francisco, Memphis, El Paso, and elsewhere. In 1906 Burnham would decide to move his company's offices to the firm's recently completed Railway Exchange Building on Michigan Avenue.

As Burnham would happily admit, for these and other projects he depended heavily on a staff of highly capable and accomplished architect/designers. None of them would ever quite fill the personal and professional void in Burnham's life left by John Root's death, but they all quickly became trusted and valuable associates destined for distinguished careers of their own. Of these colleagues, Ernest Graham had been with Burnham the longest, having served the firm dating back to the days of Burnham and Root. Frederick Dinkelberg, an associate of Charles Atwood in New York, came to Chicago in 1893 to contribute to the World's Fair and was hired into Burnham's company after the fair closed. Dinkelberg had a major role in designing 1901's triangular Fuller Building in New York—soon to be known as the distinctive, now iconic, Flatiron Building—near the point at which Broadway and Fifth Avenue converge. Peirce Anderson had joined the company in 1900 and for his first project was assigned to the mammoth new Marshall Field's department store (now Macy's) on State Street in Chicago, completed in 1902. Two other Burnham architects, Edward Probst and Howard White, would go on to join forces with Ernest Graham and Peirce Anderson to form one of the twentieth century's largest and most successful architecture firms in Chicago: Graham, Anderson, Probst and White.

Burnham's consultation services were in constant and continuing demand in this period in Cleveland and Washington and elsewhere. Little wonder that his schedule, as revealed in his diary notations, repeatedly records a man in constant motion. The travel demands of the 1890s were reaching a new level of frequency and intensity for Burnham. And his correspondence from that time depicts a man energized by activity and challenge but also yearning for respite and longer spans of time at home in Evanston.

The Philippines project would also require more travel abroad, this time—and the first time for Burnham—to Asia and the Pacific. By early October of 1904 he was hard at work in the Twin Peaks "shack" in San Francisco. On October 12 he hosted a luncheon for friends, prominent local officials, and business associates at the Pacific Union Club on Nob Hill. The next day he, his wife, and daughter Margaret, boarded a ship bound for the Far East by way of Honolulu. On October 30 the Burnhams and members of Burnham's team, which included top assistant Peirce Anderson, reached Yokohama, Japan, to begin a three-and-a-half-month sojourn in Japan, the

Philippines, and Hong Kong. At this point in the trip, Mrs. Burnham and daughter Margaret returned to Hawaii to await reuniting with Daniel once the business side of the adventure had reached completion. As with the European trips of earlier years, the journey made a lasting impression on Burnham. He commented on the "wonderful walls covered with pine trees" in Tokyo and examined the city's "great new temples," watched geisha dancers and Japanese wrestling matches, visited the Japanese emperor's "very splendid palace" in Kyoto, rode in rickshaws, and commented on the scenic effect of Hong Kong's "magnificent harbor."[44]

In January, in the ship bound for Hong Kong, Burnham had a chance to relax in white flannels and take in the cool sea air on smooth water. In this reflective mood he found his mind wandering back to a day that was to have great significance in his life and career. "This is the fiftieth anniversary," he recorded in his diary, "of the arrival of Edwin Burnham, wife, and five children in Chicago, where they arrived on the evening of the 18th of January, 1855, at the old dock of the Illinois Central Railroad, at the foot of Lake Street; Daniel Burnham then eight years and four months old." Two days later he mixed his observations of the working activities of Hong Kong Harbor with yet another sentimental memory. "January 20. Watched the loading and the harbor, especially life in the sampans. . . . This was my wedding day."[45]

On February 13 he rejoined his wife and daughter in Honolulu. By the afternoon of February 19 Burnham and Anderson were back with Edward Bennett in the house on Twin Peaks, reengaging with the firm's work on the San Francisco project. Now back in the United States, Burnham found in his quiet moments the opportunity to put his Asian experience in perspective. As he had typically done after earlier travels abroad, Burnham enthused over the fascinating otherness of what he had encountered. "The dive into the Orient has been like a dream," he recorded in his diary. "The lands, the people, and the customs are all very strange and of absorbing interest." Then he tantalizingly suggested that the sights he had seen may have altered some of his most cherished assumptions about architecture. "It surprises me to find how much this trip has modified my views, not only regarding the extreme East, but regarding ourselves and all our European precedents."[46]

Unfortunately he did not indicate with any specificity what Old World precedents he was beginning to question, and little, if anything, in the architectural work that followed can be identified as of distinctly Asian influence. As I have noted, one persistent legend surrounding William Le Baron Jenney's revolutionary use of metal skeleton construction in the Home Insurance Building has Jenney finding inspiration for his innova-

Burnham surveys a hilltop setting as part of his design for Baguio, the new summer capital of the Philippines, circa 1904–05. (Daniel H. Burnham Collection, Ryerson and Burnham Art and Architecture Archives, Art Institute of Chicago. Digital file # 194301_110614-014.)

tion in the light but sturdy supports for native huts in the Philippines. But no such eureka moment seems to have occurred to Burnham nor was one reflected in obvious ways in the firm's subsequent work.

The task of designing and building in the Philippines fell to Burnham's choice for the role: a young product of the École des Beaux-Arts named William Parsons. In Thomas Hines's words, Parsons's "best designs combined a successful mixture and abstraction of Spanish, Oriental, and modern 'industrial' architecture to forge a new architecture appropriate for a tropical climate."[47] At the same time several of the buildings, avenues, and parklands that Burnham had a hand in planning for the Philippines remained securely within the neoclassical traditions of the World's Fair and Burnham's urban-planning approaches in the United States. America's imperialist involvement in the Philippines from the time of Teddy Roosevelt has always invited critical scrutiny and impassioned controversy. But Burnham's imprint on Manila and Baguio endures and remains an accepted, perhaps even cherished, element of the Filipinos' physical cityscape. A bust of Daniel Burnham still stands in Baguio's Burnham Park, and tourists and locals alike still paddle about in the centrally located Burnham Lake.

One characteristic that Daniel Burnham and Louis Sullivan shared was the seriousness and idealism they brought to many elements of architectural thought and planning. Throughout their careers they showed little patience for cutting corners or making do with less. They could philosophize about their ambitions and intentions in ways that could both inspire and cause concern. The sincerity of their most cherished beliefs and convictions was evident to all who knew them, and their friends and associates took their opinions very seriously indeed.

Each man's ability to employ humor as an element in their professional toolkits is less well known and less appreciated. Both Burnham and Sullivan delighted in cogent—sometimes acid, sometimes gentle and self-deprecating—comic observations on their daily encounters and challenges. Sullivan used humor as something of a sword, a means to eviscerate those he saw as his "feudal" reactionary enemies on the architectural battlefield. For Burnham humor was both a natural habit—a way to take personal delight in the absurdities that surrounded him, from domestic adventures of family members to his own frailties and foibles and that of professional associates—and a useful instrument to promote his professional ambitions. The habit of humorous exchange could be used to foster a positive atmosphere within his company, to score points in efforts of persuade and cajole others into accepting his point of view, and to establish and maintain good working relationships with potential clients and influential powerbrokers.

In Burnham this could sometimes take the form of humorous anecdotes accompanied by the caricatures that frequently emerged from his penchant for making impromptu sketches and drawings. Instances of this habit are described in earlier chapters, as in 1867 when Burnham drew an exaggerated self-portrait of the angry look he claimed he could conjure up to scare off intrusive strangers or when, on the Southwest trip of 1883, he showed himself struggling to change photographic plates under loosely draped bedclothes. On a later trip, the European voyage of 1896, he rendered a quick and suggestive sketch of an "Italian tough" standing on the dock. He and other members of his gang taunted their departing friends on board by covering their ears and "chanting with hands to ears, as if enjoying the sound of their own voices, occasionally stopping to smash each other's hats, or deride their departing brothers."[48]

His own professional activities could receive light-hearted treatment, as when Burnham complained of sleeplessness during a business trip because "the sneezes had me in their grasp" or when he reported having spent a day chasing "capitalists" all over New York City before he "finally cornered them, and got some action into the business here."[49] In his L'Enfant-inspired redesign of Washington, DC, Burnham repeatedly referred to the guiding wishes of America's revered first president, whom he familiarly referred to as "our dear Uncle George," at one point declaring that "Old George's serene spirit should rule throughout [the enterprise]; let's have no jig-step in his minuet."[50]

He could make an acute observation in memorable wordplay. "A bad plan," he said once, "will defeat itself; a good plan will do its own argufying."[51] Edward Bennett, his close associate and coauthor on the *Plan of Chicago*, tried to identify the human elements that made Burnham so effective in his dealings with others. He emphasized that "over all was a rich sense of humor—perhaps that would sum up his great quality," which Burnham often expressed in the form of amusing stories or parables. Cass Gilbert remembered a man with a "keen sense of humor, a good raconteur."[52] The "reserve fund of merry wit" and fun-loving nature that Dan Jr. attributed to his father's mother seems to have, in small ways perhaps, seeped into the senior Burnham's observations on daily life and likely contributed to his easygoing relationships with fellow architects and business associates, who fondly dubbed him "Uncle Dan."

Louis Sullivan's writing could be just as high-spirited and effective and at times just as amusing. He could be charming with clients as well. An associate who knew Sullivan in his "great day" said this of him: "One saw the genius of his philosophy of action when he met the contracting parties in witty, convincing argument, all with a touch of humor. They liked him as a thinker, a companion, a man of principle and imagination, truly creative by deed and word."[53]

But self-deprecation and charm were not Sullivan's strong suit, and his most effective witticisms struck sharply at other people, particularly contemporaries who revered outworn and undemocratic "feudal" historical styles. In the last two decades of his life, Sullivan's reputation and talents were largely invested in creative and innovative designs for small Midwestern banks. So it may come as no surprise that he would also take great pleasure in mocking the common practice of building banks in the form of Greco-Roman temples. Bankers of his day believed classical columns and pediments suggested solidity, strength, and a supposedly reassuring commitment to financial conservativism, and thus such elements constituted the preferred design for bank architecture. In contrast Sullivan felt such associations were entirely alien to the business and political environment of modern America. Roman temples may have suited the culture, values, and aspirations of ancient Rome. But if banks were to be imitation Roman temples in America, said Sullivan with typical provocation, "I am going to insist that the banker wear a toga, sandals, and conduct his business in the venerated Latin tongue—oral and written."[54]

He could be just as wickedly devastating on historical approaches to domestic architecture. Responding to the castle-like fortresses Chicago businessman Potter Palmer and others of his class insisted they wanted for themselves in the US, Sullivan wrote, "If you . . . find 'battlements' upon a pretentious modern residence, you will smile and wonder why the archers are not there too."[55] Sullivan disdained traditional styles and long-dead cultures for guidance and insisted his contemporaries instead look to the "form follows function" lessons available from the world of nature. Many modern structures, he said, are as absurd to look at as if "a rattlesnake . . . standing vertically on its head, had brought forth pine cones." A building that tries to contain a steel-frame function in a disguising masonry form seemed no less strange to him than "pumpkin-bearing frogs" or "sparrows in the forms of whales, picking up crumbs from the street."[56] Analogies drenched in acid became something of a specialty to the architectural polemicist in Sullivan.

Sullivan's most famous denunciation of the architectural practices of his time appeared in the autobiography he composed shortly before his death in 1924. By the early 1920s Sullivan had observed the full effect of Burnham's fair and the City Beautiful movement it helped engender across the country and in other parts of the world. The line from the book most often quoted is Sullivan's central generalization: "The damage wrought by the World's Fair will last for half a century from its date, if not longer."[57] The same passage contains the more emphatic characterization of the problem, an extended disease metaphor comically describing the viral "infection" in architecture that he traced back to Chicago in 1893. The "virus of the World's Fair," declared Sullivan, "after a period of incubation in the architectural profession and in the population at large . . . began to show unmistakable signs of the nature of the contagion. There came a violent outbreak of the spread westward, contaminating all that it touched" until "all sense of reality was gone" and in its place illusions and hallucinations—"symptoms all of progressive cerebral meningitis: The blanketing of the brain." And things weren't getting better, he warned. Even younger architects of recent days had developed an "immunity" to common sense, vaccinated against reality with healthy doses of every known European style. The result has been a mindless outburst of historical eclecticism but not architecture. In actuality, "Architecture, be it known, is dead. Let us therefore lightly dance upon its grave, strewing roses as we glide."[58]

Burnham's and Sullivan's ability to express their sometimes diametrically opposed viewpoints in striking images for humorous or dramatic effect enhanced their roles as communicators and influencers. Their prominence was maintained by regular and frequent appearances at architectural conferences and in written contributions to professional publications. Sullivan's language could easily veer into abstruse philosophical speculations—as the early newspaper critic so aptly put it, to "large ideas tending to metaphysics." But he could just as quickly move to find linguistic anchorage in the things of this world, as when he called on his readers to visualize the absurdity of archers peering from around the castellated towers of America's Gilded Age mansions. Burnham's prose was more conventionally tempered but could also combine, in much the same way, impassioned idealism and earth-bound realism.

One of Sullivan's pointed diatribes helped secure his next significant commission, one that was to provide an economic lifeline and a new direction for his architectural legacy. "What Is Architecture: A Study in the American People of Today" was first published in the January 1906 edition of *American Contractor* and later revised for publication in *The Craftsman.* As Robert Twombly has observed in his introduction to the piece, like so much of Sullivan's writing, it is "direct and precise in places but discursive and abstract elsewhere."[59] One brief excerpt may serve to illustrate the point. Sullivan's screed against the mindless historicism of contemporary architecture employed the usual cloudy generalities only to drive the point home by calling on his readers to visualize a concrete image based on a familiar fairy-tale figure: "One longs to wash from this dirty face [of traditionalist architecture] its overlay of timidity and abasement . . . and to see if indeed there be not beneath its forlorn and pitiful aspect, the real face and form of unsuspected Cinderella."[60]

In the small rural town of Owatonna, Minnesota, local banker Carl Bennett happened to come across the *Craftsman* article and took note. Bennett had an unusual combination of traits for a Midwestern businessman: he was, writes Larry Millett, a man who "sought to live like a Renaissance prince in a world of Babbitts."[61] His most heartfelt interests did not involve the business of banking at all. A Harvard graduate, Bennett had nurtured musical and artistic ambitions during his undergraduate years, with dreams of a career as a concert pianist or conductor. But he agreed to return to Owatonna to enter the family business at the insistence of his father, Leonard Loomis Bennett. "L. L." had been a local doctor before establishing Owatonna's Farmers' National Bank in 1873 and serving as its president, and he quickly became a fixture in the town's economic life. It was understandable, and common for wealthy self-made men of this time, to want and expect the eldest son to come home to take over the family business. Carl reluctantly agreed. His wife was later to remark that Carl "would have been much happier as an artist than a banker, I'm sure."[62] Nonetheless when Carl agreed to return to Owatonna and accede to his father's wishes, he willingly embraced his civic as well as his professional duties and did not shy away from enjoying and displaying the privileges his wealth and social position made possible.

So it was not just the practical man of affairs but also the fellow enthusiast for art and music that Louis Sullivan was able to touch through his *Craftsman* article. Bennett sought a proper designer for a new bank and later described how he and associates combed through art and architectural magazines "with the hope of finding some architect whose aim it was to express the thought or use underlying a building, adequately, without fear of precedent, like a virtuoso shaping his material into new forms of use and beauty."[63]

It would be hard to find an architect whose self-regard would have provided a more perfect match for Bennett's criteria than Louis Sullivan. Several key elements of the Sullivanesque philosophy are summarized in this brief portion of Bennett's hopeful statement—that form and function flow most naturally from a kind of interior organic logic and not from historical sources, that a skilled artist (a virtuoso) of independent mind must guide the process, and that the result should express equal parts beauty and utilitarian efficiency.

Of course, Bennett's description was written in 1908 long after Sullivan had already been hired and Bennett had come to know him well. Yet he was clearly viewed from the beginning as the right man for the job. The possible red flags in Sullivan's essay—the contemptuous dismissal of fellow architects, the extravagant rhetoric, the apparent refusal to compromise—did not seem to affect Bennett's determination to offer Louis the job. Construction on the bank began in early 1907, and the completed building opened to the public in the summer of 1908. The result was a small masterpiece: boldly innovative in design, elaborately detailed in decoration, carefully planned to accommodate the needs and cultural customs of the community it was created to serve. Bennett and Sullivan took care to include a "homelike" women's room, complete with low rocking chairs and writing desks, where the wives and children of the male farmers could rest and relax; a "farmers' exchange room" where the men could gather to conduct business and discuss agricultural matters; a consultation room for private business conferences; and a gleaming bank vault plainly visible to customers in order to convey the message that their valuables will be protected in a "jewel box" that is beautiful but also solid, safe, and secure.

The National Farmers' Bank of Owatonna has a welcoming functionality in its layout, but that practical aspect disappears in the dazzling array of colors and ornamentation that engulfs the visitor from every side. Two enormous arched windows filled with luminous stained glass on the south and west sides flood the interior in carefully orchestrated earth tones of gold, green, and brown. These are complemented by expansive murals by painter Oskar Gross set within corresponding arches on the north and east depicting rural scenes of cows grazing in a field and harvesters at work. The intricate design configurations of the plasterwork, stenciling, and terra- cotta on the walls and light fixtures are typical Sullivan flourishes and are among the most elaborate of his career. The simple cube-like brick exterior structure combines a reassuring solidity with enough decorative embroidery—along with the grand arched windows framed, in a standard Sullivan move, by a rectangle—to help offset the otherwise fortress-like appearance. Bands of green terra-cotta run parallel to narrow strips of blue and gold glass mosaic.[64] Much of the detail work must be credited to the skilled hand of George Elmslie, who was intimately involved in every phase of the conception and execution of the project.

Larry Millett's comprehensive 1985 study of the Owatonna bank, *The Curve of the Arch*, provides a vivid picture of the personal connections Sullivan formed while planning and supervising the construction of the bank. When he was in Owatonna, Sullivan stayed with the Bennetts in their spacious home not far from the bank. Just as he had spent happy hours during the flush times of the early 1890s at the home of Dankmar Adler, interacting with the big chief and briefly entering the happy chaos of a noisy family life, so also did he find temporary respite from the gathering storm of financial and other problems during visits to the Bennett household. Writes Millett, "Besides good music, the Bennett home offered two other things Sullivan loved: good food and good conversation. Lydia Bennett arose early every morning to begin fixing elaborate meals for her husband and Sullivan. 'I gave these men five course dinners every day as well as their lunches and breakfasts and Mr. Sullivan found great pleasure, as we always did, in visiting over demitasses of coffee for sometimes as long as an hour.'"[65] Though a solitary, even reclusive, figure for much of his work life, Sullivan was also willing to enter into lengthy conversations—sometimes morphing into prolonged monologues—once he found an audience with whom he shared some kind of intellectual or artistic fellow feeling. This had been the case with Frank Lloyd Wright in the early days of their partnership, and such appeared to be the case now with the Bennetts.

National Farmers' Bank, Owatonna, Minnesota, completed 1908. It was the first of several rural "jewel box" banks Louis Sullivan designed in the final decades of his life. This postcard representation was sent by Sullivan employee Parker Berry in 1917 to his fellow Sullivan assistant Homer Sailor. "Wish you might see this bank," he wrote on the reverse side. "It is a wonder." (Homer Grant Sailor Papers, Ryerson and Burnham Art and Architecture Archives, Art Institute of Chicago. Digital file # 197201_150217-120.)

That Carl Bennett was satisfied with the final architectural result of this relationship is evident. The article Bennett wrote for *The Craftsman* in 1908, though clearly intended to provide positive puffery for his expensive bank, contained several passages that convey the impression of a man sincerely expressing pride in what he and his like-minded architect had wrought. "The craftsmanship displayed in the construction, fittings, and decoration of this building," wrote Bennett, "is astonishingly good for this machine-made age, showing as it does so many of the characteristics of the golden age of handicrafts. Everything is of special design and was first put on paper by Mr. Sullivan. . . . The owners of this building feel that they have a true and lasting work of art—a structure which, though 'built for business,' will increase in value as the years go by."[66] Bennett wasn't wrong. Present-day Owatonna tour guide Matthew Jessop remembers suggesting to a group of visiting architects that the cost of constructing and decorating the bank in today's dollars would likely total approximately $4 million. On hearing

Interior of the National Farmers' Bank, Owatonna, Minnesota. Louis Sullivan, architect. (Richard Nickel Archive, Ryerson and Burnham Art and Architecture Archives, Art Institute of Chicago. Digital file # 201006_110801-016.)

this, and after a close examination of the complex designs of the exterior and interior, one of the senior architects responded, "This? Nowadays? More like $100 million."

The significance of the Owatonna bank did not go unnoticed. The reputation that Sullivan had built on breathtaking designs for theaters, synagogues and church buildings, warehouses, department stores, office buildings, and skyscrapers now found a second life in the creation of smaller rural banks and financial institutions. Banking officials in other towns saw what could be done to bring attention and prestige to their places of business without resorting to the cliches of classical architecture. By the spring of 1909 Sullivan was drawing up plans for a new People's Savings Bank in Cedar Rapids, Iowa.

The successful completion of the Owatonna project and the occasional pleasures of evenings with the Bennetts, however, did little to dispel the host of emotional and financial pressures that were steadily weighing ever more heavily on Sullivan. The only other notable commissions that reached completion during this period were a Prairie Style house in Riverside, Illinois, for the Henry Babson family and an expansive home built for University of Wisconsin biochemistry professor Harold Bradley and his wife in Madison, Wisconsin. In addition, by the latter years of the decade, Sullivan's marriage to Margaret was clearly failing. Financial pressures had forced the couple to change Chicago addresses several times in less than ten years. Sullivan attempted to impose severe economies on their spending, which inevitably led to marital disagreements. Louis was spending more and more time away from the increasingly dingy dwellings they were forced to call home. Trying to drown his sorrows in frequent late-night drinking bouts just made matters worse. Elmslie remembered Margaret visiting the offices in the Auditorium tower in tears, wondering what to do with "her Louis" and complaining of having spent too many nights assisting him into bed.[67]

A true low point—though given the downward spiral of the next several years, it's hard to call it the lowest—occurred on November 29, 1909, when Sullivan listed for sale at auction a vast trove of many cherished worldly goods numbering in the hundreds. The items included oriental rugs, furniture, artwork, tapestries, and an assortment of Sullivan's books dating back to his Paris days. The full range of Sullivan's interests was evident. In addition to multiple works on architecture, the sale included historical, musical, and philosophical works; literary works such as Whitman's *Leaves of Grass*, Chaucer's *Canterbury Tales,* Mark Twain's *Roughing It,* and collections of Ibsen and Shakespeare plays; as well as scientific and geographical treatises of all kinds.[68] The sales results were a severe disappointment. He told Bennett, "The auction was a slaughter. I fully expected to realize from $2000 to $2500. I netted $1100."[69]

One week later Margaret left her husband Louis for good. Sullivan thoughtfully gave her almost all the money from the sale of his personal items to begin her new life in New York. George Elmslie, the faithful assistant who had often worked at reduced pay for Sullivan over two decades and who had been the co-designer in all but name for the Owatonna bank and other recent projects, left the firm the same year to begin a new partnership with William Purcell in Minneapolis. Before long Sullivan's financial situation had become so serious that he was forced to sell off the remaining properties at his beloved retreat in Ocean Springs, Mississippi.[70]

Sullivan knew the extent of the trouble he was in. He agreed to seek help from a friend, Dr. George Arndt, who invited Sullivan to an extended stay at Arndt's home in Mount Vernon, Ohio, for intensive treatment and, in effect, psychological counseling. "After 3 days of intense suffering, mental, moral, and physical," Louis wrote, "I began to mend and my progress was wonderfully rapid. At the end of 2½ weeks I was practically normal, my courage, strength of nerve body and brain had returned." He was also able to put a finger on the key reason behind his declining fortunes: "My crisis has, with varying fortunes been steadily approaching during the past 17 years. I have all along intuitively felt that the cause lay in a flaw in my own character which I, alone, could not discover. . . . [Dr. Arndt says it is] none other than my persistent lack of kindly feeling toward my fellow men. He is right, and I intend to change."[71]

Sullivan's association with Arndt was much more than mere doctor/patient. Once again he had found a kind of surrogate family that sporadically satisfied some missing element in his life. Arndt's daughter Mary recalled numerous visits, with Sullivan joining her father for songfests around the piano, the two of them belting out tunes in accomplished tenor voices—compositions by Schubert, Schumann, and a musical rendition of *The Rubaiyat of Omar Khayyam.* Mary remembered Sullivan helping her with French lessons and engaging in long talks with her father on "art, literature, history, philosophy, politics, human nature."[72]

Cultivating kindly feeling toward his fellow men had never been a problem for Daniel Burnham, and this gift of character often resulted in personal and professional benefits. Any intended or unintended payoff in business or reputational terms required a long gestation period. This was the case for what was to become known as the Burnham Plan for Chicago. Burnham's interest in remaking and reimagining parts of Chicago dated back to the years immediately following the World's Fair, when he started recommending plans for a renewed park system along the city's south shore, including reconfigured roads, neighborhoods, and new lakefront features. Over the years, he rarely passed up an opportunity to present his evolving ideas and sketches to business groups and political leaders, or to just about any group who expressed interest. His stated goal was to create abundant natural spaces for relaxation and recreation, especially for those located in poorer areas in the city, where he believed beautiful parkland would have the power to improve physical well-being and promote moral uplift. Of one such site nearing completion he declared, "the police say it has changed young people in the neighborhood so much that certain crimes have all but disappeared."[73] Daniel Burnham's friends and associates would always listen with attention and respect, even if the result was no immediate action.

The midpoint of the twentieth century's first decade found Daniel Burnham actively and happily involved in his varied business and public-service projects. Suggestions that he was anywhere near considering retirement during this period were met with stern rebukes. To one *Chicago Examiner* reporter in 1905 he wrote, "Will you please contradict the statement you made in the paper this morning regarding my retirement? I have no thought of doing so. . . . If you will come around and interview me about ten years from now you may possibly be able to use the line you published this morning. I am quite curious to know where you got the idea."[74]

In 1906, at about the same time Louis Sullivan was being summoned to Minnesota to initiate a new phase in his career, Burnham began to find serious support for his plans to remake Chicago. He had pinned his hopes on cooperation with the staid and generally conservative Commercial Club, but instead an organization of younger businessmen called the Merchants Club stepped forward. By chance this new opportunity in city planning occurred just as Burnham's plans for San Francisco were beginning to fall apart. The San Francisco earthquake of April 1906 had disrupted the city fathers' priorities, and many of Burnham's dreams for re-envisioning the city center were put on hold. That summer, when Burnham was returning by train from San Francisco after an uphill effort to convince local officials to revive his plan, he encountered Joseph Medill McCormick, scion of the *Chicago Tribune* Medill family and a Merchants Club member. McCormick had also served as a newspaper correspondent in the Philippines not long before Burnham's involvement there. McCormick engaged Burnham in conversations during the long ride home, and he tested Burnham's interest in shifting his attention from doing urban planning on the West Coast to doing the same for their home city. Burnham acknowledged that it would be an "enormous job" that would require support from influential civic organizations, but he was clearly open to the idea.[75]

Tired of "critical, 'pin-pricking'" at small problems and eager to undertake "a big piece of work that would really leave its imprint in the city," Merchants Club officers later approached Burnham in Chicago and convinced him to take charge of developing a blueprint for improvement along the lines he and McCormick had discussed.[76] Events moved swiftly in the months to come. Burnham agreed to take on the task, once again donating his time but stipulating that he was to assume full authority over the project. In 1907 the Merchants Club merged with the Commercial Club, maintaining the latter's name, and the newly enlarged organization set about fundraising and drumming up community support for the plan. The effort was, in fact, prodigious and yet another commitment that would absorb enormous amounts of Daniel Burnham's time, if perhaps reducing the number of cross-country journeys he took by rail.

Meetings were held over abundant lunches at long tables in Burnham's new offices in the Railway Exchange Building on Michigan Avenue across from the Art Institute. State legislators, railway executives, and city council and park board members often sat in. As Charles Moore noted, "Scarcely a day passed without a meeting."[77] The committees formed to execute the plan were once more, as with the World's Fair, composed almost entirely of Chicago's power brokers. Some of those names have become familiar to anyone who has explored the far reaches of Chicago's cityscape: the brewer Charles Wacker (Wacker Drive); Marshall Field's president John G. Shedd (Shedd Aquarium); Art Institute president Charles L. Hutchinson (Hutchinson Commons, the University of Chicago); and lumber baron Martin Ryerson (the Ryerson and Burnham Libraries, Art Institute of Chicago; Louis Sullivan's Ryerson Tomb, Graceland Cemetery). Others, with names less recognizable to today's Chicagoans, exercised enormous political and economic influence at the time: attorney and grocery king Franklin MacVeagh, later secretary of the treasury under Taft; insurance executive Charles D. Norton and railroad president Frederic Delano, two of the original Merchants Club members who recruited Burnham for the task; and Cyrus H. McCormick Jr., son of the founder of International Harvester and the company's president.

Chicago's movers and shakers assumed that they, and not grass-roots community groups or ordinary citizens, would know best how to remake the city. They also assumed, correctly, that the titans of Chicago business and politics were best positioned to generate the funds necessary for such an enterprise. They did so by soliciting pledges for "subscriptions" among themselves and their friends and associates, first set at $100 each, and later at $300 spread out over three years. Carl Smith's study, *The Plan of Chicago: Daniel Burnham and the Remaking of the American City,* reprints the initial handwritten estimates Burnham made of projected expenses, which Burnham thought would total a little under $25,000. The largest single expense of $7,200 would be reserved for Burnham's assistant Edward Bennett, who was entrusted with primary responsibility for the project and who was ultimately recognized as co-author of the finished product. The jottings included $2,500 for "2 1st Class helpers," $600 for a stenographer, and $500 for someone to edit the finished document. Burnham's estimates assumed everything could be completed in a single year. But as the scope of the project grew, the time and money expended grew as well. The final cost came to approximately $80,000.[78]

Daniel Burnham's reputation for overseeing large-scale enterprises and his willingness to reach out to possible interested parties and city leaders were critical to the plan's success. There was no question that he and his company were the guiding forces behind the operation, even to the point of constructing special rooms for the purpose on top of his Railway Exchange Building. Burnham tirelessly wrote dozens of letters early on in a frenzy of information gathering. He hosted numerous meetings of the various committee planners in his company offices. As he had done in his earlier urban planning efforts, he turned to the great European cities for inspiration and ideas, and none more so than the epic midcentury restructuring of Paris by Baron Haussmann.

During this period Burnham maintained oversight for the operations of his firm, met with clients, was called upon to consult with contacts in Washington, DC, over the placement of a presidential memorial to Ulysses S. Grant, and managed yet another trip abroad in 1907. Despite the inevitable rigors of foreign travel, Burnham viewed this as a chance to escape with his family from professional demands but also to introduce sons Hubert and Dan Jr., both of whom intended to pursue careers in architecture, to the glories of European architecture.

So from April of 1907 through most of June, Burnham toured England and France yet again to immerse himself in the architectural heritage of Old Europe. And his enthusiasm for what he saw was just as sincere and effusive as it had been during his first trip abroad in 1896. Arriving in Canterbury, he felt he was "immediately in another fairyland." The view from the iron gateway of Winchester Cathedral, he wrote, "is the most sumptuous thing inside of any church I know. . . . As a glory of rich effect, combined into one great mass of decorations, nothing exceeds it." Of a particular effect in Rouen, "So far as this sort of thing goes surely neither Paris or Amiens can surpass it." This did not mean his critical faculties or his sense of humor were entirely suppressed. He took, for instance, a kind of malicious glee in denigrating Eugène Viollet-le-Duc's nineteenth-century restoration work in the apse at Amiens Cathedral, comparing it to the draping of a garish colored tunic over Praxiteles's classical sculpture of the god Hermes. He looked forward to the day when "it can all come off . . . when France is undergoing one of her noble moments of artistic sanity."[79]

Diary entries from the trip divulge two persistent concerns for Burnham: a sharpened awareness of his own mortality and related reflections on the value of spiritual experience. In his public pronouncements Burnham repeatedly stressed the aesthetic and moral benefits of great architecture. In his private notations something like the Swedenborgian insistence on the seamless unity between the material world and the world of spirit was ever more likely to occupy his thoughts. Images suggestive of Swedenborg's

Daniel Burnham explains key concepts of the 1909 *Plan of Chicago* in his Railway Exchange offices, October 1908. (Edward H. Bennett Collection, Ryerson and Burnham Art and Architecture Archives, Art Institute of Chicago. Digital file # 197301_151023-125.)

heaven appeared, with its recognizable environment of beautiful buildings and gardens very like those on earth. Deeply moved by the cathedral at Amiens, for instance, Burnham wrote, "We intend to stay with this church until she has said much more to us—a sort of goodbye to the greatness of earth for me, an opening of the sky for the boys into that architectural heaven toward which I hope their thoughts are leading them." The sculptural excellence of Amiens was great, but Chartres, with its almost perfect union of skilled masonry and its magnificent stained-glass windows illuminating the interior with God's light, brought one even closer to heaven. "Amiens appeals as a statue does. Chartres appeals as an angel might. The color and form of the major and minor things of this great monument have lifted us outside of ourselves and above the world." And later, in the presence of such "overpowering beauty" of glass "sumptuous and of quality indescribable," he remarked, "not on earth again can we hope for the artist's higher emotion to envelop us as it has done here."[80] Compare for a moment these observations with a representative passage from Swedenborg's writings. On viewing palaces of heaven "as if made of pure gold . . . and precious stones," Swedenborg reported that "such is the architecture of heaven that you would say that art there is in its art; and no wonder, because the art itself is from heaven."[81]

Burnham returned from this European trip in June 1907. There was more to do on the Chicago plan and a variety of other projects, but that didn't prevent him from embarking on another visit to the Old World in late 1908 and early 1909. This time the itinerary began as before in England and France but then extended to Germany and ended in Rome. Burnham had been involved in promotion and fundraising for the American Academy in Rome since the years immediately following the World's Fair. The brainchild of his friend McKim, the academy had been founded as an American answer to the Ecole des Beaux-Arts in Paris. In Rome Burnham visited with school officials and reported on the progress and affairs of the academy.[82]

During this period, Burnham began to be plagued with a foot infection and eventually preliminary indicators of diabetes. At one point the infection was painful enough to require hospitalization and an operation. Burnham's diary notes that on July 31, 1907, a Dr. Phillips "found the foot was poisoned and treated accordingly."[83] Several months of doing business on crutches and in a "wheeled chair" followed. In December he could finally resume his personal exercise routine with a trainer named Carver, and it took until March of the following year for him to fit a shoe over his afflicted foot.

Edward Bennett visited Burnham during a hospital stay in February 1908 and expressed concern that Burnham "was in real danger." Said Bennett, "As usual, he was serene. We talked of Swedenborg, or, rather I listened to him discourse on the subject, and came away strengthened in purpose." A few days later, visiting Burnham in Evanston, Bennett noted that Swedenborg's teachings were very much still on Burnham's mind: "We talked of the plan [of Chicago] but more of the philosophy of life—and his belief of the infinite possibilities of material expression of the spiritual."[84]

Burnham's health throughout the last half of the decade, even as he was embracing full involvement in the plan of Chicago, was a cause of concern. Charles Norton recalled that, as early as one of those initial 1906 meetings, he and Frederic Delano received news that their new city-wide plan had secured initial financing.

> [We] raced over to tell Burnham to begin, that we were financed. He was sitting in that beautiful office, high up in the Railway Exchange Building, where for three years thereafter we were to meet so often. He was gazing out over the lake front, and he appeared to be in serious distress. "It is wonderful, Charles," he said, "but I am afraid it is no use. My doctor

has just been here to tell me that I have a mortal disease—that I have at most three years to live.[85]

The young, ambitious businessmen standing in Burnham's presence did not know how to respond to this sudden, unanticipated obstacle to completing their complicated mission. Before Norton's mind had a chance to fully process the gravity of the news, he found himself blurting out, "But Mr. Burnham, that is just time enough; it will take only three years." In response, said Norton, Burnham merely laughed and said, "You are right. I will do it."[86]

Burnham had long enjoyed the consumption habits of well-to-do capitalists of his time and class. He enjoyed a good cigar, fine wines, and rich foods served in multiple courses. He was no stranger to extravagant banquets. Despite a concurrent belief in regular exercise and conditioning, routine games of golf, occasional roughing-it expeditions to the north woods, and repeated efforts at dieting, Burnham had long ago left behind the slim, athletic youth of high-school days. Photos from as early as the 1880s show a mature man of means with an ever-thickening neck and waistline. In 1898, at the age of 52, he could still take pride in his appearance, writing in biographical notes, "Mr Burnham is 5'11" in his shoes, and weighs about 200 lbs, his eyes are blue and his hair brown, and now, at the age of 52, his hair is full and scarcely touched with grey."[87] Whether the "mortal disease" the doctor had been referring to in 1906 was related to diabetes or some other malady is unclear. But as Charles Norton was quick to point out, that particular medical prognostication turned out to be off by several years.[88]

With health issues perhaps on his mind Burnham briefly considered resigning from his consulting position on the Washington project, hoping to restrict his city planning activities to the new initiative in Chicago. In a letter written in 1907 to Charles McKim, he admitted that Chicago was now absorbing the bulk of his interest and attention, partly because it could serve as a valedictory for his career as an urban planner. "It was undertaken as a sort of last campaign and because of a sense of obligation to my own city," Burnham wrote.[89] By 1909 he was envisioning a peaceful retirement, wherein he would be expected to do nothing more than to quietly sit on a veranda and smoke his cigar.[90]

At long last Burnham's finished report, simply titled *Plan of Chicago*, was published on July 4, 1909. He and Edward Bennett shared authorship credit equally, and Charles Moore's contributions as editor were prominently noted on the title page. Kristen Schaffer has examined Burnham's early drafts of the document, with revelatory insights that articulate how strongly Swedenborgian idealism influenced Burnham's thinking throughout the process. She emphasizes how Swedenborg's ideas on usefulness and correspondence likely entered into Burnham's contributions to the *Plan*. Burnham's willingness to donate his time to the project, as he had typically done with other city-planning enterprises, was an example of the Swedenborgian dictum that one should use one's practical gifts to benefit not just the self but the many. And Schaffer notes that Burnham's concentric transportation rings mirror not just Georges-Eugène Haussman's post-revolution plan for Paris but also Swedenborg's vision of correspondence between the circles of the solar system and the similar material arrangements of heaven, amounting to "the inscription of a divine order upon Chicago." Her description of Burnham's indebtedness to one Swedenborgian article of faith—that the "internal spiritual origin [gives] birth to the physical"—even sounds vaguely suggestive of Sullivan's concept of a "seed germ" that must ultimately express the material form contained within it.[91]

As Schaffer demonstrates, Burnham's drafts and notes show an active social conscience at work in a number of his recommendations, many of which did not make it into the published version. Burnham's proposed designs included provisions for day-care facilities to relieve the burdens of working mothers, police stations in which police activity was readily visible to the citizenry to prevent unseen abuses, widely accessible public toilets in city centers, and restaurants of all price ranges in lakefront parks. She even argues that Burnham's much-criticized advocacy of the Beaux-Arts elements for public buildings had a basis in Swedenborgian mysticism: the timeless beauty represented by the White City in 1893, Burnham believed, could be replicated in permanent stone and inspire spiritual and moral uplift among all social classes. In Schaffer's words, Beaux-Arts formalism had "an imprint of cosmological significance" for Burnham. "It was a sacralization of space, a way of bringing spiritual order to the socio-economic free-for-all of early twentieth-century Chicago."[92]

It's hard *not* to see in these notes and recommendations elements of Swedenborg's light and nature mysticism. Burnham's consistent belief in the edifying and spiritually refreshing effects of parks and gardens, from the early days of his Lakefront Park plans through all of his subsequent city-planning exercises, is fully represented here in the many suggestions for expanded and well-maintained green spaces, most of which survived in the published plan's chapter 4.[93] As a rule, Burnham did not specifically discuss his religious convictions in his professional conversations (keeping private matters private was, said Charles Moore, "one of many reticences"),[94] but Swedenborgian idealism lurks not very far beneath the surface of most of his proposals and public statements.

Burnham's Swedenborgian intentions to include the healing and spiritually refreshing properties of nature in his architecture and city planning anticipate those of twenty-first-century "biophilic" architects who integrate abundant plant life with building design and city planning. In this sense he may be considered more biophilic than even Louis Sullivan, who mostly was devoted to representing natural forms in artistic configurations of terracotta and brick and iron. In a larger sense Burnham explicitly chose the term *organic* to describe the *Plan of Chicago* as a whole. To create a unified city, he said, it must be consciously designed so that "each portion will have organic relation to all other portions."[95]

Some passages in the unfinished *Plan*—in addition to those identified by Schaffer—may also suggest a Swedenborgian influence. Burnham's recommendations for school design, for instance, included a curious suggestion for classroom orientation. "It may be broadly said," Burnham wrote, "that the experience of the last few years has shown that children brought up in sun-lit rooms have some percentage of better health and better moral tone, everything else being equal, than those who have lived the majority of their lives in north rooms." Since sunlight plays an important role in strengthening body and mind, surely it was "the first and most effective agent to be used for this end." Classrooms should be situated in such a way as to maximize the infusion of natural light—in other words, no north-facing classrooms.[96] The sun has a similarly central role to play in Swedenborgian theology, in which the "first proceeding" of divine love and divine wisdom flows from the sun.[97]

Of course the need for natural light in indoor spaces had also been a practical requirement in the 1880s and 1890s, when electric lighting was still in its infancy. Even when the *Plan* was published in 1909, some assumed a continued reliance on light courts into the future, as Jules Guerin's expansive watercolor views of the projected city of the future in the *Plan* show. Carol Willis observed that architects considered natural light the most important element in setting dimensions for offices in tall buildings well into the 1940s.[98] But the fact that Burnham's unusual rationale for avoiding north-facing classrooms did not make it into the published *Plan* suggests that this notion was not seen by his fellow planners as a serious need and may, at least in part, have owed something to Burnham's more personal convictions and beliefs.

By decade's end the professional and personal fortunes of Louis Sullivan and Daniel Burnham had fully diverged. They were no longer seen as competitors and occasional partners in an identifiable Chicago movement of architectural innovation and enterprise. The invigorating world-

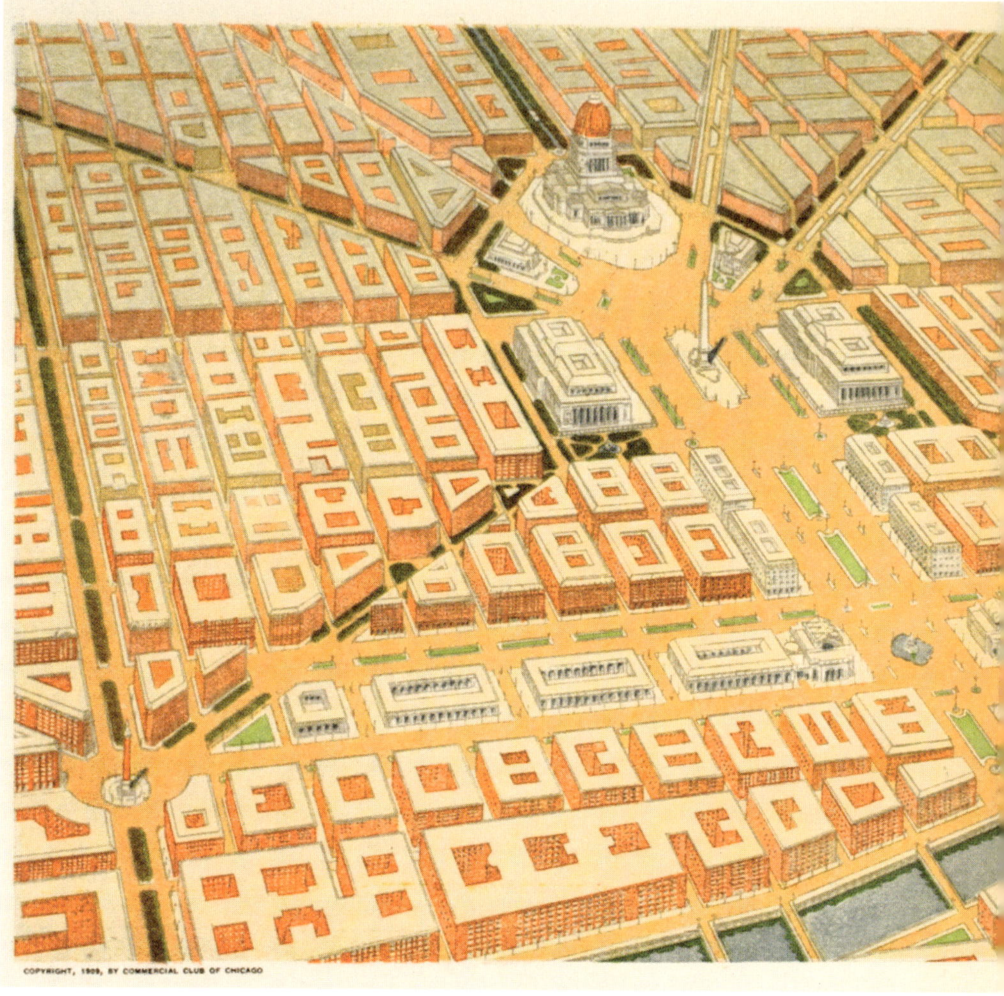

wide explosion of positive attention generated by the 1893 World's Fair was gradually receding into the background, though it continued to influence the Burnham-inspired City Beautiful movement. Sullivan continued to experience reduced commissions, brought about in part by his abrasive personality, his stubborn insistence on artistic independence, and his public expressions of contempt for the work of many of his fellow architects. These factors, along with personal crises of a failed marriage, descent into a dark phase of alcoholism, and the disappointing sale of many of his cherished personal possessions, brought him to the brink of failure. Daniel Burnham's circumstances were quite the opposite. The day-to-day work of his large firm and his talented assistants still flourished, and he was wealthy enough and

Jules Guérin's striking watercolors offered colorful depictions of the Burnham Plan's imagined future for Chicago. This image represents one proposal for the area surrounding a grandiose Civic Center west of the river. Note the convergence of a system of diagonal boulevards and railway lines, the uniform cornice heights for buildings, and the assumption that commercial structures will continue to require open central courts for light and ventilation. (Ryerson and Burnham Libraries Book Collection, Art Institute of Chicago. Digital file # 000000_140108_002.)

connected enough to donate much of his time to large visionary projects in city planning, despite increasing age and emerging health concerns.

Neither man was quite done yet. The Owatonna bank had already begun to attract notice from bankers throughout the Midwest and created opportunities for Sullivan to keep his moribund architectural practice alive, however diminished, into the next decade. Burnham was once again basking in widespread acclaim, this time for the 1909 *Plan of Chicago,* several key elements of which were soon to be set in motion. He was comfortable assuming the role of elder statesman in his field, courted and consulted by presidents, business titans, mayors, and fellow members of the architectural elite. But the sixty-three-year-old did not know how much time would be left for him to occupy this exalted station.

8

Downward to Darkness

1910s–1924

ON THE MORNING OF October 14, 1910, Daniel Burnham delivered yet another speech, this one at a town-planning conference in London before, as one correspondent put it, "a crowded assemblage of the most brilliant architects of the world."[1] It contained the most famous words he would ever utter, although by dint of a historical oversight, their very existence remained in question for more than a hundred years. What was on his mind was not the prospect of creating the words and phrases that would forever be associated with his name but a question relating to democracy itself—specifically, whether future city planners and architects would be able to change the face of great cities through democratic means. He explicitly thought they could.

"My subject," he said, "is a city of the future, under a Democratic government," citing as particular American strengths "our mixture of bloods, our new environment, our searching publicity and our growing intelligence." His points of emphasis here are revealing. A "mixed blood" populace, presumably, would not put up monolithic resistance to new ideas and change. He had made this point earlier in a note to Charles Moore, when he foresaw a "coming American," the product "of all the varied national and racial forces commingling here," who would join Chicago's "argonauts of adventurers" in welcoming purposeful democratic change.[2] And the power of publicity, as he recently had seen it practiced in Chicago and elsewhere, could overcome self-serving politicians and knee-jerk defenders of the status quo. Burnham believed democratic governance meant civic-minded power brokers united in collaborative effort to move public opinion, to convince ordinary citizens of the "value of plans to bring convenience and beauty into the hearts of cities" and thereby create an irresistible force to effect the change needed.

When Burnham told his audience, "Plenary democracies can do what we want them to do," the *we* contained more than a hint of ambiguity. Did it identify a circle of socially and professionally connected experts or the people in affected communities or the people at large? Did it imply that the interests of all these groups were essentially identical? Burnham's belief in democratic architecture contained the same tensions and contradictions as Louis Sullivan's democratic "man-search." In Sullivan's case, democracy meant the power of each individual to chart his or her own path in near-perfect freedom from the constraints of history or conventional ways of thinking. The artist should be free to create without interference. Majority sentiment or majority rule did not factor in his thinking. If people in a community were to express a preference for classical columns on banks, for instance, Sullivan would surely have contended that it was the duty of the architect to overrule them, perhaps to show them the error of their ways and to create the kinds of buildings that the architect is certain would *truly* express their democratic culture. Burnham's view was more collaborative than Sullivan's—more *we* than *I*—but it took for granted that the "best men," the charitably minded few with the expertise and power to make big things happen, could together reshape the physical environment in ways beneficial to the silent, and if necessary persuadable, multitudes.

Burnham singled out for praise several powerful benefactors in his speech. Of Montreal's railroad magnate and art collector William C. Van Horne he said, "Sir William is one of the three or four first men of Canada. He is a fair sample of the kind of people who are beginning to think and work for the realization of a new architectural and spiritual era in the great cities of the North American continent." Having neatly linked architecture to spiritual rebirth in a typical Burnham move, he then went on to acknowledge that for Van Horne, as for all those in the city-planning movement, "The most difficult task of all before us is that of raising public interest up to the level of definite action." Architects and planners design and propose and then must work to bring the people along to embrace the vision.

The spiritual note appeared again in Burnham's predictions for the city of the future. Despite the remarkable changes he had both witnessed and helped foster over the previous four decades, Chicago remained plagued by loosely regulated factories, dust, soot, a foul-smelling river, and horse manure. Against that background Burnham's listeners must have felt he was conjuring up an almost impossible urban dream.

> Our city of the future will be without smoke, dust, or gases from manufacturing plants and the air will, therefore, be pure. The streets will be as clean as our drawing-rooms to-day. Smoke will be thoroughly consumed,

> and the gases liberated in manufacture will be tanked and burned. Railways will be operated electrically, all building operations will be effectually shut in to prevent the escape of dust, and horses will disappear from the streets. Out of all these things will come not only commercial economy but bodily health and spiritual joy.

Burnham was partly right, of course. Or at least he was prescient in his conviction that environmental issues such as these would deeply matter decades hence, and that architects would be enlisted to help resolve them. He was just as certain, as he repeatedly insisted, of the moral and spiritual benefits of increased allotments of greenspace. He urged his fellow planners to build more parks because they encouraged good citizenship and offered the city dweller "the balm his spirit needs." As for waterfronts, he declared, "keep all the shore for the people."

After making an extended case for city planning in the context of democratic culture, Burnham launched into what a reporter aptly called "an apotheosis of enthusiasm, imagination, and hope":

> Make no little plans; they have no magic to stir men's blood and probably themselves will not be realized. Make big plans; aim high in hope and work, remembering that a noble, logical diagram once recorded will never die, but long after we are gone will be a living thing, asserting itself with ever-growing insistency. Remember that our sons and grandsons are going to do things that would stagger us. Let your watchword be order and your beacon beauty.

On the matter of future impact, Burnham was largely on point. The "diagram" of the 1909 *Plan of Chicago* was never fully realized, but its influence remains. Whenever major changes are proposed for the shape of the city, some interested parties are almost certain to refer back, whether positively or negatively, to the vision outlined in the Burnham Plan. For example, in 2007, the Chicago organization Friends of the Parks began revisiting the question of whether to extend the city's public lakefront all the way into the northern suburbs, including beachfront along Burnham's home turf in Evanston. The effort would highlight Burnham's vision for full public access to the city's lakefront parks and recognize the approaching hundredth anniversary of the *Plan of Chicago*.[3] Just as Burnham foresaw, the chief difficulty lay in convincing the public to go along. Residents at the northern edge of the city, many of whose high-rise homes bordered the lake, wanted no part of new parkland and bike paths pushing the shoreline away from them.

How was it that Burnham's stirring paragraph became so famous a part of his legacy when for so many years no one could determine whether he ever actually said it? Burnham's friend and associate Charles Moore included the "Make no little plans" paragraph in his two-volume 1921 biography, saying Burnham had formulated this "injunction" as early as 1907 and often repeated it, so that it had quickly become "the motto of city planners since that day."[4] But Moore's otherwise meticulously detailed and researched biography was minimally footnoted and offered no source for the quote. A version of the speech reproduced in a book published by the Royal Institute of British Architects after the London event contained segments of several sentences in the Moore quotation but left out the phrases "Make no little plans" and "Let your watchword be order and your beacon beauty."[5]

The Art Institute of Chicago has in its collection a 1918 printed card with Burnham's words, in Moore's version, enshrined within an elaborate border. San Francisco architect Willis Polk sent it as a Christmas greeting to *Plan* co-author Edward Bennett, and the card also gives 1907 as the famous lines' point of origin. Polk had apparently been sending cards like this since around 1912. Clearly Moore was correct in his assertion that the passage, including "Make no little plans; they have no magic to stir men's blood," had by then become familiar to many in the field and especially to those who knew and revered Daniel Burnham, even as the precise source remained unknown.

In 1957 Henry H. Saylor published an article that asked the key question: "'Make No Little Plans': Daniel Burnham Thought It, But Did He Say It?" Saylor essentially followed Dan Jr.'s speculation that Willis Polk created the famous paragraph by stitching together disparate lines, that Burnham had said at one time or another, into a satisfactory and inspiring whole.[6] In Carl Smith's 2006 book *The Plan of Chicago,* the "famous dictum" is noted to have been "attributed (bur never definitively) to Burnham."[7] Thomas Hines, in the second edition of his comprehensive biography, still couldn't document the source of Burnham's statement in its entirety, though he correctly deduced that most of it may have been drawn from Burnham's 1910 London speech. Hines too surmised that Burnham never actually spoke the words exactly as Moore and Polk had rendered them.[8]

All of these researchers agreed that the language used and the sentiments expressed were quintessential Burnham, but the exact origins of the key phrases remained muddled. Then in 2019 tour guide and prolific author Adam Seltzer posted on the website Mysterious Chicago a piece entitled "Burnham's 'Make No Little Plans' Quote: Apocryphal No More!" Seltzer had located an article published on October 15, 1910, in the *Chicago Record-Herald* with large portions of Burnham's London speech recorded verbatim.[9] The headline read "Stirred by Burnham, Democracy Champion," thus accurately stressing the central theme of democracy in city planning.[10]

Nonetheless there, at the end, were the words of Polk's Christmas card and Moore's excerpt, word for word, including the famous opening lines.

"The quote," observed Seltzer, "is not a compilation or a hodge-podge, but is, in fact, something that was attributed to Burnham in his lifetime, right after he said it."[11] Other papers and magazines from the period also picked up the lines as spoken in London. In July 1912, for example, the *American Architect* fully cited the famous passage, which the editors said they, in turn, had taken from an article in *Collier's* magazine.[12] Burnham's words, distributed in more than one publication at the time and possibly used on more than one occasion, would have their effect for decades to come.[13]

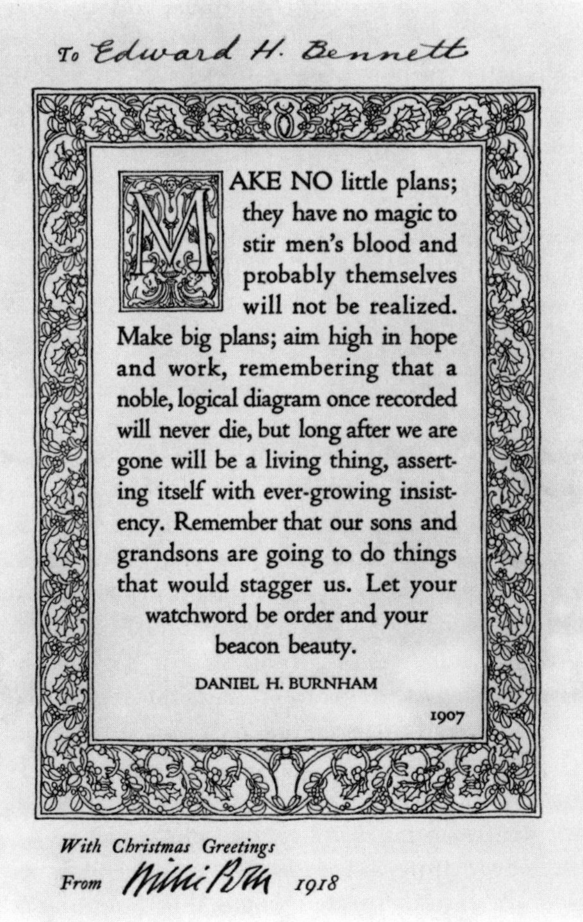

To Edward H. Bennett

MAKE NO little plans; they have no magic to stir men's blood and probably themselves will not be realized. Make big plans; aim high in hope and work, remembering that a noble, logical diagram once recorded will never die, but long after we are gone will be a living thing, asserting itself with ever-growing insistency. Remember that our sons and grandsons are going to do things that would stagger us. Let your watchword be order and your beacon beauty.

DANIEL H. BURNHAM

1907

With Christmas Greetings

From Willis Polk *1918*

Willis Polk, who served as the Burnham company's San Francisco representative, sent out this Christmas card in 1918 to friends and associates. For many years the card was one of the only sources for the entire passage containing Burnham's "Make no little plans" catchphrase. The word-for-word accuracy of the statement was finally established by Adam Seltzer in 2019. Polk's 1907 attribution remains unconfirmed. (Historic Architecture and Landscape Image Collection, Ryerson and Burnham Art and Architecture Archives, Art Institute of Chicago. Digital file #197301.nosmallplans card_mended.jpg.

The need to widen what was then the northernmost segment of Michigan Avenue and the stretch of Pine Street north of the river is evident in this pre-improvement photo of a traffic bottleneck where Michigan Avenue meets Randolph Street. (Edward H. Bennett Collection, Ryerson and Burnham Art and Architecture Archives, Art Institute of Chicago. Digital file # 48375.)

By the time Burnham delivered the London speech, efforts to make the *Plan of Chicago* a reality in his home city were already underway. A Chicago Plan Commission had been formed, with brewing magnate Charles Wacker named as its chair. His first order of business, for which Burnham advocated, was to initiate a massive effort to convince the public and policymakers to implement Burnham's plan. Wacker hired Walter L. Moody in 1911 to conduct the day-to-day business of promotion, including the creation of a reader-friendly summary of the plan, *Wacker's Manual of the Plan of Chicago*, which Moody managed to get included in civics programs in Chicago's eighth-grade classes.

Some projects got the green light early; others had to wait years, even decades, for completion. And many of the *Plan*'s recommendations, as its creators knew was inevitable, never came to fruition. Several of the envisioned transportation routes—the interconnected diagonal thoroughfares and peripheral roads and multiple consolidated rail lines—would eventually lose their primacy in moving traffic through the city, in part because of an understandable failure to foresee the development of the interstate highway system. But among the most noticeable improvements present-day Chicagoans owe, in whole or in part, to the *Plan* are these: the widening and renaming of Pine Street north of the main branch of the river to create North Michigan Avenue, a revitalized commercial district now known as the Magnificent Mile; expansion and preservation of considerable expanses of lakeshore parkland for public use, called by Ira Bach "the most stunning success of the Plan"[14]; Northerly Island, the current site of the Adler Planetarium, completed in 1930; consolidation of some railway lines and terminals, leading to the construction of a new Union Station in 1925; creation of a double-decker Wacker Drive on the south edge of the river and a corresponding two-level Michigan Avenue Bridge, now officially named the DuSable Bridge; extension and improvement of the forest preserve and park systems throughout the city; and 3,300-foot-long Navy Pier, now one of Chicago's most visited tourist attractions.

Louis Sullivan was fortunate to have found a client and friend as patient and supportive as Owatonna's Carl Bennett. Bennett's newly constructed National Farmers' Bank had opened for business in 1907, yet Sullivan continued a personal relationship with Bennett well into the 1910s. Outwardly Sullivan was a man of enormous personal pride and professional self-assurance. However, in a series of remarkable letters with Bennett, Sullivan was as uncompromising in brutally assessing himself and his situation as he was in standing up for his art. During this period he sought relief from "intense suffering, mental, moral, and physical" from his friend Dr. Arndt who, Sullivan noted, "in our heart to heart talks in Mount Vernon [Ohio] diagnosed me mentally and morally with the same simplicity and precision that he had shown in his physical examination." He emerged from his visit with Dr. Arndt determined to change and to "fight this off for all that is in me."[15]

Paul Sprague offers the intriguing and plausible suggestion that the root of many of Sullivan's troubles, both personal and professional, may have been a longstanding struggle with some form of mental illness. Sprague contends that Sullivan's decline reached a nadir in 1910 but that his psychological decline had begun in the early 1890s after the completion of the Auditorium Building. The fall-off in commissions that began in the years following 1893, when an economic depression gripped the country and doomed the partnership of Adler and Sullivan, undoubtedly caused additional stress. This was followed by other disruptions and setbacks, some of them at least partly self-induced, including the irrevocable break with his brother Albert, the estrangement from some of his architectural colleagues after Sullivan's savage attacks on their "feudal" historicism, the drinking, and separation from his wife Margaret. These and other life circumstances added pressure to what appears to have been an already troubled mind.

Sprague considers other possible sources for Sullivan's personal torments and often self-destructive behavior: alcoholism, Twombly's suggestion of suppressed homosexuality, and possible drug use dating back to his Paris apprenticeship days. But he ultimately concludes that the steady downward spiral of Sullivan's later years, with its serious consequences for his architectural practice, could only be explained by one of two things: either Louis had no business sense or he was the victim of ongoing mental illness.[16] Rochelle Elstein cites Wright's contention that Sullivan's troubles dated back to his Paris days and suggests that the condition that underlay such long-lasting personal torment was some form of bipolar disorder.[17]

It is hard to evaluate the accuracy of Sprague's assessment as he offers no clinical diagnosis of an identifiable mental disorder other than suggesting that perhaps Sullivan suffered from a generalized depression. Elstein's diagnosis is more specific but equally hard to assess at such a remove. But there is no question that Sullivan's declining personal fortunes over the last decade and a half of his life were due in no small part to increasingly irrational and erratic behavior. His actions likely resulted from something more than a demanding artistic temperament.

The depth of Sullivan's financial situation can be gauged by the number of times, over the next fourteen years, he felt compelled to approach friends and associates for money. On November 13, 1911, Daniel Burnham noted in his diary, "Louis Sullivan called to get more money."[18] The "more" in Burnham's diary notation is especially suggestive, indicating that this may not have been the first time the down-on-his-luck architect had sought financial assistance from the esteemed and prospering Uncle Dan. During this time, and before, Sullivan was an occasional visitor to Burnham's offices.[19] The fierce denunciations in which he specifically attacked Burnham and Burnham's influence were still several years in the future, but the city planner must have been aware of Sullivan's well-publicized disdain for the kinds of buildings Burnham had championed since the days of the World's Fair. Louis nonetheless felt their relationship was strong enough to presume upon their longstanding associations. Just a few months before the 1911 visit, Sullivan had called on Burnham in the Railway Exchange Building, where Burnham may have offered to buy a painting from Sullivan. On the same day he also sent original drawings of his latest project—St. Paul's Methodist Church in Cedar Rapids, Iowa—with the handwritten message, "To Daniel H. Burnham, with the best wishes of his friend Louis H. Sullivan."[20]

The Cedar Rapids connection was, at least briefly, one bright spot in an otherwise bleak period. Midwestern bankers were enthralled with the unique structure in Owatonna, and a group in Cedar Rapids wanted something similarly distinguished for their town. Sullivan had begun preparing drawings for the People's Savings Bank in Cedar Rapids in 1909, and the rigidly rectangular, fortress-like building reached completion in late 1911. The bank was marked by Sullivan's characteristic originality and gained positive critical attention in the architectural press. A second Cedar Rapids commission came Sullivan's way during this period: the Methodist church represented in the drawings he offered to Burnham. The church was eventually built but not before Sullivan abruptly quit the project when another architect was engaged to find cost-effective means to modify Sullivan's plans. In a curious twist of fate, the task of completing the project was placed in the hands of George Elmslie, now establishing himself in partnership with William Gray Purcell of Minneapolis.

The disappointment of the St. Paul's Methodist Church experience was, as it turned out, to be repeated in different ways and for different reasons in the coming years with other promising projects. Sullivan would be hired, draw up the plans, and then either lose the commission through personal conflicts with the clients, disagreements over cost, or other circumstances out of his control. Several projects would never be built. One of these, a major commission from the continuously supportive Carl Bennett, came in 1911 with the hiring of Sullivan to design a new house for the Bennett family. The plan Sullivan devised was ambitious, unique, imaginative, expansive, and of questionable value for domestic family life. It was in the form of an immense cross, with the living area away from the garden and divided from the kitchen and dining room by an elegant reception hall. An impressive and imposing structure, it would have dominated its lot and served a family accustomed to a formal, highly structured lifestyle. In William Purcell's view it was a design "wholly lacking in any feeling for the Bennetts as a living family [or] for their relation to the community."[21] Carl Bennett never followed through with the house, but he did hire Sullivan in 1913 to landscape the property, a project which also came to naught. In 1912 or 1913 Sullivan even designed a garage for his friend and physician Dr. Arndt, another project that never moved beyond the design stage.[22]

Despite Sullivan's expressed desire to do no more rural banks, the big commercial work he hoped for proved elusive, and smaller projects were the only ones that came his way. From 1913 to 1915 he worked on three relatively modest buildings in Iowa, all of which were completed: the Land and Loan Office Building in Algona for Henry Adams; the Van Allen Building department store in Clinton; and, most notably, the Merchants' National Bank in Grinnell. Each of these buildings had distinctive Sullivan touches: color-soaked stained-glass clerestory windows in the Henry Adams Building; wide horizontal windows on the Van Allen store intersected by continuous vertical bands with terra-cotta flourishes at top and bottom, reminiscent of both the Schlesinger & Mayer store and the Gage Group façade; and an outsized, eye-catching terra-cotta explosion of geometrically contained floral ornament framing a light-filled rose window by Louis Millet that crowned the entrance to the Grinnell bank, a window so richly designed that it once prompted a visiting college student to wonder whether the building may once have been a church. Two even smaller structures—the trapezoidal Purdue State Bank in West Lafayette, Indiana, and the Home Building Association Bank in Newark, Ohio—were his primary active projects through most of 1914 and into 1915. None of these commissions produced enough money to return full financial security to Sullivan's practice.

Starting sometime around 1915 Sullivan became acquainted with an architect, and Sullivan admirer, working at the Art Institute of Chicago named Karl Howenstein. A fellow employee at the Art Institute, Edith Gutterson, who eventually became Howenstein's wife, remembered sharing several dinners with Karl and Louis Sullivan at Chicago's Tip Top Inn, an upscale top-floor restaurant overlooking the Art Institute. The three of them would spend pleasant hours watching night fall over the lake.[23] Gutterson's recollections offer a vivid depiction of Sullivan's long-established habit of engaging friends and associates in long, wide-ranging, spellbinding, sometimes one-sided conversations. The talks with Howenstein and Gutterson, as she described them, undoubtedly resembled his long-ago nighttime monologues with Frank Lloyd Wright in the Auditorium tower; visits with Dankmar Adler's family in the 1890s; long, lazy afternoons and evenings with the Bennetts in Owatonna; and similar after-hours sessions with George Elmslie and others.

> We would sit there for several hours, eating cheese sandwiches and drinking beer, while Sullivan talked. Karl always felt that his words, spoken, were more fraught with meaning and carried overtones of meaning not possible in the written word, and now I know what he meant. His mind would range from one point to another, from one subject to another, but not rambling. Each thought and point grew organically out of the preceding. . . . I think the thing I remember best is the impact of his real concern for men, the human being, and his spiritual and emotional needs. There was no patronizing, or feeling that he in any way knew the answer, only a deep desire to share whatever he comprehended. There was nothing of the "Master" about him, as there was about Wright or [modernist

The front façade of Merchants' National Bank, built in 1914 in Grinnell, Iowa, is highlighted by a rose window framed by terra-cotta ornamentation. Louis Sullivan, architect. (Richard Nickel Archive, Ryerson and Burnham Art and Architecture Archives, Art Institute of Chicago. Digital file # 201006_110801-014.)

> architect Richard] Neutra. Of course Wright called him "Master," but I have the feeling Sullivan would have accepted this half humourously. I remember his eyes, gentle at times, but when really roused, fire would flash from them. He was essentially a kind man."[24]

The chats would turn at times to Sullivan's favorite philosophers. Gutterson specifically recalled discussing Rudolph Steiner, the Austrian-born social philosopher who founded a school of "anthroposophy," which posits the objective existence of a spiritual world entirely accessible to human beings.

Edith Gutterson, of course, was relying on memories several decades old, and her view of Sullivan may have been softened by the passage of time and a conscious or subconscious desire to round out the rough edges of Sullivan's personality. But her account gives us a convincing and complicated picture of a man people often enjoyed visiting with and listening to—a true raconteur who could be playful, philosophical, passionate, sincere, kind, inspiring, arrogant and modest, argumentative and receptive, all at the same time.

The projects that extended into 1915, though hardly enough to revitalize Sullivan's faltering practice, represented the last real flurry of architectural activity in Sullivan's career. He no longer could count on the assistance of the accomplished George Elmslie, who for much of his time with Sullivan had been, in fact if not in title, a co-equal and sometimes primary contributor to several of the projects. To replace Elmslie he had come to rely on a young graduate of the University of Illinois named Parker Berry. Berry had joined Sullivan's office in 1909, straight out of school at age twenty-one, and stayed with Sullivan through most of the early bank commissions. For a time Sullivan did allow Berry to pursue some small projects independently, though ultimately this became a point of conflict between them. In 1917 Carl Bennett's influence and the success of the Owatonna bank's design helped get Sullivan and Berry invited back to Owatonna to discuss their proposals for a new community high school. Unfortunately Sullivan got into an argument with one of the board members, and the commission was awarded elsewhere. Berry and another young assistant in Sullivan's office, Homer Sailor, soon left Sullivan's employ. Berry did pick up commissions after establishing his own office in Chicago, but his career was tragically cut short in 1918, when he died during the influenza epidemic. Sailor went on to a long career in Chicago, designing churches, commercial buildings, and Prairie Style homes.

Only two projects occupied Sullivan's attention for the remainder of the decade, both examples of the "jewel box" small-town banks he had earlier said he hoped he would never have to do again. The first, the People's Federal Savings and Loan Association Building in Sidney, Ohio, received the same kind of meticulous attention he habitually devoted to most commercial projects. For two long days, he perched on a curbstone in Sidney, smoking cigarette after cigarette as his vision for the new building formed in his head. When he finally approached the bank directors, he quickly drew a sketch of the structure he had in mind, offered cost estimates, and immediately encountered the now familiar objections, eliciting the equally predictable Sullivanesque response. According to bank president W. H. Wagner, "One of the directors was somewhat disturbed by the unfamiliarity of the style, and suggested that he rather fancied some classic columns and pilasters for the façade. Sullivan very brusquely rolled up his sketch and started to depart, saying that the directors could get a thousand architects to design a classic bank but only one to get this kind of bank, and that as far as he was concerned it was one or the other."[25]

Happily for the people of Sidney, Ohio, the director's momentary fancy was eventually overruled and Sullivan's plans accepted, resulting in a building some regard as the finest of Sullivan's banks, both functionally and aesthetically. As with the Owatonna bank, the entrance was crowned with a dramatic arch, this time with a carefully modulated mosaic design surrounding a golden-lettered message of "THRIFT" serving as both a reassuring message about the bank's core values and a cautionary warning to entering bank customers. Sullivan's characteristically elaborate floriate terra-cotta ornament on the front and side added considerable interest to an otherwise severe rectangular brick edifice.

The banking and office spaces inside were carefully designed for maximum efficiency. Sullivan even included structural climate controls, to enhance customer and employee comfort, with mixed results. Of the air conditioning system, bank official Gary Fullenkamp has noted, "It was called an air washing system. It pulled air through ductwork and would shoot a mist through (large, decorative urns that are still in place at the north end of the business area). It didn't work well. It was just adding humidity to an already humid, Ohio day." At the same time, the early twentieth-century ductwork was in place and remains in use today.[26]

The final full-scale bank project of Sullivan's career was reserved for the Farmers' and Merchants' Union Bank of Columbus, Wisconsin, a commission that got underway in 1919. A smaller structure than those in Owatonna or Grinnell, the Columbus bank again featured a semicircular arch on the front façade with stained glass panels that, together with five enormous side windows awash in blues and reds, invited complementary streams of colored light into the bank's interior. The lunette hovered over another elaborate explosion of terra-cotta and marble to mark a grand entry to a building of relatively modest size. As in his other recent bank projects, the sticker shock of so ambitious an architectural enterprise was initially of great concern to the bank's president, in this case J. R. Wheeler. And as before the combination of Sullivan's financial circumstances and a bank president's generosity led Sullivan to take advantage of the opportunity to stay in the president's home. Once again daily interactions, including Sullivan's willingness to engage with his hosts in philosophical reflections, deepened his relationships with members of the family. Said Wheeler, "My admiration for him, and then my liking for him, grew continually stronger" during these visits. At one point, when Wheeler was once again voicing worries over cost, Sullivan replied in characteristic fashion, "Just remember: you

Built in 1919, the Farmers' and Merchants' Union Bank of Columbus, Wisconsin, features a series of five elaborately designed arched windows that illuminate the northwest side of the building. Louis Sullivan, architect. (Photo by author.)

will have the only Louis Sullivan bank in the state of Wisconsin," a statement that turned out to be both true and a source of permanent pride for the people of Columbus.[27]

Sullivan's personal life continued to unravel. The news that his separation from Margaret had finally been made official in a 1917 divorce, together with her subsequent marriage to Davies Marshall, may have come as a relief to Sullivan, but it surely added to his sense of emotional isolation. Sullivan's primary worries, however, remained financial. In a letter written to his former assistant Frank Lloyd Wright in 1918, Sullivan revealed just how desperate his situation had become, thus initiating a reconciliation that lasted through Sullivan's remaining years. He repeatedly asked Wright for money, and Wright sometimes obliged, but it was never enough. Sullivan had been forced to leave his Auditorium office in February of 1918 and shortly thereafter was able to rent offices on South Wabash Avenue. Almost immediately he got in trouble with his new landlord. In one of the letters to

Wright he confessed that he had faced the embarrassment of being locked out of his own place of business. Little wonder that during this period he frequently expressed his anguish in no uncertain terms. "With the future blank," he told Wright in the letter that reconnected them, "I am surely living in hell." And later, "I hate to write in a panicky tone, but I can't help it. It is hell!"[28] For most practical purposes, his business address during this time was at the Cliff Dwellers Club in Burnham's Orchestra Hall, where arts-supporting club members gave him free space for writing and other projects. By June 1918 he had left his Wabash Avenue offices for good and moved the objects he had kept there into storage.

Things looked rosy for Daniel Burnham in the fall of 1910. He had just completed the *Plan of Chicago*, yet another major project with far-reaching consequences for his city and his reputation. The federal official under whom he had worked on city planning in the Philippines, William Howard Taft, was no longer a mere cabinet official but was now president of the United States. And Taft's personal secretary was the same Charles D. Norton who, as a member of Chicago's Merchants Club, had actively recruited Burnham for the *Plan of Chicago*. Little wonder that, with more designing and planning to be done in Washington, DC, and in other federal districts and properties, Taft named Burnham to chair a new permanent Commission of Fine Arts for the United States of America to oversee those tasks. Burnham accepted the appointment with customary enthusiasm and gratitude together with a quiet note of resignation on a career nearing its end. He told Norton, "Please convey to the President my deep appreciation of the honor he has conferred on me, an honor which rounds out my life in a manner unhoped for." At the same time he could not help but add a characteristic cautionary note from one accustomed to asserting clear lines of authority: "What may grow out of the office will depend on the way it is handled at first."[29]

The question of where and how to create a suitable memorial to Abraham Lincoln was one important bit of unfinished business from the 1902 Washington plan. The commission immediately set out to sort through and evaluate proposals. After much discussion and some resistance—including from Burnham's old nemesis Joe Cannon, now sitting on a congressional panel determined to provide input—the site Burnham and others originally proposed some nine years earlier was approved. Architect Henry Bacon of New York designed the memorial, sculptor Daniel Chester French created a grand statue of the revered president, and Jules Guérin, who illustrated Burnham's *Plan of Chicago*, painted two large murals. The Lincoln Memorial would rise on the western extremity of the National Mall, just above a bend in the Potomac River, on an axis that stretched directly from the Capitol through the Washington Monument and along Henry Bacon's elongated reflecting pool. The Lincoln Memorial we know today is largely consistent with Burnham's vision for the National Mall.

Burnham's life during this period, satisfactory as it was in so many respects, was not without its challenges and frustrations. He was now in his mid-sixties, and a life of relentless effort and strenuous business travel was taking its toll. His painful foot infection had not gone away. In the summer of 1911 he made what must have been a heart-wrenching decision to resign from the American Institute of Architects—the organization to which he had devoted so much of his time and energy and of which he had twice been president—over a dispute concerning architectural competitions. The same subject had sparked a minor disagreement between himself and Louis Sullivan at the fledgling WAA convention way back in 1884. The AIA had instituted a rule limiting the conditions under which members should seek to enter those competitions. Burnham felt the rule too restrictive for his company, and cited instances in which he felt constrained from entering bids on potentially large and remunerative projects. The distress he felt over the situation was exacerbated when the current AIA officials chose to ignore his resignation and sent threatening letters to him after Burnham had entered one such competition. Burnham replied angrily: "I have received notice from you . . . to appear before the Judiciary Committee of the American Institute of Architects and stand trial for disobedience to the rules of the Institute. As you are well aware, I resigned before entering this competition and have not been a member since that time."[30] The separation from an organization that had meant so much to him, and to which so many of his old friends still belonged, was clearly a bitter pill to swallow.

If Burnham felt some degree of disenchantment with his profession and the arts generally during this episode, it may have briefly found expression in a letter written in August 1911 to an unidentified female family member who was seeking his advice concerning her son's desire for a career in the arts. "It is impossible to state," wrote Burnham with straightforward candor, "how much talent your son has from a glance at the drawings you sent and which I return herewith. They seem to be copies of things he has seen. The pencil horses are good enough copies . . . but are not unusual work, though they are fairly good." The big questions were how much he wanted it and how hard the young man was willing to work. Unless the young man was relentlessly determined and willing to put in the time and effort required, warned Uncle Dan, best tell your son look to another field.

> How old is he, and what has he been doing all his life? Is he a natural hard worker? All these things bear on the problem. The field of architecture is now filled with highly trained men, many of them having had the French Art School course. Unless a young fellow has exceptional talent there is little chance for him without a very thorough training. Now, has he any remarkable gifts? If not he had better avoid the fine arts. No one ever exceeds [*sic*] in that practice unless he is gifted with and energy and capacity for constant work—early and late. The hard work part is essential in any case. . . . If your son has it in him nothing will stop him, even against all odds, but if he is not unusual, the life of an artist is a very poor one for him to enter upon. There are lots of them in the field and are a burden to themselves and every one else.[31]

The discouragingly sententious call for tenacity and "constant work" may seem somewhat hypocritical from the man who as a young adult impulsively decided to set aside his plan to become "the greatest architect in the city or country" for the tantalizing prospect of striking it rich in a mining adventure out West. But by this time in his life Burnham had undoubtedly seen enough of tragic failure among hopeful artists and architects of his acquaintance. If nothing else, the example of even the accomplished Louis Sullivan's struggles during this period would not have been lost on him. Some nine years earlier Burnham had felt obliged to give similar advice to another young family member, his brother-in-law's son John Goddard Jr., who was planning a career in medicine but who wondered if he should consider a more congenial choice. "I should advise that you stick to the thing you know," said Burnham, "and fight it out on that line. . . . There is no work that is 'congenial' and congenial all the time. Discouragement comes to every one all through life. A man stands to his gun in spite of it, and as the storm grows fiercest, he sings louder and mounts more securely. You know nothing but medicine, stand by your trade. It is a noble one."[32]

In the early months of 1912 the Burnhams were preparing for yet another trip abroad, this one to begin in France, move southward into Italy, and then up through Switzerland and into Germany. It had been only sixteen years since his very first trip to Europe. Now, after repeated trips, he was deeply familiar with many of the architectural and historic sites of the Old World. His wife Margaret, daughter Ethel, and her husband Albert Wells were with him. His foot was bothering him again, and his diabetes was getting no better, but he approached the voyage with his usual enthusiasm and interest.

Shortly before his ship sailed, in April of 1912, Burnham was again in Washington, DC, to take part in a planning session for the proposed Lincoln Memorial, a session presided over by President Taft himself. The condition with his foot had necessitated the use of a wheelchair on the train from Chicago to Washington. One wonders at the emotions Burnham must have felt as he rolled through the dramatic spaces of Union Station, the rewarding result of efforts he had helped set in motion ten years earlier.

At the planning meeting Burnham took a leading role in the discussion. He urged the commissioners to oppose those who wanted to settle for something "merely striking and picturesque and not nobly ideal." He argued that "we must disappoint them, and rise above their expectations as we did in Chicago." Burnham took issue with some of the classical designs under consideration, and he urged those present to make the right choices as to architect and sculptor. In a letter to his old friend Francis Millet, who had been in Rome attending to matters at the American Academy, he emphasized how important it was for Millet to be present when the final decision was made the following week so that their choice—a man such as Charles McKim protégé and Beaux-Arts specialist Henry Bacon—would receive serious consideration.

Burnham's letter contained remarks that could only have been made by one who had grown accustomed to working with difficult clients and contrarian committees. Of one participant who declared he wanted a statue of Lincoln "bigger than the Colossus of Rhodes," Burnham wrote, "I didn't even say a word to this, and I hope the sneer of pity in my mind did not appear in my face. When an ignorant man says, 'I don't claim to know much about architecture, but I do know what I like, and I don't need anyone to tell me,' he is hopeless, and trying to tell him anything would be like trying to show a blind man pictures." Burnham's talent for acidic figurative language, particularly when he felt the targets deserved it, reappeared a few lines later when he warned Millet about the chances for political backstabbing in Washington once Burnham was safely abroad: "I know, and you know, dear Frank, that men don't 'stay put,' and that the rats swarm back and begin to gnaw at the same old spot the moment the dog's back is turned." He urged Millet to make sure he would be at the next vote in the coming week, to "reiterate the real argument, which is that they should select a man in whom we have confidence."[33] The letter was intended to be presented to Millet when his ship docked at Pier 59 in New York.

Burnham was no stranger to direct or indirect connections to historic movements and events. He had been part of the mining fever of the Old West in the 1860s, the architectural revolution in Chicago during the final decades of the nineteenth century, the remaking of central Washington, DC, and the beginnings of comprehensive city-planning efforts in the opening decade of the new century. In 1912 he was even, by pure chance, associated with a consequential tragedy, for Millet—the man who was slated to take Burnham's place in the Lincoln Memorial discussions—was sailing on the *Titanic.* Burnham's Europe-bound ship, the *Olympic,* was in fact a *Titanic* sister ship, another luxury vessel of the White Star Line. Burnham decided to send a message to his trusted friend as the ships were in transit. The date of Burnham's cable was April 14. The message never got through.

On the morning of April 15 the steward told Burnham that there had been an accident: the *Titanic* had gone down. The *Olympic* was one of the ships initially ordered to change course to assist in the rescue, but on receiving notice that the *Carpathia* had arrived at the scene, it resumed its eastward course, although the wireless room continued to function as a clearinghouse for radio messages. Burnham spent the next couple days anxiously scanning survivor lists. "This ship is in gloom;" he noted, "everybody has lost friends, and some of them near relations." Burnham was of course distraught when he was given the news that Millet, along with another associate, a military aide to President Taft, were among those lost. The tragedy, he said, had the sad effect of severing "my connection with [Millet,] one of the best fellows of the Fair."[34]

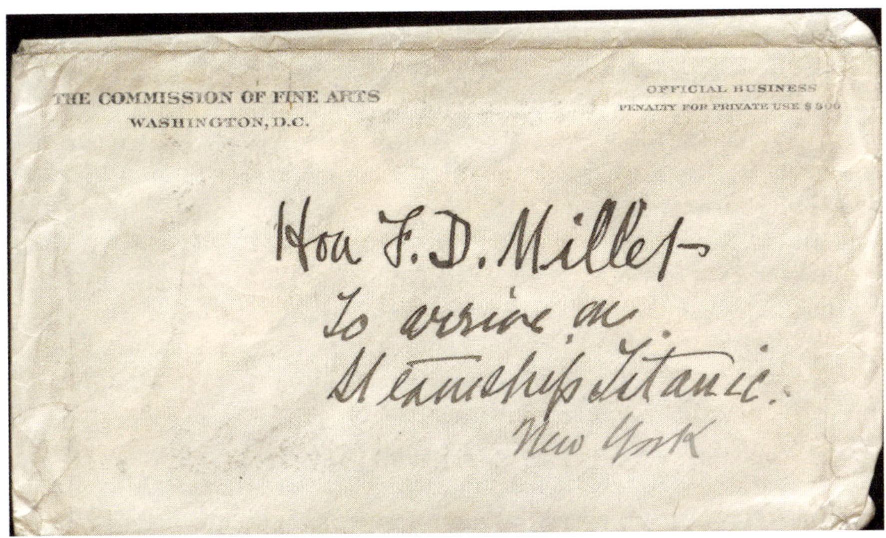

THE COMMISSION OF FINE ARTS
WASHINGTON, D.C.

OFFICIAL BUSINESS
PENALTY FOR PRIVATE USE $300

Hon F. D. Millet
To arrive on
Steamship Titanic.
New York

The envelope of the letter Daniel Burnham hoped would be given to painter and sculptor Frank Millet when the *Titanic* docked in New York. In the letter Burnham urged his friend to take his place and to represent his views on the government commission planning the design of the Lincoln Memorial. Millet did not survive the sinking. His body was eventually recovered and returned to Massachusetts for burial. (Charles Moore Collection, Manuscript Division, Library of Congress.)

He could not have known, of course, that his own death lay just a little more than a month in the future and that he would never see his home country again. His sorrow over Millet's death must have been lightened somewhat by his and Margaret's reunion with son Hubert, Hubert's wife Vivian, and the couple's baby girl in France. His impressions of Europe through most of May were as enthusiastic as ever, as he once again soaked in the natural beauties of the landscape and the architectural monuments. His diary entries seem those of an energetic and active tourist always on the move despite bothersome ailments.

In late May Burnham reached Heidelberg, where his physical condition suddenly deteriorated. He passed a difficult night, but when he woke up feeling better the next day, Margaret and Ethel were relieved enough to attend a concert in a nearby park. Burnham was hospitalized that afternoon. On May 29 he fell into a coma, which lasted three days. He died on June 1 suffering from colitis, a condition complicated by food poisoning and his diabetes.[35]

The news of Daniel Burnham's death, at the age of sixty-five, elicited pained reactions from friends, family, and associates around the globe. At a Chicago area North Shore Music Festival concert, the news broke during a performance, and conductor Frederick Stock quickly added the funeral march from Wagner's *Götterdämmerung* to the program to honor Burnham, who had also served as a director of the festival. Calling Burnham "the Father of the Skyscraper," the *Chicago Tribune* declared that "[t]here is scarcely an American architect who has completed the amount of work which Mr. Burnham has, and who has received the honors, both in America and abroad, which have been accorded him."[36] The *San Jose Mercury and Herald* conveyed a similar message that emphasized Burnham's tall-building resume; its headline read, "Skyscraper Inventor Passes Away in Germany."[37]

The most heartfelt and detailed tributes came from the legion of architects and artists who had known him through the years. The August issue of the *Architectural Record* devoted ten pages to encomia by colleagues and friends. Cass Gilbert emphasized Burnham's dominating presence: "His was indeed a rare nature, sometimes whimsical, almost pedantic, always forceful and commanding, with a dignity and presence of which he himself was not unaware." The journal also reprinted the speech Peter Wight had given at the Art Institute just days following the news of Burnham's death, which recounted his early days with Burnham and also attempted to cover the full scope of Burnham's career. Wight, like Gilbert, stressed the power of Burnham's personality.[38]

Said Wight: "If his buildings do not give him fame by their beauty and significance, his life will furnish the lesson of unselfish generosity and meekness of spirit. Yet he was born to command and have his way. He would brook no opposition or interference, but in opposing his adversaries, he did it like a gentleman." President Taft's tribute was printed as were others in the same vein by Howard Van Doren Shaw, William Holabird, Burnham's onetime employee Paul Lautrup, and Irving K. Pond. Even Frank Lloyd Wright offered his own unique appreciation of "Uncle Dan," which characteristically combined genuine praise for qualities Wright admired with a candid assessment of what he believed to be Burnham's shortcomings. He was a great man, Wright acknowledged, but "not a creative architect." "He loved the beautiful and served it," Wright allowed, then added, "but his buildings will live as architecture no longer than others of this period produced in the same way." Louis Sullivan did not contribute to this collection of remembrances, but his take would likely have echoed Wright's two-sided view.

In 1913 Charles Moore published an article entitled "Lessons of the Chicago World's Fair: An Interview with the Late Daniel H. Burnham." Moore gave no specific reasons for publishing material from an informal interview that he conducted in Burnham's offices in the Railway Exchange Building in 1908. But a passing comment in his introduction offers a clue. "[E]nough was said" in the interview, declared Moore, "to throw a strong light on the way in which the Fair work developed; and Mr. Burnham's own task of direction is shown to be much more comprehensive than is generally supposed."[39] With public memory of the Chicago World's Fair fading, Moore was eager to document Burnham's consequential role in every aspect of the enterprise. He asked the reader to consult the piece as a complement to Peter Wight's warm memorial tribute to Burnham in the August issue. Clearly Moore intended to nurture and protect Burnham's post-mortem reputation, an effort that reached full expression in his two-volume biography published in 1921.

Moore's verdict on Burnham was slightly more ambiguous in his personal memoir. "Was Daniel Burnham a great architect?" he asked. "That depends." Moore went on to emphasize Burnham's devotion to beauty but noted that beauty, for Burnham, did not depend on originality. Architecture, said Moore, seeks to construct agreeable form, and if for Burnham agreeable beauty could be achieved by looking to the past, so be it. Moore gave the example of a young architect who approached Burnham with a novel design, and when Burnham asked for the precedent, "the young man blushingly confessed it was original; the library disclosed a dozen analogous designs all better than the 'original' one." Burnham believed "originality consisted in the best possible solution of a problem [regardless of where it came from], beauty always being an essential ingredient."[40]

In the years immediately following Burnham's death, Moore's concerns about his subject's reputation seemed unnecessary. As Thomas Hines has written, "The tones and emotions of the funeral eulogies continued through the 1910s to heighten and solidify Burnham's posthumous reputation. . . . Burnham continued to be praised and revered, especially for the largeness of his vision and his plans."[41] Daniel Burnham's contributions to architecture and city planning were firmly established and well known; to most observers, his legacy could now be chiseled in stone.

In the late teens and into the 1920s, as Charles Moore was busy gathering information on Daniel Burnham for his biographical tribute, Louis Sullivan was entering the last, painful phase of his extraordinary life. A modest remodeling job for a bank in Manistique, Michigan, in 1920 and a façade design for a final Chicago building, the Krause Music Store, in 1922 represented Sullivan's only substantive architectural accomplishments of the 1920s. For the Manistique project his office staff had been reduced to two architecture students. Sullivan was able to use some office space provided by another of Sullivan's benefactors, the American Terra Cotta Company, initially at 1808 Prairie Avenue, well out of the central business district but only two and a half miles from Sullivan's humble rented living quarters at the Hotel Warner. When the company moved, in late 1921, two blocks north to a Jenney-designed mansion at 1701 Prairie Avenue, Sullivan's office accommodation moved with them.

Always a willing contributor to discussions concerning art and architecture, Sullivan turned increasingly to writing to fill his empty hours. He continued a lengthy correspondence, including desperate pleas for money, with Frank Lloyd Wright and others and, after initially hesitating, responded positively to Andrew N. Rebori's suggestion to compose his autobiography. Friends and admirers had offered several suggestions for other writing projects that Sullivan pursued, such as publishing *Kindergarten Chats* in book form in both the US and in Europe. Many in Chicago's arts community were aware of Sullivan's difficult personal circumstances and did what they could to offer support. In January 1922 the Art Institute of Chicago's Burnham Library commissioned a series of drawings, which the American Institute of Architects published the following year, along with Sullivan's notes and essays, in a book entitled *A System of Architectural Ornament, According with a Philosophy of Man's Powers.*

The two major writing projects that came to fruition during this time—the autobiography and *A System*—were perfect activities for the effectively unemployed architect. They fed his lifelong desire to teach, to philosophize,

Portrait of Louis H. Sullivan by Frank Werner, 1919. (Chicago History Museum. Image # ICHi-013745.)

to explain and justify his architectural principles and beliefs from his desk at the Cliff Dwellers Club on Michigan Avenue or from the Prairie Avenue office. The *System* project allowed Sullivan to provide a step-by-step illustration of how the "seed-germ" of an architectural idea could, through the creative power of a nature-inspired architect, emerge from seemingly inorganic geometric linear projections into swirling organic foliate designs. Sullivan's initial illustration of the seed-germ is a "typical seed" flanked by two winglike leaves (cotyledons) that will furnish the nourishment needed to help the "delicate mechanism" of the seed to find a way to express its "will to power."[42] From this simple organic starting point, the architect must mold "rigid geometry," Sullivan said, into "plastic, mobile, fluescent phases of expression."[43]

How to do this? First it must be understood that that which "appears" to be lifeless and inorganic can be brought to life through human creativity, which involves both spiritual understanding and an infusion of the creator's passion.

> By the word inorganic is commonly understood that which is lifeless, or appears to be so; as stone, the metals, and seasoned wood, clay, or the like. But nothing is really inorganic to the creative will of man. His spiritual power masters the inorganic and causes it to live in forms which his imagination brings forth from the lifeless, the amorphous. He thus transmutes into the image of his passion that which of itself has no such power. Thus man in his power brings forth that which hitherto was non-existent.[44]

In *A System* it was clear that Sullivan the architectural pugilist had not lost his penchant for aggressive advocacy on behalf of creativity and originality. David Van Zanten goes so far as to suggest the plates Sullivan created for the book were meant to "slay" his contemporary rivals in a final virtuoso display of architectural power.[45]

Sullivan's intriguing title for the other major work, *The Autobiography of an Idea,* can be interpreted as an extended elaboration of several ideas (as discussed in chapter 4) stemming from, or related to, this not-so-simple concept of releasing the life-force within inorganic materials.[46] A second provocative implication of the title is to downplay the value or importance of Louis Sullivan's lived life in favor of the story of the developing mind/spirit/passions—the growing "Idea"—within the artist who, in his brief sojourn on this tiny planet and, through this mystical creative power, has learned to reinfuse living nature into human-made physical spaces. Partly for this reason, Sullivan's biographical account concentrates almost exclusively on his formative years, especially his childhood. Fully three-quarters of his

The Germ the Seat of Power

A SYSTEM OF ARCHITECTURAL ORNAMENT

According with a philosophy of man's powers.

By Louis H. Sullivan, Architect

THE GERM.

Cotyledon

Germ

Above is drawn a diagram of a typical seed with two cotyledons. The cotyledons are specialized rudimentary leaves containing a supply of nourishment sufficient for the initial stage of the development of the germ.

The Germ is the real thing: the seat of identity. Within its delicate mechanism lies the will to power: the function which is to seek and eventually to find its full expression in form.

The seat of power and the will to live constitute the simple working idea upon which all that follows is based—as to efflorescence

This draft of the first page of Louis Sullivan's *A System of Architectural Ornament* illustrates the essence of Sullivan's "seed-germ" idea as the starting point for architectural design. (Sullivaniana Collection, Ryerson and Burnham Art and Architecture Archives, Art Institute of Chicago. Digital file # 193101_150922-001.)

autobiography is devoted to recollections from his earliest years to the age of twenty-five, when he joined the practice of Dankmar Adler and, as he put it, "Louis H. Sullivan became a full-fledged architect before the world."[47] Sullivan's self-narrative then moves into lengthy elaborations of his personal philosophy regarding nature and democracy, with only occasional mentions of significant Adler and Sullivan projects. It stops abruptly at the time of his early triumphs and the 1893 World's Fair. There is nothing about the break with Adler, marriage to Margaret, the dissolution of his relationship with brother Albert, the birth of a son given up to adoption, the apprenticeship of Frank Lloyd Wright, the Schlesinger and Mayer store, Carl Bennett, George Elmslie, the rural banks, the divorce, or the twenty-some years of struggle and hardship after the fair.

The *Autobiography* offered Sullivan a final opportunity to vent his opinions about what had gone wrong, not with his life but rather with the state of American architecture as he saw it. And the influence of the Columbian Exposition, with Daniel Burnham now one of the contributors implicitly in the crosshairs, became a principal target. Perhaps the most quoted passage in the entire autobiography was the one in which, as we have seen, he took devastating aim at the lasting, and in his view disastrous, effects of the World's Fair on American architecture. Sullivan wasn't wrong about the fair's influence. At the time he was writing, the City Beautiful movement was broadly popular and influential, emphasizing Greco-Roman, Beaux-Arts monumentalism—the latest example of which was then taking shape in the National Mall's Lincoln Memorial. And the late Burnham had for years been one of its leading and most prominent advocates.

Before this Sullivan had rarely attacked Burnham directly in his public comments. In the concluding pages of the *Autobiography*, he still was careful to acknowledge Burnham's managerial and leadership skills, but he also was not afraid to name Burnham as a key enabler of what Sullivan regarded as this ongoing curse of "feudal" historicism. In describing the initial meeting of architects prior to the World's Fair, Sullivan remembered a timid and complacent Burnham. "He was not facile on his feet," Sullivan observed, and when Burnham rose to address the group, "it soon became noticeable that he was progressively and grossly apologizing to the Eastern men for the presence of their benighted brethren of the West." When Richard Morris Hunt abruptly brought Burnham up short and urged the group to get to work, Burnham "was keen enough to understand that 'Uncle Dick' had done him a needed favor." Burnham, wrote Sullivan, "learned slowly but surely, within the limits of his understanding."[48]

Sullivan claimed in his memoir that Burnham favored the selection of Eastern architects for the fair "solely . . . on account of [Burnham's belief in] their surpassing culture." According to Sullivan, it was only after railroad executive and member of the Board of Directors Edward T. Jeffery "with exquisite delicacy and tact . . . persuaded Daniel come to judgment, to add the Western men to the list of his nominations," that Burnham agreed to allow the less tradition-bound architects from Chicago and elsewhere participation in the enterprise. This account differed in some details from Burnham's own memories and from other accounts, but it conveyed the impression that Burnham was wholly in thrall to the Beaux-Arts historicism of the East and had weakly acquiesced to what Sullivan termed the "white cloud" of reactionary thinking that was to cast a 'gauze-like pall' over American architecture for decades to come. He was aware that others had contributed to the omnipresent white cloud but noted that it was "one man's unbalanced mind" and "one man's unconscious stupor in bigness, and in the droll phantasy of hero-worship" that allowed the World's Fair to become the "appalling calamity" Sullivan was now certain it had been. In Sullivan's mind the untimely death of his friend and kindred spirit John Root deprived Burnham of the one trusted voice that could have saved the day. "Who now," Sullivan asked retrospectively, "would take up the foils [Root] had dropped on his way, from hands that were once so strong. There was none."[49] Certainly, as Sullivan saw it, not Burnham.

This supposed infection in the bloodstream of American architecture preoccupied Sullivan in the final essays he composed for the country's architectural press. A perfect opportunity arose when the *Chicago Tribune*, in 1922, announced an international competition to create "the most beautiful and distinctive office building in the world" for its towering new home near the main branch of the Chicago River on Michigan Avenue. Entries poured in from across the globe, and newspapers and magazines fueled controversy by keeping the proposed designs, and the conflicting opinions that accompanied them, before the eyes of an interested public.

The winning design, a neo-Gothic tower from the New York team of John Mead Howells and Raymond Hood, combined a modern vertical emphasis with a crown of buttresses and exterior details borrowed from historic French cathedrals. The runner-up in the competition, the design for Finnish architect Eliel Saarinen's soaring skyscraper—with its graceful setbacks, restrained ornamentation, and strong vertical emphasis that transitioned smoothly into the outward expression of the building's topmost floors—eschewed direct reference to medieval or Renaissance precursors in favor of a simplified but striking high-rise that was to influence architectural design for years after its appearance. Only a few years after the *Tribune* competition closed, John Holabird and John Wellborn Root Jr., son of Daniel Burnham's renowned first partner, combined the slim profile of the

Tribune Tower, completed in 1925. John Mead Howells and Raymond Hood, architects. Louis Sullivan critically observed that this competition-winning neo-Gothic entry existed on "the level of those works evolved of dying ideas." (Wikimedia Commons.)

Eliel Saarinen's runner-up entry in the Tribune Tower design competition. The structure was never built but remained influential in architectural circles for many years. (Prints and Photographs Division, Library of Congress. Reproduction # LC-DIG-ppmsca-51973.)

senior Root's Monadnock Building with the simple verticality and elegant setbacks of Saarinen's entry to create the landmark 333 North Michigan Avenue, on the other side of the bridge from Tribune Tower. Holabird and Root Jr.'s building constitutes a kind of "Saarinen's revenge," for as the observer looks south down the canyon of buildings on the Magnificent Mile, a bend in Michigan Avenue just before the bridge ensures that what directly confronts the eye is not the Gothic newspaper tower but rather the recognizable offspring of the competition's sleek and slender second-place finisher.

It was no secret where Sullivan's sympathies lay. Saarinen in this instance demonstrated that he was a "Master of Ideas" who was able to separate himself from the stultifying past and to restore "man's faith in himself and his power to create anew." Mead and Hood, by contrast, were among that host of contemporary architects lost in "bewilderment of thought, in a world that has lost its bearings, and submits in distress to the government of dying ideas." They were, in Sullivan's uncompromising terms, the kinds of architects who allow themselves to become "slaves by choice" who "seek shelter in the shadows of ideas." In praising Saarinen, Sullivan once again returned to his vision of heroic masculinity in architectural creation. If only Hood and Howells had found the courage to embrace the "Free Spirit" where "Man shall find Man," a real building of unpretentious power could have been created. But even then, said Sullivan, "it could be but as a foundling at the doorstep of the Finn—for it seems they breed *strong* men in Finland."[50]

Sullivan was just as insistent on the need for architects to seek release from the heavy grip of the past in his last two public papers, published in 1923 and 1924. In place of negative commentary on "dying ideas," he instead offered praise for a genuine "master of ideas," his one-time protégé Frank Lloyd Wright, and for Wright's Imperial Hotel in Tokyo, Japan. The building featured a sprawling 250-room, H-shaped hotel with wings extending around a central courtyard and reflecting pool. In true Wright fashion, the structure made use of local materials, in this case chiefly Oya stone, a local volcanic rock. There had been talk of Wright's involvement in the project from as early as 1911, but it had taken several years before he was given the commission and could begin the work in earnest. Construction began in 1917 and Wright guided the development of the structure through to completion in 1923. Sullivan had shown an interest in the project from the beginning and even, in his desperate circumstances, had hoped to join Wright in Japan as a working partner, an offer Wright chose not to accept. Despite his lack of direct involvement, Sullivan saw the ultimate product of Wright's imagination as "a high act of courage—an utterance of man's free spirit, a personal message to every soul that falters, and to every heart that hopes."[51] In other words, it displayed none of the willing subjection to the "superstitious tyranny of insane ideas" that had conceived buildings like the Tribune Tower.[52]

His final public architectural statement, in the February 1924 issue of the *Architectural Record,* also focused on Wright's Tokyo hotel, this time in the aftermath of the devastating September 1923 earthquake in Japan. It was, Sullivan said, the achievement of "this man [Wright], a poet, who had reduced thinking to simples . . . to devise a system of construction such as should absorb and dispose of the powerful shocks, waves and violent tremors, and yet maintain its integrity as a fabricated structure."[53] The Imperial Hotel did, in fact, weather the tragedy well, remaining largely intact and functional in the post-earthquake years. Over time, however, the building exhibited structural weaknesses, as the building's foundations settled unevenly in the softened subsoil, and it was demolished in 1967 to make way for a new high-rise hotel.

In praising Wright's artistry and technical skills, Sullivan seemed to be making amends for the long rupture in their relationship and showing sincere appreciation for Wright's genuine accomplishments as an architect and for the renewed friendship and generosity he now enjoyed from his former apprentice. He was also, in effect, telling the world that Wright was the person who fully represented the philosophy of architecture that Sullivan had been tirelessly advocating for almost thirty years. The Imperial Hotel, "a vast sumptuous building, in all its aspects: structural, utilitarian, and aesthetic, was the embodiment, and is now the revelation, of a single thought tenaciously held by a seer and a prophet, a craftsman, a master-builder."[54] This union of poet, philosopher, artist, technician, and fearless original thinker, Sullivan insisted, was exactly what an architect should be, and he took some credit for Wright's having become exactly that. When Wright paid his final visit to see his "beloved master," in April of 1924 in Chicago, Sullivan acknowledged that Wright was now the public face of the new American architecture, but added, tellingly, "I do not believe you could have done it without me."[55]

At the time he wrote this last essay, Sullivan's professional reputation remained strong and his personal circumstances remained dire. Sick and alternately depressed, hopeful, angry, and energized, he was entering his final days in his cramped living space in the South Side's Hotel Warner. But he enjoyed many sympathetic visitors during those final days. Frank Lloyd Wright noted the occasional presence of "a loyal little henna-haired milliner" who often came to be with him, as did numerous youthful admirers of the "master's" genius. Nothing is known of the milliner beyond this and other comments of Wright's. Whether she was in any sense a romantic partner or a casual friend or a sympathetic kind soul is anybody's guess. But it's clear that, while Sullivan suffered from loneliness at times, he wasn't entirely alone. When his condition was clearly deteriorating, he had a nurse who came to attend to his needs. As we have seen, his friends had provided writing space waiting for him at the Cliff Dwellers Club, and business associates at the American Terra Cotta Company and the Northwestern Terra Cotta Company were also involved in supporting Sullivan through these difficult times. Of the latter groups, as Wright pointed out, these businessmen "had especially good reason to befriend him" since "terra cotta in him had found a prophet!"[56]

While Wright's accounts must always be viewed through the sometimes-distorting mists of his self-dramatizing and self-serving ego, his description of Sullivan's erratic behavior in these final days have the ring of authenticity. "At times," Wright observed, "despondency would overcome his natural pride and buoyancy. Even his high courage would give way to fear for his continued livelihood. Then all would clear and come up again. But only for a little while."[57] Sullivan's letters to Wright during this period seem to confirm this picture. At times Sullivan's comments conveyed hope and confidence ("There is prospect of some work in the spring. . . . Am in pretty good health and exercising as much patience as I can"), at others misery and despair ("I seem to have lost my way").[58] Wright relates that when, at last, the author's copy of *The Autobiography of an Idea* arrived at the hotel, Sullivan said simply, "There it is, Frank"—a life's work, a life's philosophy summed up in one magnum opus. "I was sitting by him," said Wright, "my arm around him to keep him warm and steady him. I could feel every vertebra in his backbone as I rubbed my hand up and down his spine to comfort him; and I could feel his enlarged heart pounding."[59]

The next day, April 14, 1924, Louis Sullivan died in his sleep. The cause of death was kidney disease complicated by an inflammation of the heart muscle.

The funeral arrangements and unpaid debts for Louis Sullivan were attended to by several friends and associates who had also visited and assisted Sullivan in the final months of his life, among them Dankmar Adler's son Sidney and architects Max Dunning and George Nimmons. He was buried in Graceland Cemetery on the city's north side near the resting places for his father and mother and not far from the grave of his colleague, friend, and sometime nemesis Daniel Burnham.

In a somewhat ironic twist, the Burnham grave merges more quietly and "organically" into Graceland's natural landscape than Sullivan's. A simple bronze plaque displays Daniel's and Margaret's names and dates on an otherwise untouched and unaltered granite boulder on a shady islet reaching into Lake Willowmere. Any reference to architecture, to Burnham's career in city planning, to his famous pronouncement is absent. The site is nothing more than a rock, an island, and a minimally informative plaque. Sullivan's grave for several years remained unmarked, but five years after his death friends and admirers came together to create an impressive rough-hewn stone monument, designed by architect and architectural historian Thomas Tallmadge. It featured a medallion relief portrait of Louis Sullivan and decorative detailing in an instantly recognizable Sullivanesque style. On the reverse of the tombstone, a carved inscription paid tribute to Sullivan's notable career in terms that accurately highlighted the architect's own interest in assuming the role of architectural poet and prophet:

> Louis Henri Sullivan by his buildings great in influence and power; his drawings unsurpassed in originality and beauty; his writings rich in

Grave marker for Daniel and Margaret Burnham, Graceland Cemetery, Chicago. (Photo by Paul R. Burley is licensed under CC BY-SA 4.0.)

poetry and prophesy; his teachings persuasive and eloquent; his philosophy where, in "form follows function," he summed up all truth in art, Sullivan has earned his place as one of the greatest architectural forces in America. In testimony of this, his professional and other friends have built this monument.

Thomas Tallmadge-designed tombstone for Louis Sullivan, commissioned by his friends and admirers and erected five years after Sullivan's death, Graceland Cemetery, Chicago. Note the inclusion of a tall-building motif that seems to emerge naturally from the side of the stone. (Richard Nickel Archive, Ryerson and Burnham Art and Architecture Archives, Art Institute of Chicago. Digital file # 201006_110613-019.)

EPILOGUE

Take a Walk with Me Down Michigan Avenue

Daniel Burnham and Louis Sullivan, Sullivan and Burnham: the ghosts of these two architects and artists, their descendants, associates, and disciples haunt Chicago's city center.

Come along! Take a walk with me down Michigan Avenue, Chicago's answer to Fifth Avenue, Oxford Street, the Champs Élysées. Let's start on the northern segment of the DuSable (Michigan Avenue) Bridge, near the point at which the Chicago River joins Lake Michigan. We are standing at the sidewalk rail on the east side of the street near the 1925 bronze plaque "In Honor of Louis Jolliet & Pere Jacques Marquette," placed there by the Illinois Society of the Colonial Dames of America. We are facing south.

It was here, very near where we're standing, that Jean Baptiste Point DuSable established his trading post in the 1780s, and what was to become the city of Chicago was born. A bust of DuSable, a person of color likely of French/Haitian background, stands just behind us on the plaza called Pioneer Court. It was also here, as the plaque points out, that Joliet and Marquette constituted "the first white men to pass through the Chicago River," an event that occurred in September of 1673. If you turn your head sharply to the right, you'll see the imposing angular oddity of the Wrigley Building, featured in Sinatra's catchy tune and designed by Burnham's successor firm of Graham, Anderson, Probst and White to simulate the white-faced grandeur of Burnham's White City of 1893. A young William Wrigley Jr. introduced Juicy Fruit brand chewing gum at the Chicago World's Fair, which contributed to the fortune that in turn led to the creation of this unique structure.

If you direct your gaze southward across the bridge and peer down toward the canyon of skyscrapers, you will glimpse the northern edge of the original

Michigan Avenue, earlier called Michigan Boulevard or "Boul Mich." Until the early years of the twentieth century, it ended at the river. On the eastern corner just south of the bridge stands the slim art deco high-rise, 333 North Michigan Avenue, designed by John Wellborn Root Jr., the namesake son of Daniel Burnham's esteemed first partner. Root Jr.'s building is the one many believe was inspired by Eliel Saarinen's much-admired losing entry in the Tribune Tower competition of 1922 and by the senior Root's slim and sleek Monadnock Building of 1892. Produced by the son of one of the few colleagues whom Louis Sullivan regarded as a worthy peer, this "proud and soaring thing, rising in sheer exultation . . . from bottom to top" would likely have pleased the notoriously hard-to-please Sullivan. On the other hand, the contest's winning entry that stands immediately behind us, the neo-Gothic Tribune Tower capped with decorative flying buttresses, earned nothing but Sullivan's withering contempt.

At the time of the First World War, a stretch of Michigan Avenue north of the river, the street now behind us, was a narrow and largely residential roadway called Pine Street. No bridge joined Pine Street on the north to Michigan Avenue on the south. To get across the river you would have to go a half block west to Rush Street and take the angled, ugly, crowded utilitarian bridge that, in one form or another, had occupied this space since 1857. It was only after 1920, when the new double-decker Michigan Avenue (now DuSable) Bridge was completed, that a widened Pine Street became the northern extension of Michigan Avenue: today's broad, elongated upscale shopping district known to many as the Magnificent Mile. The two-level roadway was designed to ease traffic flow across the bridge, with the lower level devoted to service-vehicle traffic. It was matched in 1926 on the south side of the river with a new upper and lower Wacker Drive (formerly South Water and River Streets) conceived for the same dual purpose. The driving force behind the construction of the Michigan Avenue Bridge, the creation of the two-level Wacker Drive, and the development of the Magnificent Mile? Daniel H. Burnham's and Edward Bennett's *Plan of Chicago*.

Crossing the bridge to the south bank, we may look to the sidewalks on both sides of Wacker Drive and note the markers outlining the site of Fort Dearborn, the US outpost originally built in 1803 to secure this important entry point into the waterways that eventually made their way to the Mississippi. Descending Michigan Avenue and stopping at the sign marking East South Water Street, we can look across the street, where stands the soaring Carbide and Carbon Building (230 North Michigan Avenue, now the Pendry Hotel), another art deco skyscraper, this one designed by Daniel Burnham's two sons, Hubert and Dan Jr. The distinctive black polished granite base gives way to a green and gold terra-cotta exterior. It rises in uninterrupted vertical lines to a highly decorated crown topped by what some observers have likened to a "champagne cork," a slim tower covered in 24-carat gold leaf. Feel free to cross the street and enter the lobby of the hotel if you wish to experience the gleaming elegance of an art deco interior. Then return to the east side to rejoin the group.

Continuing down the long incline and coming to a stop on the busy corner of Randolph and Michigan Avenue, on our right on the southwest corner of the intersection we'll see the Chicago Cultural Center, for many years the city's main public library and a showcase for the world's largest Tiffany glass dome. The building was constructed in the 1890s by the Boston firm of Shepley, Rutan and Coolidge, one of the Eastern firms that came to Chicago to help assemble Burnham's exposition in the approved Beaux-Arts style. If we take a moment to turn around and view the northwest corner of Millennium Park, we'll encounter a curving peristyle of classical columns. The structure is a reduced-size replica of the colonnade designed by Burnham's close associate and *Plan* co-author Edward Bennett in 1917 to adorn the same site—one element in a larger effort to bring into being Burnham's formal and classically inspired vision for Grant Park.

We walk two blocks farther on, passing the intersections of Washington and Madison Streets. As we pass Madison, North Michigan Avenue becomes South Michigan Avenue, and the street numbering begins anew. Take a moment to examine the Willoughby Tower on the corner at 8 South Michigan, with its ghost inscription of "Haberdashers A. Sulka & Company Shirt Makers," a reminder of the time when Michigan Avenue merchants catered to style-conscious Chicagoans in search of fashionable attire. The building next door, the ornate, red-brick Chicago Athletic Association Hotel at 12 South Michigan, was designed by Henry Ives Cobb in the Venetian Gothic style to impress visitors for the upcoming 1893 World's Fair. Louis Sullivan came here in the early 1900s to take out his daily frustrations by "boxing for dear life" under the tutelage of former lightweight boxing champion—and, legend has it, inventor of the kidney punch—George Dawson.

A little farther on we stop to observe the block of buildings near the northwest corner of Michigan and Monroe. The tall Gothic Revival structure on the corner is the University Club, designed by Martin Roche. The three adjoining buildings, also products of the Holabird and Roche firm, are known as the Gage Group. The two relatively plain reddish brick buildings feature the "Chicago window," an innovation developed in the late nineteenth century consisting of a large fixed pane of glass situated between two narrower double-hung windows for increased natural light and improved ventilation. The third member of the Gage Group, the twelve-story structure adjacent to the Chicago Athletic Association Hotel, exhibits a more flamboyant and ornate façade than the other Gage buildings, with a pair of flat decorative columns that shoot from the second floor all the way to the cornice, where they explode into two outsized flower-like blooms. The façade design is the work of Louis H. Sullivan, whom the building's owners recruited specifically to ensure the presentation of a strikingly expressive, artistic face to the viewing public.

At the corner of Monroe and Michigan, we'll take a brief side trip up Monroe eastward toward the lake. We will pass the Renzo Piano-designed modern wing of the Art Institute and descend to the corner of Monroe and Columbus Drive. At the corner we'll turn to the right, take a few steps, and turn for a view of another Sullivan creation: the recovered entry arch to the old Chicago Stock Exchange. The south-facing side again reveals the interweaving decorative motifs that characterized so much of Sullivan's work.

If we have time and credit cards (and the crowds aren't too bad), we'll return up Monroe Street, pay the fee to enter the modern wing of the museum, and go inside to visit the meticulously restored Chicago Stock Exchange Trading Room. The space features Louis Sullivan's extensive and phantasmagoric intertwining patterns and multiple shadings of yellow, red, and green stenciling, molded plaster capitals, and colored glass skylights.

Next we can make our way toward the Michigan Avenue entrance and ascend the grand Women's Board staircase, near the original Art Institute lobby, to examine numerous decorative elements from now demolished buildings created by Sullivan and Burnham and other contributors to Chicago's architectural legacy. On the site of the grand staircase and nearby Fullerton Hall, World's Fair speakers and religious leaders lectured to rapt audiences on topics of cultural, scientific, and historical interest. It was here, on July 13, 1893, that Frederick Jackson Turner delivered his famous address making the influential but controversial case for the role of the frontier in forming the American character.

Returning to Michigan Avenue through the main entrance of the Art Institute, we can take a moment to turn and examine the institute's classical façade. This iteration of Chicago's Art Institute was originally conceived as an auxiliary to the 1893 World's Columbian Exposition under Burnham's direction, though the building's design was not his. It was executed by the Eastern firm of Shepley, Rutan and Coolidge, whose public library we just recently viewed at the corner of Michigan and Randolph. In a sunken courtyard off the southwest corner of the institute, we will find a tall bronze fountain sculpture by Lorado Taft representing allegorical figures of the five great lakes. Half-naked maidens pour water into a series of five basins, from the topmost figure (Lake Superior) to the bottommost (Lake Ontario). Taft's sculpture was prompted by a chance comment on the absence of such a representation at the Columbian Exposition. The source of the comment? Daniel Burnham.

We can now cross the street and continue our walk on the west side of Michigan Avenue. On the northwest corner of Michigan and Adams we'll observe D. H. Burnham and Company's creation the Peoples Gas Building, its bold Ionic columns announcing yet another expression of late nineteenth-century classically influenced architecture. The second building south of Adams, red-brick Orchestra Hall (220 South Michigan), was also designed by Burnham's firm and was originally named for the symphony conductor Theodore Thomas, Burnham's good friend. Here, in the penthouse, the Cliff Dwellers Club met, where Louis Sullivan, in his harrowing final years, found a refuge and a space to pass his days and devote himself to writing.

Just next door, at the southwest corner of Adams and Michigan, in the Tip Top Inn atop the now vanished Pullman Building, Sullivan spent long evenings over cheese sandwiches and beer, regaling his Art Institute friends with stories and philosophical reflections while watching the sun set over the lake. Just south of Orchestra Hall, at 224 South Michigan, stands the bright white Railway Exchange Building, designed by Burnham and Company and for many years topped by a gigantic "Santa Fe" sign, reminiscent of the days when this building provided office space for railway officials, whose extensive yards dominated the lakeshore on the other side of the avenue. For most of the last decade of his life, Daniel Burnham and associates occupied offices on the fourteenth floor. Much of the 1909 Burnham Plan for Chicago was hatched here. Several architectural firms still maintain offices in the Railway Exchange building, including the international mega-firm Skidmore, Owings and Merrill.

The next block to the south, at 310 South Michigan, is the Metropolitan Tower (first named the Straus Building), a skyscraper of luxury residential condos topped with a stepped pyramid. The Metropolitan was another product of Burnham protégés Ernest Graham, Peirce Anderson, Edward Probst, and Howard Judson White. At the end of this block, at the corner of Ida B. Wells Drive and Michigan Avenue, looms an early Adler and Sullivan masterpiece: the Auditorium Building. Originally designed as a combination theater, hotel, and commercial building (and now housing an urban university), the Auditorium at the time of its completion was, in the words of the Chicago Architecture Center, "the largest, tallest, priciest, and heaviest building of its time."[1] Sullivan's partner, Dankmar Adler, was credited with creating an engineering marvel featuring a theater with remarkable acoustical properties, weight-bearing masonry walls atop an innovative foundation system, and an ingenious and complex interior iron-framing structure. If Adler created the imaginative framework, the aesthetic design, both interior and exterior, was largely the inspiration of Sullivan, brought to fruition with the help of his young assistant Frank Lloyd Wright.

The immense arch that stretches above a rough-hewn rocky base and frames the main Michigan Avenue entrance reflects the influence of one of Sullivan's early heroes, Henry Hobson Richardson of Boston. Richardson's expansive Romanesque-style rusticated entry arches, either designed by himself or his imitators, can be seen in hundreds of late nineteenth- and early twentieth-century homes and office buildings across the nation. Above the arch, the relatively plain and blocklike outside—true to the Richardsonian legacy—is largely free of the complex interweaving, flowerlike extravaganzas for which Sullivan would become known. On the second-floor now-enclosed loggia, university students can look out over the vast grounds of Grant Park. The landscaped lakefront was expanded outward beginning in the weeks following the Great Chicago Fire of 1871 and eventually reimagined and reshaped in part by Burnham's and Bennett's 1909 *Plan of Chicago*.[2]

If we time our arrival to coincide with a public performance at the Auditorium, we can step inside and witness Sullivan the creative master at work: the grand staircase that sweeps dramatically upward; intricate carvings and stenciling, elaborate mosaics and plaster moldings; the detailed column capitals that recall those of the Stock Exchange Trading Room; the second-floor colored-glass skylights. Every element contributes to an overall effect of lush extravagance and elegance suitable to the operas that the theater was originally designed to showcase.

Sullivan and Burnham, Burnham and Sullivan. And this represents just a handful of sites along Michigan Avenue. If you and I have time to walk a few blocks inland, we could take in another Sullivan landmark at the corner of State and Madison: the Sullivan Center, for years known to Chicagoans as the Carson, Pirie, Scott and Company Building. On LaSalle Street we could visit the dark and towering Monadnock or the airy atrium of the Rookery, both designed by Burnham and Root. At 15–19 South Wabash, we could view Adler and Sullivan's Jewelers Building. And across the street we could examine the recently uncovered decorative work on original Schlesinger and Mayer storefronts at 18 and 22 South Wabash. A walk one block west to State Street and one block north brings us to the white terra-cotta Reliance Building at 1 West Washington, built according to a design by Root for the Burnham company and thought by some to have served as a precursor for the glass-and-steel high-rise modernism of Mies van der Rohe.

The two men connected with these creations—either directly or through their immediate associates and disciples—were hardly intimate friends and occupied different spaces in Chicago's architectural community. Yet they knew each other through many years and resembled each other in certain important ways. They both looked to American literary and cultural traditions for inspiration, and they both saw architecture as a form of spiritual expression of positively Emersonian intensity and pervasiveness. It may be hard to imagine, in a highly secular age, locating spiritual content in the stone and steel of commercial buildings. But it may be equally hard to imagine a present-day visitor—no matter how deep or shallow his or her religious convictions—resisting at least a slight spiritual lift of the heart upon experiencing the design intricacies of Burnham and Root's Rookery light court or the carefully orchestrated union of light and ornamentation in Adler and Sullivan's Auditorium Theater.

For all their artistic and philosophical predilections and preferences, they believed that commercial structures should serve the client and the client's customers. They worked ceaselessly; their projects consumed them. They embraced nature, believed people of all social classes required intimate and daily involvement in the natural world, and included it in their architectural thinking: Burnham through designs for immense expanses of parks, shorelines, and lagoons; Sullivan through an "organic" architecture that sought to inject the spirit of nature into of the very bones of his buildings.

So how did two figures so thoroughly immersed in nineteenth-century history and culture—and so inclined to locate transcendental and spiritual meaning in their physical creations—arrive at such different forms of material expression? The answer must lie in their distinct personalities and personal inclinations. From early on Daniel Burnham exhibited a respect for the work and values of his contemporaries and artistic forebears. His management of the Columbian Exposition resulted in decisions that favored the tried, true, and traditional—an orientation that lasted, for him, far beyond the confines of the World's Fair. Louis Sullivan, by contrast, carried little respect for convention, authorities, or the authority of history. The small boy for whom school represented a "vile, unspeakably gloomy . . . filthy prison for children" grew into the man for whom the cherished beliefs and assumptions of his professional colleagues amounted to little more than "symptoms of insanity." Both Burnham and Sullivan welcomed, and adapted quickly to, technical innovation in architecture. But in matters of style and form Burnham's conservative temperament gradually asserted itself, while Sullivan readily embraced the role of fearless iconoclast.

We measure our lives by what we love and what we leave behind. By these standards both men, for all their human limitations and sometimes misguided cultural assumptions, can be said to have fared well in the long view of history. Daniel Burnham's loves extended in many directions: to family members, to neighbors and business associates, to an ideal of the power of beauty and spiritual meaning that, he believed, may be embodied in the human-made physical environment. His personal warmth, humor, idealism, and sincerity made him one of the most successful architectural leaders and managers of his time and inspired extraordinary loyalty among those who worked with and for him. His signature great achievement, the World's Columbian Exposition of 1893, vanished almost entirely from the face of the earth in a few short months, but the memory of its transformative effects has never faded. Of course, Burnham also left behind architectural and urban structures that remain, for many visitors and occupants, worthy exemplars of the Swedenborgian union of utility and beauty.

Louis Sullivan's love for his fellow human beings existed on a more abstract plane. In interpersonal relationships he often failed, and his character embodied noticeable contradictions. He was deeply committed to democracy and democratic values in architecture, but at the same time he demanded something resembling autocratic control for the designing artist/architect. He could be a charming conversationalist in the right company yet also direct withering criticism at those he regarded as his artistic enemies. But his love for great, original architecture, and his belief in the need for his admirers and associates to forge their own path, was unchanging and absolute. Several key figures of twentieth-century architecture were inspired to follow his lead. Frank Lloyd Wright did not doubt the wellspring of Louis Sullivan's fervent devotion to his beliefs. "Principle," said Wright, "is all and single the reality my master . . . loved."[3] Although too many of Sullivan's greatest buildings have fallen to the wrecking ball, enough remain—from his hands and the hands of his most dedicated disciples—to remind us of the continuing strength of the Sullivan legacy.

And for those intrigued by the lives and work of Burnham and Sullivan, their friends, associates, and many others who followed in their footsteps, a walk along Michigan Avenue is just a taste of what more there is to see.

Notes

Chapter 1. Uncle Dan, Beloved Master

1. Frank Lloyd Wright, *An Autobiography* (London: Longmans, Green and Co., 1932; New York: Horizon Press, 1977), 149–52. Unless otherwise noted, all subsequent references to Wright's visit in the Waller home derive from the Horizon Press edition of this source.

2. Thomas Hines, *Burnham of Chicago: Architect and Planner*, 2nd ed. (Chicago: University of Chicago Press, 2009), 268.

3. Wright, *An Autobiography*, 125.

4. Hugh Morrison, *Louis Sullivan: Prophet of Modern Architecture* (1935; repr., New York: W. W. Norton, 1998), 149.

5. Daniel Burnham, Business Diaries, 31 January 1897, series 5, vol. 3, Daniel H. Burnham Collection, Ryerson and Burnham Art and Architecture Archives, Art Institute of Chicago.

6. Louis Sullivan, *Kindergarten Chats and Other Writings* (New York: Wittenborn, Schulz, 1947), 112.

7. Louis Sullivan, *The Autobiography of an Idea* (New York: Press of the American Institute of Architects, 1926), 291.

8. Daniel Burnham to Charles Moore, 5 May 1908, series 8, box 63.20, Burnham Collection, Art Institute of Chicago.

9. The phrase appears in early manuscript versions of *Kindergarten Chats* held at the Art Institute of Chicago. See, for example, Sullivaniana Collection, series 2, box 15.

10. Wright, *An Autobiography*, 125.

11. Louis Sullivan, "The High Building Question," in *Louis Sullivan: The Public Papers*, ed. Robert Twombly (Chicago: University of Chicago Press, 1988), 79.

12. Sullivan, *The Autobiography of an Idea*, 286.

13. Daniel H. Burnham and Edward H. Bennett, *The Plan of Chicago* (Chicago: The Commercial Club, 1909), 50.

14. Charles Moore, *Daniel H. Burnham: Architect, Planner of Cities*, vol. 2 (Boston: Houghton Mifflin, 1921), 174.

15. Louis Sullivan, "What Is the Just Subordination, in Architectural Design, of Details to Mass," *Louis Sullivan: The Public Papers*, 33; Sullivan, *The Autobiography of an Idea*, 286.

16. Robert Twombly, *Louis Sullivan: His Life and Work* (Chicago: University of Chicago Press, 1986), 400; Robert Twombly and Narciso G. Menocal, *Louis Sullivan: The Poetry of Architecture* (New York: W. W. Norton, 2000), 114–15.

17. Louis Sullivan, "What Is Architecture?" *Louis Sullivan: The Public Papers*, 190.

18. Sullivan, *Kindergarten Chats*, 99.

19. Burnham and Bennett, *The Plan of Chicago*, 117.

20. Joan Draper, "Paris by the Lake: Sources of Burnham's Plan of Chicago," in *Chicago Architecture, 1872–1922: Birth of a Metropolis*, ed. John Zukowsky (Munich: Prestel Verlag, 1987), 114.

21. Thomas Hines, "The Imperial Façade: Daniel H. Burnham and American Architectural Planning in the Philippines," *Pacific Historical Review* 41, no. 1 (February 1972): 36.

22. "Resignation of Director of Works Burnham," *Inland Architect and News Record* 22, no. 4 (November 1893): 33.

23. "Honors to D. H. Burnham," *New York Tribune*, March 26, 1893.

24. Sullivan, *The Autobiography of an Idea*, 258–59.

25. Hines, *Burnham of Chicago*, 369.

Chapter 2. "There Was a Child Went Forth"

1. Charles Moore, *Daniel H. Burnham: Architect, Planner of Cities*, vol. 1 (Boston: Houghton Mifflin, 1921), 7.

2. Frederick Douglass, *My Bondage and My Freedom* (New York: Miller, Orton, and Mulligan, 1855), 371.

3. John Lewis Peyton, "Seeing Chicago from a 'Trap'," in *As Others See Chicago: Impressions of Visitors, 1673–1933*, ed. Bessie Louise Pierce (Chicago: University of Chicago Press, 2004), 100–101.

4. John Van Osdel, "History of Chicago Architecture, Part VI," *Inland Architect and Builder* 2, no.1 (August 1883): 89. One pair of critics has likened American cities of the nineteenth century to "unplanned stewpots leaking from whatever cracks the topography inflicted," a situation the Burnham-inspired City Beautiful movement launched in the wake of the 1893 World's Fair was partly designed to address. See Steve Mannheimer and Kate Christianson, "The Second Coming of City Beautiful," *Landscape Architecture* 82, no. 4 (April 1992): 62.

5. Henry Ericsson, *Sixty Years a Builder: The Autobiography of Henry Ericsson* (Chicago: A. Kroch and Son, 1942), 150.

6. Henry David Thoreau, *The Maine Woods* (Boston: Houghton Mifflin, 1892), 6.

7. Henry David Thoreau, *Walden and Resistance to Civil Government*, ed. William Rossi, 2nd ed. (New York: W. W. Norton, 1992), 32.

8. Horatio Greenough, *Form and Function: Remarks on Art, Design, and Architecture*, ed. Harold A. Small (Berkeley: University of California Press, 1947), 118, 157, 175.

9. Daniel Burnham Jr. to Charles Moore, 1 December 1919, series 3, box 27.6, Burnham Collection, Art Institute of Chicago.

10. Robert E. Aliasso Jr. interview with Elaine Scott, email message, August 8, 2011.

11. Signe Toksvig, *Emanuel Swedenborg: Scientist and Mystic* (New Haven, CT: Yale University Press, 1948), 84.

12. Emanuel Swedenborg, *Heaven and Its Wonders and Hell, From Things Heard and Seen*, trans. John C. Ager (West Chester, PA: Swedenborg Foundation, 2009), section 186, https://swedenborg.com/wp-content/uploads/2013/03/swedenborg_foundation_heaven _and_hell.pdf.

13. Hines, *Burnham of Chicago*, 5–6.

14. Ralph Waldo Emerson, "Nature," in *Selections from Ralph Waldo Emerson*, ed. Stephen E. Whicher (Boston: Houghton Mifflin, 1957), 31, 50.

15. Ralph Waldo Emerson, "Swedenborg; or, The Mystic," in *Representative Men: Seven Lectures* (New York: Home Book Company, n.d.), 99.

16. Hines, *Burnham of Chicago*, 6.

17. J. Coleman Hart, "Unity in Architecture," *The Crayon* 6, no. 3 (March 1859): 86.

18. Hart, "Unity in Architecture," 85.

19. Hart's reference to Ruskin, quoted on page 86 of "Unity in Architecture," is taken from the opening lines of Ruskin's "Lamp of Sacrifice" in the widely influential *The Seven Lamps of Architecture* (London: Smith, Elder and Co., 1849), wherein Ruskin declared that architecture can be distinguished from mere "building" by impressing on its utilitarian form "certain characters venerable or beautiful, but otherwise unnecessary." Hart's positive comments on Emerson appear on page 85 of the "Unity" paper.

20. Moore, *Daniel H. Burnham*, vol. 1, 10.

21. "Biography of Daniel Hudson Burnham of Chicago, Notes for Editor," box 13, Charles Moore Papers, Manuscript Division, Library of Congress, Washington, DC.

22. Elizabeth Burnham to Ellen Burnham, 26 November 1848, box 13, Moore Papers, Library of Congress.

23. Elizabeth Burnham and Edwin Burnham to Edwin Burnham Jr., 3 October 1853, box 13, Moore Papers, Library of Congress. See also Hines, *Burnham of Chicago*, 6–7.

24. Daniel Burnham Jr. to Charles Moore, 1 December 1919, series 3, box 27.6, Burnham Collection, Art Institute of Chicago.

25. Clara Woodyatt, "Mrs. Elizabeth Keith Burnham," series 4, box 29.26, Burnham Collection, Art Institute of Chicago.

26. Daniel Burnham Jr. to Charles Moore, 1 December 1919, Burnham Collection, Art Institute of Chicago. An undated newspaper clipping held at the Henderson, New York, Historical Society—Elba A. Henry's "Times Good in Middletown Springs When John Burnham Was in Charge"—reported that Daniel's great grandfather John Burnham Jr. regularly attended church meetings and gave financial support to the minister but "the good people of that time did not look upon his ventures as likely to prosper for the man did not believe in the immortality of the soul!" This is further evidence that unorthodox (and locally unpopular) religious thought was not unfamiliar territory for some members of Daniel Burnham's paternal and maternal lines. See also Moore, *Daniel H. Burnham*, vol. 1, 8.

27. Daniel Burnham Jr. to Charles Moore, 1 December 1919, Burnham Collection, Art Institute of Chicago. See also Hines, *Burnham of Chicago*, 7–8.

28. Thomas E. Tallmadge, *Architecture in Old Chicago* (Chicago: University of Chicago Press, 1941), 62.

29. Donald Miller, *City of the Century: The Epic of Chicago and the Making of America* (New York: Simon & Schuster, 1996), 89.

30. Miller, *City of the Century*, 96.

31. Louis Sullivan, *The Autobiography of an Idea*, 36. In *Louis Sullivan: His Life and Work* Robert Twombly points out (page 10) that Sullivan's birth records in Boston listed the birth name as "Henry Louis" but adds that this was likely a clerical mistake, in that his mother's name was also misspelled and that the boy was consistently referred to as "Louis Henry" by the family. As Timothy Samuelson has noted, "Sullivan probably never anticipated that by attributing his middle name as a tribute to maternal grandfather, Henri List, an alternate spelling would proliferate." See *Louis Sullivan's Idea* (Chicago: Alphawood Foundation, 2021), n.p.

32. Twombly, *Louis Sullivan: His Life and Work*, 10.

33. Sullivan, *The Autobiography of an Idea*, 15–16, 19–20.

34. Walt Whitman, *Leaves of Grass* (Brooklyn: W. Whitman, 1855), 92. All subsequent Whitman quotations in this chapter derive from this source.

35. Sullivan, *The Autobiography of an Idea*, 19.

36. Sullivan, *The Autobiography of an Idea*, 19.

37. Richard P. Adams, "Architecture and the Romantic Tradition: Coleridge to Wright," *American Quarterly* 9, no. 1 (Spring 1957): 58. See also David S. Andrew, *Louis Sullivan and the Polemics of Modern Architecture* (Urbana: University of Illinois Press, 1985), 70–72. For a scholarly argument holding that Louis Sullivan's thought may legitimately be traced to Emerson and other early transcendentalists, see Edward Madden, "Transcendental Influences on Louis Sullivan and Frank Lloyd Wright," *Transactions of the Charles S. Peirce Society* 31, no. 2 (Spring 1995): 286–321.

38. Sullivan, *Kindergarten Chats*, 25.

Chapter 3. Pathways

1. Report card for Daniel Burnham, Garden City Institute, 11 January 1856, series 4, box 29.26, Burnham Collection, Art Institute of Chicago.

2. "Alumni Who Are a Credit: Noted Graduates of the Old Central High School," *Chicago Sunday Tribune*, December 29, 1895.

3. "Alumni Who are a Credit," *Chicago Sunday Tribune*.

4. Twombly, *Louis Sullivan: His Life and Work*, 12.

5. Sullivan, *The Autobiography of an Idea*, 21–22.

6. Sullivan, *The Autobiography of an Idea*, 24.

7. Twombly, *Louis Sullivan: His Life and Work*, 13.

8. "Biography of Daniel Hudson Burnham of Chicago, Notes for Editor," box 13, Moore Papers, Library of Congress.

9. William Keith to Daniel Burnham, n.d., box 13, Moore Papers, Library of Congress.

10. Hines, *Burnham of Chicago*, 11.

11. Moore, *Daniel H. Burnham*, vol. 1, 15.

12. Daniel Burnham to Edwin Burnham, 21 January 1866, series 2, box 25.2, Burnham Collection, Art Institute of Chicago.

13. Daniel Burnham to Edwin Burnham, 21 January 1866, Burnham Collection.

14. Daniel Burnham to Elizabeth Burnham, 24 November 1867, series 2, box 25.2, Burnham Collection, Art Institute of Chicago.

15. Daniel Burnham to Elizabeth Burnham, 15 December 1867, series 2, box 25.2, Burnham Collection, Art Institute of Chicago.

16. Daniel Burnham to Elizabeth Burnham, 27 April 1868, series 2, box 25.2, Burnham Collection, Art Institute of Chicago.

17. Daniel Burnham to Elizabeth Burnham, 24 November 1867, Burnham Collection, Art Institute of Chicago.

18. Daniel Burnham to Elizabeth Burnham, 24 November 1867, Burnham Collection.

19. Daniel Burnham to Elizabeth Burnham, 15 December 1867, Burnham Collection, Art Institute of Chicago.

20. Daniel Burnham to Elizabeth Burnham, 24 November 1867, Burnham Collection, Art Institute of Chicago.

21. Daniel Burnham to Elizabeth Burnham, 24 November 1867, Burnham Collection.

22. Daniel Burnham to Elizabeth Burnham, 24 November 1867, Burnham Collection.

23. Daniel Burnham to Elizabeth Burnham, 15 December 1867, Burnham Collection, Art Institute of Chicago.

24. Daniel Burnham to Elizabeth Burnham, 24 November 1867, Burnham Collection, Art Institute of Chicago. Burnham added that there was an architectural school he might attend but that he expected to receive most of his training in the office. The school he was referring to may have been Illinois Industrial

University, later to be renamed the University of Illinois. In May 1867 Illinois became, after MIT, one of the first American schools to announce plans to offer a program for professional training in architecture.

25. Edwin Burnham to Elizabeth Burnham, 9 December 1867, Burnham Collection, Art Institute of Chicago.

26. Daniel Burnham to Elizabeth Burnham, 1 December 1867, Burnham Collection, Art Institute of Chicago.

27. John Ruskin, *The Stones of Venice: The Foundations*, vol. 1 (New York: John B. Alden, 1885), 132.

28. Daniel Burnham to Elizabeth Burnham, 11 May 1868, Burnham Collection, Art Institute of Chicago.

29. See Joanna Merwood-Salisbury, *Chicago 1890: The Skyscraper and the Modern City* (Chicago: University of Chicago Press, 2009), 48, who has suggested that "terra-cotta tile is as important a material as steel in the creation of an aesthetic for modern architecture."

30. Twombly, *Louis Sullivan: His Life and Work*, 19.

31. Sullivan, *The Autobiography of an Idea*, 75. The passages that follow describing Sullivan's summer in Newburyport are drawn from *The Autobiography of an Idea*, 79–86.

32. Sullivan, *The Autobiography of an Idea*, 98–99.

33. Sullivan, *The Autobiography of an Idea*, 100–101.

34. Paul M. Wright, "Louis Sullivan Woke Up Here," *The Massachusetts Review* 28, no. 2 (Summer 1987): 328.

35. Sullivan, *The Autobiography of an Idea*, 122–23.

36. Paul M. Wright, "Louis Sullivan Woke Up Here," 329.

37. Sullivan, *The Autobiography of an Idea*, 101. All subsequent Sullivan-related passages derive from this source, pages 103 through 127.

Chapter 4. Apprenticeship

1. Arnold Lewis, *An Early Encounter with Tomorrow: Europeans, Chicago's Loop, and the World's Columbian Exposition* (Urbana: University of Illinois Press, 1997), 1.

2. Harold M. Mayer and Richard C. Wade, *Chicago: Growth of a Metropolis* (Chicago: University of Chicago Press: 1969), 106.

3. Donald Miller, *City of the Century: The Epic of Chicago and the Making of America* (New York: Simon & Schuster, 1996), 132.

4. Lewis, *An Early Encounter with Tomorrow*, 105.

5. Lewis Mumford, *The Brown Decades: A Study of the Arts in America, 1865–1895* (New York: Dover, 1971), 2–4.

6. Thomas Tallmadge, *Architecture in Old Chicago*, 65, 69, 72.

7. Mayer and Wade, *Chicago: Growth of a Metropolis*, 52.

8. Daniel H. Burnham Jr. to Charles Moore, 4 May 1920, series 3, box 27.8, Burnham Collection, Art Institute of Chicago.

9. "The Democratic Ticket," *Elko Independent*, October 8, 1870.

10. Daniel Burnham to his sisters, 13 March 1870, series 2, box 26.22, Burnham Collection, Art Institute of Chicago.

11. Daniel Burnham to Ellen Burnham, 30 April 1870, series 2, box 26.22, Burnham Collection, Art Institute of Chicago.

12. Mark Twain, *Roughing It* (Berkeley: University of California Press, 1972), 141, 393.

13. See Michael Kowalewski, "Romancing the Gold Rush: The Literature of the California Frontier," *California History* 79, no. 2 (Summer 2000): 204–25.

14. Daniel Burnham to Ellen Burnham, 30 April 1870, series 2, box 26.22, Burnham Collection, Art Institute of Chicago.

15. Essay on the mountain breeze, 29 July 1870, series 4, box 34.29, Burnham Collection, Art Institute of Chicago.

16. Essay about Jones and a shootout, n.d., series 4, box 34.38, Burnham Collection, Art Institute of Chicago.

17. Essay on mines and people in Nevada, n.d., series 4, box 34.40, Burnham Collection, Art Institute of Chicago.

18. "When a mining camp gets well known and is doing well," wrote Burnham, "the Bank immediately puts out a feeler in its midst, and from that time all healthy enterprise ceases, and like a poor consumptive, who recognizes the finger of disease, and the near approach of the light weight death, the place looses [*sic*] energy and calmly sits down to meet its fate." Essay on life in Nevada, n.d., series 4, box 34.39, Burnham Collection, Art Institute of Chicago.

19. Sullivan, *The Autobiography of an Idea*, 129.

20. Sullivan, *The Autobiography of an Idea*, 141–42. As with all the years-removed recollections in his *Autobiography*, Sullivan's accounts must be viewed as highly subjective and as the sometimes-questionable impressions of a deeply dewy-eyed boy and young man. Minnie may well have told Louis of her interest in him, or Louis may have assumed he could read her mind. What remains unquestionable is the strong emotional connection Louis felt at the time. Most biographers report the girl's full name as "Minnie Whittlesey," based on the assumption that the girl he encountered on the veranda that day must have been Walter and Jennie Whittlesey's daughter. However records suggest Minnie's last name was actually Culver—no relation to Aunt Jennie and Uncle Walter. See George E. Pettengill, "Who Was Sullivan's Minnie?" *Journal of the Society of Architectural Historians* 47, no. 2 (June 1988): 177–78.

21. Sullivan, *The Autobiography of an Idea*, 156–57.

22. Twombly, *Louis Sullivan: His Life and Work*, 25.

23. Sullivan, *The Autobiography of an Idea*, 166.

24. Louis Sullivan, "The Young Man in Architecture," *Louis Sullivan: The Public Papers*, 137.

25. Moore, *Daniel H. Burnham*, vol. 1, 16.

26. Edwin Burnham to Asher Carter, 5 August 1872, series 1, box 3.70, Burnham Collection, Art Institute of Chicago.

27. Peter B. Wight, "Daniel Hudson Burnham: An Appreciation. A Paper Delivered at a Meeting Held at the Art Institute of Chicago, June 11, 1912," *Architectural Record* 32, no. 2 (August 1912): 178.

28. Harriet Monroe, *John Wellborn Root: A Study of His Life and Work* (Boston: Houghton, Mifflin, 1896), 23.

29. Sullivan, *The Autobiography of an Idea*, 184–88.

30. Louis H. Sullivan and John H. Edelmann, Lotus Club Notebook, 1872–1880, 1–2, Special Collections, Avery Architectural and Fine Arts Library, Columbia University.

31. Sullivan, *The Autobiography of an Idea*, 188–189.

32. Sullivan, *The Autobiography of an Idea*, 182.

33. Sullivan, *The Autobiography of an Idea*, 191–93.

34. Twombly, *Louis Sullivan: His Life and Work*, 42–43.

35. Sullivan, *The Autobiography of an Idea*, 194.

36. Isaiah Ellis, "The Inscrutable Spirit of Louis Sullivan: Transcendentalism and American Architecture at the Turn of the Twentieth Century" (Master of Arts Thesis, University of North Carolina at Chapel Hill, 2017), 21, 27; William H. Furness, "Closing Address, Proceedings of the Fourth Annual Convention of the American Institute of Architects, November 8–9, 1870," in *The Literature of Architecture: The Evolution of Architectural Theory and Practice in Nineteenth-Century America*, ed. Don Gifford (New York: E. P. Dutton, 1966), 394–95. In William Henry Furness's talk, he referred to the "blood relationship of architecture to nature" before quoting from Emerson's poem "The Problem," which describes a universal force in nature—unmediated by churches or churchmen—that has inspired the great human-made structures we so admire. Peter B. Wight, who shortly thereafter welcomed both John Root and Daniel Burnham into his firm, was in attendance and served as the organization's secretary.

37. Sullivan, *The Autobiography of an Idea*, 195.

38. Sullivan, *The Autobiography of an Idea*, 196–197.

39. Sullivan, *The Autobiography of an Idea*, 197.

40. Miller, *City of the Century*, 178.

41. Tallmadge, *Architecture in Old Chicago*, 95, 115.

42. Monroe, *John Wellborn Root*, 24.

43. Monroe, *John Wellborn Root*, 23–24.

44. Moore, *Daniel H. Burnham,* vol. 1, 20–21.

45. Moore, *Daniel H. Burnham,* vol. 1, 20–21.

46. Wight, "Daniel Hudson Burnham: An Appreciation," 178.

47. Monroe, *John Wellborn Root*, 14, 44.

48. Sketchbook of architectural details, series 4, box 28.9, Burnham Collection, Art Institute of Chicago.

49. Monroe, *John Wellborn Root*, 35.

50. Monroe, *John Wellborn Root*, 12.

51. Monroe, *John Wellborn Root*, 25.

52. Moore, *Daniel H. Burnham*, vol. 1, 21.

53. Moore, *Daniel H. Burnham*, vol. 1, 22.

54. Daniel H. Burnham Jr. to Charles Moore, 21 February 1918, series 3, box 27.3, Burnham Collection, Art Institute of Chicago.

55. Mary (Burnham) Goddard to Daniel Burnham, 18 March 1875, series 2, box 26.22, Burnham Collection, Art Institute of Chicago.

56. Moore, *Daniel H. Burnham*, vol. 1, 23.

57. Daniel H. Burnham Jr. to Charles Moore, 21 February 1918, Burnham Collection.

58. Sullivan, *The Autobiography of an Idea*, 204. See also Roxanne Kuter Williamson, *American Architects and the Mechanics of Fame* (Austin: University of Texas Press, 1991), 34–35.

59. Sullivan, *The Autobiography of an Idea*, 203–4.

60. Sullivan, *The Autobiography of an Idea*, 206.

61. Sullivan, *The Autobiography of an Idea*, 207.

62. Twombly, *Louis Sullivan: His Life and Work*, 80.

63. Samuelson, *Louis Sullivan's Idea*, n.p. The architect Irving K. Pond also made the acquaintance of John Edelmann in these early days. Newly arrived in Chicago and living with college roommates, Pond was present at an evening visit from Edelmann in which John "talked transcendentalism of a sort" and tossed off quick sketches of "spiky shapes and budlike things" that had a distinctly Sullivanesque look. Only natural, Edelmann is reported to have said, "as originally he had given Louis the idea." See David Van Zanten, "Sullivan to 1890," in *Louis Sullivan: The Function of Ornament*, ed. Wim de Wit (New York: W. W. Norton, 1985), 34.

64. Edmund Morris, *The Rise of Theodore Roosevelt* (New York: The Modern Library, 2001), 51.

65. Sullivan, *The Autobiography of an Idea*, 211–12. Sullivan recalled that the club had been named after a bed of lotus located on the banks of the stream the club bordered. He also asserted that Edelmann favored the Greek spelling "lotos" for the club, which is the spelling observed here.

66. Sullivan and Edelmann, Lotus Club Notebook, 62.

67. Sullivan, *The Autobiography of an Idea*, 220–21.

68. Wright, *An Autobiography*, 129.

69. Sullivan, *The Autobiography of an Idea*, 311.

70. Louis Sullivan to Albert Sullivan, 7 December 1874, series 1, box 1.1a, Sullivaniana Collection, 1780–2018, Ryerson and Burnham Art and Architecture Archives, Art Institute of Chicago.

71. Wright, *An Autobiography*, 289. See also Samuelson, *Louis Sullivan's Idea*, n. p.

72. Sullivan, *The Autobiography of an Idea*, 234.

73. Sullivan, *The Autobiography of an Idea*, 234–35.

74. Sullivan, *The Autobiography of an Idea*, 234.

75. See, for example, drawings 65, 66, 67, 71 in "Catalogue of Drawings 1867–1923," in Twombly and Menocal, *Louis Sullivan: The Poetry of Architecture*, 217–20.

76. Sullivan, *The Autobiography of an Idea*, 240–41.

77. Hines, *Burnham of Chicago*, 29.

78. See Daniel Hoffman, *The Architecture of John Wellborn Root* (Chicago: University of Chicago Press, 1973), 143–48.

79. Wight, "Daniel Hudson Burnham: An Appreciation," 178.

80. Sullivan, *The Autobiography of an Idea*, 233.

81. Sullivan and Edelmann, Lotus Club Notebook, 88–89, 190, 186, 200, 163, 171, 175.

82. Chicago Foot Ball Club program, series 1, box 1.19, Sullivaniana Collection, Art Institute of Chicago; "Athletic. The Chicago Football Club," *Chicago Daily Tribune*, May 28, 1876.

83. "The Fourth of July at Calumet," *New York Sportsman*, 15 July 1876, series 1, box 1.22, Sullivaniana Collection, Art Institute of Chicago.

84. Dave Revsine, *The Opening Kickoff: The Tumultuous Birth of a Football Nation* (Guilford, CT: Rowman and Littlefield, 2014), 24.

85. "Football Match at Evanston," *Chicago Daily Tribune,* February 23, 1876

86. "Football Match at Evanston," *Chicago Daily Tribune,* February 23, 1876; "Locals," *The Tripod,* February 24, 1876. See also Larry LaTourette, *Northwestern Wildcat Football* (Charleston: Arcadia, 2005), 9–10.

87. Sullivan, *The Autobiography of an Idea,* 244–45.

88. H. H. Starr, "Erection of the Kentucky River High Bridge," *Railway Age Gazette*, 50, no. 17 (April 28, 1911): 984.

89. Sullivan, *The Autobiography of an Idea*, 247.

90. Sullivan, *The Autobiography of an Idea*, 245, 249–250.

91. "Opening Services at D. L. Moody's Chicago Avenue Church," *Chicago Daily Tribune*, June 2, 1876.

92. Twombly, *Louis Sullivan: His Life and Work*, 94.

93. See Twombly, *Louis Sullivan: His Life and Work,* 94–96, and Charles E. Gregersen, *Louis Sullivan and His Mentor, John Herman Edelmann, Architect* (Bloomington, IN: AuthorHouse, 2013), 19.

94. Sullivan, *The Autobiography of an Idea*, 252–53.

95. The first professional architecture program in America was established by the Massachusetts Institute of Technology (MIT) in 1868, a mere four years before Sullivan enrolled there. MIT's example was followed by Cornell (1871), the University of Illinois (1873), Columbia (1881), and Tuskegee (1881). The first architecture professional organization, the American Institute of Architects (AIA), was organized in 1857, with Richard Morris Hunt, fresh from the École des Beaux-Arts in Paris, as one of the founding members. Licensing requirements came much later. In 1897 Illinois became the first state to make such requirements a matter of law.

Chapter 5. Fruition

1. Manhattan builders held an advantage over their counterparts in Chicago since, as Jason Barr has pointed out, the island "is really just one long . . . boulder." However, Barr goes on to note that the "boulder" is not flat, that bedrock depth

varies considerably, and that in any case skyscraper construction on Manhattan depended more on economic factors than on geology. See "The Bedrock Myth and the Rise of Midtown Manhattan (Part I)," *Building the Skyline: The Birth and Growth of Manhattan's Skyscrapers*, July 29, 2019, https://buildingtheskyline.org/bedrock-and-midtown-i.

2. Monroe, *John Wellborn Root*, 193–94.

3. "The Grannis Block," *Chicago Daily Tribune*, May 1, 1881.

4. Moore, *Daniel H. Burnham*, vol. 1, 24.

5. Tallmadge, *Architecture in Old Chicago*, 142–43.

6. Ericsson, *Sixty Years a Builder*, 45.

7. Tallmadge, *Architecture in Old Chicago*, 143.

8. As recently as 1975, *The Oxford English Dictionary* listed an 1891 article in the *Boston Journal* as the first appearance of "skyscraper" in reference to tall buildings. It may well be that a pre-1883 print reference to the term used in this sense remains to be discovered.

9. "New York Gossip." *Chicago Daily Tribune*, February 25, 1883.

10. M. A. Lane, "High Buildings in Chicago," *Harper's Weekly*, October 31, 1891, 856–57.

11. "More Cloud Supporters," *Chicago Tribune*, July 7, 1889.

12. Ralph B. Peck, "History of Building Foundations in Chicago," *University of Illinois Bulletin* 45, no. 29 (January 2, 1948): 21.

13. Hines, *Burnham of Chicago*, 53.

14. *Inland Architect and Builder* 4, no. 4 (November 1884): 1.

15. "The Convention," *Inland Architect and Builder* 4, Extra Number (November 1884): 8.

16. "The Convention," *Inland Architect and Builder* 6, no. 5 (November 1885): 69, 71.

17. The Montezuma Hotel burned down only five months later, prompting another southwestern trip for Burnham when the firm received the commission to rebuild the luxury hotel. Burnham decided to relocate the structure on Reservoir Hill to take full advantage of the play of sunshine on the property and to afford visitors a more striking view of Gallinas Canyon and the region's mountain scenery. The new hotel was completed and opened to the public on April 20, 1885. See Louise Harris Ivers, "The Montezuma Hotel," *New Mexico Architecture* (May-June 1977): 13–25.

18. Daniel Burnham, Mexico and San Francisco Diary, series 3, box 28.12, Burnham Collection, Art Institute of Chicago. Unless otherwise noted, all subsequent references to Burnham's diary entries of the 1883 Mexico and California trip derive from this source.

19. Tallmadge, *Architecture in Old Chicago*, 153.

20. "Development of Construction," *Economist* 55, no. 26 (June 24, 1916), https://chicagology.com/goldenage/goldenage144.

21. See Twombly, *Louis Sullivan: His Life and Work*, 99–101 for a discussion of Sullivan's occasional work projects with Adler during this period.

22. "Development of Construction," *Economist*, https://chicagology.com/goldenage/goldenage144.

23. Sullivan, *The Autobiography of an Idea*, 256.

24. Twombly, *Louis Sullivan: His Life and Work*, 101.

25. Twombly, *Louis Sullivan: His Life and Work*, 96.

26. Sullivan, *The Autobiography of an Idea*, 258.

27. Sullivan, *The Autobiography of an Idea*, 285–86.

28. Sullivan, *The Autobiography of an Idea*, 286.

29. Sullivan, *The Autobiography of an Idea,* 288–89.

30. Sullivan, *The Autobiography of an Idea*, 288.

31. "Amusements," *The Daily Inter-Ocean*, August 12, 1882.

32. "Amusements," *The Daily Inter-Ocean*, August 12, 1882.

33. Monroe, *John Wellborn Root*, 25.

34. Hines, *Burnham of Chicago*, 22–24.

35. Rochelle Elstein, *Dankmar Adler: A Biography* (Chicago: Arthur S. Elstein, 2017), 309, https://artic.contentdm.oclc.org/digital/api/collection/mqc/id/70186/download.

36. Elstein, *Dankmar Adler*, 158.

37. "The Music Hall," *Chicago Daily Tribune*, December 5, 1879.

38. Twombly, *Louis Sullivan: His Life and Work*, 96.

39. Twombly, *Louis Sullivan: His Life and Work*, 134.

40. "The Great Chicago Exposition," *Land Owner*, June 1873, https://chicagology.com/rebuilding/rebuilding016.

41. "A $250,000 Fire," *Chicago Daily Tribune,* February 20, 1885.

42. "The Grannis Block," *Chicago Daily Tribune,* May 1, 1881.

43. For a thorough discussion of fireproofing technologies developed during this period, see Sara E. Wermiel, *The Fireproof Building: Technology and Public Safety in the Nineteenth-Century American City* (Baltimore: Johns Hopkins University Press, 2000).

44. Ericsson, *Sixty Years a Builder*, 217–18.

45. Ericsson, *Sixty Years a Builder*, 185.

46. Al Chase, "Experts Settle Long Dispute on 1st Skyscraper," *Chicago Tribune*, November 22, 1931. Some architectural historians have noted that New York architects such as George Post and Richard Morris Hunt created masonry structures in the 1870s that rose well above the conventional five stories and so were designing buildings that could be considered skyscrapers or at least proto-skyscrapers. But architecture critic Carter Wiseman has argued that the standard approach by Post and Hunt and others was to make these buildings look like little more than "amplified short ones." See "The Rise of the Skyscraper and the Fall of Louis Sullivan, *American Heritage* 49, no. 1 (February/March 1998), https://www.american heritage.com/rise-skyscraper-and-fall-louis-sullivan.

47. Blair Kamin, "The Same People Who Demoted Willis Tower Could Strip Chicago of Another Skyscraper Title," *Chicago Tribune*, November 7, 2019, https://www.chicagotribune.com/2019/11/07/column-the-same-people-who-demoted-willis-tower-could-strip-chicago-of-another-skyscraper-title.

48. Thomas Leslie, "Built Like Bridges: Iron, Steel, and Rivets in the Nineteenth-Century Skyscraper," *Journal of the Society of Architectural Historians* 69, no. 2 (June 2010): 236.

49. Thomas Leslie, *Chicago Skyscrapers: 1871–1934* (Urbana: University of Illinois Press, 2013), 52.

50. Sullivan, *The Autobiography of an Idea*, 311, 313.

51. Louis Sullivan, *Kindergarten Chats*, 30.

52. Jeffrey Karl Ochsner, *H. H. Richardson: Complete Architectural Works* (Boston: Massachusetts Institute of Technology, 1982), 381.

53. Montgomery Schuyler, *American Architecture: Studies* (New York: Harper and Brothers, 1892), 133, https://www.gutenberg.org/ebooks/58697.

54. Tallmadge, *Architecture in Old Chicago*, 168.

55. Sullivan, *The Autobiography of an Idea*, 294.

56. Sullivan, *The Autobiography of an Idea*, 303.

57. Louis Sullivan, "Essay on Inspiration," *Inland Architect and Builder* 8, no. 8 (December 1886): 61.

58. Sullivan, "Essay on Inspiration," 63.

59. Sullivan, *The Autobiography of an Idea*, 302.

60. Sullivan, *The Autobiography of an Idea*, 303.

61. Louis H. Sullivan to Walt Whitman, 3 February 1887, series 1, box 1.2b, Sullivaniana Collection, Art Institute of Chicago. In the letter, Sullivan recalled the title of the poem as "Elemental Rights."

62. The 1909 auction of books from Sullivan's personal library shows that, at that time, Sullivan possessed the 1860–61 edition published in Boston, in which "Elemental Drifts" opens the *Leaves of Grass* section on page 195. See Walt Whitman, *Leaves of Grass* (Boston: Thayer and Eldridge, 1860–61).

63. Sullivan, *The Autobiography of an Idea*, 22–23.

64. Sullivan to Walt Whitman, 3 February 1887, Sullivaniana Collection, Art Institute of Chicago.

65. Lauren Weingarden, "Naturalized Technology: Louis H. Sullivan's Whitmanesque Skyscrapers," *The Centennial Review* 30, no. 4 (Fall 1986): 481, 485. See also Naomi Tanabe Uechi's *Evolving Transcendentalism in Literature and Architecture* (Newcastle upon Tyne, UK: Cambridge Scholars Publishing, 2014), in particular chapter 2, "Sullivan and Whitman."

66. Louis Sullivan, "What is the Just Subordination, in Architectural Design, of Details to Mass?" *Louis Sullivan: The Public Papers*, 31.

67. Sullivan, "What is the Just Subordination, in Architectural Design, of Details to Mass?" 33. Sullivan frequently discussed architectural features in terms suggestive of "correspondences" between the physical and metaphysical worlds, though he did so without reference to Swedenborg. In the 1934 version of *Kindergarten Chats* he said that "[E]verything in life is, for us, a symbol. . . . which stands as a middle term between ourselves and the Infinite, in the marvelous mathematics of the universe." A concrete example, with echoes of both Swedenborg and John Ruskin, would be the simple pier, which Sullivan asserts represents upward aspiration and growth (the "rhythm of life") at the same time that its

solid anchorage in the ground suggests the counter-rhythm of "decadence, of destruction, of that which would crush to earth." See Sullivan, *Kindergarten Chats: On Architecture, Education and Democracy*, ed. and introduced by Claude F. Bragdon (n.p.: Scarab Fraternity Press, 1934), 202–03, 162.

68. Narciso Menocal, *Architecture as Nature: The Transcendentalist Idea of Louis Sullivan* (Madison: University of Wisconsin Press, 1981), 25. Sullivan biographer Robert Twombly also entertains the idea that a Swedenborgian concept of a masculine/feminine divide influenced Sullivan's thinking. See *Louis Sullivan: His Life and Work* and the book he co-wrote with Menocal, *Louis Sullivan: The Poetry of Architecture.* Lauren Weingarden also sees "manliness" as an attribute Sullivan sought to embed in his early buildings, but she views this largely in terms of Walt Whitman's influence. See *Louis H. Sullivan and a 19th-Century Poetics of Naturalized Architecture* (Farnham, UK: Ashgate, 2009), 242.

69. Wright, *An Autobiography*, 111–114, 514.

70. Daniel Burnham to Elizabeth Burnham, n.d., series 2, box 25.2, Burnham Collection, Art Institute of Chicago.

71. Daniel Burnham Jr. to Charles Moore, 27 May 1920, series 2, box 27.8, Burnham Collection, Art Institute of Chicago.

72. Daniel Burnham to Elizabeth Burnham, n.d., Burnham Collection, Art Institute of Chicago.

73. Daniel Burnham Jr. to Charles Moore, 27 May 1920, Burnham Collection, Art Institute of Chicago.

74. The Burnham Michigan Avenue home was located only five blocks from the site of the house that jazz great Louis Armstrong bought in the mid-1920s, when the area was rapidly becoming known, culturally and historically, as Chicago's Black Metropolis. For much of the 1880s, however, the Black population in Chicago was largely concentrated west of State Street between 16th and 24th Streets on the South Side, well north of the Burnhams' 43rd Street home, though not far from Millionaires' Row in the Prairie Avenue district. See Heidi Sperry, Susan Perry, and Terry Tatum, "Chicago's Black Renaissance Literary Movement," Department of Zoning and Land Use Planning, City of Chicago, n.d., https://www.chicago.gov/dam/city/depts/ zlup/Historic_Preservation/Publications/Lorraine_Hansberry_House_Landmark_Report.pdf.

75. "Grand Boulevard," *The Electronic Encyclopedia of Chicago* (Chicago: Chicago Historical Society, 2005), www.encyclopedia.chicagohistory.org/pages/537.html.

76. "Red War," *Chicago Daily Tribune,* July 26, 1877.

77. Miller, *City of the Century*, 471–72.

78. Irving K. Pond, "Home," *Inland Architect and News Record*, 10, no. 6 (November 1887): 61, 63–65.

79. Daniel Burnham to Samuel Bowles, 13 June 1905, series 1, box 1.7, Burnham Collection, Art Institute of Chicago. Burnham's linking of "free-trade" and "communism" may seem strange to twenty-first-century readers. In the nineteenth century free trade was a position often associated with classical

liberalism in opposition to "protectionist" policies that many saw as serving favored industrial interests of wealthy capitalists—especially those in the northern states.

80. Burnham to Samuel Bowles, 13 June 1905, Burnham Collection.

81. Jean F. Block, *Hyde Park Houses: An Informal History, 1856–1910* (Chicago: University of Chicago Press, 1978), 22.

82. Barbara J. Buchbinder-Green, *Evanston: A Pictorial History* (St. Louis: G. Bradley, 1989), 95.

83. Daniel Burnham to Elizabeth Burnham, n.d., Burnham Collection, Art Institute of Chicago.

84. Burnham to Elizabeth Burnham, n.d., Burnham Collection.

85. Hines, *Burnham of Chicago*, 265.

86. *Rand, McNally and Co.'s Bird's-Eye Views and Guide to Chicago* (Chicago: Rand, McNally, 1893), 145.

87. Hines, *Burnham of Chicago*, 57.

88. Schuyler, *American Architecture: Studies*, 143.

89. Jay Pridmore, *The Rookery* (San Francisco: Pomegranate, 2003), 35.

90. Pridmore, *The Rookery*, 11.

91. Daniel Burnham to Margaret Burnham, 23 January 1888, series 2, box 25.3, Burnham Collection, Art Institute of Chicago. An indication of Burnham's gift for inspiring deep and lasting friendships can be seen in an undated note William Keith included with a shipment of several canvases he sent to the Burnham family, including one for Burnham's mother, whom Keith referred to as "Saint Elizabeth." In a spontaneous addendum Keith openly addressed Burnham in the language of expressive intimacy that would not have seemed unusual or untoward among nineteenth-century correspondents: "I open this," wrote Keith, "to tell you that I think of you with real love lots of times in the daytime & when I lie awake at night." William Keith to Daniel Burnham, n.d., box 13, Moore Papers, Library of Congress.

92. "Fell with a Crash," *Chicago Tribune*, March 1, 1888.

93. Daniel Burnham to Margaret Burnham, 3 March 1888, series 2, box 25.3, Burnham Collection, Art Institute of Chicago.

94. "More Cloud Supporters," *Chicago Tribune*, July 7, 1889.

Chapter 6. Triumph

1. *Arguments Before a Special Committee of the United States Senate by Hon. DeWitt C. Cregier, Mr. Thos. B. Bryan, and Mr. Edward T. Jeffery, in Support of the Application of the Citizens of Chicago for the Location in Their City of the World's Exposition of 1892* (Washington, DC, Government Printing Office, 1890), 9, 10, 12.

2. Hines, *Burnham of Chicago*, 71.

3. Merwood-Salisbury, *Chicago 1890*, 56–69.

4. Monroe, *John Wellborn Root*, 122–23.

5. Monroe, *John Wellborn Root*, 198.

6. Paul Starrett, *Changing the Skyline: An Autobiography* (New York: Whittlesey House, 1938), 29, 33. An article in *Engineering and Building Record* (January 11, 1890): 83–84, titled "The Organization of an Architect's Office," included a diagram of the Burnham and Root office layout and highlighted unique approaches to business such as the inclusion of a gymnasium space ("equipped by the firm with foils and masks, several pairs of Indian clubs, and a set of chest weights"), the provision of an engineering superintendent for each important building, paid Saturday afternoons free, and "a vacation every year for old hands, during which their salaries go on."

7. Starrett, *Changing the Skyline*, 18, 42.

8. Monroe, *John Wellborn Root*, 260–62.

9. Daniel Burnham, interview notes by Charles Moore, 26 April 1908, box 13, Moore Papers, Library of Congress.

10. Daniel H. Burnham, "The Organization of the World's Columbian Exposition," *Inland Architect and News Record* 22, no. 1 (August 1893): 6.

11. John W. Root, "Art of Pure Color," *Inland Architect and Builder* 1, no. 6 (July 1883), 82; Merwood-Salisbury, *Chicago 1890*, 72.

12. Monroe, *John Wellborn Root*, 242–43.

13. Burnham, "The Organization of the World's Columbian Exposition," 6.

14. Charles Moore, "Lessons of the Chicago World's Fair: An Interview with the Late Daniel H. Burnham," *Architectural Record* 33, no. 1 (January 1913): 43–44.

15. Of value, especially for visual representations of the fair, are Stanley Appelbaum, *The Chicago World's Fair of 1893: A Photographic Record* (New York: Dover, 1980); R. Reid Badger, *The Great American Fair* (Chicago: Nelson Hall, 1979); Norman Bolotin and Christine Laing, *The World's Columbian Exposition: The Chicago World's Fair of 1893* (Urbana: University of Illinois Press, 1992, 2002); and Neil Harris et al. *Grand Illusions: Chicago's World's Fair of 1893* (Chicago: Chicago Historical Society, 1993).

16. Moore, *Daniel H. Burnham*, vol. 1, 54–56.

17. David Silkenat, "Workers in the White City: Working Class Culture at the World's Columbian Exposition of 1893," *Journal of the Illinois Historical Society* 104, no. 4 (Winter 2011): 283. Silkenat maintains that the experience of enduring difficult working conditions at the fair turned some of the workers—including Elias Disney (father of Walt)—into lifelong socialists. See Silkenat, 287.

18. For a full discussion of the African American experience of the World's Fair, see Anna R. Paddon and Sally Turner, "African Americans and the World's Columbian Exposition," *Illinois Historical Journal* 88, no. 1 (Spring 1995): 19–36. For extended critiques of the treatments of marginalized peoples at the fair, see Neil Harris et al., *Grand Illusions: Chicago's World's Fair of 1893*. For insight into the original intentions of some of the fair planners, see "A World's Fair Historical Architectural Exhibit," *Inland Architect and News Record* 16, no. 5 (November 1890): 56, in which writers for the publication envision a "habitations of man" exhibit featuring Native American structures and early settler log cabins "to show

how this country had an architecture when the world was young that rivaled some of the works of these latter days."

19. Daniel Burnham, "The Uses of Expositions," transcript of speech given at Chicago Literary Club, 15 April 1895, series 6, box 58.13, Burnham Collection, Art Institute of Chicago.

20. Henry Justin Smith, *Chicago's Great Century: 1833–1933* (Chicago: Consolidated Publishers, 1933), 104. See also "World's Fair Chicago's Magic Masterpiece," *Chicago Commerce* (6 October 1923): 10. Daniel Burnham was careful to highlight the independence of architect Sophia Hayden. Not only did she oversee construction but also "examination of the facts show," he assured his male colleagues, "that this woman had no help whatever." See Burnham, "The Organization of the World's Columbian Exposition," 7.

21. "Honors to D. H. Burnham," *New York Tribune*, March 26, 1893.

22. "A Hall for the People," *The Daily Inter Ocean*, December 10, 1889.

23. "Dedicated to Music and the People," *Chicago Tribune*, December 10, 1889.

24. "Dedicated to Music and the People," *Chicago Tribune*, December 10, 1889.

25. "Chicago Real Estate," *Chicago Tribune*, December 15, 1889. See also Twombly, *Louis Sullivan: His Life and Work*, 177–78.

26. Sullivan, *The Autobiography of an Idea*, 295.

27. Sullivan, *The Autobiography of an Idea*, 297.

28. The houses stood, through various restorations, for more than a century, but in 2005 Hurricane Katrina destroyed Sullivan's house and severely damaged the Charnley property. Architects from around the country volunteered their services in a communal effort to rebuild the house, which is now restored and known as the Charnley-Norwood House.

29. Sullivan, *The Autobiography of an Idea*, 297.

30. Sullivan, *The Autobiography of an Idea*, 298.

31. Claude Bragdon, *More Lives Than One* (New York: Knopf, 1938), 157. Donald Hoffman disputes almost all of Sullivan's assertions, arguing that the Wainwright used heavy masonry, did not express the steel frame, and was built for purely utilitarian purposes. See *Frank Lloyd Wright, Louis Sullivan, and the Skyscraper* (Mineola, NY: Dover 1998): 21–25.

32. Louis Sullivan to Daniel Burnham, 11 November 1893, series 1, box 1.5, Sullivaniana Collection, Art Institute of Chicago.

33. George R. Davis, *Picturesque World's Fair: An Elaborate Collection of Colored Views* (Chicago: W. B. Conkey, 1894), 5.

34. "France Honors Louis H. Sullivan," *Inland Architect and News Record* 25, no. 2 (March 1895): 20.

35. Daniel Burnham to Louis Sullivan, 11 February 1891, series 1, letterpress copybooks, vol. 1, Burnham Collection, Art Institute of Chicago.

36. Louis Sullivan to Daniel Burnham, 11 November 1893, Sullivaniana Collection, Art Institute of Chicago.

37. Brendan Gill, *Many Masks: A Life of Frank Lloyd Wright* (New York: G. P. Putnam's Sons, 1987), 100.

38. Twombly, *Louis Sullivan: His Life and Work*, 325–26.

39. A thorough presentation of this time-consuming dispute is covered in Hines's *Burnham of Chicago*, 125–33.

40. DHB Diaries, 21 and 23 August 1883, series 4, box 28.12, Burnham Collection, Art Institute of Chicago.

41. Years after the World's Fair closed, Burnham paid tribute to landscape architect and fellow fair planner Henry Codman in terms that Louis Sullivan would have regarded as an architect's ultimate compliment: "Nature spoke through him direct." See Moore, "Lessons of the Chicago World's Fair," 41.

42. "Soon to Bloom in Beauty," *Chicago Chronicle*, June 4, 1895.

43. Henry Blake Fuller, *With the Procession* (New York: Harper & Brothers, 1895), 87.

44. Moore, *Daniel H. Burnham,* vol. 2, 101.

45. Moore, *Daniel H. Burnham,* vol. 2, 101–102.

46. Burnham and Bennett, *The Plan of Chicago*, 8.

47. "Building of a Year," *Chicago Daily Tribune*, January 1, 1895, 22.

48. Siegfried Giedion, *Space, Time, and Architecture: The Growth of a New Tradition*, 5th ed. (Cambridge, MA: Harvard University Press, 1967), 388.

49. Joanna Merwood, "The Mechanization of Cladding: The Reliance Building and Narratives of Modern Architecture," *Grey Room* no. 4 (Summer 2001): 66.

50. See Thomas Leslie, "The Mysterious Life and Death of Charles Bowler Atwood," *Architecturefarm*, April 25, 2011, https://architecturefarm.wordpress.com/2011/04/25.

51. Burnham, interview notes by Charles Moore, 26 April 1908, Moore Papers.

52. Daniel Burnham, "Charles Bowler Atwood," *Inland Architect and News Record* 26, no. 6 (January 1896): 56–57.

53. Daniel Burnham, DHB Diaries, series 4, boxes 28.13 and 28.14a, Burnham Collection, Art Institute of Chicago. Unless otherwise noted, all subsequent references to the Mediterranean cruise derive from this source.

54. "Requirements of a Master Architect," *The Fulcrum* 1, no. 1 (November 1897), series 4, box 34.30, Burnham Collection, Art Institute of Chicago.

55. Hines, *Burnham of Chicago*, 137.

56. Burnham, "The Uses of Expositions," 47.

57. "World's Fair Chicago's Magic Masterpiece," *Chicago Commerce*, October 6, 1923.

58. Louis H. Sullivan, "The Tall Office Building Artistically Considered," *Inland Architect and News Record* 27, no. 4 (May 1896): 33.

59. Sullivan, "The Tall Office Building Artistically Considered," 34.

60. Sullivan, "The Tall Office Building Artistically Considered," 33–34. In a lengthy 1895 article on Chicago architecture, Montgomery Schuyler likens the seeming architectural attachment to a three-apart structural scheme to "the Aristotelian precept of a beginning, a middle and an end" in dramatic narratives.

See Schuyler, "Great American Architect Series—No. 2, Part I—Architecture in Chicago, Adler and Sullivan," *Architectural Record* (December 1895): 25.

61. See Twombly, *Louis Sullivan: His Life and Work*, 207–209, and Willard Connely, *Louis Sullivan as He Lived: The Shaping of American Architecture, a Biography* (New York: Horizon Press, 1960), 203.

62. Pauline A. Saliga, "Gage Group, 1898–99," in *The Sky's the Limit: A Century of Chicago Skyscrapers*, ed. Pauline A. Saliga (New York: Rizzoli, 1990), 57.

63. "Real Estate Review," *Chicago Sunday Tribune*, July 5, 1896.

64. Lyndon P. Smith, "The Schlesinger & Mayer Building," *Architectural Record* 16, no. 1 (July 1904): 59.

65. Joseph M. Siry, *Carson Pirie Scott: Louis Sullivan and the Chicago Department Store* (Chicago: University of Chicago Press, 2012), 148.

66. The reference to Schlesinger and Mayer's occurs in chapter 7 of the novel. The store's name was later changed in Dreiser's novel to "Partridge's" on the advice of an editor who sought to avoid identifying actual stores. The original names were restored in the 1981 Pennsylvania Edition of *Sister Carrie*. Compare, for instance, the Partridge's reference in the widely distributed Riverside Edition of 1959 (Boston: Houghton Mifflin), page 62, to the restored original in the Pennsylvania Edition (Boston: Houghton Mifflin), page 67.

67. Siry, *Carson Pirie Scott*, 166.

68. Siry, *Carson Pirie Scott*, 179.

69. Twombly, *Louis Sullivan: His Life and Work*, 356.

70. Connely, *Louis Sullivan as He Lived*, 210.

71. Samuelson and Ware, *Louis Sullivan's Idea*, n.p. Robert Twombly has questioned Elmslie's role in disposing of much of Sullivan's memorabilia, suggesting that the loss of many personal items may have had more to do with Sullivan's frequent changes in living quarters than with attempts to protect Sullivan's posthumous reputation. See Twombly's "Small Blessings: The Burnham Library's Louis H. Sullivan Collection," *Art Institute of Chicago Museum Studies* 13, no. 2 (1988): 146–57.

72. Twombly, *Louis Sullivan: His Life and Work*, 356, 399.

73. Paul Sprague, "Louis Sullivan's Mid-Life Crisis: 1890–1910," *Arris* 15 (2002): 60. Mario Manieri Elia sees Sullivan's resolve to strive for a kindlier "feeling for [his] fellow men" in response to a later personal crisis as "unequivocal evidence of his homosexuality." See *Louis Henry Sullivan* (New York: Princeton Architectural Press, 1996), 152.

74. Twombly, *Louis Sullivan: His Life and Work*, 357.

75. Paul Sprague, "A New Chapter in the Life of Louis Sullivan: Margaret Hattabough Sullivan and Lester Sullivan," *Arris* 13 (2002): 40.

76. Sprague, "A New Chapter," 42.

77. Daniel Burnham, Business Diaries, 5 January-23 February 1900, series 5, vol. 6, Burnham Collection, Art Institute of Chicago.

78. Daniel Burnham to Margaret Burnham, 6 November 1895, series 2, box 25.6, Burnham Collection, Art Institute of Chicago.

79. Thomas Leslie, "'Buildings Without Walls': A Tectonic Case for Two 'First' Skyscrapers," *International Journal of High-Rise Buildings* 9, no. 1 (March 2020): 59.

80. Leslie, "Built Like Bridges: Iron, Steel, and Rivets in the Nineteenth-Century Skyscraper," 252.

81. Henry Blake Fuller, *The Cliff-Dwellers* (Peterborough, ON: Broadview, 2010), 59.

82. George Ade, "After the Sky-Scrapers, What?" in *Stories of Chicago*, ed. Franklin J. Meine (Urbana: University of Illinois Press, 2003), 104–5.

Chapter 7. Divergence

1. Sherman Paul, *Louis Sullivan: An Architect in American Thought* (Englewood Cliffs, NJ, Prentice-Hall, 1962), 56.

2. Sullivan, "The Young Man in Architecture," 131, 133.

3. Sullivan, "The Young Man in Architecture," 132, 136.

4. Twombly, *Louis Sullivan: His Life and Work*, 364.

5. Twombly, *Louis Sullivan: His Life and Work*, 325–26.

6. See Paul Sprague, "A New Chapter in the Life of Louis Sullivan," *Arris* 13 (2002): 39–53, for a full discussion of what is known of the circumstances surrounding the birth of Lester Sullivan.

7. Sullivan, *Kindergarten Chats*, 15.

8. Sullivan, *Kindergarten Chats*, 100. It's tempting to see a young Frank Lloyd Wright as one of the models for the anonymous youthful apprentice of the *Chats*. In his autobiography Wright claimed that his radicalism in architecture was strengthened through his early talks with Sullivan, building on the "kindergarten training" he had received from his own mother. See Wright, *An Autobiography*, 125.

9. Stuart Graff, "Organic Architecture and the Sustaining Ecosystem," *The Whirling Arrow: News and Updates from the Frank Lloyd Wright Foundation*, July 11, 2018, https://franklloydwright.org/organic-architecture-and-the-sustaining-ecosystem.

10. David Pearson, *The New Organic Architecture: The Breaking Wave* (Berkeley: University of California Press, 2001), 72.

11. Sullivan, *Kindergarten Chats*, 99.

12. Sullivan, *Kindergarten Chats*, 45.

13. Sullivan, *Kindergarten Chats*, 45.

14. See Katherine Gilbert, "Clean and Organic: A Study in Architectural Semantics," *Journal of the Society of Architectural Historians* 10, no. 3 (October 1951): 3–7, for an extended discussion of the disparate meanings that reside within the term "organic."

15. Ericsson, *Sixty Years a Builder*, 212.

16. Sullivan, "The Young Man in Architecture," 135.

17. In his final book-length architectural statement, Sullivan even included, deliberately or coincidentally, echoes of transcendentalist Henry Thoreau's famous intention to boldly "brag as lustily as Chanticleer on the morning, if only

to wake my neighbors up" when Sullivan called on the power of one's spiritual self to "awaken man as by the call of a transcendent chanticleer, in the dawning hour to consciousness of himself." See Louis Sullivan, "The Inorganic and the Organic" in *A System of Architectural Ornament According with a Philosophy of Man's Powers* (New York: The Eakins Press, 1967), n.p. For a thorough discussion of nineteenth-century organic architectural theory as informed by science—very much akin to Louis Sullivan's thinking—see Barry Bergdoll, "Of Crystals, Cells, and Strata: Natural History and Debates on the Form of a New Architecture in the Nineteenth Century," *Architectural History* 50 (2007): 1–29.

18. Sullivan, *The Autobiography of an Idea*, 298; Hugh Dalziel Duncan, *Culture and Democracy: The Struggle for Form in Society and Architecture in Chicago and the Middle West During the Life and Times of Louis H. Sullivan* (Totowa, NJ: Bedminster Press, 1965), 242.

19. Claude Bragdon, "Foreword," in Sullivan, *The Autobiography of an Idea*, 7–8. Bragdon was one of Sullivan's disciples who traced the roots of his advocacy of organic architecture directly through Sullivan to the transcendentalist Ralph Waldo Emerson. In *Architecture and Democracy* (New York: Knopf, 1918), 49, he quoted from "The Problem"—the same Emerson poem William Furness cited in his 1870 address to the AIA—and enjoined every architect to learn the poem by heart.

20. Twombly, *Louis Sullivan: His Life and Work*, 363, 375.

21. Connely, *Louis Sullivan as He Lived*, 224–25.

22. Twombly, *Louis Sullivan: His Life and Work*, 383ff. and 453. For the 1903 statistics on Burnham and Company, see Hines, *Burnham of Chicago*, 380.

23. Twombly, *Louis Sullivan: His Life and Work*, 387. See also Edward J. Vaughn, "Louis Sullivan and the University of Michigan," *Prairie School Review* 6 (First Quarter 1969): 22.

24. *The Capital of Our Country* (Washington, DC: The National Geographic Society, 1923), 12.

25. Moore, *Daniel H. Burnham*, vol. 1, 134.

26. "Permanent Plan for the City of Washington," *Inland Architect and News Record* 37, no. 1 (February 1901): 1.

27. Moore, *Daniel H. Burnham*, vol. 1, 136.

28. Daniel Burnham to Margaret Burnham, 26 March 1901, series 2, box 25.7, Burnham Collection, Art Institute of Chicago.

29. Charles Moore, unpublished memoir, box 21, 79, Moore Papers, Library of Congress.

30. Daniel Burnham to Margaret Burnham, 1 April 1901, series 2, box 25.7, Burnham Collection, Art Institute of Chicago.

31. Moore, *Daniel H. Burnham*, vol. 1, 143.

32. Moore, *Daniel H. Burnham*, vol. 1, 142.

33. Moore, *Daniel H. Burnham*, vol. 1, 154–55.

34. Moore, *Daniel H. Burnham*, vol. 1, 168.

35. Moore, *Daniel H. Burnham*, vol. 1, 202.

36. Hines, *Burnham of Chicago*, 167–68.

37. Hines, *Burnham of Chicago*, 177.
38. Hines, *Burnham of Chicago*, 180.
39. Moore, *Daniel H. Burnham*, vol. 2, 170–71.
40. Daniel Burnham, Business Diaries, 2 April 1903, series 5, vol. 9, Burnham Collection, Art Institute of Chicago.
41. See Timothy A. Hickman, "A Chicago Architect in King Arthur's Court: Mark Twain, Daniel Burnham, and the Imperialism of Gilded Age Modernity." *Journal of American Studies* 48, no. 1 (February 2014): 99–126.
42. Hines, *Burnham of Chicago*, 198.
43. Hines, *Burnham of Chicago*, 198–99.
44. Moore, *Daniel H. Burnham*, vol. 1, 236–43.
45. Moore, *Daniel H. Burnham*, vol. 1, 242.
46. Moore, *Daniel H. Burnham*, vol. 1, 245.
47. Hines, *Burnham of Chicago*, 211.
48. DHB Diaries, 28 January 1896, series 4, box 28.13, Burnham Collection, Art Institute of Chicago.
49. Daniel Burnham to Margaret Burnham, 19 September and 28 August 1894, series 2, box 25.5, Burnham Collection, Art Institute of Chicago.
50. Daniel Burnham to Margaret Burnham, 10 April 1901, series 2, box 25.7, Burnham Collection, Art Institute of Chicago; Moore, *Daniel H. Burnham*, vol. 1, 232. One can also see elements of habitual playfulness in Burnham's first partner, John Root. At the 1885 meeting of the Western Association of Architects, the debate focused on the question of what could be said to constitute an architect's "sole occupation." Following a comment by Louis Sullivan, a member asked, "But suppose my friend, Mr. Sullivan, was president of a bank?" Root teasingly remarked, "That is too violent a supposition," and the group erupted in laughter—a bit ironic, given Sullivan's later exclusive work in designing rural banks. On another occasion, during the cornerstone ceremony of the Burnham and Root skyscraper for Frances Willard's Women's Christian Temperance Union, Root reportedly responded to a children's group singing "Saloons Must Go" by turning to his friends and suggesting that it was time for them to go have a drink. See "The Convention," *Inland Architect and News Record* 6.5 (November 1885): 71, and Hoffman, *The Architecture of John Wellborn Root*, 194.
51. Moore, *Daniel H. Burnham*, vol. 2, 4.
52. Edward Bennett, "Remarks of E. H. Bennett at the 'Burnham Library Dinner' of the American Institute of Architects in 1929," series 4, box 29.28, Burnham Collection, Art Institute of Chicago; Cass Gilbert, "Daniel Hudson Burnham: An Appreciation," *Architectural Record* 32, no. 2 (August 1912): 176.
53. Louis H. Sullivan, William Gray Purcell, Hugh Morrison, and H. W. Fridlund, "What Is Architecture: A Study in the American People of Today," *Journal of the American Society of Architectural Historians* 4, no. 2 (April 1944): 11.
54. Sullivan, *Kindergarten Chats*, 37.
55. The line does not appear in all editions of *Kindergarten Chats*. For this quotation, see the 1934 edition edited by Bragdon: Sullivan, *Kindergarten Chats: On Architecture, Education and Democracy*, 208.

56. Sullivan, "The Young Man in Architecture," 139.

57. Sullivan, *The Autobiography of an Idea*, 325.

58. Sullivan, *The Autobiography of an Idea*, 325–26.

59. Sullivan, "What Is Architecture: A Study in the American People of Today," *Louis Sullivan: The Public Papers*, 174.

60. Sullivan, "What Is Architecture: A Study in the American People of Today," *Louis Sullivan: The Public Papers*, 189.

61. Larry Millett, *The Curve of the Arch: The Story of Louis Sullivan's Owatonna Bank* (St. Paul: Minnesota Historical Society Press, 1985), 9.

62. Millett, *The Curve of the Arch*, 12.

63. Carl Bennett, "A Bank Built for Farmers: Louis Sullivan Designs a Building Which Marks a New Epoch in American Architecture," *Craftsman* 15, no. 2 (November 1908): 183.

64. Millett surmises that the green bands may be intended to represent the rich farmland of the region while the blue "flows alongside the terra cotta like a life-giving river." See *The Curve of the Arch*, 87.

65. Millett, *The Curve of the Arch*, 52.

66. Bennett, "A Bank Built for Farmers," 185.

67. Connely, *Louis Sullivan as He Lived*, 244.

68. Auction Catalog, series 3, box 6.13, Sullivaniana Collection, Art Institute of Chicago.

69. Robert R. Warn, "Part 1: Bennett & Sullivan, Client & Creator," *Prairie School Review* 10, no. 3 (Third Quarter 1973): 14.

70. Twombly, *Louis Sullivan: His Life and Work*, 399.

71. Warn, "Part 1: Bennett & Sullivan, Client & Creator," 14–15.

72. Warn, "Part 1: Bennett & Sullivan, Client & Creator," 10.

73 Daniel Burnham to Richard Watson Gilder, 12 September 1904, letterpress copybooks, series 1, vol. 15, Burnham Collection, Art Institute of Chicago.

74. Daniel Burnham to James S. Evans, 31 July 1905, letterpress copybooks, series 1, vol. 15, Burnham Collection, Art Institute of Chicago.

75. Carl Smith, *The Plan of Chicago: Daniel Burnham and the Remaking of the American City* (Chicago: University of Chicago Press, 2006), 68.

76. Frederic A. Delano to Walter D. Moody, 7 July 1915, box 13, Moore Papers, Library of Congress.

77. Moore, *Daniel H. Burnham*, vol. 2, 15.

78. Smith, *The Plan of Chicago*, 74–75.

79. Moore, *Daniel H. Burnham*, vol. 2, 33–40.

80. Moore, *Daniel H. Burnham*, vol. 2, 40, 42–43.

81. Swedenborg, *Heaven and Its Wonders and Hell*, section 185.

82. Apparently Burnham's openness to women in the profession had its limits. He was comfortable enough allowing Louise Bethune into the Western Association of Architects in 1885 and engaging a female architect for the Woman's Building at the World's Fair. But having women assume supervisory roles in the American Academy in Rome was a step too far. "This Academy needs a master and not a presiding lady," he wrote to Frank Millet. "There should be no woman

in the Mirafiore [the villa that housed the school]. The students there are not boys. They do not need 'the influence and refinements of a home.'" See Moore, *Daniel H. Burnham*, vol. 2, 95.

83. Daniel Burnham, Business Diaries, 31 July 1907, series 5, vol. 13, Burnham Collection, Art Institute of Chicago.

84. Moore, *Daniel H. Burnham*, vol. 2, 174.

85. Charles D. Norton, "The Merchants Club and the Plan of Chicago," in *The Merchants Club of Chicago, 1896–1907* (Chicago: The Commercial Club of Chicago, 1922), 98–99.

86. Norton, "The Merchants Club and the Plan of Chicago," 98–99.

87. "Biography of Daniel Hudson Burnham of Chicago, Notes for Editor," box 13, Moore Papers, Library of Congress.

88. Michael P. McCarthy suggests that the medical diagnosis was terminal cancer. See "Chicago Businessmen and the Burnham Plan," *Journal of the Illinois State Historical Society* 63, no. 3 (Autumn 1970): 231.

89. Moore, *Daniel H. Burnham*, vol. 2, 19.

90. Daniel Burnham to Francis S. Swales, 29 September 1909, letterpress copybooks, series 1, vol. 18, Burnham Collection, Art Institute of Chicago.

91. Kristen Schaffer, "'The beautiful and useful laws of God': Burnham's Swedenborgianism and the Plan of Chicago," *Planning Perspectives* 25, no. 2 (April 2010): 245, 247. Irving D. Fisher has posited a theory similar to Schaffer's, in which he links Swedenborg's concept of three differentiated heavens to Burnham's recommendations for three central areas in Chicago marked by arterial roads. See "An Iconology of City Planning—The Plan of Chicago," in *Swedenborg and His Influence*, ed. Erland J. Brock et al. (Bryn Athyn, PA: Academy of the New Church, 1988), 452–54.

92. Schaffer, "'The beautiful and useful laws of God,'" 249–50.

93. Those who have loved knowledge and cultivated rationality, Swedenborg wrote, in the afterlife will "dwell in gardens where flower beds and grass plots are seen beautifully arranged, with rows of trees round about, and arbors and walks, the trees and flowers changing from day to day. The entire view imparts delight to their minds in a general way, and the variations in detail continually renew the delight; and as everything there corresponds to something Divine." See *Heaven and Its Wonders*, section 489.

94. Moore, *Daniel H. Burnham*, vol. 1, 148.

95. Burnham and Bennett, *The Plan of Chicago*, 100.

96. Kristen Schaffer, "The Fabric of City Life: The Social Agenda in Burnham's Draft of the *Plan of Chicago*," introduction to the facsimile reprint of the *Plan of Chicago* by Daniel H. Burnham and Edward H. Bennett, ed. Charles Moore (New York: Princeton Architectural Press, 1993), ix.

97. Emanuel Swedenborg, *Divine Love and Wisdom*, trans. John Ager (West Chester, PA: Swedenborg Foundation, 2009), section 154, https://swedenborg.com/wp-content/uploads/2013/03/swedenborg_foundation_divine_love_and_wisdom.pdf.

98. Carol Willis, *Form Follows Finance: Skyscrapers and Skylines in New York and Chicago* (New York: Princeton Architectural Press, 1995), 24.

Chapter 8. Downward to Darkness

1. "Stirred by Burnham, Democracy Champion," *Chicago Record-Herald*, October 15, 1910. Unless otherwise noted, all subsequent references to Burnham's speech derive from this source.

2. Daniel Burnham to Charles Moore, 5 May 1908, series 8, box 63.20, Burnham Collection, Art Institute of Chicago.

3. See Noreen Ahmedullah, "Lakefront Park Opposed," *Chicago Tribune*, March 21, 2008, https://www.chicagotribune.com; and "Last Four Miles," Friends of the Parks, https://www.fotp.org/last-four-miles.html.

4. Moore, *Daniel H. Burnham*, vol. 2, 147.

5. Daniel H. Burnham, "A City of the Future Under a Democratic Government," *Transactions, The Town Planning Conference London, 10–15 October 1910* (London: The Royal Institute of British Architects, 1911), 368–78.

6. Henry H. Saylor, "'Make No Little Plans': Daniel Burnham Thought It, But Did He Say It?" *Journal of the American Institute of Architects* 27, no. 3 (March 1957): 95–99.

7. Smith, *The Plan of Chicago*, 98.

8. Hines, *Burnham of Chicago*, 401.

9. Adam Selzer, "Burnham's 'Make No Little Plans' Quote: Apocryphal No More!" *Mysterious Chicago*, March 3, 2019, https://mysteriouschicago.com/finding-daniel-burnhams-no-little-plans-quote.

10. On October 14, 1910, the *Chicago Daily News* carried the same article and placed a similar emphasis on Burnham's democratic message, its headline reading "Democracy to Last, Says D. H. Burnham." The *Chicago Tribune* did not include the famous lines and instead emphasized in its headline the architect's environmental vision for the future: "Burnham Predicts Smokeless City."

11. Selzer, "Burnham's 'Make No Little Plans' Quote," n.p.

12. "The Late Daniel H. Burnham," *American Architect* 102, no. 1908 (July 23, 1912): 23.

13. Charles Norton claimed to have been inspired by the "bugle blast" of Burnham's famous lines when undertaking the Plan of Chicago. See *The Merchants Club of Chicago, 1896–1907*, 100. If true, this could confirm Moore's placement of the origin of the passage to as early as the 1907 date noted on Polk's Christmas card.

14. Ira Bach, "A Reconsideration of the 1909 'Plan of Chicago,'" *Chicago History* 2, no. 3 (Spring-Summer 1973): 138. Burnham's vision was noticeably lacking in foresight concerning building height and uniformity of design. As Daniel Bluestone points out, and as the Jules Guérin illustrations in the *Plan* confirm, the Chicago downtown that Burnham proposed would involve a uniform cornice line for the major commercial buildings and no structure higher than fourteen

stories. As to existing skyscrapers that already exceeded that height, he simply "wished them away." See *Constructing Chicago* (New Haven: Yale University Press, 1991), 195–96.

15. Warn, "Part I: Bennett & Sullivan, Client & Creator," 14–15.

16. Paul Sprague, "Louis Sullivan's Mid-Life Crisis: 1890–1910," *Arris* 15 (2002): 67.

17. Rochelle Berger Elstein, "Adler and Sullivan: The End of the Partnership and Its Aftermath," *Journal of the Illinois State Historical Society* 98, nos. 1/2 (Spring-Summer 2005): 64.

18. Daniel Burnham, Business Diaries, 13 November 1911, series 5, vol. 20, Burnham Collection, Art Institute of Chicago.

19. Daniel Burnham, Business Diaries, 28 January 1906, series 5, vol. 12, Burnham Collection, Art Institute of Chicago. Burnham recorded that he "had a long talk with Louis Sullivan in office at 9:30," a discussion that could have included financial matters.

20. Daniel Burnham, Business Diaries, 25 August 1911, series 5, vol. 20, Burnham Collection, Art Institute of Chicago; Hines, *Burnham of Chicago*, 232. Hines believes the painting mentioned in the August entry may have been offered as a gift, but Burnham's diary on that day lists among his callers "Louis h. Sullivan, agreeing to send me his painting by Ricci," which could also imply a friendly offer on Burnham's part to purchase. Such an agreement would be consistent with Sullivan's efforts to address his difficult financial circumstances at the time.

21. Twombly, *Louis Sullivan: His Life and Work*, 414–15.

22. Twombly, *Louis Sullivan: His Life and Work*, 415.

23. The multi-room Tip Top Inn was located in the massive Richardsonian Romanesque Pullman Building, designed by Solon S. Beman, at the corner of Adams and Michigan Avenue. The building housed headquarters for the Pullman company as well as rentable office space and so-called "bachelor apartments." The tables Gutterson described would have offered panoramic views of Chicago's expansive lakefront.

24. Robert R. Warn, "Part II: Louis H. Sullivan, ' . . . an air of finality.'" *Prairie School Review* 10, no. 4 (Fourth Quarter 1973): 18.

25. Twombly, *Louis Sullivan: His Life and Work*, 425.

26. Patricia Speelman, "'Jewel Box' Bank Marks 100 Years," *Sidney Daily News*, May 23, 2018, https://www.sidneydailynews.com/2018/05/23/jewel-box-bank-marks-100-years.

27. Twombly, *Louis Sullivan: His Life and Work*, 432. See also John Szarkowski, *The Idea of Louis Sullivan* (Boston: Little, Brown, 1956), 3–14.

28. Frank Lloyd Wright and Bruce Brooks Pfeiffer, *Letters to Architects* (Fresno: The Press at California State University, 1984), 5.

29. Daniel Burnham to Charles D. Norton, 20 June 1910, letterpress copybooks, series 1, vol. 18, Burnham Collection, Art Institute of Chicago.

30. Daniel Burnham to R. C. Sturgis, 29 January 1912, letterpress copybooks, series 1, vol. 21, Burnham Collection, Art Institute of Chicago.

31. Daniel Burnham to "Dear Cousin," 26 August 1911, series 2, box 26.27, Burnham Collection, Art Institute of Chicago.

32. Daniel Burnham to John Goddard Jr., 1 April 1902, series 2, box 26.24, Burnham Collection, Art Institute of Chicago.

33. Daniel Burnham to Francis Millet, 12 April 1912, box 13, Moore Papers, Library of Congress.

34. Moore, *Daniel H. Burnham*, vol. 2, 155; Hines, *Burnham of Chicago*, 433. Hines notes that Burnham's last diary has been lost since Charles Moore used it in his 1921 biography. Thus the source for these quotations is from Moore's transcription.

35. Hines, *Burnham of Chicago*, 360. See also Moore, *Daniel H. Burnham*, vol. 2, 157–58.

36. "Daniel Burnham, Architect, Dead," *Chicago Sunday Tribune*, June 2, 1912.

37. "Skyscraper Inventor Passes Away in Germany," *San Jose Mercury and Herald*, June 2, 1912.

38. 'Daniel Hudson Burnham: An Appreciation," *Architectural Record* 32, no. 2 (August 1912): 175–85. References to tributes from Wight, Taft, Shaw, Holabird, Lautrup, Pond, and Wright in the two paragraphs that follow are all taken from this source.

39. Moore, "Lessons of the Chicago World's Fair," 36.

40. Charles Moore, personal memoir, box 21, Moore Papers, Library of Congress.

41. Hines, *Burnham of Chicago*, 367.

42. Always the pedagogue, Sullivan directed nature-deprived architecture students to *Gray's School and Field Book of Botany* to gain elementary knowledge of plant life.

43. Sullivan, *A System of Architectural Ornament,* plate 4, n.p.

44. Sullivan, "The Inorganic and the Organic," *A System of Architectural Ornament*, n.p.

45. David Van Zanten, *Sullivan's City: The Meaning of Ornament for Louis Sullivan* (New York: W. W. Norton, 2000), 150.

46. In *A System,* plate 4 for example, Sullivan seems to suggest that the architect will somehow be able to intuit the "will" contained within the seed germ and subordinate his or her own will accordingly: "The plant organism derives its impulse from the seed-germ, and in its growth develops sub-centers of further growth. The seed-germ may thus be considered also as a container of energy, forming of its own will sub-centers of energy in the course of its functioning development toward the finality of its characteristic form—the expression of its identity." So who or what has the actual power to create—the seed germ of the

plant organism that possesses "its own will" or the "man in his power [who] brings forth that which hitherto was non-existent," as cited in the previous passage?

47. Sullivan, *The Autobiography of an Idea*, 257.

48. Sullivan, *The Autobiography of an Idea*, 320.

49. Sullivan, *The Autobiography of an Idea*, 319–25.

50. Sullivan, "The Chicago Tribune Competition," *Louis Sullivan: The Public Papers*, 224, 226, 230–31.

51. Sullivan, "Concerning the Imperial Hotel, Tokyo, Japan," *Louis Sullivan: The Public Papers*, 233.

52. Sullivan, "The Chicago Tribune Competition," *Louis Sullivan: The Public Papers*, 230.

53. Sullivan, "Reflections on the Tokyo Disaster," *Louis Sullivan: The Public Papers*, 248.

54. Sullivan, "Reflections on the Tokyo Disaster," *Louis Sullivan: The Public Papers*, 250.

55. Wright and Pfeiffer, *Letters to Architects*, 41.

56. Frank Lloyd Wright, *Genius and the Mobocracy* (New York: Duell, Sloan and Pearce, 1949; New York: Horizon Press, 1971), 89.

57. Wright, *Genius and the Mobocracy*, 90.

58. Wright and Pfeiffer, *Letters to Architects*, 18, 20.

59. Wright, *Genius and the Mobocracy*, 91.

Epilogue

1. "Auditorium Building," Chicago Architecture Center, https://www.architecture.org/learn/resources/buildings-of-chicago/building/auditorium-building.

2. For a detailed treatment of the influence of the *Plan* on the development of Grant Park, see Smith, *The Plan of Chicago*, 141–45.

3. Wright, *An Autobiography*, 292.

Select Bibliography

For readers who wish to explore the lives and work of these two architectural icons in greater depth, the definitive comprehensive biographies remain Robert Twombly's *Louis Sullivan: His Life and Work* (1986) and Thomas S. Hines's *Burnham of Chicago*, 2nd ed. (2009). Firsthand accounts by the principals themselves, like Sullivan's *The Autobiography of an Idea* or Burnham's accounts of his involvement in the 1893 World's Fair, are clearly of great interest, but they are subject to possible distortions due to faulty memory or self-serving perspectives. The same could be said of Burnham associate and admirer Charles Moore, whose two-volume 1921 biography offers much important information and a firsthand account of the latter portions of Burnham's career. But his close relationships with Burnham and the Burnham family color the narrative. A selection of other full-length biographies, critical studies, histories, and contemporary accounts that illuminate the period and the lives and works of these individuals are listed below.

Several of the articles shown here relating to Sullivan and Burnham from the 1880s into the early part of the twentieth century were published in the *Inland Architect and News Record* (originally the *Inland Architect and Builder*) and are readily available online.

Andrew, David S. *Louis Sullivan and the Polemics of Modern Architecture*. Urbana: University of Illinois Press, 1985.

Bennett, Carl. "A Bank Built for Farmers: Louis Sullivan Designs a Building Which Marks a New Epoch in American Architecture." *Craftsman* 15, no. 2 (November 1908): 176–85.

Berger, Miles L. *They Built Chicago: Entrepreneurs Who Shaped a Great City's Architecture.* Chicago: Bonus Books, 1992.

Bethune, Louise. "Women in Architecture." *Inland Architect and News Record* 17, no. 2 (March 1891): 20–21.
Bluestone, Daniel. *Constructing Chicago.* New Haven: Yale University Press, 1991.
Bragdon, Claude. *Architecture and Democracy.* New York: Alfred A. Knopf, 1926.
Bragdon, Claude. *More Lives Than One.* New York: Alfred A. Knopf, 1938.
Bruegmann, Robert. *The Architects and the City: Holabird & Roche, 1880–1918.* Chicago: University of Chicago Press, 1997.
Bruegmann, Robert et al. *A Guide to 150 Years of Chicago Architecture.* Chicago: Chicago Review Press, 1985.
Burnham, Daniel. "Charles Bowler Atwood." *Inland Architect and News Record* 26, no. 6 (January 1896): 56–57.
Burnham, Daniel. "A City of the Future Under a Democratic Government." *Transactions, Town Planning Conference London, 10–15 October 1910.* London: Royal Institute of British Architects, 1911, 368–378.
Burnham, Daniel. "The Organization of the World's Columbian Exposition." *Inland Architect and News Record* 22, no. 1 (August 1893): 5–8.
Burnham, Daniel. "What an Architectural Association Should Be. Remarks Made by Architect D. H. Burnham Before the State Association of Illinois Architects." *Inland Architect and Builder* 5, no. 2 (March 1885): 20–21.
Burnham, Daniel. "White City and Capital City." *Century Magazine* 63 (February 1902): 619–620.
Burnham, Daniel, and Edward H. Bennett. *Plan of Chicago.* Edited by Charles Moore. Chicago: The Commercial Club of Chicago, 1909.
Burnham, Daniel, and Francis Davis Millet. *The World's Columbian Exposition: The Book of the Builders.* Chicago: Columbian Memorial Publication Society, 1894.
Cannon, Patrick F. *Louis Sullivan: Creating a New American Architecture.* San Francisco: Pomegranate, 2011.
Condit, Carl. *The Chicago School of Architecture.* Chicago: University of Chicago Press, 1964.
Condit, Carl. *The Rise of the Skyscraper.* Chicago: University of Chicago Press, 1952.
Connely, Willard. *Louis Sullivan as He Lived: The Shaping of American Architecture, a Biography.* New York: Horizon Press, 1960.
Cronon, William. *Nature's Metropolis: Chicago and the Great West.* New York: W. W. Norton, 1991.
Crook, David H. "Louis Sullivan and the Golden Doorway." *Journal of the Society of Architectural Historians* 26, no. 4 (December 1967): 250–58.
De Wit, Wim. "Apartment Houses and Bungalows: Building the Flat City." *Chicago History* 12, no. 4 (Winter 1983–84): 18–29.
De Wit, Wim, ed. *Louis Sullivan: The Function of Ornament.* New York: W. W. Norton, 1986.
Duncan, Hugh Dalziel. *Culture and Democracy: The Struggle for Form in Society and Architecture in Chicago and the Middle West During the Life and Times of Louis H. Sullivan.* Totowa, NJ: Bedminster Press, 1965.

Elmslie, George Grant. "The Chicago School: Its Inheritance and Bequest." *Journal of the American Institute of Architects* 37 (July 1952): 32–40.
Elmslie, George Grant. Letter to Frank Lloyd Wright. Reprinted in "Letters to the Editor." *Journal of the Society of Architectural Historians* 20, no. 3 (October 1961): 140–41.
Elstein, Rochelle Berger. "Adler and Sullivan: The End of the Partnership and Its Aftermath." *Journal of the Illinois State Historical Society* 98, nos. 1/2 (Spring-Summer 2005): 51–81.
Elstein, Rochelle Berger. "The Architecture of Dankmar Adler." *Journal of the Society of Architectural Historians* 26, no. 4 (December 1967): 242–249.
Elstein, Rochelle Berger. *Dankmar Adler: A Biography.* Chicago: Arthur S. Elstein, 2017.
Ericsson, Henry. *Sixty Years a Builder: The Autobiography of Henry Ericsson.* Chicago: A. Kroch and Son, 1942.
Fisher, Irving D. "An Iconology of City Planning—The Plan of Chicago." In *Swedenborg and His Influence*, edited by Erland J. Brock, et al., 449–464. Bryn Athyn, PA: Academy of the New Church, 1988.
Frazier, Nancy. *Louis Sullivan and the Chicago School.* New York: Knickerbocker Press, 1998.
Frei, Hans. *Louis Henry Sullivan.* Zurich: Artemis Verlag, 1992.
Gebhard, David. "Louis Sullivan and George Grant Elmslie." *Journal of the Society of Architectural Historians* 19, no. 2 (May 1960): 62–68.
Giedion, Sigfried. *Space, Time, and Architecture: The Growth of a New Tradition.* Cambridge, MA: Harvard University Press, 1967.
Gifford, Don, ed. *The Literature of Architecture: The Evolution of Architectural Theory and Practice in Nineteenth Century America.* New York: E. P. Dutton, 1966.
Goldberger, Paul. "Skyscrapers and the City." *Chicago History* 12, no. 4 (Winter 1983–84): 7–17.
Goldberger, Paul. *Why Architecture Matters.* New Haven: Yale University Press, 2009.
Greenough, Horatio. *Form and Function: Remarks on Art, Design, and Architecture.* Berkeley: University of California Press, 1947.
Grube, Oswald W., Peter C. Pran, Franz Schultze, and Museum of Contemporary Art. *100 Years of Architecture in Chicago: Continuity of Structure and Form.* Translated by David Norris. Chicago: J. Phillip O'Hara, 1976.
Harris, Neil et al. *Grand Illusions: Chicago World's Fair of 1893.* Chicago: Chicago Historical Society, 1993.
Hines, Thomas S. *Burnham of Chicago.* 2nd ed. Chicago: University of Chicago Press, 2009.
Hines, Thomas S. "The Imperial Façade: Daniel H. Burnham and American Architectural Planning in the Philippines." *Pacific Historical Review* 41, no. 1 (February 1972): 33–53.
Hines, Thomas S. "The Imperial Mall: The City Beautiful Movement and the Washington Plan of 1901–1902." *Studies in the History of Art* 30 (1991): 78–99.

Hines, Thomas S. "No Little Plans: The Achievement of Daniel Burnham." *Art Institute of Chicago Museum Studies* 13, no. 2 (1988): 96–105.
Hines, Thomas S. "The Paradox of 'Progressive' Architecture: Urban Planning and Public Building in Tom Johnson's Cleveland." *American Quarterly* 25, no. 4 (October 1973): 426–48.
Hoffman, Donald. *The Architecture of John Wellborn Root.* Chicago: University of Chicago Press, 1988.
Hoffman, Donald. *Frank Lloyd Wright, Louis Sullivan, and the Skyscraper.* Mineola, NY: Dover, 1998.
Johnson, Philip. "Is Sullivan the Father of Functionalism?" *Art News* 55, no. 8 (December 1956): 44–46, 56–57.
Kaufmann, Edgar, Jr., ed. *Louis Sullivan and the Architecture of Free Enterprise.* Chicago: The Art Institute of Chicago, 1956.
Keegan, Edward. *Chicago Architecture: 1885 to Today.* Chicago: Chicago Architecture Foundation, 2008.
Lane, M. A. "High Buildings in Chicago." *Harper's Weekly* 35 (October 31, 1891): 853–57.
Larson, George, and Jay Pridmore. *Chicago Architecture and Design.* New York: Harry N. Abrams, Inc., 1993.
Leslie, Thomas. "'As Large as the Situation of the Columns Would Allow': Building Cladding and Plate Glass in the Chicago Skyscraper, 1885–1905." *Technology and Culture* 49, no. 2 (April 2008): 399–419.
Leslie, Thomas. "'Buildings Without Walls': A Tectonic Case for Two 'First' Skyscrapers." *International Journal of High-Rise Buildings* 9, no. 1 (March 2020): 53–60.
Leslie, Thomas. "Built Like Bridges: Iron, Steel, and Rivets in the Nineteenth-Century Skyscraper." *Journal of the Society of Architectural Historians* 69, no. 2 (June 2010): 234–61.
Leslie, Thomas. *Chicago Skyscrapers: 1871–1934.* Urbana: University of Illinois Press, 2013.
Leslie, Thomas. "Dankmar Adler's Response to Louis Sullivan's 'The Tall Office Building Artistically Considered': Architecture and the 'Four Causes.'" *Journal of Architectural Education* 64, no. 1 (September 2010): 83–93.
Leslie, Thomas. "Glass and Light: The Influence of Interior Illumination on the Chicago School." *Journal of Architectural Education* 58, no. 1 (September 2004): 13–24.
Leslie, Thomas. "The Mysterious Life and Death of Charles Bowler Atwood." *Architecturefarm*, April 25, 2011. https://architecturefarm.wordpress.com/2011/04/25.
Lewis, Arnold. *An Early Encounter with Tomorrow: Europeans, Chicago's Loop, and the World's Columbian Exposition.* Urbana: University of Illinois Press, 1997.
Lewis, Lloyd, and Henry Justin Smith. *Chicago: The History of Its Reputation.* New York: Harcourt, Brace, 1929.

Madden, Edward H. "Transcendental Influences on Louis Sullivan and Frank Lloyd Wright." *Transactions of the Charles S. Peirce Society* 31, no. 2 (Spring 1995): 286–321.

Manieri Elia, Mario. *Louis Henry Sullivan*. New York: Princeton Architectural Press, 1996.

Mayer, Harold M., and Richard C. Wade. *Chicago: Growth of a Metropolis.* Chicago: University of Chicago Press, 1969.

Menocal, Narciso G. *Architecture as Nature: The Transcendentalist Idea of Louis Sullivan.* Madison: University of Wisconsin Press, 1981.

Merwood, Joanna. "The Mechanization of Cladding: The Reliance Building and Narratives of Modern Architecture." *Grey Room* 4 (Summer 2001): 52–69.

Merwood-Salisbury, Joanna. *Chicago 1890: The Skyscraper and the Modern City.* Chicago: University of Chicago Press, 2009.

Miller, Donald. *City of the Century: The Epic of Chicago and the Making of America.* New York: Simon and Schuster, 1996.

Millett, Larry. *The Curve of the Arch: The Story of Louis Sullivan's Owatonna Bank.* St. Paul: Minnesota Historical Society Press, 1985.

Monroe, Harriet. *John Wellborn Root: A Study of His Life and Work.* Boston: Houghton, Mifflin, 1896.

Moore, Charles. *Daniel H. Burnham: Architect, Planner of Cities.* 2 vols. Boston: Houghton Mifflin, 1921.

Moore, Charles. "Lessons of the Chicago World's Fair: An Interview with the Late Daniel H. Burnham." *Architectural Record* 33, no. 1 (January 1913): 34–44.

Morrison, Hugh. *Louis Sullivan: Prophet of Modern Architecture.* New York: W. W. Norton, 1998. First published 1935 by W. W. Norton.

Mumford, Lewis. *The Brown Decades: A Study of the Arts in America, 1865–1895.* New York: Dover, 1971.

Murphy, Kevin D., and Lisa Reilly, eds. *Skyscraper Gothic: Medieval Style and Modernist Buildings.* Charlottesville: University of Virginia Press, 2017.

Nickel, Richard, Aaron Siskind, John Vinci, and Ward Miller. *The Complete Architecture of Adler & Sullivan.* Chicago: The Richard Nickel Committee, 2010.

Norton, Charles D. "The Merchants Club and the Plan of Chicago." In *The Merchants Club of Chicago, 1896–1907.* Chicago: The Commercial Club of Chicago, 1922. 95–103.

Paddon, Anna R., and Sally Turner. "African Americans and the World's Columbian Exposition." *Illinois Historical Journal* 88, no. 1 (Spring 1995): 19–36.

Paul, Sherman. *Louis Sullivan: An Architect in American Thought.* Englewood Cliffs, NJ: Prentice-Hall, 1962.

Pearson, David. *New Organic Architecture: The Breaking Wave.* Berkeley: University of California Press, 2001.

Pettengill, George E. "Who Was Sullivan's Minnie?" *Journal of the Society of Architectural Historians* 47, no. 2 (June 1988): 177–78.

Pridmore, Jay. *The Reliance Building: A Building Book from the Chicago Architecture Foundation.* San Francisco: Pomegranate, 2003.
Pridmore, Jay. *The Rookery: A Building Book from the Chicago Architecture Foundation.* San Francisco: Pomegranate, 2003.
Rebori, A. N. "The Architecture of Democracy: Three Recent Examples of the Work of Louis Sullivan." *The Architectural Record* 39, no. 5 (May 1916): 436–65.
Rebori, A. N. "The Work of Burnham & Root, D. H. Burnham—D. H. Burnham & Co., and Graham, Burnham & Co." *The Architectural Record* 38, no. 1 (July 1915): 33–168.
Rinehart, Melissa. "To Hell with the Wigs: Native American Representation and Resistance at the World's Columbian Exposition." *American Indian Quarterly* 36, no. 4 (Fall 2012): 403–42.
Root, John Wellborn. "The Art of Pure Color." *Inland Architect and Builder* 1, no. 6 (July 1883): 80–82.
Root, John Wellborn. "A Great Architectural Problem." *Inland Architect and News Record* 15, no. 5 (June 1890): 67–71.
Root, John Wellborn. *The Meanings of Architecture: Buildings and Writings by John Wellborn Root.* Collected and with an introduction by Donald Hoffman. New York: Horizon Press, 1967.
Saliga, Pauline A., ed. *The Sky's the Limit: A Century of Chicago Skyscrapers.* New York: Rizzoli, 1990.
Samuelson, Timothy, and Chris Ware. *Louis Sullivan's Idea.* Chicago: Alphawood Foundation, 2021.
Saylor, Henry H. "'Make No Little Plans': Daniel Burnham Thought It, But Did He Say It?" *Journal of the American Institute of Architects* 27, no. 3 (March 1957): 95–99.
Scanlon, Lawrence E. "Louis Sullivan's 'Idea.'" *American Quarterly* 11, no. 4 (Winter 1959): 521–25.
Schaffer, Kristen. "'The beautiful and useful laws of God': Burnham's Swedenborgianism and the Plan of Chicago." *Planning Perspectives*, 25, no. 2 (April 2010): 243–52.
Schaffer, Kristen. *Daniel H. Burnham: Visionary Architect and Planner.* New York: Rizzoli, 2003.
Schaffer, Kristen. "The Early Chicago Tall Office Building: Artistically and Functionally Considered." ICOMOS: Journals of the German National Committee 54 (2015), 148–56.
Schaffer, Kristen. "Fabric of City Life: The Social Agenda in Burnham's Draft of the Plan of Chicago." Introduction to the facsimile reprint of the *Plan of Chicago*, v–xvi. New York: Princeton Architectural Press, 1993.
Schaffer, Kristen. "The Plan of Chicago as a Map of Heaven: Daniel Burnham's Swedenborgianism." Symposium on Urbanism, Spirituality, and Well Being. Architecture, Culture, and Spirituality Forum (ACSF) 5, Harvard University, June 7, 2013. https://www.youtube.com/watch?v=7rcK0S7HZvw.

Schuyler, Montgomery. *American Architecture and Other Writings.* Edited by William H. Jordy and Ralph Coe. 2 vols. Cambridge, MA: Harvard University Press, 1961.
Schuyler, Montgomery. "Architecture." *Inland Architect and News Record* 17, no. 1 (February 1891): 5.
Schuyler, Montgomery. "Glimpses of Western Architecture 1.—Chicago." In *American Architecture Studies* (New York: Harper and Brothers, 1892), 113–68.
Schuyler, Montgomery. "Great American Architect Series—No. 2, Part I—Architecture in Chicago, Adler and Sullivan." *Architectural Record* (December 1895): 3–48.
Schuyler, Montgomery. "Great American Architect Series—No. 2, Part II—Architecture in Chicago, D. H. Burnham & Co." *Architectural Record* (December 1895): 49–72.
Selzer, Adam. "Burnham's 'Make No Little Plans' Quote: Apocryphal No More." *Mysterious Chicago.* March 3, 2019. https://mysteriouschicago.com/finding-daniel-burnhams-no-little-plans-quote.
Silkenat, David. "Workers in the White City: Working Class Culture at the World's Columbian Exposition of 1893." *Journal of the Illinois Historical Society* 104, no. 4 (Winter 2011): 266–300.
Siry, Joseph M. *Carson Pirie Scott: Louis Sullivan and the Chicago Department Store.* Chicago: University of Chicago Press, 2012.
Siry, Joseph M. *The Chicago Auditorium Building: Adler and Sullivan's Architecture and the City.* Chicago: University of Chicago Press, 2002.
Smith, Carl. "The Best Thing: The Daniel H. Burnham and Edward H. Bennett Collections and the 1909 Plan of Chicago." *Art Institute of Chicago Museum Studies* 34, no. 2 (2008): 66–70.
Smith, Carl. *The Plan of Chicago: Daniel Burnham and the Remaking of the American City.* Chicago: University of Chicago Press, 2006.
Smith, Henry Justin. *Chicago's Great Century: 1833–1933.* Chicago: Consolidated Publishers Inc., 1933.
Smith, Lyndon P. "The Home of an Artist-Architect." *Architectural Record* 42, no. 6 (June 1905): 471–90.
Smith, Lyndon P. "The Schlesinger & Mayer Building: An Attempt to Give Functional Expression to the Architecture of a Department Store." *Architectural Record* 16, no. 1 (July 1904): 53–60.
Sprague, Paul. "Adler and Sullivan's Schiller Building." *Prairie School Review* 2, no. 2 (Second Quarter 1965): 5–20.
Sprague, Paul. *The Drawings of Louis Henry Sullivan.* Princeton, NJ: Princeton University Press, 1979.
Sprague, Paul. "Louis Sullivan's Mid-Life Crisis: 1890–1910." *Arris* 15 (2002): 56–71.
Sprague, Paul. "The National Farmer's Bank of Owatonna, Minnesota." *Prairie School Review* 4, no. 2 (Second Quarter 1967): 5–21.

Sprague, Paul. "A New Chapter in the Life of Louis Sullivan: Margaret Hattabough Sullivan and Lester Sullivan." *Arris* 13 (2002): 39–53.
Sprague, Paul, and Donald Egbert, "In Search of John Edelmann." *AIA Journal* 45 (February 1966): 35–41.
Starrett, Paul. *Changing the Skyline: An Autobiography.* New York: Whittlesey House, 1938.
Sullivan, Louis. *The Autobiography of an Idea.* New York: Press of the American Institute of Architects, 1926.
Sullivan, Louis. *Democracy: A Man Search.* Detroit: Wayne State University Press, 1961.
Sullivan, Louis. *Kindergarten Chats: On Architecture, Education and Democracy.* Edited and introduced by Claude F. Bragdon. n.p.: Scarab Fraternity Press, 1934.
Sullivan, Louis. *Kindergarten Chats and Other Writings.* New York: Wittenborn, Schulz Inc.,1947.
Sullivan, Louis. *Louis Sullivan: The Public Papers.* Edited by Robert Twombly. Chicago: University of Chicago Press, 1988.
Sullivan, Louis. *A System of Architectural Ornament According with a Philosophy of Man's Powers.* New York: The Eakins Press, 1967.
Szarkowski, John. *The Idea of Louis Sullivan.* Boston: Little, Brown, 1956,
Twombly, Robert. "Beyond Chicago: Louis Sullivan in the American West." *Pacific Historical Review* 54, no. 4 (November 1985): 405–58.
Twombly, Robert. *Louis Sullivan: His Life and Work.* Chicago: University of Chicago Press, 1986.
Twombly, Robert, and Narciso Menocal. *Louis Sullivan: The Poetry of Architecture.* New York: W. W. Norton, 2000.
Uechi, Naomi Tanabe. *Evolving Transcendentalism in Literature and Architecture.* Newcastle upon Tyne, UK: Cambridge Scholars Publishing, 2013.
Van Zanten, David. *Sullivan's City: The Meaning of Ornament for Louis Sullivan.* New York: W. W. Norton, 2000.
Waldheim, Charles, and Katerina Ruedi Ray, eds. *Chicago Architecture: Histories, Revisions, Alternatives.* Chicago: University of Chicago Press, 2005.
Warn, Robert R. "Part I: Bennett & Sullivan, Client & Creator." *Prairie School Review* 10, no. 3 (Third Quarter 1973): 5–15.
Warn, Robert R. "Part II: Louis H. Sullivan, ' . . . an air of finality." *Prairie School Review* 10, no. 4 (Fourth Quarter 1973): 5–19.
Weingarden, Lauren S. "The Colors of Nature: Louis Sullivan's Architectural Polychromy and Nineteenth-Century Color Theory." *Winterthur Portfolio* 20, no. 4 (Winter 1985): 243–60.
Weingarden, Lauren S. *Louis H. Sullivan: The Banks.* Boston: MIT Press, 1987.
Weingarden, Lauren S. "Louis H. Sullivan: Investigation of a Second French Connection." *Journal of the Society of Architectural Historians* 39, no. 4 (December 1980): 297–303.
Weingarden, Lauren S. *Louis H. Sullivan and a 19th-Century Poetics of Naturalized Architecture.* Farnham, UK: Ashgate, 2009.

Weingarden, Lauren S. "Naturalized Nationalism: A Ruskinian Discourse in the Search for an American Style of Architecture." *Winterthur Portfolio* 24, no. 1 (Spring 1989): 43–68.

Weingarden, Lauren S. "Naturalized Technology: Louis H. Sullivan's Whitmanesque Skyscrapers." *Centennial Review* 30, no. 4 (Fall 1986): 480–95.

Weingarden, Lauren S. "A Poetics of Organic Expression: Louis Sullivan's Transcendentalist Legacy in Word and Image." In *Mixed Messages: American Correspondences in Visual and Verbal Practices*, edited by Catherine Gander and Sarah Garland, 18–33. Manchester: Manchester University Press, 2016.

Wight, Peter B. "Daniel Hudson Burnham: An Appreciation. A Paper Delivered at a Meeting Held at the Art Institute of Chicago, June 11, 1912." *Architectural Record* 32, no. 2 (August 1912): 176–84.

Wight, Peter B. "Daniel Hudson Burnham and His Associates." *Architectural Record*. 38, no. 1 (July 1915): 1–12.

Willis, Carol. *Form Follows Finance: Skyscrapers and Skylines in New York and Chicago.* New York: Princeton Architectural Press, 1995.

Wiseman, Carter. "The Rise of the Skyscraper and the Fall of Louis Sullivan." *American Heritage* 49, no. 1 (February/March 1998). https://www.americanheritage.com/rise-skyscraper-and-fall-louis-sullivan.

Woods, Mary N. *From Craft to Profession: The Practice of Architecture in Nineteenth-Century America.* Berkeley: University of California Press, 1999.

Wright, Frank Lloyd. *An Autobiography.* New York: Horizon Press, 1977. First published 1932 by Longmans.

Wright, Frank Lloyd. *Genius and the Mobocracy*. New York: Horizon Press, 1971. First published 1949 by Duell, Sloan and Pearce.

Wright, Frank Lloyd and Bruce Brooks Pfeiffer. *Letters to Architects.* Fresno: The Press at California State University, 1984.

Wright, Paul M. "Louis Sullivan Woke Up Here." *The Massachusetts Review* 28, no. 2 (Summer 1987): 325–30.

Zabel, Craig. "George Grant Elmslie and the Glory and Burden of the Sullivan Legacy." In *The Midwest in American Architecture*, edited by John S. Garner, 1–41. Urbana: University of Illinois Press, 1981.

Zukowsky, John. *Building Chicago: The Architectural Masterworks.* New York: Rizzoli, 2016.

Zukowsky, John, ed. *Chicago Architecture, 1872–1922: Birth of a Metropolis.* Munich: Prestel Verlag, 1987.

Index

TRYGVE THORESON is Professor Emeritus of English and Humanities at William Rainey Harper College. At Harper, he designed and developed architecture tours of downtown Chicago for students in the humanities and in retirement has served as a volunteer host at the Chicago Architecture Center. Professor Thoreson is the author of *Harper College, The First 50 Years: William Rainey Harper College: 1967–2017*; his academic work has appeared in publications such as *The South Carolina Review*, *Journal of the Illinois Historical Society*, *Studies in American Humor*, and *Mark Twain Journal*.

The University of Illinois Press
is a founding member of the
Association of University Presses.

Composed in 11.5/13 Adobe Garamond Pro
with Bernhard and Gotham display
by Jim Proefrock
at the University of Illinois Press
Manufactured by Versa Press, Inc.

University of Illinois Press
1325 South Oak Street
Champaign, IL 61820-6903
www.press.uillinois.edu